301.36 Taylor, Lee, 1930–
Tay   Urbanized society

DATE DUE

URBANIZED SOCIETY

Lee Taylor
University of Texas, Arlington

Goodyear Publishing Company, Inc. • Santa Monica, California

Library of Congress Cataloging in Publication Data

Taylor, Miller Lee, 1930-
  Urbanized society.

  Bibliography at the end of each chapter.
  Includes index.
  1. Urbanization.   2. Sociology, Urban.
  3. City and town life.   4. City planning.
  I. Title
  HT151.T35   301.36   79-18145
  ISBN 0-8302-9265-9

Copyright © 1980 by Goodyear Publishing Company, Inc.
Santa Monica, California 90401

All rights reserved. No part of this book may be reproduced in any form or by any means without permission in writing from the publisher.

ISBN: 8302-9265-9
Y-9265-3

Text designer: Linda M. Robertson
Production editor: Pam Tully
Cover photograph: Frank Siteman for The Stockmarket
Compositor: Composition Type/Playa del Rey

Current printing (last number)
10 9 8 7 6 5 4 3 2 1

Printed in the United States of America

For Jacquelin Kugel Taylor

Contents

Preface xi

PART ONE
Cities, Urbanization, and Social Organization   **1**

1 The Urban Invention   **3**
The City as a Social Invention   3
Urbanized Social Organization   7
Planning for Urbanization   9
Implications   11
References   11

2 Historic Urban Forms and Social Interaction   **15**
Historic Urban Processes   15
Social Institutions   21
Matching Social Needs and Physical Forms   26
Implications   32
References   32

3 An Urbanized Planet   **35**
Concepts and Orientations   35
Urbanization: A New Stage in Social Evolution   38
Residence Patterns in Urbanized Society   45
Solutions to the Urbanization Challenge   49
Implications   51
References   52

PART TWO
Urbanization and Theory 55

4 Urban Ecology 57
Urban Ecology Models 60
Consequences of Urban Ecology 64
Ecology Issues and Developments 72
Implications 78
References 78

5 Urban Centers 83
Urban Centers and Social Institutions 85
Central Place Theory 88
Pedestrians and City Centers 97
Implications 99
References 100

6 Urban Regions and Metropolitan Government 103
Components of Regional Planning 105
Metropolitan Government and Social Organization 116
Urban Regional Planning and Management 120
Implications 121
References 122

PART THREE
People and Space 125

7 Space Meaning and Use 127
Symbolic Space Meanings 128
From Neighborhood to Total Life Systems 131
Town Planning, Urban Renewal, and Neighborhoods 136
Social Space and Personal Space 140
Defensible Space 145
Implications 147
References 147

8 Land Use and Subdivision 151
Land Use Concepts 152
Urban Land Use Planning 154
Subdivisions 159
New Town Land Use 164
Implications 165
References 167

PART FOUR
Urban Problems and Institutions   169

9 Housing, Jobs, and Transportation   171
Issues   171
Housing and Activity Systems   178
Jobs and Activity Systems   189
Transportation and Activity Systems   191
Implications   194
References   194

10 Education and Religion   197
Education in Urbanized Society   198
Religion in Urbanized Society   206
Implications   211
References   212

11 The Arts and Recreation   215
The Arts at the Apex of Urban Civilization   215
Recreation and Urbanization   224
Implications   229
References   229

12 Health, Welfare, and Crime Deterrents   233
Health and Urban Planning   234
Welfare and Urban Planning   242
Crime Deterrents and Urban Planning   246
Implications   247
References   248

PART FIVE
Planning and Urban Prospects   251

13 Urban Activity Systems and Comprehensive Planning   253
The Societal Context of Planning   254
Social Activity Systems and Planning   256
Comprehensive Planning   260
Implications   266
References   267

14 Urban Renewal   269
The Need for Urban Renewal   272
Urban Renewal in the United States   272
World Urban Renewal Experiences   274
Social Organization and Urban Renewal   277
Implications   279
References   279

15 New Towns — 281
Nature and Social Organization 282
New Town Models 287
British New Town Experiences 288
New Town Experience in the United States 290
Continental European New Town Experiences 296
*New Towns in Africa, Latin America,
   the Near East, and the Orient 300*
Implications 303
References 304

16 Urban Policies — 309
Urban Policy Elements 310
World Urban Policies 311
National Urban Policies 312
Regional Urban Policies 315
Local Urban Policies 317
Implications 319
References 321

Index 323

Preface

This book is written primarily for people with a serious interest in urban life. It is for students, professionals and others with a passion for cities, frustration about cities, and a hope for improved urban living.

Life on the planet earth is rapidly becoming increasingly urbanized. The human potential reaches great apexes in urban culture, and human misery falls to deep abysses in city slums.

Urbanized living is quite new. It is still changing and developing. Its potentials are far from reached — indeed, they are not yet fully known.

Urbanization is a worldwide experience. This book takes a worldwide focus where multinational data are available. Cities, suburbs, and urban areas are now often societal in scale. This book examines many urban problems and prospects at societal levels.

Urban living includes both people and the built environment. Nevertheless, the two subjects are seldom examined together. This book is specifically designed to explore the interface between social planning and physical planning. Together they are an exciting and rewarding challenge. The reader is presented with a review of traditional urban sociology concepts and traditional city and regional planning concepts, the latter being somewhat abbreviated. Current multinational data about human activity systems are presented. Activity systems are seen in conflict and manifesting an array of social problems. The primary focus of the book, however, is on planning human urban systems for high-quality living. The book helps the reader to be more prospect- than problem-oriented. While several chapters include a bit of urban history, in the main the book points the reader positively toward the future.

The author of a book embracing many complex urban issues owes numerous intellectual and technical debts. Only a few can be recognized here; they include: Thomas Busam (city and regional planning-USA), Howard E. Bracey (economics and sociology-England), Jorge Chaver Camacho (sociology-Costa Rica), A. K. Constandse (planning and sociology-The Netherlands), Joseph Foresi, Jr. (education-USA), Charles Glasgow (sociology-USA), Samir Maamary (planning and sociology-Pakistan and USA), Don Martindale (sociology-U.S.A.), James D. McComas (education-U.S.A.), James W. Newton (church planning-U.S.A), Sten Nilson (political science-Norway), A. Piotrowska (sociology-Poland), Elena Sessions (sociology-U.S.A.), K. Sindwani (social welfare-India and U.S.A.), John Tinney (city and regional planning-U.S.A.), and Robert Zall (rural urban planning-U.S.A).

Mrs. Ruth West typed the manuscript with exceptional care and made that part of our work easy. My wife Jacquelin read and reread each draft with critical and constructive assistance. She is a lifelong urbanite in style and intellect. Our daughter Michelle, a lover of cities on three continents, raised questions and made observations which sharpened our understanding of data and intensified our search for additional information. Sylvia Taylor, my mother, was persistent in encouragement. To all of these and many others, I express special appreciation.

The editorial staff at Goodyear Publishing Company has been encouraging and helpful to such an extent that I want particularly to acknowledge James C. Boyd, Editor; Pam Tully, Production Editor; and Cheri Adrian, Copyeditor.

I hope the reader will find this book as enjoyable and useful as I have found the task of researching and writing it.

URBANIZED SOCIETY

PART ONE

Cities, Urbanization, and Social Organization

Cities are a human invention. They are the result of a deliberate effort to expand social life and to make it more satisfying. In the more than forty thousand years of human existence, the invention of agriculture some ten thousand years ago and the invention of cities some fifty-five hundred years ago have marked major forward movements. More complex social organization resulted from each of these inventions. Longer life spans, larger populations, expanded knowledge and education, improved health, expanded welfare, and proliferation of the arts and of recreational activities are major aspects of the urban way of life.

Growing out of agricultural village settlements, early cities developed government, commerce, and religion as distinct activities and occupations. During the first few thousand years of city living, the new urban way of life was clearly different from the rural way of life. For a period the walls surrounding cities even marked this difference physically. But urban social organization continued to grow beyond walls and city limits. Cities are people — ideas of culture and science — more than they are physical buildings or geographical places.

Urbanization in the last one hundred years has saturated many of the world's societies. The attitudes, values, and life styles associated with cities are dominating and even obliterating those associated with rural areas. City-generated life styles are now spreading so rapidly that we may expect them soon to urbanize the entire planet.

The chapters in Part One explore the development of urban living. Chapter one acquaints the reader with the invention and development of the city. Chapter two presents views of the city through history, which provide a basis for understanding contemporary city life. Chapter three focuses on the problems and prospects of city expansion to suburbs and metropolitan areas. In these three chapters, not only urbanization but also cities themselves are seen as processes. They are places of plurality — competition, conflict, and cooperation.

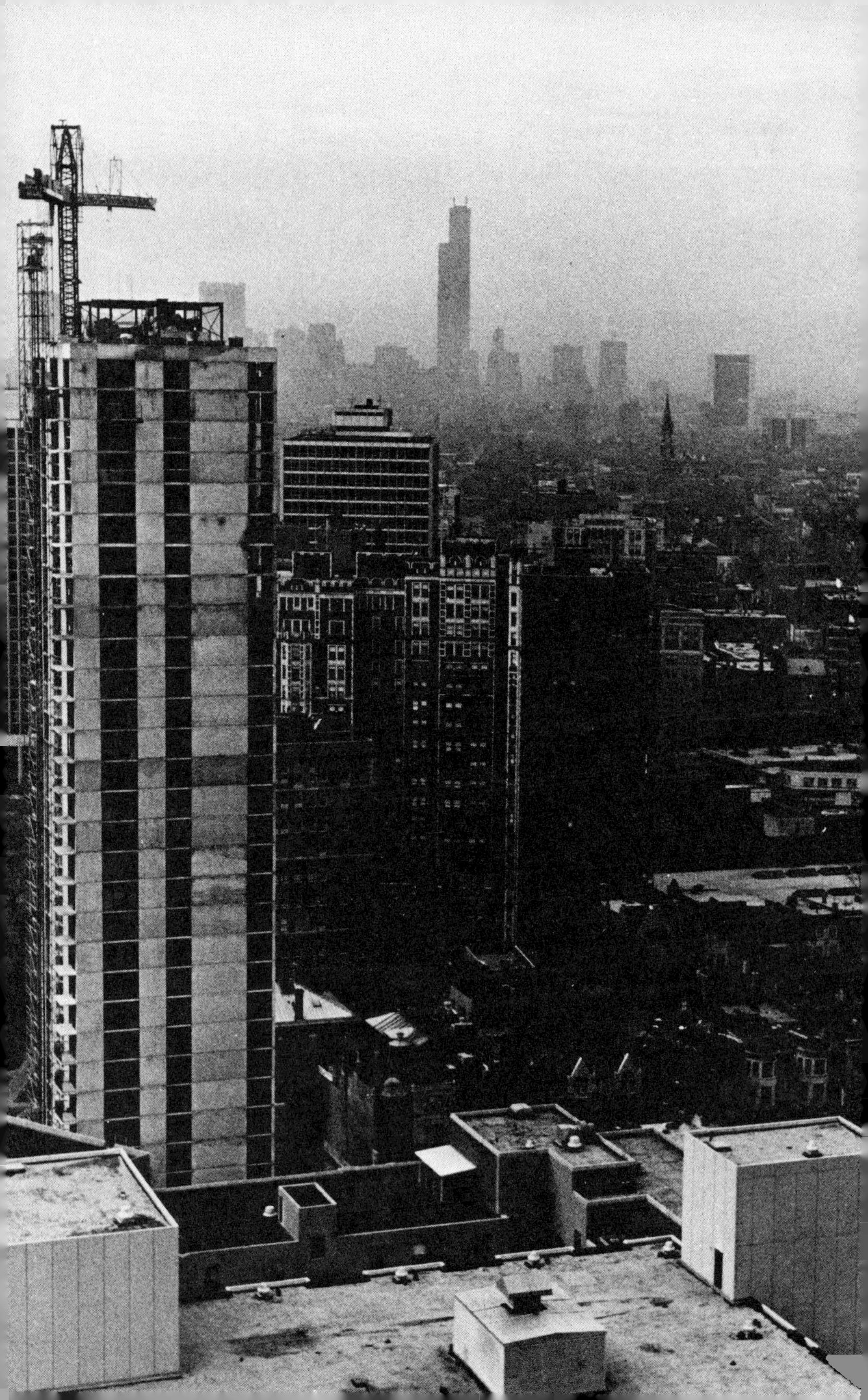

The Urban Invention 1

Historically speaking, cities are a recent form of social life. Homo sapiens sapiens man came into existence in the Pleistocene Age — forty thousand years ago. Human beings were primarily migratory for more than their first thirty thousand years. More recently, humans have tilled the soil. Agricultural villages like Jericho and Jarmo came into existence some eight and seven thousand years ago, respectively (Hamblin 1973). Continual social change stimulated the invention of cities and most recently the development of urbanization.

THE CITY AS A SOCIAL INVENTION

The social invention of the city is most frequently dated 5,500 years ago. This invention took place between the Tigris and Euphrates Rivers in the Near East, in the area now called Iraq.

The city is characterized by more and different forms of social life than those associated with migratory food gathering and agricultural village existence. Preurban society is dominated by primary social interaction — relationships tend to be personal and long-term. In city life relationships tend to be impersonal, fleeting, and determined by exchanges like buyer-seller, employer-employee, teacher-student. Over the years, secondary social interaction has come to dominate, and in some cases nearly to obliterate, primary social patterns of life in the city.

This view of Chicago shows urban building forms still being invented and constructed. (Photo: Jean-Claude Lejeune for The Stockmarket.)

The content of the new urban life style was largely religious, governmental, and mercantile. This led to the development of a middle-class category of people. Complex and advanced forms of religious rituals became significant elements of early city life in many places, and a priestly class or caste led the religious activities. The city's social organization utilized an increasingly large civil servant class; new forms of government for maintaining order among pluralistic city life styles were extensive. Most numerous of all were the urban workers — commercial laborers and others. They were the makers and distributors of products and services.

In many cases the elements of urban life interfaced so intensively that they were hard to distinguish. For example, the ruins of cities like Tikal in Guatemala and Chichén Itzá and Uxmal in Mexico are examples of what archaeologists believe to have been theocratic city-states in the New World. In such cities religious and political life were intertwined with politics dominated by religion. (In other societies the opposite has been true; currently in the Soviet Union, political structures dominate religious activities so extensively that some observers suggest that the political structures are "the real religion.")

The urban invention spread gradually to the East and to the West. In India, ruins at Mohenjo-Daro and Harappa reveal early urban development. Farther to the East there were early city developments in China along the Yellow River. In the West the use of the city form of social organization became intensified in southern Europe. Cities proliferated rapidly there until about the fifth century. The physical boundaries of early European cities were precisely designated by walls around the periphery. Avila in Spain and Carcasonne in France are well-preserved examples.

Between the fifth and the ninth centuries in southern and western Europe, cities fared badly. So much was this the case that some writers refer to this era as the Dark Ages, when Europe suffered wars, plagues, and general social disintegration, and the city nearly went out of existence. Members of the mercantile and governing classes were greatly reduced in number. Cities were largely depopulated except for persons in priestly roles. During times of siege and war, cities were inhabited by large itinerant populations seeking protection behind the walls. When hostilities ceased, the population moved back to the countryside.

With the advent of the Renaissance Era in western Europe, city growth and expansion accelerated . Science, an expansive and eventually predominant method for producing and verifying knowledge, became a major factor in the urban experience. Initially it was applied to food production and health care. Food production increased rapidly, and life spans nearly doubled. Improved food production and health care were major factors in the growth of city populations.

High urban densities create new challenges and problems for the city invention. Urban culture is characterized by the juxtaposing of man's highest achievements with plagues, famines, riots, crime, pollution, and other social problems. There are now few cities in the world with less than 10,000 people per square mile, and some, like Delhi and Calcutta, have densities of 400,000 persons per square mile in some parts. These densities stagger the imagination, yet urban planners suggest that 30,000 persons per square mile may soon be typical (Jones 1966).

City ecology

The densely settled urban environment has focused attention on human ecology, the study of people-land relationships. Nowhere are these relationships more interesting or important than in cities. The distribution of people throughout the geographical territory of cities varies considerably. The social significance and prestige of land range widely.

One first must observe that census data record city populations where they sleep. This means that the distribution of urban population is recorded by place of residence rather than by place of work, recreation, or commerce. Place of residence data are useful, but they are incomplete and often even misleading from an ecological point of view. Most people spend eight or fewer hours per day sleeping. In the highly mobile urbanized society, it is increasingly normative for urban people to spend ten or fewer hours a day in their place of residence. Typically only the very young and very old, whose ability to move about independently is limited, spend long hours in nurseries, rest homes, or other residences. Large populations are found on highways and transit routes in the early morning and late afternoon. Population densities may be high in central business districts during the mid-day hours and very low during the night hours. Population densities in large urban educational and recreational areas may be high on certain days and during certain hours and low at other times. Daily movement of people is a major characteristic of city ecology. It needs more quantification from a sociophysical and a socioeconomic point of view than is available from mere traffic origin and destination studies.

When cities were relatively small, that is until the last one hundred years, urban ecology had minimal complexity. Urban shopkeepers often resided above their stores. Separation of work and residence was more vertical than horizontal. Most movement about the city was on foot. Streets were narrow, and changes in elevation frequently involved climbing steps, for example, like the now famous Spanish Steps in Rome. In other cases streets were made wide for pedestrian promenading, as exemplified by the Champs Elysées in Paris. Plazas became significant places for meeting and social interaction, as illustrated by the Piazza San Marco in Venice.

When horse-drawn carriages, streetcars, automobiles, and other people-moving conveyances became widespread, the geographical area of cities expanded. Telephone communication, electric lighting, and improved sanitation are other technological changes which facilitated the centrifugal movement of urban populations.

By the beginning of the twentieth century, particularly in North America, new patterns of urban ecology which separated — indeed segregated — places of residence from places of work, upper social classes from lower social classes, and ethnic type from ethnic type became normative. Zoning was invented as a specific social mechanism intended to facilitate orderly urban land use. Now with some fifty years of zoning experience behind us, many are asking hard questions about whether it in fact supports or inhibits positive urban social life. The organizational complexity of urban ecology is a recent addition to the city invention.

Urban-rural differences

In the middle of the twentieth century much research was done which attempted to differentiate qualities of city living and countryside living (Sorokin 1930; Dickenson 1957; Kurtz and Eicher 1958; Stewart 1958; Dewey 1960; Taylor and Jones 1964; Taylor 1968; Bracey 1970). Now with even a short period of hindsight, it is clear that the studies of rural life demonstrated the dominance of primary human relationships and those of urban life the dominance of secondary kinds of relationships. But most of the research has been done in industrial nations — probably at their industrial peak. In the context of these industrial societies, the so-called rural life that was being researched was in fact a transitional life style between rural and urban living.

It is becoming clear in the latter part of the twentieth century that the industrial societies, and post-industrializing societies, are reaching total urbanization, a new stage in the urban invention. Food and fiber production and mineral extraction in the countryside are dominated by scientific research and technology which are produced and controlled in cities. Recreation, even that in open-country wilderness areas, has become a matter of scientific study and direction from urban areas (Clawson 1948; Brockman 1959). What at first appeared to be rural cultures with real differences in behavior are in fact cultural islands in an urbanized world. Some small units of nonscientific agricultural production are allowed to continue, but neither the resulting product nor the producing labor force are needed to sustain the urban population. Some small ideologically-oriented communes and religious groups are allowed to maintain an essentially prescientific, bucolic existence, but their contributions are not typical and are not needed by the larger society.

There are continuing primary human relationships and certain rural attitudes and values found in densely populated urban settlements. Strauss (1961) and others assert that urbanites gardening in flower pots on balconies is a kind of bucolic expression. Pocket parks and larger green spaces are frequently planned in some urban areas. These are extensions or retentions of elements of rural society.

Throughout the urbanized twentieth century, increasing emphasis has been placed on green space. The most used model in urban planning is the garden city. This model was developed by Ebenezer Howard in England in the 1890s (Howard 1965). The garden city is characterized by low density and maximum green space. It has contributed extensively to suburbanization in the last of the twentieth century. The garden city is in effect an antiurban model. The architect Le Corbusier poured scorn on the garden city, referring to it as a despicable delusion that is suburb-like and a product of a society stricken with blindness. But urban living has had its critics since industrialization began; Rousseau wrote that "cities are the final pit of the human spirit," and Shelley that "hell is a city just like London" (Jones 1966). The debate concerning the social height or depth of cities and the importance of rural and urban values continues into the present, as illustrated by books like *Cities in a Race for Time* (Lowe 1958), *The Death and Life of Great American Cities* (Jacobs 1961), *Arcology: The City in the Image of Man* (Soleri 1969), *Defensible Space* (Newman 1972), *Great Cities of the World* (Robson 1972), and *For Everyone a Garden* (Safdie 1974).

Studies of urban-rural differences open the way to intellectual understanding of suburban development, urban regionalism, and ecumenopolization.

URBANIZED SOCIAL ORGANIZATION

Demographic evidence shows that in the last one hundred years, not only rural living but even the city as a form of social invention is being replaced by massive urbanization (Doxiadis 1968; Soleri 1969; Davis and Papaioannou 1970). Urbanization is the permeating, tearing down, and often obliterating of rural lifestyles that are separate from city lifestyles. Urbanization is the domination of whole societies by city-generated ideas and values. In urbanized societies there are few socioeconomically significant urban-rural differences. Social organization, mass communication, mass marketing, and mass transportation make life within the political limits of cities and life outside those political limits essentially the same. This is the case in megalopolis areas like the American Northeast from Boston through New York to Washington, D.C., an area often called "Bo-Wash"; Central England from London to Liverpool and Manchester; and Southcentral Japan from Tokyo through Nagoya and Osaka to Kobe. In these areas some cities are totally surrounded by other cities, and some municipal areas are connected in strip developments forming large suburban patterns. Sociologically speaking, whether one lives in an open-country area or in a high-rise megastructure building in these conurbation areas, the social patterns of life are insignificantly different.

Two of the most stimulatingly controversial books treating the phenomenon of urbanization are *Ekistics* by C.A. Doxiadis and *Arcology* by Paolo Soleri. Doxiadis introduces the concept of "ecumenopolis," a strip-city development that becomes interconnected nationally, continentally and even worldwide. Ecumenopolis is, in essence, worldwide city. In America one sees it developing from the peninsula of Florida along the entire east coast to Boston, and from Boston inland to Chicago. On America's west coast it is developing from Seattle in the north through San Francisco to Los Angeles and San Diego in the south. Patterns of developing ecumenopolis are also clearly discernible in Europe and in Asia.

"Arcology," a megastructure concept developed by Soleri, is in sharp contrast with and proposed as an alternative to ecumenopolis. Soleri envisions vast megastructures, mile-high buildings, as the setting for the totality of human social life. In large single structures, people will have housing, jobs, hospitals, schools, industry, government, recreation, worship, and all other necessities of high-quality life. Many of the megastructures will have millions of people living out life within their physical boundaries. Soleri visualizes the arcologies to be places of highly satisfying human social interaction. Their environments would be largely recycled. The natural landscape outside would be preserved for agricultural and recreational use rather than destroyed by urban sprawl and ecumenopolis.

Doxiadis anticipates that the world will reach the ecumenopolis condition by 2150. By that year there is a possibility that the world population will reach more than 50 billion, as contrasted with the 4 billion of the 1970s. For either the ecumenopolis or the megastructure environment, scholars project the possibility of higher quality social life than has been achieved to date in either rural or city societies. Therefore much expansion of urban planning including new models for urban planning is anticipated.

PLANNING FOR URBANIZATION

The social history of urban planning is brief. Although all cities were new at some time in history, most had no broad-scale initial conceptualization or plan.

One of the longest experiences with national planning, and in effect with urbanization planning, has been in the Netherlands. More recently the Soviet Union and Canada each have planned and built new towns for interior territorial development. Often the primary purpose of these towns has been to support industrial development and/or mineral extraction. Though conceptualized as new towns, they are also a generic part of their society's expanding urbanization. In the United States there are industrial new towns like Kingsport, Tennessee and Kohler, Wisconsin. There are new towns initiated by the government: Norris, Tennessee to support the development of the Tennessee Valley Authority; and Boulder City, Nevada to support the development of the Hoover Dam; Los Alamos, New Mexico to support the development of atomic energy research. In Israel there is much new town building, primarily to move people inward from the seashore for agricultural and industrial development and to support the securing of frontiers. There are numerous other new towns being built for specific reasons, for instance Brasilia, a showplace capital for Brazil; Ciudad Guayana for hinterland industrialization and mineral extraction in Venezuela; and Chandigarh, a regional capital in India.

Conceptualized city planning for its own sake and on a broad societal scale originated in England in 1946. In that year the Parliament passed the Town and Country Planning Act, which gave endorsement to the Ebenezer Howard garden-city model. This low-density, suburban-like development model has been used extensively in Britain. It has also been quickly transferred to other nations. In 1968 the Congress of the United States passed the New Communities Act. The garden city again was implicitly accepted as the dominant new town form (Mields 1973).

In recent time only Brasilia (Haskell 1960) and Chandigarh (Evanson 1969) constitute strong alternatives to the garden-city model. Both Brasilia and Chandigarh are Grand Design or Baroque Design cities. Their scale is monumental, suprahuman. The megastructure model has been most imaginatively and forcefully proposed by Soleri and also in the Minnesota Experimental City, but no real prototype exists. Soleri's town Arcosanti, in Arizona, is too small to be a viable prototype of arcology.

Formal organization in urban planning

Little real conceptualization of social organization, social institutions, and social interaction exists in current urban building or in abstract theoretical models. Implicitly, if not explicitly, the urban planning models are physically or architecturally deterministic (Gutman 1965). Architects and urban planners typically try to achieve ideal social environments through physical designs (Reiner 1963).

Determinism by the built environment is a misconception. Human values, social status, primary and secondary social organization, and land tenure are all powerful variables in creating a high-quality urbanized social environment (Broady 1969).

Urbanization is a development of the last one hundred years, and its conceptualized planning is as recent as the last thirty years. It is with a sense of optimism that we join British urban sociologist Broady and others in turning to a concept that may be used as a mechanism for creating a higher quality urban environment, namely, formal social organization.

In the past twenty years sociologists have engaged in considerable research and writing concerning formal organizations (Blau and Scott 1962; Caplow 1964; Bertrand 1972). Much of this research has been conducted in industrial settings, welfare agencies, and military bureaucracies. To date, no major research has been done on the city or the new towns as formal organizations (Sessions 1979). However, when Athelton Spillhaus and his colleagues planned the Minnesota Experimental City as a megastructure-type new town for 250,000 people, they proposed that it be operated as a formal organization using the hotel as a model (Spillhaus 1968; MXC 1969; Alcott 1971).

Broady suggests that formal organization theory can be directly used in the planning and management of cities. As possible difficulties, however, he observes that the boundaries of cities are less clearly defined than those of industrial organizations, and that the purposes of cities are less precise than those of other organizations to which formal organizational theory is applied. As a starting point, however, new towns offer considerable promise. Their geographical boundaries are highly specified. Their anticipated populations are stated. Their specific goals are enumerated. Time schedules for building by stages are stipulated. They lack only the systematic integration of institutional spaces — family, education, industry, government, religion, health, welfare, recreation, and science. Planning for these institutions needs to be brought into a formally articulated model. Private property holding or socialized property are variables in the formal organizational model. Citizen participation, neighborhood organization, and community development are futher elements to be included.

Hard questions for formal organizational theory concern the relationships of one municipality to another or one urbanized region to another in an ecumenopolizing world. But in a theoretical sense, questions about such organizational interface are not different from those concerning the relationship of welfare agencies to health agencies, to protection agencies, and so forth. Neither are they different from those concerning the formal organizational relationships of military bureaucracy to governmental bureaucracy and to economic bureaucracy. Thus there are precedents that can serve in the analysis of more complex organizational relationships.

IMPLICATIONS

When cities were invented they were small. Their geographical space was minimal, and the number of people who inhabited them was few. Their unique functions were commercial, governmental, and religious. As cities have grown and as societies have become more urbanized, most of the social functions of life have begun to take place within urban areas and their immediate sociophysical environs. There was nothing in the initial concept of city to cope with, much less manage, the totality of human existence. As urbanization expands, it is clear that a high need of the urban environment is integrated management of institutional and physical spaces for total social life. Organization and management become major challenges for urbanized environments. Before exploring those challenges in detail, we turn first to a brief historic examination of urban forms in order to focus our perspectives and instruct our thinking concerning the developing urbanized condition.

REFERENCES

ALCOTT, J. A national proving ground: Minnesota experimental city. *American Institute of Architects Journal*, 1971, *56*, 37–39.
BERTRAND, A. *Social Organization*. Philadelphia: F.A. Davis, 1972.
BLAU, P. M., & SCOTT, W. R. *Formal Organization*. San Francisco: Chandler, 1962.
BRACEY, H. E. *Industry and the Countryside*. London: Routledge & Kegan Paul, 1970.

BROADY, M. The social context of urban planning. *Urban Affairs Quarterly*, March, 1969, pp. 355 – 78.
BROADY, M. The sociology of the urban environment. *Architectural Association Quarterly*, 1969, *1*, 65 – 71.
BROCKMAN, C. *Recreational Use of Wild Lands*. New York: McGraw – Hill, 1959.
CAPLOW, T. *Principles of Organizations*. New York: Harcourt, Brace & World, 1964.
CLAWSON, M. *Statistics on Outdoor Recreation*. Washington, D.C.: Resources of the Future, 1948.
DAVIS, K. & PAPAIOANNOU, J. G. Future urbanization patterns in Europe. *Ekistics*, 1970, *29*, 382 – 86.
DEWEY, R. The rural – urban continuum: real but relatively unimportant. *American Journal of Sociology*, 1960, *66*, 60 – 66.
DICKENSON, E. The geography of commuting: the Netherlands and Belgium. *Geographical Review*, 1957, *47*, 521 – 38.
DOXIADIS, C. A. *Ekistics*. New York: Oxford University Press, 1968.
EVANSON, N. *Le Corbusier: The Machine and the Grand Design*. New York: George Braziller, 1969.
GUTMAN, R. The questions architects ask. *Transactions of the Bartlett Society*, *4* (1965 – 1966).
HAMBLIN, D. *The First Cities*. New York: Time – Life Books, 1973.
HASKELL, D. Brasilia: a new type of national city. *Architecture Forum*, 1960, *113*, 126 – 33.
HOWARD, E. *Garden Cities of Tomorrow*. Cambridge: M.I.T. Press, 1965, 1898.
JACOBS, J. *The Death and Life of Great American Cities*. New York: Vintage, 1961.
JONES, E. *Towns and Cities*. New York: Oxford University Press, 1966.
KURTZ, R. A., & EICHER, J. B. Fringe and the suburb. *Social Forces*, 1958, *37*, 32 – 34.
LOWE, J. R. *Cities in a Race for Time*. New York: Vintage, 1968.
MIELDS, H., JR. *Federally Assisted New Communities*. Washington, D.C.: Urban Land Institute, 1973.
MXC: A Compendium of Publications Related to Socio – Economic Aspects. Minneapolis: University of Minnesota — MXC Project, 1969.
NEWMAN, O. *Defensible Space*. New York: Macmillan Co., 1972.
REINER, T. A. *The Place of the Ideal Community in Urban Planning*. Philadelphia: University of Pennsylvania Press, 1963.
ROBSON, W. A. & REGAN, D. E. *Great Cities of the World*. Beverly Hills, California: Sage Publications, 1972.
SAFDIE, M. *For Everyone a Garden*. Cambridge: M.I.T. Press, 1974.
SESSIONS, E. F. New towns: a social organizational analysis. Unpublished M.A. Thesis, University of Texas, Arlington, 1979.
SOLERI P. *Arcology*. Cambridge: M.I.T. Press, 1969.
SOROKIN, P. A. et al. *A Systematic Source Book in Rural Sociology*. Minneapolis: University of Minnesota Press, 1930.
SPILHAUS, A. The experimental city. *Science*, 1968, *159*, 710 – 15.
STEWART, C. T., JR. The urban – rural dichotomy. *American Journal of Sociology*, 1958, *64*, 52 – 58.
STRAUSS, A. L. *Images of the American City* New York: Free Press, 1961.

TAYLOR, L. *Urban – Rural Problems.* Los Angeles: Dickenson Publishing Co., Inc., 1968.

TAYLOR, L. & JONES, A. R. *Rural Life in Urbanized Society.* New York: Oxford University Press, 1964.

WARREN, R. Two models of social planning. In *Truth, Love, and Social Change and Other Essays on Community Change.* Chicago: Rand McNally, 1971.

WORTH, L., Urbanization as a way of life. *American Journal of Sociology,* 1938, 44, 1–24.

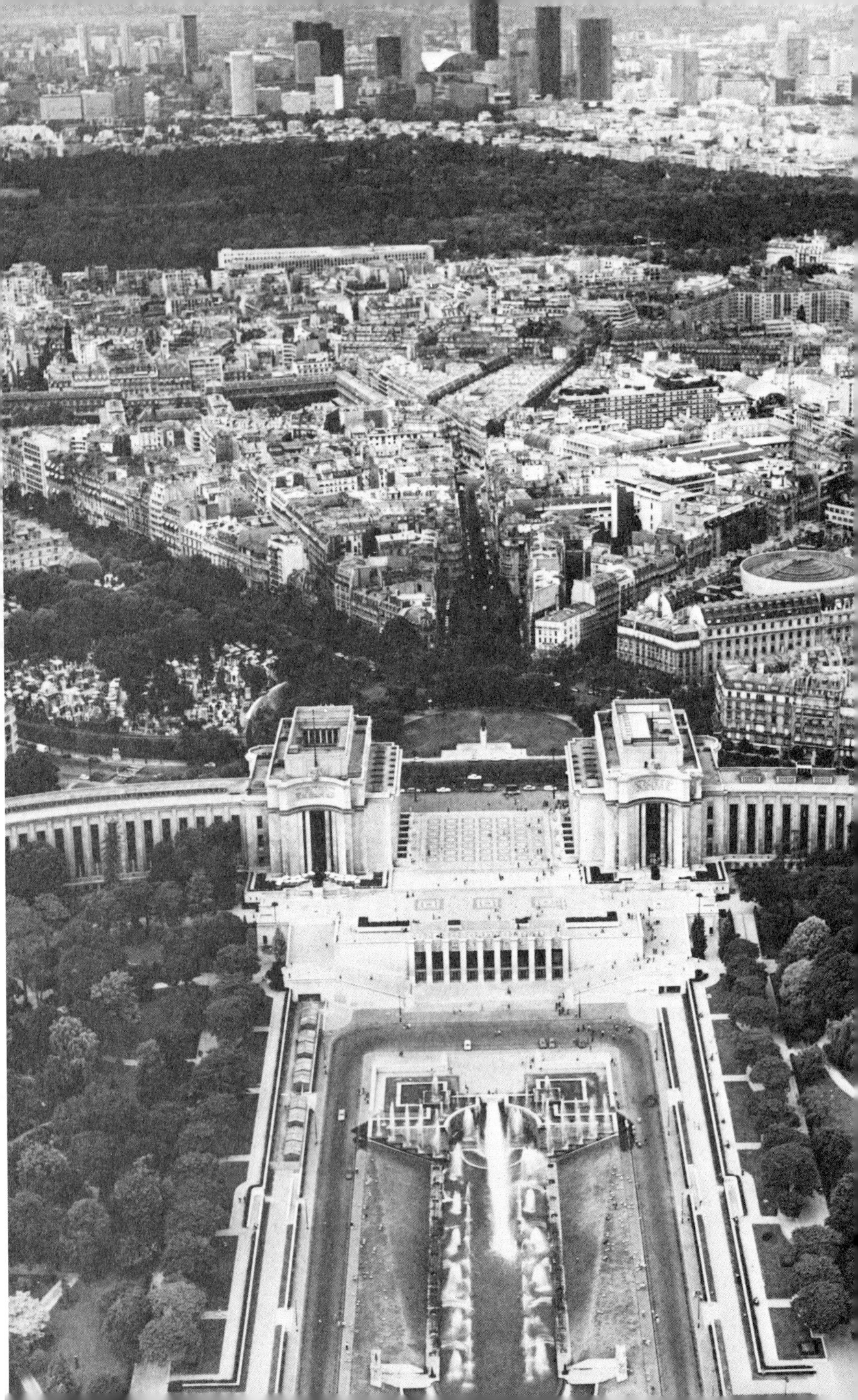

Historic Urban Forms and Social Interaction 2

People have dreamed of great cities. For some, the dreams become realities. Other urbanites live in circumstances ranging from nightmares to chaos.

The urban invention is a continuing process. This chapter is a survey of the past so that we may understand the present and set the stage to examine future urban directions.

HISTORIC URBAN PROCESSES

The task of understanding the reciprocal relationships between urban social life and the physical forms of cities is facilitated by historical perspectives. Neither sociocultural nor architectural or physical deterministic views can alone account for the changing nature of urban life.

When one asks why cities exist, what functions they perform, what purposes they fill, how they grow and expand, history reveals that urban physical forms have followed human mental images of the city and of urban patterns of social life. The process of urban invention involves first ideas, then social interaction to disseminate the ideas, and finally physical forms to embody the ideas. Social interaction occurs within the physical forms, and subsequently urban citizenry react to the physical forms. The physical forms, in turn, become a part of human perception. In this way the urban process involves ongoing interaction between ideas and the built environment.

Paris parks and streets are historic spaces for urban social interaction. (Photo: Mark Antman for Stock, Boston.)

The urban implosion

As human culture evolved through the long Paleolithic Era and through the Neolithic Era, social interactional complexities increased. Archaeologists find evidence of permanent settlements dating from fifteen thousand years ago in the late Paleolithic Era (Cavalli-Sforza 1974). After several hundred years of innovation and experimentation with embryonic Neolithic village settlements, the city was invented some fifty-five hundred years ago (Sirjamaki 1964).

One indication of the transition from rural values was the transformation in the conception of certain deities. "Mother Earth" and fertility goddesses dominated in early cultures. As agrarian social organizations came to be dominated by urbanism, "Mother Earth" deities became love goddesses like Astarte (Mumford 1961a), Aphrodite, Diana, and Juno, goddesses replete with sexuality, beauty, and erotic stimulation.

Early agricultural villages had houses, shrines, and roadways, but they lacked sufficient commercial specialization to give them the quality of cities. It was the greater level of commercial specialization that most differentiated cities from agricultural villages.

Some village elements have been known for over ten thousand years. It was the organizational conceptions of kings, later evolving into institutional kingships, and then evolving into the institution of government, that brought the urban elements into the city invention. The urban implosion, dominated by kings, brought together an array of elements that created a new way of life: commerce, ceramics, water transportation, metallurgy, mathematics, astronomy, the calendar, and writing.

In the early cities, religion was hardly less central than the institution of kingship. Sacred and secular power were close, sometimes taking the form of theocracy as occurred in Near Eastern and in Pre-Columbian cities. In accordance with these dominant kinds of social interaction, the early city's physical forms included palaces, temples, and granaries. These were forms for the support of government, religion, and commerce. Streets were for people — places for regular daily social life.

It is estimated that Ur occupied 220 acres, Khorsabad 740 acres, and Nineveh 1,800 acres (Mumford 1961a). These cities existed in what is now Iraq. There are difficulties in estimating the populations of these early cities. Sjoberg (1960) writes that even the largest probably had only between 5,000 and 10,000 people. Wooley (1954), excavator of Ur, on the other hand estimates that it had 34,000 people. By twentieth-century standards, early city populations were small, similar in size to modern neighborhoods. Yet the early cities were large enough to need

water, sewerage, and sanitation facilities. Accordingly, these were provided for in their built environment.

Conflict, violence, and warfare characterized the time when early cities were built. Walls were provided for protection. Here too, physical forms followed the primary needs of the inhabitants.

Purposes of cities

Paramount among the purposes of cities have been commerce and culture. Through these purposes new apexes in civilization have been achieved (Mumford 1961b; Sirjamaki 1964). The first social structures for achieving commerce and culture were dominated by kings and priests. The physical forms of early cities supported the institutionalization of these ideas.

In Greece, the urban invention matured so that the Greek polis was significantly different from its Mesopotamian predecessors. Greek cities were more human in scale. Gods and goddesses were still revered, and proper architectural spaces were provided for them — often in prime locations like the Acropolis in Athens. Nevertheless, the Greek cities by the fifth century B.C. were more characterized by the marketplace, a merchant middle class, and democracy. The agora, or marketplace, was a communal meeting place for political, social, and economic activities. Though a major bifurcation did exist between the free and the enslaved, for citizens, life in the Greek cities was often characterized by openness, citizen inquiry, and veneration of the mind. Activities in council and in court, in the workshop and in the marketplace, were as open as was nudity of the body in the gymnasium.

Achieving urban purposes

As ideas of social exchange were invented, matured, and modified, the physical forms of the city grew, contracted, and deteriorated. Urban power characterized the Roman Empire. To a considerable extent, the Empire was a city-building enterprise throughout most of Europe, Northern Africa, and Asia Minor (Mumford 1961a). After a thousand years of city building, the Roman Empire fell. At Rome's height, the capital was a city of a million inhabitants — the largest known metropolis of the time.

It is not the history of Rome, or of the Empire as such, which is our primary interest. Instead we are concerned with the social ideas, conflicts, and exchanges, as well as the built environment, which supported that urban power. Urbanism under the Romans was mobility — roads, traffic, and communication. Congestion on streets became so great that Julius Caesar banned wheeled traffic from Rome during the day. This made noise pollution at night so great that sleeping was difficult. In the expansive Roman cities, sewerage systems and water aqueducts were extensive. Great arenas for massive sporting events and other entertainment were erected; the Roman cities were sensate — sensual and material par excellence. Distinctions in social class were pronounced. And in the end there was a failure to integrate the complex city culture into meaningful patterns of social organization.

With the hindsight of history, the collapse of this extensive urban power may be charged to an excessive utilization of a suprahuman scale. The collapse was followed by an urban Dark Ages. In the Dark Ages the medieval small towns contributed little to achieving high urban purposes. Medieval urban life was simple and localized, with a high degree of territoriality. Walls precisely marked the boundaries. The medieval town was a mixture of burghers' shops and houses, fragrant flowers and orchards, with stables and horse dung. Medieval towns were full of little beauties and simple charm. Pageantry and dress were colorful. The sounds of birds and church chimes alternately filled the air. Workdays and marketing hours were signaled by sounding bells. Songs from monks and ballad singers emanated from places of worship and work. The detail of craft was a matter of faith and joy in life. But few urban apexes were achieved. This was a moratorium time in great urban building.

As the urban experience moved through the Middle Ages, many cities again became increasingly active in commerce and trade. For example Bruges, on the western part of the Hanseatic League, became enormous for that time. In the fourteenth century it may have had a population as large as 150,000. It was a city rich in trade, with its market square or Grand Place at its physical and social center. Social class distinctions were sharpened toward the end of the medieval city era; eventually the burgher classes dominated as a ruling oligarchy. They kept the lower classes in their place. Visible class distinctions in work, clothing, and housing were mechanisms used to achieve the stratification purposes of the medieval city (McMullen 1969).

As the medieval city matured and grew larger, its organization became more complex and its social class distinctions more precise. The economic institution expanded in importance. In effect, the city was outgrowing the small and human scale. Large-scale baroque urban forms were invented to accommodate the new social interactional needs. Swift and large-scale movement of people and goods were matters of high priority, and streets were widened. Baroque sociophysical models focused on central places and urban squares, which facilitated massive social exchanges. Many medieval cities evolved into baroque cities. Indeed, very few cities have been initially planned in the baroque style.

The evolution from the medieval city to the baroque involved more than just creating wide streets. In the medieval city, upper-, middle-, and lower-class people were thrust together for interaction in the streets, marketplaces, and cathedrals. In the baroque city, the rich rode in carriages and the poor walked. Social classes became more separated. The baroque city increasingly enabled the elites to protect themselves against the masses. Indeed, the broad streets could be used for police and military movement.

Napoleon III commissioned Haussmann to undertake what in effect was an urban renewal program in the baroque style in Paris between 1852 and 1870. Narrow streets were widened into broad avenues. A dozen streets, including the Champs Elysées, radiate from the Arc de Triomphe in Paris (Saalman 1971).

The Industrial Revolution marked another turning point for the urban invention. With large-scale industrialization, new urban purposes could be achieved. An entirely new sociophysical form, the factory, appeared on the urban landscape. Soon it was accompanied by the railroad, a mechanism for mass movement of materials, goods, and later people. Eventually railroads, like baroque avenues, dissected cities and permeated to their central core.

With industrialization, social class divided along Marxian lines into bourgeois and proletarian categories. With considerable rapidity, the proletarian workers came to inhabit large urban slums. The bourgeois and the new capitalists gradually moved to the periphery of the city and later into exclusive suburbs.

Industrial pollution and noise were elements of the early industrial city. Air circulation was poor, and lighting was often inadequate. Artificial gas lighting was invented to make possible extended hours of work — ultimately shift work. Subsequently, electric lights, telephones, and automobiles were invented and used to accelerate the expansion of the industrial city to new purposes. Problems of health and crime were exacerbated. Throughout the nineteenth century, places of work and places of residence were increasingly separated for the middle class and above. Poor people lived and worked in the slums.

With the automobile and improved communications in the early twentieth century, suburbanization expanded rapidly. As a physical form, suburbs were used for intermixing green space and open-area amenities with residential, commercial, and other service spaces (Lesser 1974). Suburbs are not new. They are identified with early cities like Ur. However, the suburb serves more dramatic and pronounced social and interactional needs for the industrial city. Suburbs are often differentiated by social class. They are frequently places for relaxing and leisure — the location of a goods-consuming newly rich. The suburb is also designed to reestablish some of the face-to-face, small-community life reminiscent of both the medieval city and the earlier ruralized societies. Suburbs continue to be experiments in modified urban ecology.

The phenomenon of mass urbanization continues at a rapid pace. About ten thousand years ago, the world population was estimated to be between 1 and 10 million. By 1 A.D., the population had grown to approximately 200 million. At the time of the early industrial city, 1750, the world population had increased to 0.7 billion. With the growth of the industrial city, population exploded upward. By 1850 there were 1.2 billion people on the planet Earth, by 1950 2.4 billion people, and by the 1970s 4 billion people (Thomlinson 1976). According to some demographers it is almost inevitable that the world population will be near 8.5 billion by 2050, in spite of some movement toward zero population growth (Freedman 1974). The problem of high civilization and multiple purposes for city development are sharply challenged in the face of this precipitous population growth. Much of the intensely urbanized part of the world is now moving toward zero population growth. It is in the Third World and less urbanized parts of the world that population growth is greatest. World population growth may not be stabilized before the total reaches 10 to 15 billion — and some even suggest 50 billion by 2150 (Papaioannou 1970).

Urban population density may increase along with the increase in total population. The history of the urban response to increased densities is two-directional. On the one hand, there is the development of high-rise buildings (Jensen 1966; Soleri 1969; Dantzig 1973; Mixed-Use Buildings 1975). And on the other hand, horizontal dispersion, which becomes conurbation and megalopolis, moves toward ecumenopolis (Gottman 1967; Doxiadis 1968). Increasingly, high-rise buildings serve multiple urban purposes including residences, offices, shopping, schools, health and recreational facilities. These large multipurpose buildings are megastructures.

With the increasing amount and the high density of urban population, problems of pollution, crime, health, and sanitation all frustrate the challenge to achieve the urban purpose of high-quality civilization. Ecological balance and recycling are responses that receive increased attention in cities facing these problems. The problems are not new, but with more large cities they become intensified. Numerous scholars in a variety of different ways have asserted that the city is more than its physical form and its individual citizenry. Mumford (1961) and Geddes (1915) have submitted that the city is a matter of spirit, community, and overriding collectivity. Doxiadis (1974) suggests that the city is an urban system in which all citizens should profit from the use of all urban land and all urban space.

The history of cities reveals urban people experimenting increasingly with planned environments. Furthermore, there is a gradual spreading of the idea that the city may be a formal organization. From this viewpoint, the high purposes of the city, namely, planned civilization, will be achieved more frequently and more expeditiously when specific goals are articulated and specific methods are established for achieving these goals.

SOCIAL INSTITUTIONS

Social institutions are important societal building blocks for stable urban life. They are found in all societies. Since ruralized social organization predates urbanized social organization, a significant amount of the folkway content of social institutions has been rural rather than urban. During the period of early urban history, the disproportionate rural content of social institutions was an impediment to city growth. Early cities were much too small to be complete societies. But with the industrial cities of the nineteenth century, large populations came to live out their total lives in urbanized environments. The city's culture spread far beyond its physical limits. By the twentieth century, industrial nations became saturated with urban culture. Consequently, the social institutions that support all the society are in effect challenged to support orderly urbanized society.

Government institutions are problematic in urban areas. To a considerable extent, government in the early cities was dominated by kings. These central figures expanded their powers to national levels. Gradually, it became traditional for municipal governments to be chartered by national governments. The authority of the municipal governments is historically limited and sharply subjugated to national governments. Nevertheless, some cities have exceeded their physical limits. The Roman cities were cities of the world. The Hanseatic League cities traded widely in multiple national areas. By the twentieth century, many cities had world trade centers, international seaports, and international airports. The relationships between modern cities and their national governments varies widely; contemporary British cities have much local autonomy, while French cities are extensively controlled by the central government. The government and regulation of activities within cities, between cities, and among cities continue as major problems.

In a technical sense, one municipal government has no authority over another municipal government. Indeed city governments compete with each other for internal and external influence and superiority. The

Doge's Palace in Venice is an impressive physical building located in the center of the city to share prestige and power only with the adjacent cathedral. The town halls in Amsterdam, Copenhagen, Stockholm, and Oslo, for example, are all situated at places of prominence. They have banqueting halls and other large, imposing public gathering facilities. In physical scale and grandeur they express a power greater than that which the charter renders to the "city hall." In the United States, the new city hall in Boston follows in the tradition of those of the great cities of Europe in its symbolically grand physical scale.

In modern Moscow, city government focuses more on district councils than on physical buildings. In Toronto, Canada and in Miami, Florida, the thrust of government is federated and consolidated, respectively, with smaller urban municipalities. The forms of urban governments, both socially and physically, increasingly are oriented toward metropolitan areas and urban regions.

Historically the institution of religion has been prominent in cities. As with other elements of urban culture, the city manifestation of religion is complex. A simple notion of Mother Earth's producing an abundant harvest was a dominating theme in much rural life. In urban life, priestly forms of religious rites expanded. Urban priests articulated the ideas of justice, equity, and fellowship. On the other hand, in early cities the gods were often conceived as vengeful, and urban areas waged war against each other in defense of their gods and with their "direction."

Religion and government in urban areas have at times engaged in hostile competition and at other times existed in peaceful and supportive coexistence. Religious leaders often bless the installation of political leaders, and in juxtaposition, political leaders have at times exercised considerable control over priestly activities. In Mesopotamian and Pre-Columbian cities, ziggurats and pyramids for places of worship and pageantry were prominent (Hammond 1973). In the medieval city too, the church was the most prominent physical feature on the landscape.

In the industrial city, religious buildings became dwarfed by manufacturing plants and high-rise skyscrapers. Separation of religion from municipal governments has become ubiquitous. Privileges of property tax exemption for places of worship are more and more being questioned. In many cities there remains even little tokenism in having representation from the priestly classes participate in the affairs of government. In the central city the physical religious facilities deteriorate and are torn down. Attempts to provide religious spaces in big urban airports, hospitals, and schools often fail. Some observers suggest that the industrial city, if characterized by religion at all, is characterized by civil religion. They suggest that the real meaning of human equity, justice, and morality is being carried out in municipal ordinances and legislation related to open housing, civil rights, and equal employment opportunities.

From the earliest cities to the present, literacy and learning have been major characteristics of urban life. Centers of learning have been highly developed in the cities. Their forms range from preschool nurseries to universities and continuing education programs. Yet even the greatest universities in cities embody but small parts of urban socialization. The totality of life in the plural culture of the city is a dynamic socializing and educational experience.

Diverse urban cultures produce knowledge, and the physical form of the city becomes a kind of historical record of that knowledge. Great cities are replete with libraries, archives, museums, symphonies, and theaters. High accomplishments in civilizations are preserved and venerated in the city. Cities support the generation of new ideas. For example, the artist-in-residence program that supported the sculptor Vigeland in the city of Oslo gave that city a landmark of artistic distinction, an entire park filled with sculpture. Cities have supported the growth of knowledge by encouraging great research hospitals and other research centers. Great universities and major cities have numerous overlapping interests. In the past, learning in the cities took place in such areas as the Greek agora; in the Middle Ages the university was a wandering university. Today, vast physical facilities with enormous libraries and research hardware are part of the socialization-education-knowledge base of contemporary cities.

Commerce, the economic institution, historically has been a major component of urban life. City people are producers and distributors of goods and services. Historic specializations have included craftsmen, burghers, priests, and rulers. City people produce parts of their means of livelihood and trade for other needed materials.

Early physical forms to support commercial social interaction were streets, squares, and shops. As production and trading proliferated, still more physical forms were added to support commercial needs. Ports and warehouses were constructed. Docks and equipment for loading and unloading were provided. Stores were gradually separated from workshops. Factories, rail transportation, truck transportation, and air transportation have been added.

As trade and commerce intensified in central city areas, concepts like the central business district evolved. The ecology of the city was modified so that along with naming the central area as a business district, zoning ordinances supported the movement of residential areas to the periphery of the city. Separation of businesses and residences became normative. Commercial activities were typically limited to the day time, while production activities could be carried out in multiple shifts or continuously on a twenty-four-hour basis.

In today's cities, limited access freeways and bus systems have been designed to move masses of people centripetally to the core of the city in the early daylight hours and centrifugally to the periphery of the city in the late afternoon. The transportation form of the city would be substantially different if virtually all trading and all production were put on a twenty-four-hour basis. People-movement systems could be used more efficiently. Peak transit hours would be reduced, with movement distributed more evenly throughout the day.

In urbanized society many industries, even the food production industry, are moving to a twenty-four-hour system. Lights on equipment expand a harvest day, and poultry units are operated around the clock. Recent city history suggests that economic institutions might undergo still more substantive modifications to reduce problems of transportation and pollution.

Housing and family procreative institutions in urban populations are experiencing considerable innovation and modification. Historically, urban dwelling places have been attached, not separated by lot lines. In early cities, shops were at the street level and residential quarters were above them, with gardens and patio spaces in the rear for some food production, service activities, and general social interaction. As cities became larger and mechanized transportation systems became typical, commercial production areas more gradually separated from residential areas.

In complex urban social organization, procreation gradually became separated from general socialization and education. Specialized childrearing centers and schools were established separate from, although often proximic to, residential areas. Nuclear families rather than extended families are characteristic of the city. Health care and care for the aged have been gradually removed from the family. Hospital and gerontological facilities are expanded in cities.

It is in the city environment that secondary institutional activities like art, science, recreation, health care, and welfare reach their highest form. They give definitive character and special flavor to great urban cultures. The city-scape of Sidney, Australia is known for its opera house. Lincoln Center for the Performing Arts in New York City is world renowned. Scientific research institutes are found in the world's major cities. Some large new towns in the Soviet Union lead in scientific research and production. Spectacular recreational events have occurred in cities, from the coliseum events of Ancient Rome to the Olympic Games of the twentieth century. Practically all of the world's greatest hospitals and health research centers are located in cities or in megalopolis areas. Welfare institutions for people of all ages are distributed through large cities, whereas few are in the open country.

Much of the tradition of cities is a history of expanding social institutions supported by physical buildings designed for specific types of social exchange.

Urban life social patterns

In addition to the social institutions and activity systems described thus far, there are three social patterns of urban life which, while not institutional, are characteristic of cities through history. One is the distinction of social classes. Another is the development of transportation systems to move people in the city from place to place. Another is the problem of various kinds of pollution in the city environment.

Social class distinctions take visible social forms (*Cities* 1973). Social classes are discernible by where people sit in music halls and opera houses; boxes and dress circles have a special high prestige, and seats are often specifically reserved in them for officials and high-ranking persons. On a much larger scale, decaying slums and affluent suburbs bear physical witness to social class differences. Uniforms and occupational titles, which are widely used in cities, mark further class distinctions.

Transportation is a central concern in cities. Cities maintain street and transportation departments. Port authorities for both sea and air are typical parts of urban culture. Elevator construction and maintenance are often regulated by city building codes and ordinances. The vertical movement of people in elevators is generally free of charge on a direct-service basis, whereas horizontal movement of people in cars and buses and by railway is usually a matter of pay-as-you-go on the part of customers. Seldom are municipal transportation systems free, although rates do vary for some hours, some days, and some ages. The history of urban social structures illustrates continuing innovation in regard to transportation.

Pollution is not new to the city. Some degree of pollution has been found in cities through the ages. But in the large industrializing cities of the twentieth century, pollution is a more pressing problem than in the past. In the Tokaido megalopolis of Japan, air pollution is so intense at times that head masks are worn. In Mexico City and Los Angeles, air pollution is often so great that respiratory disorders are serious. Noise pollution near airports, railways, and construction sites has also become oppressive and detrimental to health ("Noise" 1975).

MATCHING SOCIAL NEEDS AND PHYSICAL FORMS

The importance of urban history for urban sociology and contemporary city planning is to demonstrate the social needs of urban people, so that sociophysical responses can be developed to meet those needs. The physical forms of cities are manifestations of their social functions (Gallion and Eisner 1963).

Classic cities

The period of classic cities extended from about 800 B.C. to about 500 A.D. in the areas of Greece and Rome (Glotz 1929). This was the first era of extensive urban living after the initial thrust of the city invention some two thousand years earlier. Among the Greeks the city gradually developed a wealthy and powerful class of people who challenged the authority of kings. Along with the land-owning wealthy, there developed a merchant middle class. After a considerable power struggle between the land owners and the merchants, a balance was reached whereby they both selected leaders for the city. In this process, the city became a place where laws were formulated by free citizenry. By the fifth century B.C., democracy had become a new and dominant form under the leadership of Pericles. Though slavery did exist, citizens enjoyed many freedoms, including freedom of speech and assembly. Public service was recognized with prestige and dignity. Knowledge was encouraged as a basis for democratic law and order. Social norms were established which provided citizens with a full opportunity to participate in the conduct of urban affairs. Reason, logic, and science were foundation stones for the organization of these classic cities. In the classic city more emphasis was placed on social organization and democratic ideology than on physical form. There were spaces for common assembly — usually in open-air amphitheaters. Citizens came to debate urban affairs. For the commercial middle class, the marketplace was a center of activity. The principal market was located at or near the geographical center of the city.

By the fifth century A.D., city planning was given systematic attention. The architect Hippodamus advanced what is now known as the grid street system. To some extent a perpendicular street system was known in Mesopotamia and in the ancient cities along the Indus River. In the classic city it was elevated to a systematic plan whereby all citizens would have a more equal access to the places for public meetings and marketing. The grid was not for urban design. It was a system created to facilitate the social organization of democracy in the city. The blocks were of a size and shape to enable people to move expeditiously between their modest places of residence and the centers of major social activities. In the cities' centers there gradually developed, in addition to the marketplace, assembly halls, council halls, and council chambers for public service and community functions. A part of this early city planning was the notion of rights-of-way. Building restrictions reserved the integrity of the street to be open to traffic and prohibited second and higher floors from projecting over the first floors adjacent to streets.

In the fourth century B.C., the power and leadership of Greek cities had begun to decline and that of the Roman cities to increase. The continuing growth and prosperity of classic cities shifted to Rome and other European parts of the Roman Empire. The Romans added expertise and achievement in engineering and other technical areas. While the Greeks had been achievers in democracy, they were underachievers in technological developments like water and sewerage systems. In these, and in road and street building, the Romans excelled; they also expanded the scale of cities to be much larger than those of the Greeks. Monuments to Roman power were built on a suprahuman scale. But in Rome social justice and democratic organization were eroded. By 400 A.D., slums in the cities of the Roman Empire were large. The affluent moved to the country or at least to the fringe areas of the cities. The classic cities met their demise when they were overrun by barbarians. The light of urban civilization was nearly extinguished. The period of the urban Dark Ages followed.

Medieval cities

Cities survived the Dark Ages but with great difficulty. It took five hundred years to make a substantive comeback. By the eleventh century, small cities were being built or existing towns were being restored to a vital new life. New city charters were granted. Citizens were given rights and privileges seldom known by the serfs who had farmed the land of medieval nobles. Urban population grew steadily. Merchants and craftsmen organized themselves into guilds and thereby established a new social order. The guilds provided for occupational specialization in metalwork, textiles, stonework, mining, carpentry, glassmaking, and so forth. The merchant classes grew and eventually overpowered the earlier landowning rural classes.

Churches and church plazas were located at the center of dominance in medieval cities. The church plazas often became urban market places. Town halls and guild halls were built near the cities' centers. These were key elements of the new urban town centers. The population of medieval cities was small, and most traffic was by foot. Streets were frequently curvilinear, and ascent from lower to higher levels was aided by steps. Medieval cities were walled. Cities were sharply different from rural areas in physical form as well as in social aspects such as occupational specialization.

The medieval cities gave what little support there was during this period to intellect and the arts. Research in monasteries, sometimes open and sometimes clandestine, provided inquiry and training in law, medicine, and the arts. By the twelfth and thirteenth centuries, universities grew up in Bologna, Paris, Cambridge, Krakow, and Salamanca. Some hospital facilities also were supported by the church.

Pageantry, song, and drama were added to the spirit and color of medieval cities by the church. These activities were participated in enthusiastically by most urban inhabitants. Although there were social class distinctions between merchants, artisans, peasants, and others, the small medieval cities were structured to provide for high rates of social interaction.

The knowledge base and social-organizational diversification continued to proliferate into and through the Renaissance. Cities grew larger. In the fourteenth and fifteenth centuries, it was not uncommon for urban populations to reach between 50,000 and 200,000. Technology lagged behind population growth. Congestion and disease became rampant in some of the larger cities. Epidemics of the Black Death (bubonic plague) and typhus reduced the urban population by nearly one-half in the fourteenth century (Gallion and Eisener 1963). By the sixteenth and early seventeenth centuries, sanitary systems and water systems were developed and expanded.

Renaissance cities pulsated with creativity and participation in the arts. Wealthy merchants and churchmen became patrons of the arts. Painting, sculpture, music, and architecture all were occupational specializations. Some cities were expanded and rebuilt in the grand style, incorporating the arts.

Baroque urban forms

Baroque city planning and building are high forms of urban culture. The baroque city plans are monumental — suprahuman in scale. They glorify urbanized social organization as a thing in and for itself.

The baroque urban form focuses on central places or squares connected by wide avenues that facilitate the rapid movement of people and goods for both economy and pleasure. The grandiose scale of the avenues also facilitate military, political, and economic display. Such avenues allow for automotive or other mechanical movement of masses of people, in sharp contrast to the modest pedestrian streets of the small medieval city (Mumford 1961a; Koenigserb 1968). Versailles, Washington, D.C., and Vienna are built in the baroque form. Christopher Wren attempted some rebuilding of London in the Baroque model following the great fire in that city in 1666. Of social organizational significance is that Wren planned to place the London Stock exchange at the central focus, in contrast to a traditional palace or cathedral. In the mid-nineteenth century, Paris was rebuilt in the baroque model.

Brasilia, Brazil and Chandigarh, India are baroque cities of the second half of the twentieth century. They are designed for large populations and have major areas connected by wide avenues with grandiose buildings. The architecture of these cities is plain and severe, displaying none of the elaborate decorative details associated with the façades of earlier baroque buildings.

The baroque urban form is intended to match the needs of complex urban social life.

Industrial cities

By the late eighteenth and early nineteenth centuries, industrial production became large-scale. Baroque avenues and squares were by themselves inadequate to meet the needs of industrialization. The industrial city needs space for manufacturing, and this must be supported by rail, water, truck, and air transportation.

The assembly line for mass production enabled the size of factories to grow and the number of workers to be increased. Capitalism provided models for money accumulation to support the expansion of manufacturing and distribution of products. In this milieu, population densities increased and urban traffic congestion grew. Large tracts of urban land were used for factories and for rail and roadways to bring in raw materials and return manufactured products. Early factory buildings were plain and unappealing. The physical environment around them was frequently polluted. The middle and upper classes moved to peripheral areas of the cities and to suburbs. Tenant slum areas grew around factories.

The new form of industrial cities rapidly became one in which land use was sharply differentiated. By the first quarter of the twentieth century, the idea of zoning was invented, and municipal zoning ordinances were rapidly passed and upheld by the courts. Zoning provided for heavy industry, light industry, commercial areas, detached residential areas, attached residential areas, recreational areas, school sites, church sites, and hospital sites.

In some important respects the industrial city was a conglomerate — even a noncity. There were few spaces large enough for social interaction for all the types and classes of people. Industrial cities were in effect highly stratified and sharply segregated. But while they lost the high quality of social interaction characteristic of medieval cities, industrial cities excelled in introducing and distributing goods and in supporting science and education. In sum, the industrial city was a material success but an interpersonal frustration. Antisocial behavior, in particular crimes against people and property, accelerated.

Suburbs, megalopolis, and ecumenopolis

By the middle of the twentieth century, the suburbs became a typical appendage to the industrial city. A big city's affluent population attempts to escape from the problems and antisocial behavior of the declining industrial city core. In some cases the affluent attempt to isolate themselves in small residential municipalities that are totally surrounded by big industrial cities. In other cases the affluent commute to suburban municipalities that are exclusive in their zoning and deed restrictions. But exclusionary zoning and suburbanization fail to enable the urban population to achieve much of the city's original purpose.

At the end of the twentieth century, new inventions in urban forms are being attempted. Superblocks and planned developments are designed for rebuilding the industrial city as well as for building new towns. These are attempts to integrate residential space, open and/or green space, commercial space, and employment space in a sociophysical form that will support both high technical production and positive social interaction.

With rapid urbanization, cities and suburbs are growing together in large conurbations. They are also growing together in megalopolis forms as in Tokaido, Japan and Bo-Wash, U.S.A., with populations larger than many nations. Future-oriented concepts like ecumenopolis suggest that by the twenty-second century, twentieth century conurbations and megalopolises will be connected in continental and even worldwide strip cities.

High-rise and megastructure forms

High-rise buildings express a clear urban mentality (Jensen 1966). They illustrate advances in late-nineteenth-century building technology. Great density pressure was felt in the central areas of the old industrial cities. High-rise buildings enable more offices, stores, and related facilities to be located in the densely populated central business areas. High-rise hotels and apartments are also added to cities' central areas.

There are numerous questions concerning the economic costs and the quality of social life in high-rise buildings. One view is that high-rise buildings are efficient in cost and land utilization, and provide desirable living-working conditions. They can be designed with balconies for gardens and green spaces, and with halls and other kinds of facilities to support positive social interaction (Wood 1961). Le Corbusier (1971) has designed high-rise cities in which there would be extensive green space to support a quality environment.

An opposing view regards the high-rise as a human jungle that is economically costly and disproportionately generative of antisocial behavior. Doxiadis (1971), for example, argues that high-rise buildings isolate human beings from each other and work against man's social nature, increasing the probability of crime. He believes that children in high-rise buildings lose direct contact with nature. It is also argued that the neighborhood unit is eroded in the high-rise building environment. Critics of the high-rise observe that the increased densities they bring contribute to cognitive overload (excessive mind and/or mental stimulus confusion), to thoroughfare congestion, and to breakdowns in services. Finally, those who argue against high-rise buildings charge that they destroy the urban landscape. Churches and civic centers were once the tallest buildings in cities; now they are dwarfed and obscured by commercial and residential skyscrapers.

Oscar Newman (1972) is more empirical in his argument against high-rise spaces. Typical buildings, between seven and fifteen stories, house from 100 to 150 or more families. There is little opportunity for primary-group social control, or control by close personal friendships. Consequently, unless there are protective electronic devices, patterns of entrance and exit in elevators and in interior halls can be carefully observed by deviants so that muggings, rapings, and other antisocial behavior can occur there with impunity. In New York, Newman found that 80 percent of the crime in housing projects took place within the buildings — crimes of mugging, burglary, larceny, rape, and assault. Muggings constitute some 95 percent of the crimes in the public spaces in buildings, and burglaries 90 percent inside individual apartments. It is Newman's thesis that buildings up to six or seven stories high designed in cross shapes maximize defensible space, while high-rise buildings in rectilinear shapes minimize defensible space. In lower buildings there are many windows, which give people visual contact with entry areas. Both interior and exterior spaces around the entrances may become social spaces. Not only can people observe who enters and exits, they can become acquainted with persons who frequent the buildings. All of these characteristics are generally absent in the high-rise building. The point argued is that natural surveillance through acquaintance and social exchange is superior to mechanical surveillance through television cameras and emergency call devices.

Yet when one carefully analyzes neighborhood and community experiences in the city, and socioeconomic characteristics of persons interacting in high-rise spaces, the issues become more complex. Much of the antisocial behavior identified by Newman was in high-rise buildings populated by persons in the lower-middle and upper-lower classes. It appears that in high-rise buildings inhabited by persons in the upper-middle classes and above, there are no significant problems with antisocial behavior and few if any significant problems with social interaction of a neighborhood type.

Indeed, as megastructures are being planned, the possibility for positive social interaction increases. The megastructure model developed by Soleri (1969) is specifically designed to be large enough for all of the social-institutional experiences of life to be carried out within it. The possibility for neighborhood and community social interaction of a positive type is real in the megastructure. In sum, one finds that the history of the high-rise is recent and rapidly changing. Only at the end of the twentieth century is it being conceptualized fully as an appropriate place for total urban living. Its satisfactoriness for that end remains to be tested.

IMPLICATIONS

The city and its urbanisms are social inventions with physical expressions. Urban people interact in built environments. The built environment and the natural environment are among the variables which reciprocally influence behavior. Human beings learn to respond to characteristics of their built environment. Some forms of physical environment contribute to a higher or lower quality of social interaction. Penal institutions with solitary confinement cells contribute to one kind of social interaction, university campuses with quadrangles contribute to another kind of social life, and shopping malls support still other patterns of social activities.

The history of mankind illustrates that the urban experience is comparatively new. The social history of the city reveals that the secondary social organization which characterizes it is contrived, manmade, not natural. The medieval city, the superblock, and the garden city express related forms of urban, if not antiurban, social interaction. They are oriented to low density and primary social interaction. The baroque urban forms and the now-developing megastructure forms are intensely urban in character. As the social organization of the urban invention matures, physical forms are being designed to embody it. The extent to which humans can be socialized for urbanity, and for its goal of high-quality civilization, remains to be tested in the more complete use of new urban forms.

REFERENCES

CAVALLI-SFORZA, L. L. The genetics of human population. In *Human Population*. San Francisco: W. H. Freeman, 1974, 41–52.
Cities: Their Origin, Growth, and Human Impact. San Francisco: W. H. Freeman, 1973.

DANTZIG, G. G., & SAATY, T. L. *Compact City: A Plan for a Liveable Urban Environment.* San Francisco: W. H. Freeman, 1973.
DOXIADIS, C. A. *Ekistics.* New York: Oxford University Press, 1968.
DOXIADIS, C. A. The great urban crimes we commit by law. *Ekistics,* 1974, *219,* 85 – 88.
FREEDMAN, R., & BERELSON, B. The human population. In *The Human Population.* San Francisco: W. H. Freeman, 1974.
GALLION, A. B., & EISNER, S. *The Urban Pattern* (2nd ed.). New York: Van Nostrand, 1963.
GEDDES, P. *Cities in Evolution.* New York: Harper and Row, 1971.
GLOTZ, G. *The Greek City and Its Institutions.* London: Kegan Paul, Trench Trubner, 1929.
GOTTMAN, J. *Megalopolis.* Cambridge: M.I.T. Press, 1967.
HAMMOND, N. The planning of a Maya ceremonial center. In *Cities.* San Francisco: W. H. Freeman, 1973, 72 – 81.
JENSEN, R. *High Density Living.* New York: Praeger, 1966.
KOENIGSERB, M. D. Urban development: an introduction to the theories of Lewis Mumford. In S. Fava (Ed.), *Urbanism in a World Perspective.* New York: Crowell, 1968.
LE CORBUSIER. *The City of Tomorrow and Its Planning.* Cambridge: M.I.T. Press, 1971.
LESSER, W. Patrick Geddes, the practical visionary. *Town Planning Review,* 1974, *45,* 311 – 27.
MCMULLEN, R. The life and death of Bruges. *Horizon,* 1969, *11,* 74 – 90.
MUMFORD, L. The city in history. *Horizon,* 1961a, *3,* 32 – 64.
MUMFORD, L. *The City in History.* New York: Harcourt, Brace & World, 1961b.
NEWMAN, O. *Defensible Space.* New York: Macmillan Co., 1972.
Noise: new regulations reflect growing concern about noise pollution. *The Futurist,* 1975, *9,* 63.
PAPAIOANNOU, J. G. Future urbanization patterns in Europe. *Ekistics,* 1970, *29,* 382 – 86.
SAALMAN, H. *Haussmann: Paris Transformed.* New York: George Braziller, 1971.
SIRJAMAKI, J. *The Sociology of Cities.* New York: Random House, 1964.
SJOBERG, G. *The Pre-Industrial City.* Glencoe, Ill.: Free Press, 1960.
SOLERI, P. *Arcology.* Cambridge: M.I.T. Press, 1969.
STEPHENS, S. Mixed-use buildings: microcosms of urbanity. *Progressive Architecture,* 1975, *56,* 37 – 51.
THOMLINSON, R. *Population Dynamics* (2nd ed.). New York: Random House, 1976.
WOOD, E. *Housing Design: A Social Theory.* New York: Citizen's Housing & Planning Council of New York, 1961.
WOOLEY, L. *Excavations at Ur.* London: Benn, 1954.

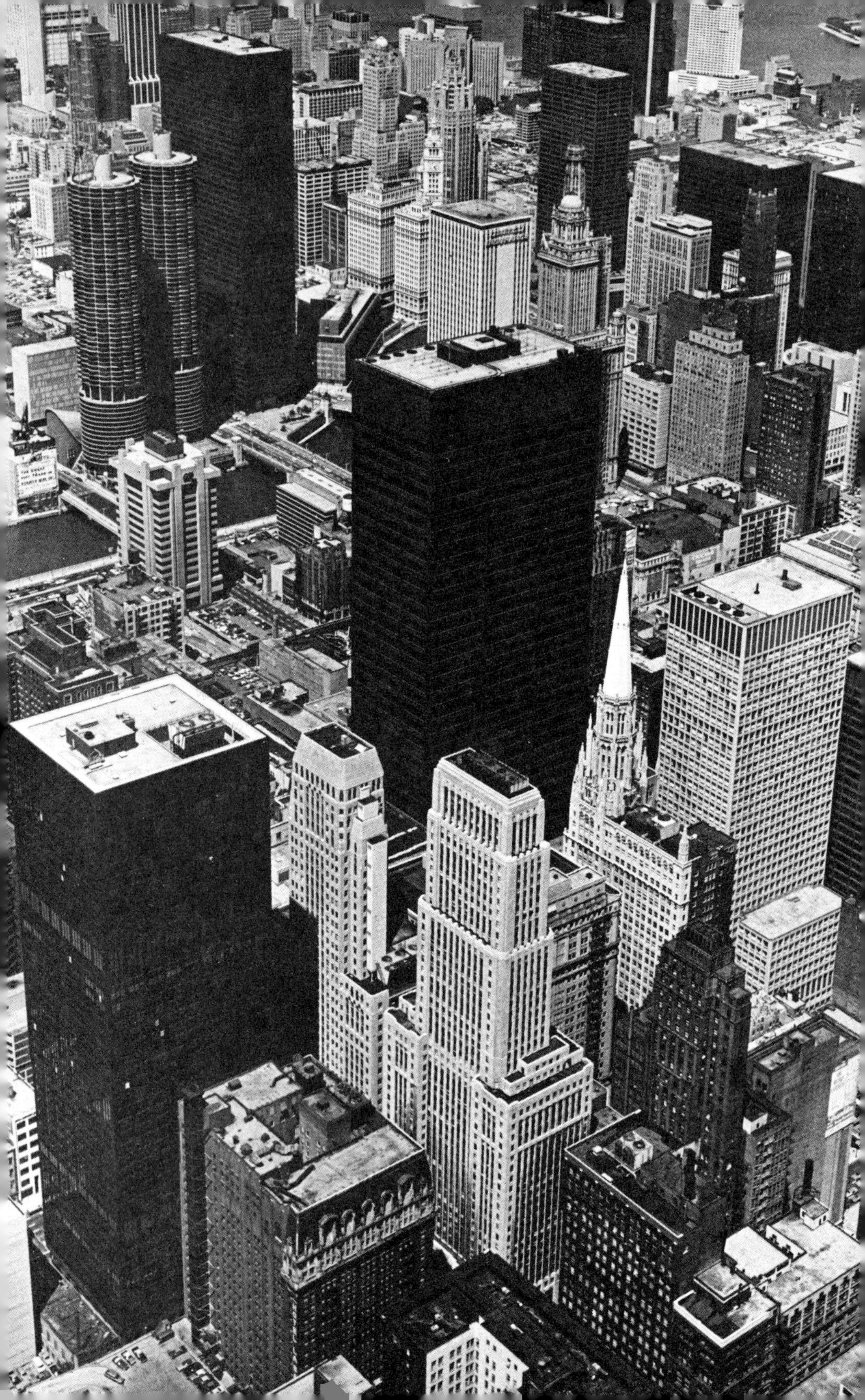

An Urbanized Planet 3

Urbanization is an experience of the last one hundred years. It originated in the industrial West, and it is rapidly becoming worldwide. By the year 2000 it is expected that half of the world's population will be urban. By 2150, some planners expect that ecumenopolis, worldwide city life, will dominate society.

The recency and rapidity of urbanization explains why so many problems of urban life are not yet solved. Intellectually and practically, urban challenges are still unfolding. Those who predict the decline and fall of urbanization do so before it has even passed through its tumultuous adolescence (Forrester 1971; Meadows 1972). Urban problems are many, but so are urban prospects. Doxiadis and others suggest that worldwide urbanization offers the possibility of a higher quality civilization than humans have ever known (Doxiadis 1968; Berry 1974).

CONCEPTS AND ORIENTATIONS

The city concept

There is no widespread agreement on the definition of city, much less of urbanization. There are, however, numerous operational definitions. The U.S. Bureau of the Census uses as the minimum definition of city a place of 2,500 or more people. On a worldwide basis city definitions generally range between populations of 1,000 and 10,000 (Smith 1976). These definitions are useful but limited. For the purposes of un-

The planet Earth urbanizes. (Photo: Jean-Claude Lejeune for The Stockmarket.)

derstanding cities and seeking to build high-quality civilizations, the core of the urban concept is neither a particular number of people nor a particular physical space, but the quality and quantity of social exchange that differentiates urban from rural life. From a sociological perspective, what distinguishes the city is that it is a place characterized by extensive secondary (impersonal, transient) social interaction, by plural cultures, by diverse occupations, and by extensive production and distribution of goods and services.

An urbanized society is characterized by patterns of behavior, social structures, and ideologies which originate in the city and dominate beyond the city limits throughout the total society (Taylor 1964; Davis 1968). By contrast, a ruralized society is one in which the social structures guide, direct, and embody social life both inside cities and in the open country with a bucolic content, even though boundaries might be precisely marked, as with physical walls. From the seventh to the tenth centuries in Western Europe, social life was largely ruralized. While some cities continued to exist throughout this time, there was little difference in the content and quality of life on either side of the city walls (Pirenne 1925). Clergymen and craftsmen in the walled cities often had little "light" or learning to distinguish them from peasants.

Urban life is often assumed to be superior to rural life. Accordingly, some contemporary societies, like the People's Republic of China, are systematically attempting to minimize urban elitism and maximize urban-rural cooperation (Lewis 1971). In any event it is assumed that in urbanized society, urban-rural differences should minimize as urbanisms tend to obliterate ruralisms.

Urbanized Areas and Standard Metropolitan Statistical Areas

In the United States the Bureau of the Census defines Urbanized Areas as places with a minimum population of 50,000 plus the population of their surrounding areas, where 50 percent or more of the population are engaged in nonagricultural work. The Bureau of the Census also uses the Standard Metropolitan Statistical Area (SMSA) concept, defined as a city or cities having a combined total population of 50,000 or more, plus the total population of the county or counties in which the municipalities are located. Demographics may reveal that there is considerable acreage that is in open-country or agricultural use in an SMSA. San Bernardino County in California is a large geographical area extending from near the Pacific Ocean inward to the desert. Most of its population is densely settled in the portion nearest the ocean. Similarly, in Minnesota the SMSA for the city of Duluth extends all the way to the Canadian border, with most of that area a rugged forest wilderness.

Both the Urbanized Area and the Standard Metropolitan Statistical Area concepts recognize and address parts of the reality of urbanized life. Yet both are inadequate concepts for urban social planning. Like "conurbations" or "megalopolis regions," "Urbanized Area" and "Standard Metropolitan Statistical Area" are concepts that treat urbanization as a territorial issue. They are static rather than dynamic concepts. In fact, cities and urbanized areas are more matters of ways-of-life than of physical territory.

Much of the world's population still resides in small agricultural villages. People go out to their fields daily to cultivate plants and attend animals. The content of their social behavior is dominated by things agrarian and bucolic. In the urbanized society, whether the people live in central cities, suburbs, or open-country areas, the content of their social exchanges are characterized by urban attitudes and values. Even flower-pot gardening on urban balconies, or suburban gardening on lots, often involves urban values such as social status or prestige, more than real bucolic value orientations.

Size is a significant component of the urbanization concept. Urbanized areas involve large masses of people, frequently of a societal size — for example, New York with 15 million people, Tokyo with 14 million, London with 12 million, and Mexico City with 11 million. The American megalopolis of Bo-Wash has a population in the magnitude of 60 million; Japan's Tokaido megalopolis has a population approaching 80 million.

Doxiadis (1974) asserts that there is little hope of creating desirable cities and urbanized areas until we have a concept of those situations which deals simultaneously and dynamically with social, economic, political, technological, and cultural behavior. This is similar to Broady's (1970) suggestion that cities be conceptualized as formal organizations.

The first step in refining city and urbanization concepts in terms of formal organizations is to specify their goals. The means for achieving the goals must be clear and accessible to the masses of people. Historically, the goals or functions of cities were conceived as limited. Essentially cities were seen as providing streets, sewage disposal, police protection, fire protection, and, more recently, recreational and health services. The goals of cities have not included enough societal elements to enable city-planning organizations to give forceful leadership to high-quality social interaction and civilization. Clearly, people have jobs in cities, and in some cases cities have passed ordinances or used other forms of regulation to guide and control conditions of work. But few of the people who earn a living in cities are employed by them. The ability of cities to create jobs and to control working conditions is minimal. Similarly, large numbers of people live in cities, but most cities provide little or no housing for their citizenry. Through the ages cities have had some control over buildings and structures, but their posture has been defensive rather than offensive. Many people attend schools from kindergarten to postgraduate and professional training centers in cities, but most schools are not operated or controlled by cities. There is much more formal and informal learning which takes place in cities in museums, science halls, music auditoriums, and research laboratories. In most cases cities have even less direction over these places, even though there may be fire ordinances regulating the number of people who may occupy seats at a given time in an auditorium, or health ordinances governing sanitary conditions, and so forth. The traditional concept of the city clearly has not included functions that would be needed for planning at societal levels. By the last of the twentieth century, a third of the world's people live in cities and urbanized areas that need to operate at societal levels.

Today there are, in many of the large urbanized areas of the world, multiple generations of people who are born, live out their lives, and die in cities and urbanized environments. The urban invention has become a societal organization. Conceiving the city or urbanized area as a formal organization would mean defining goals and means for achieving goals related to jobs (production and distribution of goods and services); residential units (including procreational and family-activities spaces); government (within cities and among cities); socialization spaces for people of all ages; health and welfare facilities; art and recreational facilities; and scientific research facilities.

URBANIZATION: A NEW STAGE IN SOCIAL EVOLUTION

Some seven thousand years ago, or just prior to the initial invention of cities, it is estimated that the world's population was between 5 and 10 million people. By 1300 A.D., in the middle of the Dark Ages, population is estimated to have increased to 400 million. By 1650, in the era of revitalization and rebuilding of cities, population is estimated to have been 0.5 billion. By 1850, the earth's population had grown to an estimated 1.2 billion. This was the demographic launching of urbanization. By 1900, there were 1.6 billion persons on the planet Earth. By 1950 the total reached 2.4 billion, and by the 1970s some 4 billion. The dynamics of this population growth may be more clearly understood if we note that if the growth rate reached in the 1970s, about 2 percent per year, continues, the world's population will double in twenty years — reaching more than 8 billion prior to 2000. In 1650 when the new wave of city-building started, the rate of increase was 0.1 percent per year, and at that rate it would have taken a thousand years to double the world's population (Thomlinson 1976).

Put another way, cities 5,500 years ago were small — meaning 5,000 to 10,000 people. A medieval city of 10,000 population was considered of substantial size. Industrial cities ranged from 100,000 to 500,000 persons. In the last one hundred years, city populations have aggregated into megalopolis areas with populations of up to 80 million. Many of the world's nations, for example Canada, Chile, Costa Rica, Switzerland, Norway, and Sweden, have populations much smaller than those of major megalopolis areas. Urbanization represents a new dimension of social development that is supranational.

The process of urbanization

In 1968 Davis asserted that while the world was not then fully urbanized, it soon would be. In 1973 Ward estimated that 1.5 billion of the world's people lived in cities with a population of 20,000 or more, while 2 billion resided in smaller places or rural areas. Ward went on to observe that by 2000 we should anticipate 3.5 to 4 billion people living in cities and 3 billion living in the country. In the second half of the twentieth century, mankind is living through a major demographic shift from small-city social life to urbanized social organization.

England, in the late nineteenth century, was the first nation to go through such a change. For all practical purposes it took England seventy years to become saturated by urbanized social organization after its demographic shift from rural to urban. In the United States the population census of 1920 was the first to report more people living in cities than in rural areas. It took the United States fifty years to become saturated by urbanized social organization. There are conflicting views concerning how long it will take the world to be saturated by urbanization.

The world's urbanization process is moving forward at a potential crisis speed (Ward 1964). While estimates suggest that the world's population growth rate is about 2 percent a year, big-city areas are growing at a rate of between 5 and 8 percent per year. This unprecedented scale of growth brings with it an equally unprecedented need for new buildings — residential, commercial, and industrial. In order to avoid the worst built environment human beings have ever known, as well as massive social disintegration, sociophysical research is needed to produce working models for regional planning and regional action. Slums, barrios, and favellas — all low-quality social environments with different names — are growing within older cities as well as around their periphery. In Brazil and in India, population growth rates are 3 percent or more a year (Lewis 1966). In Lima, Peru and Caracas, Venezuela, half of the population are slum squatters. In Calcutta, India, more than half a million persons have no shelter at all and sleep in the streets.

Along with the rapid growth in urban population there is a reduction in the rate of job increase (Ward 1973). Even the "Green Revolution" in agriculture is capital-intensive as opposed to being people- or job-intensive. The urbanizing planet is moving toward machines replacing manual work. Urbanized society is moving toward postindustrialization, in which computerized production will replace mass numbers of workers (Bell 1973).

The process of urbanization is accelerated by advances in health care and disease prevention. In the past, one of the chief obstacles to urbanization was high mortality. In the present and the foreseeable future, mortality is low and combined with an increasing longevity.

The urban society is complex and costly. Services such as transportation, sanitation, and the production and distribution of goods need to be made more efficient. Problems such as air and noise pollution need to be solved. In a highly disciplined society, health preservation and birth control add to the urban cost. Arms races are increasingly urbanized and expensive.

Ecumenopolis, should it obtain, would be one of the most enormously complex social organizations man has experienced. Doxiadis suggests that a logical extension of the conurbations and megalopolises which are now developing would be to connect them in urban regions, then in urban continents, and finally intercontinentally into worldwide cities or ecumenopolis (see Figure 3-1).

There are suggestions that the population in ecumenopolis could reach 50 billion. By straight mathematical projection, the population would be over 45 billion by the year 2150 should the present rate of growth continue. Even with such an enormous world population, ecumenopolis thinkers suggest that the possibility of achieving a high-quality social organization and civilization is possible. The ecumenopolis views are in sharp contrast to the "limits of growth" concerns expressed by the distinguished international scholars of the Club of Rome (an organization of futurist thinkers), and in the work of several Massachusetts Institute of Technology scholars (Forrester 1971; Meadows 1972; Mesarovic 1974).

Ecumenopolis is seen as a stage in urbanization development. The Doxiadis ekistics scale of human settlements starts with the small neighborhood and proceeds through neighborhood, small town, town, large city, metropolis, conurbation, megalopolis, urban region, urban continent, to ecumenopolis.

In the third quarter of the twentieth century there are clear trends toward ecumenopolization in the form of developing sociospatial interdependency urbanizing corridors. One ecumenopolizing pattern is developing east from Moscow along the Trans-Siberian Railroad. A second corridor follows the "Asian Highway" from Northern Iran via Afghanistan through Pakistan on through the Ganges Valley

An Urbanized Planet 41

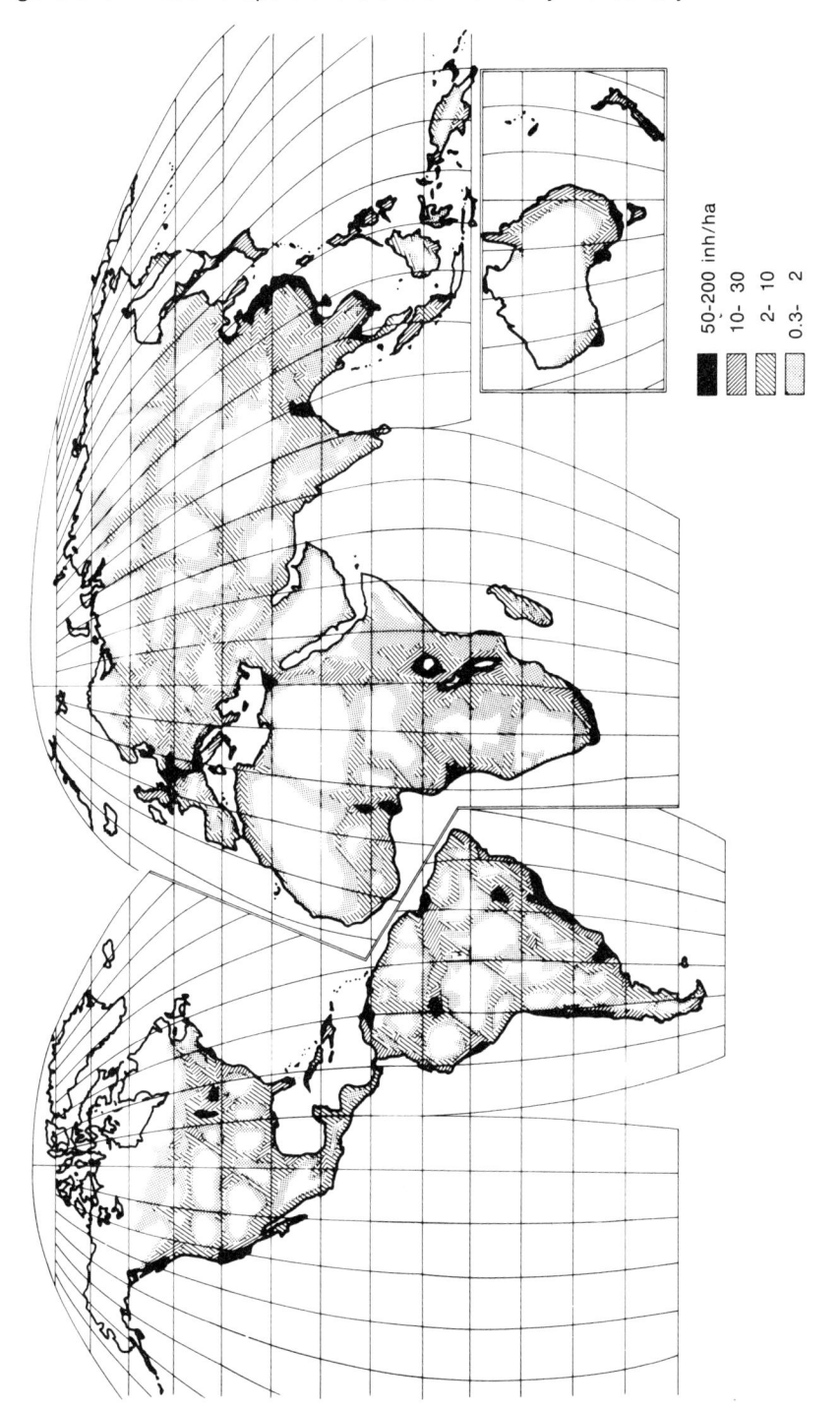

Figure 3-1 Ecumenopolis at the end of the twenty-first century

to Indochina. Third, ecumenopolizing Europe looks across the Atlantic to ecumenopolizing America with strong sea and air connections. Papaioannou (1970) suggests that these urbanizing corridors will continue to accelerate in growth in the last quarter of the twentieth century and on into the early part of the twenty-first century. It is expected that succeeding steps toward ecumenopolis will also continue.

Within the continent of Europe itself, more detailed ecumenopolizing developments are identifiable. Through London, Paris, and the Randstad there is a major ecumenopolizing concentration. Running to the northeast, this development connects with Berlin, Warsaw, and Moscow. Another developing corridor runs from Poland, to Kiev, through the Caucasus toward Asia. A population corridor connecting Bavaria, Vienna, and Budapest expands to the Black Sea. Finally, there is a corridor running southwest along the Mediterranean coast connecting northern Yugoslavia, northern Italy, southern France, Spain, and Portugal. Additionally, there are smaller corridors intercepting these major ecumenopolizing patterns.

The stimulus for European ecumenopolizing trends is the existing conurbations and megalopolises. For example, the region from London to Birmingham and Manchester is a conurbation growth area. On the continent the Rhine conurbation extends from the Randstad in the Netherlands through the Ruhr Valley to Frankfurt and Stuttgart. Another conurbation area connects the Randstad, Brussels, and Paris. Hanover and Leipzig are connected to Berlin. These European conurbations and megalopolis networks are expected to continue their evolution into urbanized regions. Other conurbation areas are developing in Poland, southern Italy, Mediterranean Spain, Scandinavia, and the Soviet Union from Leningrad through Moscow to Gorki and perhaps even to Kazan. It would appear that Europe may be expected to move firmly into the urbanized continental stage in the first half of the twenty-first century.

Ecumenopolizing patterns in Canada, the United States, Mexico, and Central America are newer and even more dramatic than in Europe. Most of Canada's over 22 million people are located in cities near to or connected with American cities from Seattle through Minneapolis, Chicago, and on to Boston — connecting with Bo-Wash in the East. Along the Pacific Coast, the megalopolis from San Francisco through Los Angeles to San Diego is developing north for an ecumenopolis hook-up with the Seattle area, and developing southeast to connect with the Gulf Coast, on to Mexico, and through Central America. Major metropolitan areas in Texas will eventually connect in a corridor with Mexico City through Wichita and on to Minneapolis. From Metropolitan New Orleans north along the Mississippi River to Chicago, another megalopolis pattern is developing. From the peninsula of Florida through Washington, D.C., New York, and on to Boston, an Eastern Seaboard megalopolis is growing. The Eastern and Northwestern magalopolis areas are combining into another urban region. It appears that these patterns may continue until North America becomes an urbanized continent.

In South America also, urbanizing patterns that can be expected to grow toward ecumenopolis are evident: the entire Pacific Seaboard from Cali, Colombia through Ecuador to Lima, Peru, and on through Chile; on the Atlantic Seaboard from Buenos Aires through Montevideo, Sao Paulo to Rio de Janeiro; and from Venezuela through central Colombia and along the full length of the Amazon.

In Africa and Asia, further urbanizing population developments may be observed. Northern Mediterranean Africa from Egypt through Morocco connects an urban population with Atlantic Africa from Morocco to the Ivory Coast and then east through Central Africa to Tanzania and south along the Indian Ocean to South Africa. India and China have for all practical purposes become urbanized subcontinents. Japan and much of Indonesia are already urbanized into megalopolis patterns. Even the distribution of population in sparsely settled Australia shows accumulation along the southern and eastern seaboards (Doxiadis 1970).

New urbanization forms

Intensified urban patterns require complex changes in social structures. For example, one such change might be the reduction of local government's importance in urban regions and continents. It is possible that in urban regions, traditional municipal and even provincial or state government functions may be better performed by new urbanized regional governments, two-level governments, or some combination of these. The New York-New Jersey Port Authority is an existing example. Similarly, national governments in urbanized continental areas may come into new cooperation with, or be subservient to, urbanized continental governments. Urbanized continental governments might ultimately be subservient to ecumenopolis government structures (*Constitution for the Federation of Earth* 1977).

Some social structures that begin to set the stage are illustrated by increasing numbers of multinational industries. It is entirely possible that multinational industrialization will develop closer loyalties with continental areas than with nation states (Vernon 1971; Barnet and Muller 1974; Tavel 1975). Common Market developments constitute another social structural situation which implicitly, if not explicitly, supports urbanized continental development. Similarly, international cooperation with weather satellites and satellite communication supports multinational urbanization and lays the foundation for structures on which ecumenopolis can be built. Scientific cooperation in space exploration between major powers like the United States and U.S.S.R. become an additional cultural building block to support ecumenopolis. The increasingly common use of the metric measuring system is another example of a social structure which implicitly, if not explicitly, supports ecumenopolis. On the other hand, differences in spoken and written languages continue to be social structural barriers inhibiting ecumenopolizing trends.

New urbanization sociophysical supports

The world's ecumenopolizing tendencies suggest the need for constructing new buildings at an unprecedented speed. Ward (1964) expresses the magnitude by indicating that between the 1960s and the year 2000, the amount of new building required will equal that of the entire previous history of humanity. If this magnitude of building is required for a population expected to be 7 to 8 billion, the magnitude needed for a population of 50 billion or more requires new and innovative thinking concerning the nature and form of the built environment as well as the social interaction to take place in it. The challenges for education, jobs, health, and so forth are of equally gigantic proportions.

Feeding the urbanized population, and anticipating feeding an ecumenopolis-sized population, present another challenge. Whether or not mankind can meet this challenge for food is a matter of considerable debate and conjecture (Brown 1974). Urbanized food production is a complex matter, involving scientific research and technology, economic production and distribution, the exploitation of natural resources, and the development of energy resources. Scientific agriculture is not new; much of it started in the 1750s in England with the Bakewell experiments (Taylor 1968). But scientific inquiries into animal husbandry and plant genetics have become major urban priorities. Food production combined with death reduction, or disease control, are key variables in the goals of urban culture. Thus most food and fiber are no longer produced as a way-of-life tradition. It is the urbanized and sensate-science-oriented populations which provide the markets for food and fiber production and which control them.

Urban utopianists like Robert Owen in the New Harmony Experiment directly related food and fiber production to city organization (Sargeant 1860; Lockwood 1902). New-town planners like Ebenezer Howard called for direct relationships between open-country land for food and fiber production and urban land. To a somewhat lesser degree, Frank Lloyd Wright's proposals for a Broadacre City implied a direct interfacing between food and fiber production and urban life

(Wright 1970). But the essence of these ideas remained more intellectual than applied. Nowhere are there viable examples of city-states which governmentally and economically directly control surrounding land areas for food and fiber production. Soleri's arcology megastructure idea implies a balance between population in the megastructure and its supporting food production both in and outside of the megastructure. Nevertheless, the Soleri proposal focuses on internal social organization more than on external land relationships.

Lester Brown (1974) identifies several food problems related to economics. He observes that much of the world's population in the 1970s spend some 80 percent of their income on food. Consequently, he suggests there is little or no margin for increasing food prices for much of the world's population. He sounds another alarm by noting the nearly 2 percent annual population growth rate and its concomitant requirement for doubling food production in slightly more than a decade. There is little probability of achieving such an accelerated rate of agricultural production, he suggests, given the current status of human knowledge and values.

Energy, fertilizer, and water supplies are all key variables which must be manipulated for food and fiber production in the urbanizing environment. New kinds of foods and new food preferences must be achieved. For example, some advantage could be gained by shifting massively from beef consumption to soybean consumption for major quantities of protein. Farming the oceans for fish and other food commodities has been considered for some time, but only limited achievements have been made. Hydroponic food production is a subject of experimental research but currently has only limited economic use.

There still prevails a dominant view that food and fiber production is "out there" in open space. Considerable physical and intellectual energy is currently devoted to preserving agricultural lands around the periphery of growing urbanized areas. Little intellectual and economically aggressive attention is given to the possibility of food and fiber production in skyscrapers and megastructures. Some food production is planned for in Soleri's arcology megastructures. Such urban food production ideas must adhere closely to environmental recycling considerations. The view that resources could be totally recycled, and the formal organization view of the urban environment contribute positively and hopefully to the ecumenopolis prospect.

RESIDENCE PATTERNS IN URBANIZED SOCIETY

In the 1970s the trend for place of residence in urbanized societies is suburban. Most people apparently prefer to live beyond the "walls" of cities.

The great cities of the world contain a small part of their urban population (Hall 1966; Robson 1972). Several do not have particularly large populations, and some of them have more population outside their political limits than inside:

	Population	
	City	Total Metropolitan Area
Amsterdam	860,000	1,040,000
Chicago	3,300,000	6,800,000
Copenhagen	600,000	900,000
London	7,000,000	11,500,000
Los Angeles	2,800,000	6,000,000
Moscow	7,000,000	9,000,000
New York	7,800,000	15,000,000
Paris	2,900,000	9,000,000
Tokyo	10,000,000	22,000,000

Additionally, cities like Cairo, Mexico City, Sao Paulo, and Stockholm differ little from their metropolitan population because of extensive annexation. Demographic studies in many great cities and their surrounding areas reveal that over the past two decades, the centrifugal movement of people is greater than the centripetal movement. Some of the world's great cities have lost population in absolute numbers while others have experienced slower rates of growth than their suburbs and surrounding areas. Conurbation growth in England between London, Liverpool, and Manchester illustrates the dramatic increase in population in both urban and nonurban places beyond the major cities. Numerous new towns have been systematically planned in the English conurbation corridor since 1946. Greenbelts, along with controlled expansion of existing cities, are important parts of the developing pattern of urbanization.

On the European Continent the long experience of urbanization in the central Netherlands with the Amsterdam conurbation on the north and the Rotterdam conurbation on the south has been systematically developed into the Randstad Urban Region. It is about thirty miles across and contains a population near 5 million, or 40 percent of the Netherlands' total. It occupies 5 percent of the nation's land. Its famous old central cities have relatively small populations: Amsterdam, 860,000; Rotterdam, 600,000; Haarlem, 170,000; and Leiden, 100,000. Some urban planning has gone on in the Netherlands for centuries. In recent decades renewed efforts have been made to maintain agricultural green wedges in densely populated areas. The net effect has been increasingly to stabilize the populations of the older central cities and to expand suburban areas systematically.

Paris is another of the world's great cities, and the region of Paris is one of its large urbanized areas. The city is of Roman origin and dates from the Middle Ages (Hall 1966). It was small until the seventeenth century; then new unplanned growth began. In the Mid-nineteenth century in Haussmann's massive urban renewal programs, much obsolete housing was torn down and many narrow winding streets were eliminated. In their place were constructed the elegant townhouses and modern wide boulevards which have contributed to the city's fame. Displaced poor people were moved to the city's periphery, where slum areas developed.

Today the Paris region has become a massive suburbanized area of 9 million people. The region's population constitutes approximately 20 percent of the nation's population. The rate of growth in the Paris region is high, nearly 2 percent per year.

In 1965 a master plan for the Paris region was developed (Merlin 1971). The plan is oriented to the year 2000. It anticipates a population of 14 million inhabitants. It projects a decrease in the annual rate of growth to 1 percent per year by 2000, and anticipates that the regional proportion of the French urban population will be 23 percent, considerably less than it would be without planning. Three million people are to be housed in new towns in the region by 2000. The new towns will be large, with populations of about 500,000 each.

Metropolitan Moscow illustrates a different type of development. Most of the population live in the central city, though the general pattern of urban residences moving centrifugally is evident. Seven million people reside in the city of Moscow and another 2 million in its fringe or suburban areas. The territorial growth of Moscow has been great. In the 1930s Soviet planners attempted to control the rate of Moscow's growth, but that has largely failed. Accordingly, most of Moscow's population now lives in relatively new urbanized locations that might have been considered suburban if they had not been incorporated into the city's political limits.

In order to handle the large urban population, organizationally the city of Moscow has been divided into "microdistricts." These are called *mikrorayons*, the suffix *"rayon"* meaning "district" or "borough." Microdistricts have populations between 5 thousand and 15 thousand people. They include residential areas, public restaurants, nurseries, kindergartens, clubs, public workshops, a library, a pool, a park, and other related facilities.

In 1962 a new ring highway was opened around the city. It marked the outer edge of the city, beyond which there is a ten-mile-wide greenbelt. Beyond the greenbelt are satellite cities with populations of approximately 100,000 each. Much of the population in these satellite cities commutes daily across the greenbelt to employment in Moscow. Beyond the development of satellite cities the major policy in Soviet urban planning is to develop new towns, particularly in the U.S.S.R.'s eastern areas, where there are minimum population densities.

Tokyo is still another example of metropolitan population dominance outside the central city. The 10 million population of the city of Tokyo is exceeded by a fringe population of 12 million. Furthermore, Tokyo is in the Tokaido megalopolis complex with nearly 80 million population (Nagashima 1972). In many respects the large population of Tokyo and its region makes it something of a new town. In 1785 the population of Tokyo was estimated to be 1.4 million. Due to rapid nineteenth and twentieth century population growth and due to the military destruction of much housing during World War II, a substantial part of Tokyo is new. Many smaller satellite towns are part of the city's urbanized region. There is massive daily movement in the region between the central city, the surrounding fringe areas, and the surrounding satellite towns (Hall 1966).

These few examples illustrate that the trend is for urbanized populations to live in suburban areas — which often have lower densities than the older major central cities. In Tokyo, Moscow, and Stockholm, the urbanization pattern provides for and facilitates diurnal commuting of the population between the fringe areas and the central cities. Around London, Paris, and the Randstad, planning deemphasizes daily movement on a mass basis, attempting to construct suburban areas that are sufficiently large to provide for major population services.

The observation that urbanized Americans now typically live in big-city suburbs needs to be refined in several ways. By the 1970 Census some 73 percent of all Americans lived in urban places. Thirty-one percent resided in big cities, 34 percent lived in big-city suburbs, and 8 percent lived in small towns. Of the balance, 21 percent resided in rural nonfarm areas, many adjacent to big cities and their suburbs, and only 6 percent on farms, some of which are in intensely urbanized areas like the megalopolis East. Twenty years earlier the distribution was as follows: 31 percent in big cities, 24 percent in big city suburbs, 10 percent in small towns, 17 percent in rural nonfarm areas, and 18 percent on farms (Hellman 1970). It is expected that by the end of the century the 73 percent of Americans living in urban areas will have increased to between 90 and 95 percent.

Other census data reveal that not only are more than half of all Americans urban, but that 69 percent live in more than 240 Standard Metropolitan Statistical Areas (U.S. Bureau of the Census 1970; Smith 1976). Residentially, urban Americans attempt to move to low-density areas. This presents numerous problems for an urbanizing nation and an urbanizing planet. Efficiency in transportation, utilities, schools, and many other services is reduced by the spreading out of large urban populations in suburban areas. While some housing experts suggest that most new-home starts in urban America in the next twenty years will be attached, zero lot line, or medium high-rise, such thinking is in considerable conflict with the cultural value placed on detached, low-density residences.

The United States, like many other urbanized areas of the world, is still experiencing in fact and in ideology a spreading out of population in relatively low densities. This is in the opposite direction of the development of megastructures and the exploring of other possibilities for high-quality social interaction between and among people in high-density living. In many respects urbanizing America, like the urbanizing planet, is developing along a model that is still implicitly anti-city.

SOLUTIONS TO THE URBANIZATION CHALLENGE

We present here two of the major elements of a solution to the challenge of an urbanizing planet. The first is population control. This is widely discussed in intellectual circles and increasingly confronted in political circles as well. Technologies for population control are still being developed (Ravenholt 1976). The ideology of population control, however, remains controversial. From one side we hear phrases like "population explosion," "standing room only," and "baby boom"; from the other "the right to live," "abortion is criminal," and a general notion that Christian religion teaches people to "be fruitful and multiply." Both views express emotionalism.

In sociology and urban planning one needs to look at population projections and try to discern their meaning for an urbanizing planet. Some scholars suggest that the planet will have more than 7 billion population by the year 2000, 12 billion by 2033, 24 billion by 2066, and 48 billion by 2100 (Miles 1971). Some demographers suggest that 12 billion people will create a world of "standing room only." Other research specialists indicate that it is not probable that 50 billion people can be sustained on the planet earth. Doxiadis and associates, although not advocating it, suggest the possibility of a higher quality urban civilization with 30 billion people than is currently experienced.

Sociologists take the view that balanced and recyclable urban social organization is more important than absolute numbers of people. This is to say that humans, natural resources, and the built environment must exist in a socioecological balance. For instance, the prehistoric American Indian population was small and at times struggled for an existence above the poverty level. With new technologies and new ideologies, a population of over 200 million is supported in the same geographical area by utilizing some resources obtained in other parts of the world. The challenge facing urbanized and postindustrializing areas of the world is not just local provision, but social and technological systems that will enable a maximum achievement of high-quality urban life on a planetary basis. Large rural populations like those found in India and China are characterized by great poverty. Population control alone should not be expected to eradicate either urban or rural poverty. Such improvements require significant changes in social organization as well.

A second element in the solution of the challenge facing the urbanizing planet is formal organizational theory. In several different ways, scholars like Michael Broady, Athelstan Spilhaus, Paolo Soleri, and C.A. Doxiadis have suggested that urban society be viewed as a formal organization. Viewing it as such would allow a more integrated approach to population control. Moreover, formal organizational theory would allow for multiple contents and thus could encompass the plurality of urban life.

Municipalities, urban regions, and megastructures all may be viewed as formal organizations with specified goals and widely accepted means for achieving goals if new apexes of urban civilization are to be achieved. The essence of urban civilization involves both complex organization and high densities.

Now that cities and urban areas are societal in size, it is incumbent upon leaders to conceptualize the urban environment as more than a street department, fire department, police department, and so forth. In many respects, cities have been places of rugged individualism. Particularly from the Middle Ages to the present in the Western World there has been an ideology that people who are free manifest their freedom in the city.

Cities in the last of the twentieth century are places of plural culture and enormous freedom for their inhabitants. But it is grossly inconsistent with the magnitude of the world's urban population, and the opportunities for high-quality civilization, to presume that "by chance" people interacting in large secondary environments will create high-quality civilization. Civilization is a cultural and ideological view of society. It is not random. Four billion people, 8 billion people, 12 billion people, and so forth improve their odds for achieving urban civilization by establishing goals and agreeing upon ways for achieving the goals.

Urbanized society means by definition that life has evolved beyond both ruralization and the city. Urbanized society is total society. Therefore, the concepts and goals in planning must be comprehensive, encompassing all aspects of urban life: art, health, spiritual meaning, social order, procreation, production, recreation, science, socialization, and welfare. Police departments, fire departments, street departments, recreation departments, and so forth may have been appropriate mechanisms for achieving city goals. They are not ends in themselves. The "home-rule" city charter (or its equivalent), which is found in many big urbanized societies, is in effect misnamed. "Home rule" is an invalid definition of the situation. Such charters typically do not allow city residents to control social institutions within the city limits. Currently, municipalities have little authority over schools, jobs, family life, health services, welfare services, church organizations, and special district governments. Furthermore, most city charters make inadequate provision for interfacing one city with another city in an urban region.

The city concept is inadequate for the urbanized society. The concept of the city suggests an either/or situation: one can live either in a town or in the country, and expect life's circumstances to be different accordingly. In earlier ruralized societies which had agricultural villages, the values of living were rural whether one lived in a village or in the open country. Similarly, the experience of urbanized society suggests that the values of life will be urban whether one lives within the corporate limits of a municipality, in an urban-rural fringe, or in the open country.

IMPLICATIONS

The prospects for the urbanizing planet are many. Urban civilization never before has had so much support. In those parts of the world where all people — food and fiber producers, factory workers, as well as scientists and knowledge generators — live within an urbanized ideology, the formal organization of urban life is an appropriate model for achieving civilization.

Large municipalities may be viewed as societal, and small municipalities may be viewed as parts of urbanized societal regions. Their formal organizations must be adequate to enable people to achieve all the necessary life supports whether they reside in a large or a small urbanized area. To say that the city concept is too small for urbanized society is not a utopianistic call for the abolition of municipalities. It is a challenge, however, to plan urban formal organizations and urban activity systems on a sufficiently large scale, even if that involves the cooperation of numerous smaller municipalities, to provide for high-quality life services. Given this definition of the situation, there are many sociological and planning mechanisms that may be utilized for urban civilization's support. Multinational cooperation in planning for urban development is still in its infancy but is growing rapidly (Raiffa 1975). The chapters which follow deal with urban planning in an increasingly multinational and global perspective.

REFERENCES

BARNET, R., & MULLER, R. *Global Reach*. New York: Simon & Schuster, 1974.
BELL, D. *The Coming of the Post-Industrial Society*. New York: Basic Books, 1973.
BERRY, A. *The Next Ten Thousand Years*. New York: Mentor Books, 1974.
BROADY, M. *Planning for People*. London: The Bedford Square Press, 1968.
BROADY, M. The sociology of the urban environment. *Ekistics*, 1970, *34*, 187–90.
BROWN, L. R. Global food insecurity. *The Futurist*, 1974, *8*, 56–64.
Constitution for the Federation of Earth. Lakewood, Colo.: World Constitution & Parliament Assoc., 1977.
DAVIS, K. The urbanization of the human population. In (Ed.) *Cities*. New York: Alfred A. Knopf, 1968, 3–24.
DOXIADIS, C. A. *Ekistics*. New York: Oxford University Press, 1968, 330.
DOXIADIS, C. A. The great escape. *Ekistics*, 1974, *38*, 221–24.
DOXIADIS, C.A. Man's movement and his settlement. *Ekistics*, 1970, *34*, 210–27.
Feeding the World in the Year 2000. *The Futurist*, 1975, *9*, 294–309.
FORRESTER, J. W. *World Dynamics*. Cambridge: Wright-Allen Press, 1971.
HALL, P. *The World Cities*. New York: McGraw-Hill, 1966.
HELLMAN, H. *The City in the World of the Future*. Philadelphia: J. B. Lippincott Co., 1970.
LEWIS, D. (Ed.) *Pedestrian in the City*. Princeton: Van Nostrand, 1966.
LEWIS, J. W. (Ed.) *The City in Communist China*. Stanford, Calif.: Stanford University Press, 1971.
LOCKWOOD, G. B. *The New Harmony Communities*. Marion, Ind.: The Chronicle Co., 1902.
MEADOWS, D. et al. *The Limits to Growth*. New York: Universe Books, 1972.
MERLIN, P. *New Towns: Regional Planning and Development*. London: Methuen and Co., 1971, 146–75.
MESAROVIC, M., & PESTEL, E. *Mankind at the Turning Point*. New York: Dutton, 1974.
MILES, R. E. Three ways to solve the population crisis. *The Futurist*, 1971, *5*, 200–204.
MOLITOR, G. T. T. The coming world struggle for food. *The Futurist*, 1974, *8*, 169–78.
NAGASHIMA, C. Megalopolis in Japan. In G. Bell and J. Tyrwhitt (Eds.), *Human Identity in the Urban Environment*. Baltimore: Penguin Books, 1972.
PAPAIOANNOU, J. G. Future urbanization patterns. *Ekistics*, 1970, *34*, 368–81.
PIRENNE, H. *Medieval Cities*. New York: Doubleday Anchor Books, 1925.

RAIFFA, H. A multinational institute explores global problems. *The Futurist,* 1975, *9*, 147–49.
RAVENHOLT, R. T. Winning the battle against overpopulation. *The Futurist,* 1976, *10*, 64–68.
ROBSON, W. A., & REGAN, D. E. *Great Cities of the World.* Beverly Hills, Calif.: Sage Publications, 1972.
SAALMAN, H. *Haussmann: Paris Transformed.* New York: George Braziller, 1971.
SARGENT, W. L. *Robert Owen.* London: Smith, Elder & Co., 1860.
SMITH, T. L., & ZOPF, P. E., JR. *Demography.* New York: Alfred Publishing Co., 1976.
SOLERI, P. *Arcology.* Cambridge: M.I.T. Press, 1969.
TAVEL, C. *The Third Industrial Age.* Homewood, Ill.: Dow Jones-Irwin, 1975.
TAYLOR, L. *Urban-Rural Problems.* Los Angeles: Dickenson Publishing Co., Inc., 1968.
TAYLOR, L., & JONES, A. R., JR. *Rural Life and Urbanized Society.* New York: Oxford University Press, 1964.
THOMLINSON, R. *Population Dynamics* (2nd ed.). New York: Random House, 1976.
U.S. Bureau of the Census. *U.S. Census of Population: 1970, Number of Inhabitants,* Final Report DC(1)-Al, U.S. Summary, 1971. Washington, D.C.: U.S. Government Printing Office, 1971.
VERNON, R. *Sovereignty at Bay.* New York: Basic Books, 1971.
WARD, B. The process of world urbanization. *Ekistics,* 1964, *28*, 274–80.
WARD, B. An urban planet. *Ekistics,* 1973, *37*, 428–33.
WRIGHT, F. L. *The Living City.* New York: New American Library, 1970.

PART TWO

Urbanization and Theory

The study of urbanization assumes the past historical development of individual cities and focuses on society-wide urban influences. Urbanization is analyzed in comparison with organizational theory. Special insights are drawn from exchange and symbolic interactionist theories. Urbanized areas are places of dynamic and plural exchanges as well as places of vastly differing symbols and meanings.

Chapter four examines people-land relationships. Different growth patterns of urbanization are explored. Social class and stratification patterns are studied. Planned efforts to direct, to minimize, or to maximize stratification impact on urbanization are evaluated. The changing meanings and often deteriorating nature of neighborhoods are considered in some detail. Urban scale, density, and zoning receive special attention.

In chapter five the urban core is studied. The purpose of the city center has changed through time from domination by one institution to multiinstitutional domination. Special focus is placed on new physical forms like large megabuildings to facilitate urban living at societal levels.

In chapter six the governance of urban regions is highlighted. One of the most challenging problems of mass urbanization is alienation. The scale of urban living is so large that many people experience "overload." Significant numbers of people in all social classes find it difficult to identify positively with the urban environment. New forms of urban government are needed to deal effectively with societally sized problems and at the same time to maximize meaningful citizen participation. While long-range solutions seem far from at hand, several of the current efforts at governance-citizen participation resolutions are explored. The viability of urbanized social organization to a considerable extent hangs on the resolution of these problems.

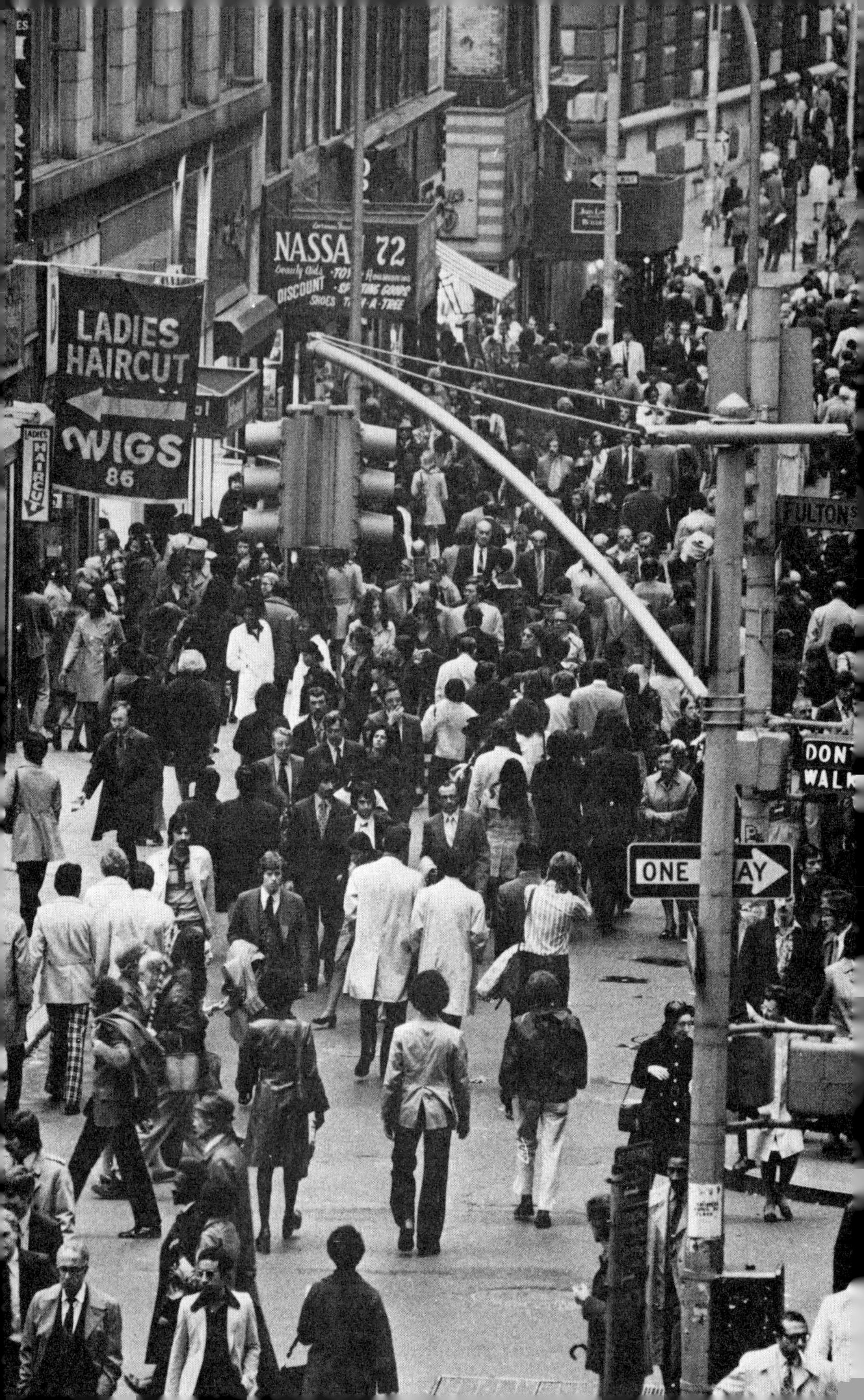

Urban Ecology 4

Social ecology concerns people-land relationships. In urbanized society, people-land relationships occur in cities, suburbs, metropolitan regions, open-country recreation areas, and open-country food and fiber production areas. In this chapter we focus on urban ecology situations while acknowledging that in a post-industrializing and ecumenopolizing world, there are few people-land relationships that fall outside the "urban" category.

People- and space-densities are basic urban problems. Some observers suggest that people should modify their physical and built environments in accordance with their societal meaning. Others argue that physical space and the built environment determine human behavior. These positions are sometimes referred to as social determinism, geographical determinism, and architectural determinism. In the end, oversimplistic deterministic positions earn little credibility.

In 1947, for example, Firey did a study of land use in Boston which revealed the dominance of social values over physical or economic values. According to Firey, land use on Boston's Beacon Hill was explained more by social values than by economic costs. One finds that certain land areas take on a sacred or quasi-sacred societal meaning. This is exemplified further in cases like New York City's Central Park, San Francisco's Golden Gate Park, London's Regency Park, and Venice's Piazza San Marco. Some places are venerated for historical meanings — Independence Hall in Philadelphia for Americans, the Vatican City for Roman Catholic Christians, the Acropolis for Greeks, the

This crowded New York street illustrates the need for ecological balance. (Photo: Cary Wolinsky for Stock, Boston.)

pyramids for Egyptians, and Teotihuacán for Mexicans. In Boston's West End, Gans (1962) found land and dwellings occupied by the poor to have strong positive meaning. This was their turf, and they wanted to remain even though some viewed their buildings as a slum.

There are other kinds of examples of the effects of social values on urban ecology. Some urban spaces are divided by sex, for example the separation of restrooms for men and for women in most public buildings in America. At the peak of industrial culture there was considerable separation of eating places by sex, with many clubs having men's bars, men's grills, and men's dining rooms. By the mid-1970s many of these separations by sex for eating spaces have been eliminated, but their elimination too illustrates the impact of social values in urban ecology.

Urban planners face questions concerning space and site arrangements for environmental quality. In the United States in recent years there has been an effort to construct some two million residential units annually, but with limited knowledge concerning how they relate to high-quality social living. The nagging problems resulting from insufficient theory and empirical evidence concerning residential space is thrown into sharp focus by the failure of the Pruitt-Igoe Project in St. Louis, Missouri. There a slum was cleared and thirty-three buildings erected at a cost of $40 million in the mid-1950s. Soon antisocial behavior became so great in the housing project that many of the buildings had to be torn down. Currently a new form of social organizational management by residents is being implemented.

The relationship between site planning, individual behavior, and social organization is increasingly relevant as urbanized society sustains massive increases in population. The relationships of propinquity or social distance between people and physical units are increasingly paramount (Gans 1961; Lynch 1962; Gutman 1966).

Urban ecology is related to size-of-place considerations. The question is: how big should cities be? There is no agreed-upon answer, but some size principles are suggested in terms of desired service levels. The urban neighborhood unit is an ecological concept used by physical planners since the 1920s (Gallion 1963). The physical planning use of the neighborhood concept was dramatically moved forward in 1946 when it was embodied in the British New Town Act (Dahir 1947; Dahir 1951). In the mid-twentieth century physical planners often targeted 30 to 40 thousand population as the optimum size for a city. By the 1970s 150,000 to 300,000 population was more prevalently accepted as an optimum city size. Beyond that size, there is support for the notion of urban regions rather than the continual enlargement of single cities.

The greenbelt is something of a companion concept for optimum city size. From one point of view, the optimum city size question is ultimately answered by a boundary area—historically a wall and more recently a greenbelt. The idea of the greenbelt was suggested by Queen Victoria of England. She proposed containing the growth of London by establishing a greenbelt around the city. In 1938 the London greenbelt was finally designated. Many other greenbelts have been established in recent years (Creswell 1974; Ash 1974).

In most of what has been said above, there is an implicit assumption that urban ecology is tied to territory. But city neighborhoods and communities in urbanized societies are increasingly found to be mental constructs as well as physical territories (Suttles). In the 1950s Goode (1957) identified occupational communities by the social interaction of selected professionals in the same kind of work rather than by their physical locations. As physical and social mobility have accelerated in the urbanized society and as the dominance of the family has declined, increased proportions of people have interacted more in terms of significant others than of residential locations. Only the very young and the very old, for whom mobility is limited, exist primarily in an urban ecology based on territoriality. Separation of place of work from place of residence, along with land-use zoning restrictions, are contributing to the demise of urban ecology by territoriality.

Webber (1963) discusses place and nonplace communities. Effrat (1974) views community as a multidimensional variable. The community is not an absolute territory, but may be defined operationally that way for purposes of empirical investigation. Further, community is a matter of degree rather than kind. Sociologists and planners talk about more or less "communitiness" rather than the simple presence or absence of community. Effrat emphasizes that there may be more communitiness in some urban situations and less communitiness in others. The neighborhood nevertheless still appears in terms of territory in most new-town plans the world over. Physically, the neighborhood concept attempts to cluster people in units of between 5,000 and 10,000 population. Much emphasis is placed on maintaining walking distances from place of residence to neighborhood centers, schools, health facilities, and transportation stops. Minimal attention is focused on the fact that mass numbers of people spend most of their waking hours away from their places of residence. Moreover, much social behavior in places of residence is influenced by stimuli like television, the telephone, newspapers, and magazines rather than from the neighborhood itself. Urban parks, cul-de-sacs, planned unit developments, community centers, and many other sociophysical entities are used to create situations that give the feeling of small groups. Nevertheless, large proportions of urban people do not have friendships according to neighborhood proximity. Alienation and urban overload remain critical issues.

URBAN ECOLOGY MODELS

Urban ecology concerns interrelationships between variables including population, organization, technology, and environment (Duncan 1959). Space and land distributions are made in relation to these variables using one of three types of models: classic, factorial, or density.

Classic models

Studies of urban ecology since the 1920s have shown that cities develop in three different ways (Park and Burgess 1925). The three major classic models are concentric circle, sector, and multiple-nuclei (see Figure 4 – 1). The concentric circle model is associated with the work of Burgess (1925) in Chicago. Area 1 is the central business district or CBD. It is characterized by intensive commercial activity, civic life, complex transportation, office buildings, museums, theaters, restaurants, and so forth. During the working hours of the day, population density is high in area 1, and during the hours from midnight to 8:00 A.M., population densities are low. The second area is a place of transition. As the central business district moves centrifugally, area 2 is characterized by some industrial and commercial activity but primarily is a residential slum. Area 3 is characterized primarily by residential sites for manual workers, and services related to their needs. Area 4 is characterized by single-family detached residences for white collar and professional workers, and services related to their needs. Area 5 is a commuter residential location, often beyond the city limits. It has some

Concentric Circle   **Sector**   **Multiple Nuclei**

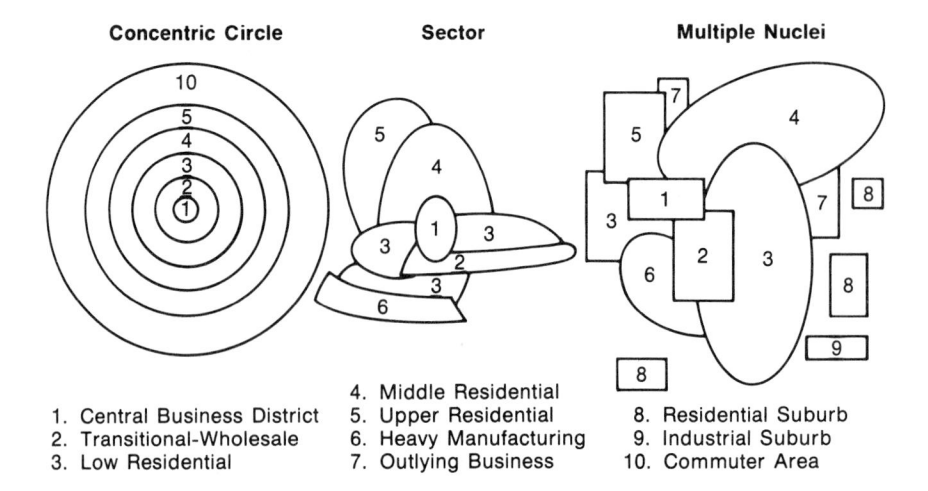

1. Central Business District
2. Transitional-Wholesale
3. Low Residential
4. Middle Residential
5. Upper Residential
6. Heavy Manufacturing
7. Outlying Business
8. Residential Suburb
9. Industrial Suburb
10. Commuter Area

Figure 4–1   Three Classic Urban Ecology Models

mixed suburban and satellite land use ranging from high-quality residential estates to mediocre housing, some industrial park development, and some agricultural land use.

The sector model of city growth was developed by Hoyt (1937). This model is typically found where rivers, mountains, or other geographical influences modify the shape and growth patterns of cities. Pittsburg and New Orleans are frequently cited as cities whose early growth was sectorial, primarily because of rivers.

The third of the classic models is the multiple-nuclei form of city growth. This model was developed by geographers Harris and Ullman (1945). This model is the most prevalent for megalopolis-type urban growth.

The classic models are all based on the view that gross distributional urban patterns are a result of sociogeographic forces. The theory is that individual urbanites select the living and working areas which are closest to their social characteristics and needs.

Classic urban ecology models are used primarily for description after the fact. The sector model explains most urban growth and development in Latin America (Amato 1970). Ecology patterns have been studied in Bogota, Colombia; Quito, Ecuador; Lima, Peru; and Santiago, Chile. Each of these cities was established under Spanish colonial direction. Initially they were planned around a central plaza in accordance with the 1573 Laws of the Indies. Over their several hundred years of existence, all except Quito have grown to populations of over 2 million. Quito is approximately one-half million. Initially the upper class lived near the center of the city, but over the years the middle class has remained in the higher densities near the city's center, the upper-class sectors are located beyond the middle class, and the lower-class sectors are further peripheral from the city's center. Given these ecological patterns, the upper-class residents experienced the lowest density, the middle-class residents the highest density, and the low-income residents an intermediate density.

Mexico City has more than 600 years of urban experience. During most of this time, the population growth was limited. By 1900 there were only 350,000 persons in Mexico City (Hayner 1966). In recent years the population has grown to 9 million. Most of the growth has been sectorial. Toward the south and the west are the more affluent population sections. In the north and east are the poorer sections. The National University is in the extreme south near the affluent areas. An area near the central business district and extending west to the highlands beyond Chapultepec Forest is a section of upper-class residences. In the late 1860s the Emperor Maximilian built a wide and pretentious street, the Paseo de la Reforma, in the baroque style. It connects the upper-class residential area with the central city. Climate and altitude have influenced some of the sectorial developments. The better climate is in the higher altitudes; therefore they have become the residential areas of the more affluent citizenry.

In Europe, urban ecology is most described by the sector and the multiple-nuclei models (Hauser 1951). This is illustrated by analysis of London, Paris, Vienna, and Stockholm. The city of London originated in Roman times at a ford over the Thames River near the present London Bridge. Twentieth-century London's ecology, however, dates from the middle of the seventeenth century with the city's industrial expansion. Also, much of the city has been destroyed by fires and rebuilt sectorially along the river. Industrial development and transportation were influenced by the direction of the river and by proximity to it. Residential areas are developed sectorially along parks and larger green spaces, a number of which originally had been held by nobility or wealthy land owners.

Paris originally was a fortress city built on an island in the River Seine. The Seine River played a lesser role in the growth of Paris than did the Thames for London. During the nineteenth century, Paris grew in population. The most affluent areas were on the West Bank and other western locations. When Baron Haussmann planned and rebuilt much of the city, the west end was designated as a high-rent quarter. The University of Paris is located in the south part of the city. Many of the people there were unmarried males and prostitutes living in rooming houses. This has become known as the Latin Quarter. The northern sector of the city became a predominantly working-class residential area. It juxtaposed places of residence and shops. The eastern part of Paris also became a large working-class area. Wide baroque streets were built to connect these sectors.

Vienna's importance as an urban center is of more recent origin than that of London and Paris. Its significant growth also came after 1700. It merged with nine suburban communities, giving it a multiple-nuclei character. Modern Vienna is made up of more than twenty districts. Original land division centered around government, monastery, university, and craft areas. Initially the upper-class residential area was in the government zone; the university residential area was a Latin Quarter; and the manufacturing area was a working-class district.

Stockholm's ecological development in many respects is the most systematically planned. Stockholm's population began an accelerated growth in the 1870s. By 1904 the city was authorized to purchase land outside of its political limits for future expansion. Specific provision was given to improve some of the land and leave other parts of it in a natural or unimproved state. New communities have been planned and built by the city outside its original area. These become satellites in the multiple-nuclei ecological pattern.

Factorial models

There are two distinct but related models in this category. The first, social area analysis, is the most prevalently used (Shevky and Williams 1949; Shevky and Bell 1955; Anderson 1961; Orleans 1966). The social-area model suggests that for American cities, an understanding of ecological development requires the analysis of three variables: class or prestige; family type or stage in the family cycle; and ethnicity or race. This model is concerned with factor clustering and scale development. As societies modernize and increase in size, societal differentiation increases; this is accompanied by more complex urban land use. In smaller and less differentiated societies, land use is more related to family form. In large-scale and highly differentiated societies, neighborhoods are sharply separated in terms of status characteristics.

The factorial ecology model, the second in this category, differs from social area analysis primarily by the use of a wider range of variables and more inductive reasoning (Berry 1969; Merdie 1969). The factorial model uses a data matrix containing measurements on M variables for N units of observation. The units of observation may be census tracts, wards, or other territorial areas. There is difficulty in comparing the factorial analysis of one urban area to that of another because of the relatively unique data inputs. Social-area analysis is generally not hampered by this difficulty because its variables are stabilized by the theoretical framework.

The factorial models are used in analyzing social change and modernization in urban areas (Abu-Lughod 1969; Berry 1969).

Density models

The density-distance models suggest that the d-d curve resembles a volcano, with the lower densities at the center or the crater area, followed by the higher densities, and then the lowest densities on the periphery (Hoover 1968). It is immediately noted that the d-d curve is partly a function of the operationalized residential definition which excludes hotel residents. In many cities, if hotel populations in the central business district areas were included as residential, the d-d curve would peak rather than crater. The density-distance model further suggests that the decline of people with distance is due to the rate at which citizens are willing to trade residential site spaces for time and money costs in transportation. Further, Hoover argues that (1) bigger cities have greater central densities; (2) the largest municipalities have the flattest d-d curves; (3) growing cities in developed societies develop flatter d-d curves; (4) city age influences density because early transportation systems inhibit new horizontal expansion; and (5) even as cities have population increases, central densities tend to decline along with flattening d-d curves.

All three sets of major urban ecology models — classic, factorial, and density — are weighted toward territoriality. Useful as these models are, already it has been noted that in an ecumenopolizing kind of world, interaction within residential territorial spaces is less and less characteristic of urban people. This needs to be further understood, however, for purposes of planning residences in relation to other social activities. But the more pronounced urban challenges concern mobility, quality of social interaction, and defensibility — in short, competition and conflict — in all urban spaces.

CONSEQUENCES OF URBAN ECOLOGY

The consequences of urban people-land relationships are both positive and negative. On the positive side, the complex urban ecology stimulates production of goods, scientific ideas, and high culture. But often the components of urban ecology become so complex that mental overload and alienation results. Social class meanings become intensified. The experience of territorial neighborhoods is eroded. For many people the complex urbanized society is characterized by frustration, conflict, and overload. Accordingly, city dwellers develop patterns for reducing the number and intensity of inputs and conserving their sociopsychic energy. Examples of these adaptive mental overload mechanisms include superficial relationships with a large number of acquaintances (Simmel 1950); less time spent on each personal contact; considerable disregard for low-priority inputs (for example, the city person may disregard the drunk, the sick, and the maligned in street crowds); activities shifted to other persons or machines (for example, bus drivers no longer make change for passengers and elevator operators are replaced by automation); social screening and input blockage (for example, executives ask secretaries who is calling before granting admission to their offices, and unlisted telephone numbers are used); superficial forms of involvement (for example, messages may be left through secretaries to avoid face-to-face contact); specialized institutions to handle overload problems (for example, welfare, health, science, recreation, and the arts all become institutional patterns of behavior in extensively urbanized societies) (Milgram 1970).

Urban overload is responded to both by individuals and by social systems (Meier 1962). Libraries increasingly become computerized as data banks. Medical and banking records similarly are computerized.

Urbanized culture has become too complex for individuals to conveniently internalize. Accordingly, adaptive mechanisms are created which enable urban people to relate to a few categories of circumstances rather than to the enormous multiplicity of individual situations. There is a limited willingness to trust and assist strangers, as urban social structures are established to provide special types of assistance like traveler's aid, legal aid, and emergency medical aid. The unknown and the uninvited are seldom admitted to urban places of residence. Doorbells, one-way glass, intercom systems, remote television, and domestic telephone answering services are all techniques used to provide selective levels of privacy. In small towns customers of stores are known as individuals — often by complete name and by many family and social characteristics. In large areas customers are known by credit ratings and receive form letters produced by computers.

Cognitive mapping (mental images) of cities grows in importance (Lynch 1960). Some cities have high imagability while others are nondescript. Some cities are known by their distinctive districts — for example, Chinatown in San Francisco, the French Quarter in New Orleans, Rockefeller Center in New York City, and Georgetown in Washington, D.C. Cities may be known for their interactional personalities, assumed from famed festivals like Mardi Gras in New Orleans, Carnival in Rio de Janeiro, Semana Santa (Holy Week) in Seville, the Mozart Festival in Salzburg. New York City is known for its skyscrapers; Paris for its low skyline and wide baroque streets; Brasilia for its grandiose and starkly modern impersonal buildings; and Venice for its canals and piazzas. Many of the Western World's new towns are found to be homogeneous — a polite way of saying dull and uninteresting. But in contrast to urban overload, the homogeneity of new towns and smaller residential neighborhoods may mean tranquility and rest from urban pressure.

Social stratification and social class

Stratification is widely observed even in open-class urban societies. In the United States social stratification is identified in a series of now classic case studies: Yankee City (Newburyport, Massachusetts) studied in the 1930s when it had a population of 17,000, Jonesville (Morris, Illinois) in the 1940s when the population was 6,000, both by Warner; Georgia Town (Statesboro, Georgia) studied in the late 1940s and early 1950s when it had a population of 7,000; Middletown (Muncey, Indiana) studied by the Lynds in 1929 when there were 35,000 people and again in 1935 when the population had grown to 50,000; Deep South (Natchez, Mississippi) studied in the late 1930s by Allison and Davis when the population was 13,000; New Haven, Connecticut studied in 1958 by Hollingshead and Redlick when the population was 250,000; Chicago, Illinois studied by Martineau in 1955 – 56 and by Simmons and Associates in 1960; and Kansas City, Missouri studied in 1954 – 55. Five distinct social classes were found in these urban areas although their characteristics varied (Coleman 1971). The percentage of the urban population in the respective social classes for six of these areas is shown in Table 4 – 1. Both in residential neighborhoods and in occupations, the urban upper classes were separated from the urban lower classes.

TABLE 4–1   Social Class Distributions In Six American Communities

SOCIAL CLASSES[a]	Yankee City (Early 1930s)	Jonesville (Early 1940s)	Georgia Town (Early 1950s)	New Haven (Early 1950s)	Chicago[b] (1956, 1960)	Kansas City (Mid-1950s)
	\multicolumn{6}{c}{ADULTS AT EACH SOCIAL LEVEL — Percent}					
Upper Class	3.0	2.7	3.2	2.7	2.1	1.8
Upper Middle	10.1	12.0	15.7	9.8	8.1	11.6
Lower Middle	28.3	32.2	27.3	21.4	21.6	33.3
Working Class	33.3	41.0	27.4	48.5	43.6	40.2
Lower Class	25.3	12.1	26.4	17.6	24.6	13.1
TOTAL	100	100	100	100	100	100

[a] In the New Haven Study, the classes were referred to by Roman numerals, I through V; in Yankee City, Jonesville, and Georgia Town the Working Class was called Upper-Lower, and the Lower Class, Lower-Lower.

[b] The percentages for Chicago are averages based on two different studies, Martineau (1957) and Simmons and Associates (1960). For the Martineau study based on 3,600 households, a modified version of the Warner I. S. C. was used, producing the following class distribution: 0.9 percent Upper, 7.2 percent Upper-Middle, 28.4 percent Lower-Middle, 44.0 percent Working Class, and 19.5 percent Lower Class. The second study was conducted by W.R. Simmons and Associates, a New York research firm, in a study of the Chicago area market for the Chicago Sun-Times and Chicago Daily News newspapers. It was based on a sample of 4,374 Chicago area residents, classified by the Hollingshead two-factor Index of Status Position. The class distribution of metropolitan Chicago estimated by Simmons and Associates was: 3.3 percent Upper, 8.9 percent Upper-Middle, 14.8 percent Lower-Middle, 43.2 percent Working Class, and 29.8 percent Lower Class.

Source: Richard P. Coleman and B. L. Neugarten, Social Status in the City (San Francisco: Jossey-Bass Inc., 1971), p. 260.

In Mexico City Hayner found social classes to be separated geographically (Hayner 1966). The city's upper classes were identified by being listed in Who's Who in Latin America. Persons in this listing resided disproportionately in the Lomas de Chapultepec district. It is a hilly area just southwest of the center of the city. Also a higher class area is located ten miles south of the central city and just west of the National Autonomous University in the Pedregal Gardens area. Poor districts are primarily north and northeast of the central business and government areas. Although slums and low-income areas are found in several different locations, they are disproportionately in the eastern and northern sections. The architectural style of homes varies sharply between the upper-income and lower-income areas. In the upper-income areas the homes tend to be detached, with spacious green yards surrounding the exteriors. The low-income area residences are characterized by the zero lot line construction of traditional Latin America, with rooms and high walls facing directly on the streets and small patios in the interior.

New-town planners usually suggest that new towns' virtues include a balance in social classes and physical ecology. Whatever their virtues may be, they have generally failed to achieve a social class balance. They are disproportionately middle-class ghettos. Few really low-income people can afford to live in most new towns, and few really well-to-do people find much of challenge or way of life gratification in them (Heraud 1968; Bolwell 1969; Keller 1969). Keller points out that people in both old and new towns use housing type and residential area to support their expression of status and prestige. Social mobility is generally accompanied by residential mobility. Particularly for the higher social classes, housing is more symbolic for its status than for its utilitarian value. Even in new towns, social class distinctions are established by home furnishing styles, differences in childrearing, and so forth. Gardens quickly become status symbols. Working-class areas are characterized by extensive family and kinship visiting. Middle-class people are selective and more personal in accepting friendships. Upper-class people are more exclusive in their relationships with other persons, use distinctive architecture, attend fashionable churches, and send their children to private schools.

The experience of English new towns, according to Heraud (1968), is the gradual shifting of the working classes into the middle classes. Instead of real social class balance, there is some tendency for working classes to move up. Table 4–2 shows the class structure of selected London ring new towns compared to England and Wales and to the Greater London population.

Neighborhoods and social class

There was a unique application of the neighborhood idea in the superblock built by Clarence Stein in Radburn, New Jersey in 1929. It was unique in that one block was essentially a complete neighborhood. Considerable discussion of the superblock neighborhood followed for another fifteen years, but with little application.

TABLE 4-2 Class Structures of New Towns, with Comparisons

SOCIAL CLASS	Crawley 1961	Harlow 1957	Hemel Hempstead 1960	England and Wales 1961	Greater London 1961	Dagenham 1958
I. Professional	3.7%	5.0%	5.9%	3.8%	4.8%	1%
II. Intermediate professional	13.4%	13.0%	20.1%	15.4%	15.8%	4%
III. Unskilled non-manual and skilled manual	63.6%	63.0%	54.6%	51.1%	52.2%	56%
IV. Semi-skilled manual	13.1%	} 19.0%	14.4%	20.5%	18.1%	22%
V. Unskilled manual	6.2%		5.0%	9.2%	9.1%	17%
MIDDLE CLASS (Classes I & II)	17.1%	18.0%	26.0%	19.2%	20.6%	5%
WORKING CLASS (Classes III, IV, AND V)	82.9%	82.0%	74.0%	80.8%	79.4%	95%

Source: B.J. Heraud, "Social Class and the New Towns," Urban Studies 5 (February 1968), 39.

In England there were various reports concerning housing and new towns from the 1920s through the Second World War. Immediately following the War, there was a great need to restore old housing and to build new housing. In 1946 the British Parliament passed the New Town Act in effect officially adopting the neighborhood as the tool with which to build quality living and working environments. The neighborhood concept emphasized open space, a population sufficiently small to be served by one elementary school (this ranged from 3,000 to 10,000 persons), and the location of shops on the edge of neighborhoods so that traffic flows and shopping centers could be formed at the junction of several neighborhoods. In the British new town, residential densities were targeted at between 30 and 40 persons per acre. Goss surveyed the results of this planning notion for several neighborhood units in British new towns and found close adherence (Goss 1961): one neighborhood was selected in each of ten new towns, and the average net residential density was thirty-six persons per acre. The range was a high of fifty-one to a low of thirty. The same neighborhoods ranged in total planned population from a high of 21,000 to a low of 5,400, or an average size of 9,875 persons. Both density and neighborhood size are close to what the theory recommended.

One elementary school was planned in the smallest neighborhood and six elementary schools were planned in the largest. The Dudley Report recommended that one grocery shop be built for every 100 to 150 persons in neighborhoods. Goss found a considerable deviation from this, reporting some 374 persons per shop. Cinemas, libraries, and youth centers were in generally short supply at the neighborhood levels.

Social class balance was anticipated at the neighborhood level. In several of the British new towns effort has been made to intermix standard rented houses and flats for middle- and higher-income groups with those for lower-income groups. Some degree of success has been achieved, but a total class balance has not yet been reached.

Howard Bracey has studied neighboring patterns in Bristol, England and Columbus, Ohio (Bracey 1964). He discovered much greater propensity for block social interaction in Columbus neighborhoods than in Bristol neighborhoods. Americans develop welcoming committees, churches have special programs to integrate newcomers, and so on. Even in neighborhoods where many residents consider themselves to be temporary, associations and social action programs are supported. In suburban areas there are high rates of social interaction in voluntary associations like country clubs, P.T.A.'s, and scouting groups. Many of these voluntary association "identities," however, can be easily moved to a new community.

From the 1950s to the 1970s, social interaction patterns in residential neighborhoods have been studied in America (Merton 1951; White 1956; Van der Ryn 1965; Carey 1972; Maps 1972). In a study of Massachusetts Institute of Technology housing for married students, Festinger found that the physical distance between dwelling residences and the orientation of dwellings to each other are both variables which influence neighborhood group interaction. Robert Merton's earlier study of friendship formation in Craftown similarly found that residential propinquity and the orientation of residential structures influenced social interaction.

In Lake Vista, a planned residential area in New Orleans, Filipich and Taylor (1971) found that superblocks and cul-de-sacs do increase social interaction. Both children and adults had increased knowledge of persons on their cul-de-sacs and across the lanes from them on superblocks. Adult women had more social interaction than adult men in these areas, but the differences were only a matter of degree.

In San Francisco a special study of amenity attributes of residential locations was undertaken by University of California professors for the Author D. Little Corporation. The purpose of the research was to identify amenity elements in residential environments; to determine how these elements influenced decisions of users about their residential locations; to further understanding of interaction systems between different social classes of users; and finally to interpret this information in the design of appropriate high-quality renewal for different neighborhoods. Amenity elements were operationalized to be features considered to be sufficiently desirable to generate intracity movements by residents. It was further noted that some elements of the environment would be amenities for certain residents but not for others. The amenity elements concept was also operationalized to refer to both physical and social attributes of places.

As is often the case, in San Francisco most residents — two-thirds to three-fourths — had relatively high satisfaction with their location. For those who were the most satisfied, the social characteristics of their neighborhoods were said to be their reasons for satisfaction. Similarly, among those residents who were dissatisfied, social characteristics of the neighborhoods were the prime causes. The study was designed to produce data that would allow the clustering of San Francisco's 108 census tracts into 10 to 15 amenity residential classes. It is impressively clear that even in San Francisco where physical views are so important, Van der Ryn (1965) asserts that most people still decide where to live in accordance with the kind of neighbors they expect to have. The second amenity factor is proximity to the life of the city — meaning density, the level of street activity, and ownership. The other two amenity factors are the topography and historical status of the neighborhood. In most areas of San Francisco, hill locations are more status-giving than lower physical locations. Also for many residents in San Francisco there is status attached to living in a neighborhood that has a sense of history. Many once-blighted areas, for example, like Telegraph Hill, are being updated and made fashionable.

San Francisco has a long history for an American city (founded in 1776), but its built environment is essentially new, dating after the earthquake and fire in 1906. Accordingly, some 90 percent of dwelling units fit one of ten or twelve stereotyped plans. As dilapidated housing is removed, more expensive units are put in its place, forcing many families out of the city who would prefer the more urban style of life. The San Francisco neighborhood studies bring into sharp focus the view that a neighborhood is first and foremost people and second a physical location.

In 1975 Taylor studied neighborhood patterns in three locations in the Dallas-Fort Worth Standard Metropolitan Statistical Area (Taylor 1975). The East Dallas neighborhood is a central city slum with a mixed white, black, and brown population. The Las Colinas neighborhood is a suburban, new-town-like development between Dallas and Fort Worth. It has its own private country club and eventually will have shopping facilities. Its population is upper-middle- and lower-upper-class. The Woodhaven neighborhood is in the city of Fort Worth, but suburban in character. Most houses, condominiums, and apartments have views of and direct access to a golf course and country club development in the area. Woodhaven has a predominantly upper-middle-class population. The primary reason for moving to these neighborhoods was given as "liked the environment" by 63 percent in Woodhaven and 54 percent in Las Colinas; and as "house was a good buy" by 21 percent in East Dallas. The typical housing types are for Woodhaven and Las Colinas, 96 percent single family detached; and for East Dallas, 56 percent apartments. (Woodhaven and Las Colinas are, in fact, new areas still being developed. There will be more multiple housing units in these areas in the next decade.) In all three neighborhoods, nearly 60 percent of the respondents failed to count neighbors among their closest friends. Moreover, there was no difference in the three neighborhoods in respect to getting to know "best friends" since the residents moved there. In all cases there is an absence of friendship by proximity. About half of the respondents in Woodhaven and Las Colinas do go to some activities like picnics and movies with neighbors on some occasions, but only 20 percent of the East Dallas residents participate similarly with their neighbors. The least amount of neighboring is found in East Dallas. Finally, in the East Dallas area there was limited use of yard spaces because they were considered to be unsafe. Yards in Las Colinas and Woodhaven were considered to be safe spaces, but they were mostly used for status and prestige.

The "people view" of the neighborhood is sharply acknowledged by Webber's (1963) concepts of "place community" and "nonplace community." Theoretically, Webber views urban communities first of all as places where individuals interact (place communities) and secondly as large urban areas of influence (nonplace communities). The point of his distinction is that individuals, firms, organizations, and institutions increasingly have contacts and transactions on a global urban basis. This is another way of demonstrating the developing trend toward ecumenopolis. Webber also refers to the nonplace communities as "urban realms." He asserts that even the social interaction in place communities must be interpreted in the framework of urban realms. Most urban individuals participate in some place communities but also participate extensively during much of their life in nonplace communities related to employment, the arts, recreation, health, and education. Accordingly, Webber views the city as a "dynamic system in action."

ECOLOGY ISSUES AND DEVELOPMENTS

Since the mid-twentieth century, the major socioecological concerns of urban planners have been questions of land use, density, scale, and zoning. These are rarely mutually exclusive issues. Zoning, for example, is often used to enforce land use plans. Nevertheless, each is used with sufficient distinction to justify separate examination.

Comprehensive planning and land use analysis

Comprehensive planning developed in the first quarter of the twentieth century. It became widespread in America when Congress passed and funded the 701 Comprehensive Planning Title in the 1954 Housing Act. For some twenty years, 701 Comprehensive Planning was the nation's largest program for land use planning. By the mid-1970s over 11,000 grants totaling $610 million had been awarded. Initially, small communities received most of the planning support, but from the late 1960s onward larger metropolitan areas were primary recipients (Cohen 1975).

A part of the land use planning tradition that gives a ready overview of physical ecology is the color-coded land use map. A detailed color code list is found in de Chiara and Koppelman, *Urban Planning and Design Criteria*, 1975. The principal land use categories are residential: single-family dwellings (lemon yellow), multiple dwellings (dark brown), and hotel-motel structures (purple). Business and commercial land use is divided into local or neighborhood business (pink) and general business (scarlet). Industrial land use is divided into heavy industry (black) and light industry (light grey). Public and quasipublic spaces include parks (true green), schools (grass green), public spaces (true blue), churches (indigo blue), and cemeteries (aquamarine). Agricultural land (apple green) is separately designated. Vacant land is signified by no color. Social-institutional activities are represented in the color code maps as follows: residential land use relates to procreative spaces; business, commercial, and industrial land use support production and distribution institutional space; schools provide much of the socialization space; churches relate to institutional spaces; and civic centers embody much of the government institutional space. Parks provide space for recreation and leisure, and hospitals relate to the institutional space concerning health care.

Less widely adopted but still used are physical planner color-coded maps that report the age of buildings, square footage per lot per family, and zoning.

Land use maps describe the results of human action. Comparative analysis of past patterns of land use assist planners in predicting the amounts of land required for future use. However, such predictions are limited because they do not enable decision makers to consider changes in ideology and in technology, both of which may impact heavily on desired future land use by citizens.

Urban density

Physical planners have placed much emphasis on the issue of urban density. Frank Lloyd Wright proposed 1 dwelling per acre in his Broadacre design. At an upper extreme Le Corbusier proposed a vertical city with some 300 dwellings per acre. Ebenezer Howard called for 8 to 12 dwellings per acre in his garden city new-town model. This middle-range density prevails most. Table 4 – 3 shows the common specifications for land area per family in different size neighborhoods ranging from a low of 1,000 persons to a high of 5,000 persons. In small neighborhoods, yard and house square footage range up to 9,060. In neighborhoods of 5,000 people, multidwelling units thirteen stories high provide only 1,400 square feet per family. This American land use is ample when compared to smaller European standards.

Table 4 – 4 shows land area use per family in a large neighborhood. The table indicates the greater efficiency of land use with multifamily dwellings.

These various densities range from much open space, frequently found in suburban areas, to vertical cities like New York's Manhattan and proposed megastructure cities. Such differences in density raise questions concerning the impact of urban scale on human behavior.

Urban scale and visual environment

Authors like Ebenezer Howard and Lewis Mumford have extolled the virtues of small human scale and maximum open green space. These are illustrated in the garden city new-town model developed by Howard, and in the small medieval cities praised by Mumford. Others expound the advantages of high-rise buildings and megastructures, as illustrated in the proposals for a vertical city for 3 million people by Le Corbusier, and for arcologies large enough for 6 million people by Soleri.

It is hypothesized by Lozano (1974) that visual dissatisfaction is part of man's major conflict with his built environment. He also hypothesizes that human beings need different types of visual spaces in their environments. Visual spaces may be positive integrating forces in urban areas. For example, shopping areas, parks, and worship spaces may be visually complementary. Lozano cites the failure of the Pruitt-Igoe Housing Project in St. Louis, Missouri as one of the most serious examples of environmental failure. Other similar failures are described by Blake (1974), who charges that most buildings are shaped in accordance with plumbing, electrical, wiring, heating, and air-conditioning specifications rather than by design for high-quality social living. He opposes an urban visual design which attempts to provide green and open spaces on street levels. He suggests that what people really want is a tightly structured urban space filled with shops, restaurants, theaters, and offices. He opposes the expansion of transportation systems and proposes that cities be designed on an interactional scale that will make mass urban transportation systems unnecessary.

TABLE 4–3 Common Allowances of Family, by Type of Dwelling, for Neighborhoods of Various Sizes

	NEIGHBORHOOD POPULATION				
	1,000 persons	*2,000 persons*	*3,000 persons*	*4,000 persons*	*5,000 persons*
DWELLING TYPE	*275 families*	*550 families*	*825 families*	*1,100 families*	*1,375 families*
	Square Feet per Family[a]				
One- or Two-Family Dwellings					
One-family detached	9,060	8,600	8,520	8,460	8,440
One-family semidetached or Two-family detached	6,460	6,000	5,920	5,860	5,840
One-family attached (row) or Two-family semidetached	4,360	3,900	3,820	3,760	3,740
Multifamily Dwellings					
Two-story	3,425	2,960	2,885	2,825	2,795
Three-story	2,825	2,360	2,285	2,225	2,195
Six-story	2,210	1,745	1,670	1,610	1,580
Nine-story	2,095	1,630	1,555	1,495	1,465
Thirteen-story	2,030	1,565	1,490	1,430	1,400

[a]Calculated with street allowances added.

Source: Joseph de Chiara and Lee Koppelman, Urban Planning and Design Criteria, 2d. ed. *(New York: Van Nostrand Reinhold Co., 1975), p. 358.*

TABLE 4-4 Common Allowances of Land Area Use per Family, by Type of Dwelling, for Neighborhood of 5,000 Persons (1,375 Families)[a]

DWELLING TYPE	Not residential	Streets serving dwellings[b]	Community facilities	Streets serving com. fac.[c]	Total
One- or Two-Family Dwellings					
One-family detached	6,000/71%	1,800/22%	530/6%	110/1%	8,440/100%
Two-family semidetached or Two-family detached	4,000/68%	1,200/21%	530/9%	110/2%	5,840/100%
One-family attached (row) or Two-family semidetached	2,400/64%	700/19%	530/14%	110/3%	3,740/100%
Multifamily Dwellings					
Two-story	1,465/53%	600/21%	610/22%	120/4%	2,795/100%
Three-story	985/45%	480/21%	610/28%	120/6%	2,195/100%
Six-Story	570/36%	280/18%	610/39%	120/7%	1,580/100%
Nine-story	515/35%	220/15%	610/42%	120/8%	1,465/100%
Thirteen-story	450/32%	220/15%	610/44%	120/9%	1,400/100%

[a]Assumed average family size: 3.6 persons. Organization of this and later tables by dwelling types does not imply that a neighborhood should consist of one dwelling type alone.
[b]Will vary locally with volume of traffic, street widths, parking scheme, etc.
[c]Allowance is approximately 20 percent of area of community facilities.
Source: Joseph de Chiara and Lee Koppelman, Urban Planning and Design Criteria, 2d. ed. *(New York: Van Nostrand Reinhold Co., 1975), p. 358.*

Lynch (1962) asked respondents a series of questions concerning the visual impact of city life in Boston, Jersey City, and Los Angeles. He asked residents: (1) what is it that visually comes to mind when you think of describing your city; (2) what would you explain to strangers when describing the downtown or central part of your city; (3) what do you see on your normal trip from your place of residence to your place of work; and (4) which elements of your central city do you believe are most distinctive.

Through all of these techniques of physical ecology analysis from land use, to densities, to perceptions of visual scale, it has been found that the overriding concern is people's satisfaction with people. When people are satisfied with others with whom they must interact, they have a high tolerance for modification of the built environment.

Zoning and planned developments

Zoning is potentially one of the strongest ecological tools used by urban planners. It is a technique for bringing balance between individual land uses and community needs. Also it is a technique for regulating people movement, light intensity, air flow, and general amenities (Rody 1960). Throughout twentieth-century America, even with a private property ideology, there is wide recognition that property owners must not use their possessions in ways that are harmful to other persons. The Supreme Court of the United States began upholding this view in 1905 in the zoning case of *Jacobson* v. *Massachusetts*. In 1916 the Court specifically upheld the legality of zoning ordinances. By 1922 the U.S. Department of Commerce developed a standard state zoning act. This has become the model for many subsequent zoning acts. Typical municipal zoning acts now specify the designation of land for residential, commercial, and industrial uses. Zoning ordinances further specify administrative procedures related to permits, records, adjustments, and enforcement (Bassett 1940).

As society becomes increasingly urbanized, large numbers of people are planned for at one time in terms of residences, jobs, commercial activities, health activities, education, and transportation. This brings increased pressure for large-scale zoning. The Planned Unit Development (PUD), or more recently the Planned Development (PD), is an approach that has come into increasingly prevalent use in the second half of the twentieth century (Huntoon 1971). PDs allow for the bringing together of housing, jobs, commerce, and recreation into new neighborhoods, new communities, and new towns. PDs are extensive departures from traditional zoning and therefore require enabling legislation and specific PD ordinances. One of the most notable examples of a Planned Development is Heritage Village, which opened in Southbury, Connecticut in 1965 to provide for a population of 2,500 senior-citizen families. This involved the clustering of townhouses in a bucolic wooded environment around shops and a full range of urban facilities.

With rapid urban and suburban growth there is pressure to increase multiple housing units, and apartment and townhouse developments permeate the suburbs. Convenience shopping centers and, eventually, proximity to jobs become a part of consumer demand in the new and rapidly changing urban environment.

PDs are designed to have social interaction amenities and advantages. Cul-de-sacs and common recreational areas provide safety and social facilities. Economically, PDs should be cheaper to build because of minimal street distance and reduced construction costs for utility services. More usable open space can be provided in common areas while clustering and zero lot lines reduce wasted space between units. Table 4–5 shows the economic advantage of PD planning over traditional zoning for municipalities.

In the pluralized urban society there is a need for multiple ecology models to be experienced by different categories of the urban population at different times in the life cycle. Ecological patterns must simultaneously provide for heterogeneity and homogeneity. Urbanized society is an explicitly secondary form of social organization. Sociophysical ecological structures, in order to be effective, must support secondary social organization.

TABLE 4–5 Traditional Zoning and PD Zoning Compared

	UNDER EXISTING ZONING	UNDER APPROVED PD
Number of housing units	282	1,368
Types of units	all single-family	60 single-family detached; 140 single-family attached; 1,168 apartments and townhouses (also commercial and office buildings)
Number of school pupils	560	550
Value	$4,250,000	$11,300,000
Tax revenues	$ 170,000	$ 452,000
Educational costs	$ 136,000	$ 134,000
Total service costs	$ 184,000	$ 256,000
Total service costs per housing unit	$ 650	$ 114
Benefit or loss to town	$ 14,000 loss	$ 196,000 surplus

Source: Maxwell C. Huntoon, Jr., PUD: A Better Way for the Suburbs (Washington, D.C.: Urban Land Institute, 1971), p.72.

IMPLICATIONS

People and their space relationships constitute one of the most critical issues facing urban planners. In small-scale ruralized societies there were few specialized space uses. More importantly, where specialized land use did exist it was proximic to all other land uses.

As cities have grown and matured, and as societies become urbanized, land use specializations proliferate and become separated by many blocks — often even by multiple miles. Commuting for multiple miles between place of residence and place of work is typical. The mass movement of urban people becomes costly in time, money, energy, health, and sociophysical pressure. As identities are confused and lost, the cost of urban movement is high in antisocial behavior. Many social systems are inefficient in rendering services accordingly.

Social institutions and land use are being integrated in sociophysical planning to create a new urban ecology. Efforts to revitalize downtown areas focus on providing detached, middle-rise, and highrise residential units particularly for the middle classes and above. Philadelphia's Society Hill district is one among many examples. Shopping-mall streets and central-city recreational facilities are being strengthened by the return of adjacent residential populations.

Cloward and Piven in *The Politics of Turmoil* (1974) point to the urban crisis of poverty, a matter significantly related to ecology. The day populations of urban offices come essentially from middle- and upper-class suburban areas. The night populations of central urban areas come from adjacent slum transitional zones. New urban ecology plans are changing this by integrating the full range of activity systems with a full social class distribution of populations.

REFERENCES

ABU-LUGHOD, J. L. Testing the theory of social area analysis: the ecology of Cairo, Egypt. *American Sociological Review,* 1969, 34, 198 – 211.
AMATO, P. W. A comparison: population densities, land values and socioeconomic class in four Latin American cities. *Land Economics,* 1970, 41, 447 – 55.
ANDERSON, T., & BEAN L. The Shevky-Bell social areas. *Social Forces,* 1961, 40, 119 – 24.
ASH, M. Green belt, or the green city? *Town and Country Planning,* 1974, 42, 7 – 9.
BASSETT, E. M. *Zoning.* New York: Russell Sage Foundation, 1940.
BERRY, B., & REES, P. The factorial ecology of Calcutta. *American Journal of Sociology,* 1969, 74, 445 – 91.
BLAKE, P. The folly of modern architecture. *The Atlantic,* 1974, 234, 59 – 66.
BOLWELL, L., & TOWEL, J. Social class in a new town. *Urban Studies,* 1969, 6, 93 – 96.

BRACEY, H. E. *Neighbours*. Baton Rouge: Louisiana State University Press, 1964.

BURGESS, E. W. The growth of the city. Park, R. E., Burgess, E. W., & McKenzie, R. D. (Eds.), in *The City*. Chicago: University of Chicago Press, 1925.

CAREY, L., & MAPS, R. *The Sociology of Planning*. London: B. T. Batsford, Ltd., 1972.

CHAPIN, F. S., JR. *Urban Land Use Planning*. Urbana: University of Illinois Press, 1970.

CLOWARD, R. A. & PIVEN, F. F. *The Politics of Turmoil*. New York: Pantheon Books, 1974.

COHEN, B. Stung and shaken, but surviving. *Planning: The ASPO Magazine*, 1975, *41*, 8–11.

COLEMAN, R. P., & NEUGARTNER, B. L. *Social Status in the City*. San Francisco: Jossey-Bass, 1971.

CRESWELL, P. In the defense of green belts. *Town and Country Planning*, 1974, *42*, 227.

DAHIR, J. What is the best size for a city? *The American City*, August 1951, 104–5.

DAHIR, J. *The Neighborhood Unit Plan*. New York: Russell Sage Foundation, 1947.

DE CHIARA, J., & KOPPELMAN, L. *Planning Design Criteria*. New York: Van Nostrand, 1975.

DUNCAN, D. Human Ecology and Population Studies. In P. M. Hauser and O. D. Duncan (Eds.), *The Study of Population*. Chicago: University of Chicago Press, 1959.

EFFRAT, M. P. *The Community: Approaches and Applications*. New York: Free Press, 1974, 1–34.

FESTINGER, L. *Social Pressures in Informal Groups*. New York: Harper & Brothers, 1950.

FILIPICH, J., & TAYLOR L. *Lakefront New Orleans*. New Orleans: Louisiana State University, Urban Institute, 1971.

FIREY, W. *Land Use in Central Boston*. New York: Greenwood Press, 1947.

GALLION, A., & EISNER, S. *The Urban Pattern*. New York: Van Nostrand, 1963, 252–53.

GANS, H. J. *The Urban Villagers*. New York: Free Press, 1962.

GANS, H. J. Planning and social life. *Journal of the American Institute of Planners*, 1961, *27*, 134–40.

GOODE, W. J. Community within a community: the professions. *American Sociological Review*, 1957, *22*, 194–200.

GOSS, A. Neighborhood units in British new towns. *Town Planning Review*, 1961, *32*, 66–82.

GUTMAN, R. Site planning in social behavior. *Journal of Social Issues*, 1966, *22*, 103–15.

HARRIS, C. D., & ULLMAN, E. L. The nature of cities. *The Annals of the American Academy of Political and Social Science*, 1945, *242*, 7–17.

HAUSER, F. L. In T. L. Smith & C. A. McMahan (Eds.), *The Sociology of Urban Life*. New York: Dryden Press, 1951, 370–88.

HAYNER, N. S., & HAYNER, U. M. *New Patterns in Old Mexico*. New Haven, Conn.: College and University Press, 1966, 76.

HERAUD, B. J. Social class in new towns. *Urban Studies*, 1968, *5*, 33–58.

HOOVER, E. M. The evolving form and organization of metropolis. In H. S. Perloff & L. Wingo, Jr. (Eds.), *Issues in Urban Economics*. Baltimore: Johns Hopkins Press, 1968.

HOYT, H. City growth and mortgage risk. *Insured Mortgage Portfolio*, December, 1936 – April, 1937, Vol. I.

HOYT, H. *The Structure and Growth of Residential Neighborhoods in American Cities*. Washington, D.C.: Government Printing Office, 1937.

HUNTOON, M. C., JR. *PUD: A Better Way for the Suburb*. Washington, D.C.: The Urban Land Institute, 1971, 22.

KELLER, S. Social class in physical planning. *Urban Studies*, 1969, 6, 57 – 65.

LOZANO, E. E. Visual needs in the urban environment. *Town Planning Review*, 1974, 45, 351 – 74.

LYNCH, K. *The Image of the City*. Cambridge: M.I.T. Press and Harvard University Press, 1960.

LYNCH, K. *Site Planning*. Cambridge: M.I.T. Press, 1962.

MAPS, R. *The Sociology of Planning*. London: B. T. Batsford, Ltd., 1972.

MEIRER, R. L. *A Communications Theory of Urban Growth*. Cambridge: M.I.T. Press, 1962.

MERDIE, R. A. *Factorial Ecology of Metropolitan Toronto*. Chicago: University of Chicago Press, 1969.

MERTON, R. K. The social psychology of housing. In D. Wrong et al. (Eds.), *Current Trends in Social Psychology*. Pittsburg: University Press, 1951, 163 – 217.

MILGRAM, S. The experience of living in cities. *Science*, 1970, 167, 1461 – 68.

NEWMAN, O. *Defensible Space*. New York: Macmillan Co., 1972.

ORLEANS, P. Robert Park and social area analysis: a convergence of traditions in urban sociology. *Urban Affairs Quarterly*, 1966, 1, 5 – 19.

PARK, R. E., & BURGESS, E. W. *The City*. Chicago: University of Chicago Press, 1925.

PURLOFF, H. S., & WINGO, L., JR. *Issues in Urban Economics*. Baltimore: Johns Hopkins Press, 1968.

RODY, M. J., & SMITH, H. H. *Zoning Primer*. West Trenton, N.J.: Chandler-Davis Publishing Co., 1960.

SHEVKY, E., & BELL, W. *Social Area Analysis*. Stanford: Stanford University Press, 1955.

SHEVKY, E., & WILLIAMS, M. *The Social Areas of Los Angeles*. Los Angeles and Berkeley: University of California Press, 1949.

SIMMEL, G. *The Sociology of George Simmel* (K. H. Wolff, Ed.) New York: Macmillan Co., 1950.

SUTTLES, G. *The Social Order of the Slum*. Chicago: University of Chicago Press, 1968.

TAYLOR, L. Original research data collected 1975.

Town and Country Planning Act, 1946. London: Her Majesty's Stationery Office, 1946.

VAN DER RYN, S. *Amenity Attributes of Residential Locations: San Francisco Community Renewal Program*. Boston: Arthur D. Little, Inc., 1965.

WEBBER, M. Order in diversity: community without propinquity. In L. Wingo (Ed.), *Cities and Space*. Baltimore: Johns Hopkins Press, 1963.

WEBBER, M. M. The urban place and the non-place urban realm. In M. M. Webber (Ed.), *Explorations into Urban Structure*. Philadelphia: University of Pennsylvania Press, 1964.

WHITE, W. H., JR. *The Organization Man*. New York: Simon and Schuster, 1956.

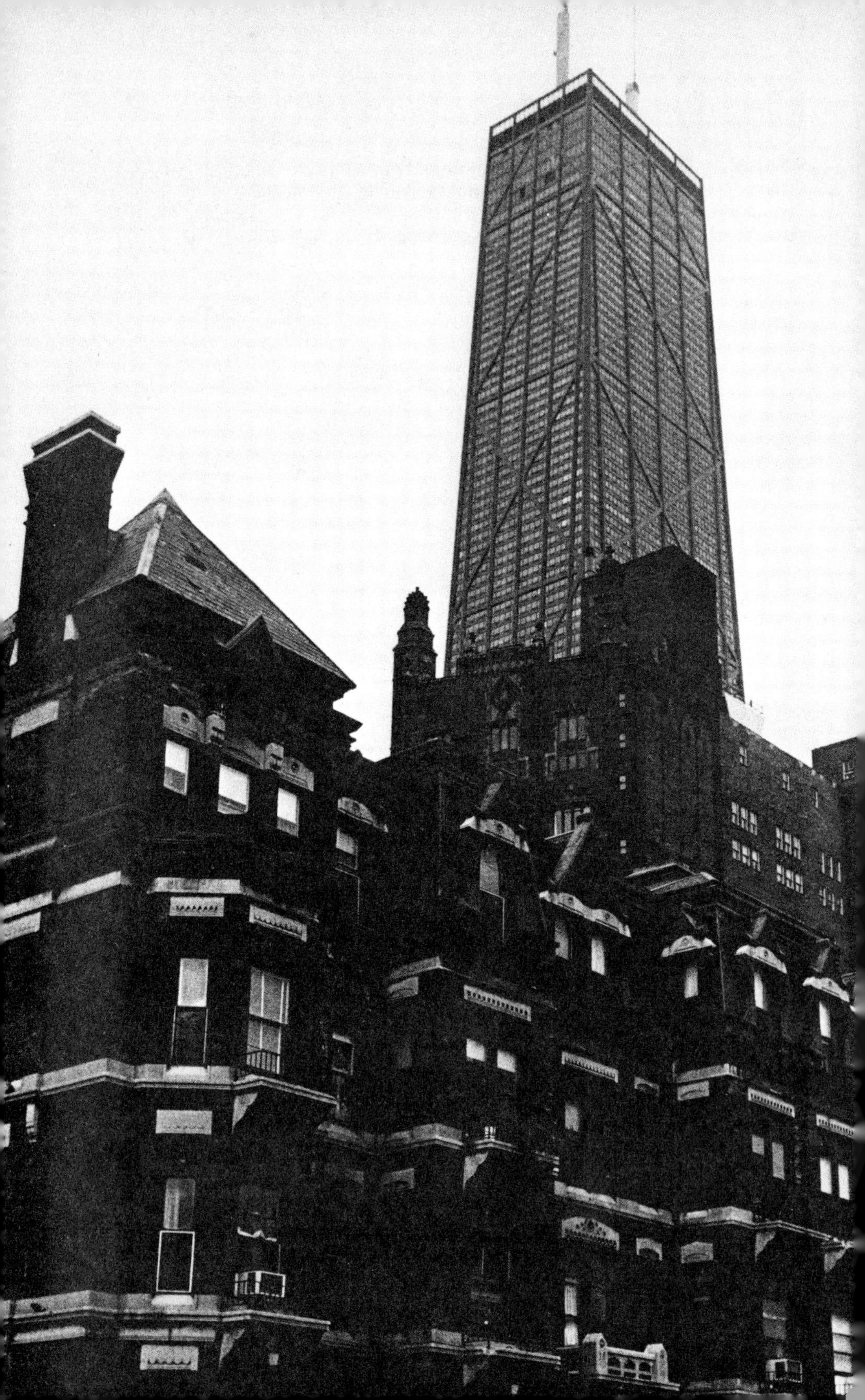

Urban Centers 5

Throughout most of urban history, physical and social city centers have largely overlapped. Generally city centers have the largest commercial buildings, largest government buildings, largest religious buildings, and so forth. The major plazas, streets, and cultural facilities are in or near city centers. Much social interaction takes place in streets and squares as people walk from one location to another. They may engage in commercial fairs, cultural extravaganzas, religious pageantry, and related activities.

In the early city people lived in small residential quarters near the center, frequently over shops. Education took place more informally than formally in families and in craft guilds — often near city centers.

As cities grew both social organizationally and physically, division of labor and specialization proliferated. Central land uses too gradually became specialized. Urbanized societies moved through an intensive era of industrialization and in the industrialized city, the central area became increasingly unifunctional. Its major purpose became commerce. It was only a matter of time until the central business district concept was developed. Later in this chapter we look at this concept in some detail, examining its characteristics and discussing its measurements.

Along with the industrialized city came the seeds of post-industrial urban social organization. Starting in the late nineteenth century, improvements in communication and transportation made suburbanization possible. Suburbanization has continued at an accelerated

The John Hancock megastructure in Chicago is one example of urban centers reaching new heights. (Photo: Jean-Claude Lejeune for The Stockmarket.)

pace for nearly a century (Johnson 1967). By the latter part of the twentieth century, urban megalopolis regions are developing in patterns which suggest further post-industrialization and future ecumenopolis.

The single-purpose economic city center is being eroded. With computerized record keeping and automated distribution systems, many of the business functions of the early twentieth century cities are being moved to suburbs. The pendulum is swinging away from the single-purpose land use that was characteristic of the peak of industrial urbanization. Greater multiple land use by the integration of living, recreational, and business spaces into common geographical territories is taking place. Some "downtown" areas are becoming virtual ghost towns. Efforts to revive downtown areas by creating pedestrian malls are in fact an expression of a shift from single to multiple purposes in the urban core.

Urbanized society has reached such a large scale that many cities and many urban regions provide social space for all major societal activities from economics to the arts. The early urban cores, which were multifunctional, were inhabited only by people who opted for what they considered to be the culture and other advantages of city life. Urban living for such early urbanites was a distinctly desirable way of life characterized not only by business and commerce but by high achievement in painting, music, theater, dance, religion, education, and (later) science. Furthermore, the urban way of life included the sometimes elegant dining-out and cafe living. Both drama and status were reflected in the style of clothing of urbanites in the early multifunctional cities.

Most people who did not opt for this urban style of life had clear alternatives in rural and bucolic life styles. But with the urbanization of life in the Western World, the rural and bucolic life patterns of behavior have been eroded to virtual nonexistence. The force of city culture which causes rural erosion is embodied in business and economics. Land use priorities were given to business functions. Office skyscrapers soon towered over the churches and cathedrals which in an earlier urban era had dominated the city landscape. With changes in technology which made possible massive suburbanization, large numbers of people whose life was not directly related to central-city economic functions moved to suburbs.

The vacuum in many central cities is gradually being refilled with residents who desire the cultural plurality of city-center life. The population is heterogeneous in multifunctional urban areas.

In the last of the twentieth century, city planning and urban regional planning must recognize that world ecumenopolizing trends make it both possible and necessary to design urban centers at many different scales and with different functional levels. Some will be regional centers, some community centers, and some neighborhood centers. All of these centers must be planned in cognizance of their social and physical places at a societal level.

URBAN CENTERS AND SOCIAL INSTITUTIONS

Urbanized society involves multiple levels of social organization. Some urban centers can have a scale of smallness and social intimacy, and others can have a scale of grandness or baroqueness which diminishes the importance of individuals, even causing some to feel dehumanized.

In an urbanized world, whether the urban center is small and primary or large and secondary in its provision of social relationships, it must interface in an organizational network that is societal in scale. Theoretically, this is to say, no city in the last of the twentieth century is so small or so isolated that it is beyond the limits of the impact of urbanized society. City centers must be understood and planned either as unifunctional or multifunctional. Both types can be viable when their positions are articulated societally.

Urban planners need to ascertain what types of people desire to live in planned unit developments, what types like large plural environments, and what types like small, primary-scale environments. Some individuals may hope to reduce urban overload by living in small-scale, unifunctional urban environments. In all of these cases, the success of urban designing is improved when it is directly related to societal institutions.

Megastructures, ecumenopolis, and central places

Urban planners are with increasing frequency developing different megastructure models. Some proposals constitute dramatically important innovations in urban forms (Soleri 1969; Sadao 1969; Dantzig and Saaty 1973). Some megastructures are physical buildings of substantial size, designed to support institutional activities including residence, work, leisure, education, health, and worship. The John Hancock Building and the Marina Towers in Chicago and the Olympic Towers in New York City are examples of limited megastructures. They have the potential for extensive primary social interaction and considerable reduction of urban overload. The Olympic Towers building will in effect become an upper-class ghetto. The residents of some 250 exclusive condominiums will have their own skyscraper park, complete with a three-floor-high waterfall. Office facilities, exclusive shops, limited medical facilities, and so forth will be available to residents within the premises of the building. To some extent one can live in such a high-rise megastructure as if one were removed from the pressures of the larger society.

Other megastructures are both physically and socially on larger urban scales. They contain their own city centers. The Minnesota Experimental City would, if built, be a megastructure environment for 250,000 people. All life-support needs would be provided for in the city. But the survival of the city would require direct interfacing and articulation with the larger society for natural and socioeconomic resources (Spilhaus 1968; Minnesota Experimental City 1969). "Compact City" is a similar megastructure design for initially 250,000 people and containing space for all social institutions (Dantzig and Saaty 1973). Ultimately Compact City would grow to 1 million population. Among the largest megastructure models are the arcologies proposed by Soleri (1969). The largest of Soleri's arcologies would provide for a population of 6 million. This large population would carry out all of its social-institutional functions within a single physical structure. From one point of view, this megastructure-arcology is suprahuman in scale. Many of the world's nations have fewer than 6 million people. Nevertheless, the possibility of creating a high-quality, smooth-functioning social organization is increased in such megastructures. All social relationships would be provided for in them. Individuals would have both privacy and community on a systematic and higher quality basis than in the less planned urban environments.

The ecumenopolis form of urban life, like urbanized worldwide strip regions, will have high-density center nodes in some places, with low-density, garden-city-like spaces between them (Doxiadis 1968). The concept of ecumenopolis implies a network of integrated urban centers on a worldwide scale. A few of these urban centers are expected to exercise worldwide influence. Most urban centers, however, would extend their influence all the way to regional and national levels. Large numbers of neighborhood centers would proliferate throughout lower density ecumenopolis areas. All levels of urban centers in ecumenopolis would be systematically articulated with social institutions.

Central places in traditional cities, in megastructure cities, and in ecumenopolis are more viable and contribute more to high-quality urban environment when conceptualized as parts of social institutions and seen functioning in formal organizations.

New towns and town centers

Most conceptualized new towns have been built since 1945. By definition part of their sociophysical space is designated as a town center. Without significant exception, the town center is a place of commerce. But in most cases the new-town center is also multifunctional.

In addition to commerce, often the principal government offices, schools, health facilities, recreational facilities, and some housing are found in the town center (Osborn 1969; Merlin 1971; Bailey 1973; Mields 1973; Campbell 1976). Frequently the transportation system is designed in support of the town center.

In most of the new towns that follow the garden-city model (Howard 1965), there are, in addition to the town center, multiple neighborhood centers. Neighborhood centers are designed on smaller scales, intended to support primary group relationships, and oriented primarily toward two functions, namely convenience shopping and elementary education. On a very limited scale some other services may be provided.

In many respects the garden-city new town is in fact the anticity (Le Corbusier 1929; Gruen 1973). Many garden-city new towns and other middle-size suburban towns have land use separated for the civic center, the medical center, the educational center, the industrial center, the office center, the financial center, the shopping center, the cultural center, the amusement center, and so forth. The net effect may be little or no city life. To some extent the converse of dividing urban areas into unifunctional spaces is found in the megastructure new-town model used in Cumbernauld, Scotland and Jonathan, Minnesota. In both of these cases, the town centers are planned as megastructures with residential neighborhoods and some industrial sites located on the periphery of the megastructure. The megastructure town center is designed to be multifunctional, combining shopping, finance, offices, civic functions, some medical facilities, cultural areas, educational spaces, and amusement facilities.

In the new town of Valencia, a satellite of Los Angeles, a population of 250,000 is anticipated. The town center includes some ninety-three acres near the geographical center of Valencia. The multifunctionality of the town center is illustrated by the following distribution of revenue-producing spaces:

Space Function	Square Feet
Retail facilities	2,500,000
Offices	4,500,000
Apartments	6,000,000
Government facilities	150,000
Cultural facilities	200,000
Entertainment facilities	100,000
Hotels	100,000
Institutional facilities	600,000
TOTAL	14,150,000

In addition to the town center, Valencia is divided into a number of smaller neighborhoods with village centers. Other land use functions are segregated into industrial, medical, religious, and open space.

Barbican is a new-town-in-town in the city of London. It is a thirty-five-acre site in part of the old Roman-built area of London. Barbican is in effect urban renewal in an area almost completely devastated during World War II where the only remaining and rebuilt structure is St. Giles Church. Barbican is built largely on a pedestrian platform under which is provided the utility service, transportation, and parking facilities. The new area physically centers around St. Giles, but the multiple functions include 2,100 residential units (flats, maisonettes, and houses); 300,000 square feet of office space; a girls' school; a swimming pool; the Guild Hall School of Music and Drama; a cultural center providing a library, an art gallery, a theatre, a concert hall, and a meeting house. Also included in Barbican is a water garden and open public spaces (Gruen 1973).

Another example of a multifunctional town center as a new-town-in-town development is the proposed Houston Center in Texas. This is a seventy-five-acre project adjacent to the existing central business district. It would provide 5,000 residential units in the form of apartments and townhouses. Other services would include offices, hotels, retail stores, plus cultural and recreational facilities (Gruen 1973).

Around London, Paris, and Stockholm are areas called "ring towns." These follow predominantly the garden-city model. The three Stockholm satellite new towns are the smallest, each approximately 50,000 population. The eight London ring new towns are middle sized, between 50,000 and 100,000 population each, and the five Paris new towns are the largest, each projected for 500,000 people. They have in common the designation of multifunctional town centers with surrounding land area specifically designated for housing, recreation, industry, employment, highways, rapid transit, and other functions related to appropriate major and minor social institutions.

CENTRAL PLACE THEORY

Central Place Theory is generally attributed to geographers like Walter Christaller and August Losch (Johnson 1967). Christaller and Losch developed different but related type-hierarchies of cities, ranging from hamlets to villages to towns to cities. These are ideal-type hierarchies. The work of these geographers has been expanded to include the concept "range of goods," which refers to the distance people will travel for a particular type of goods or service, and also the concept "threshold," which refers to the amount of purchasing power necessary to support a service in a particular size of place. The more specialized and unique goods and services must have a greater range or require a larger threshold. These concepts were developed toward the end of the rural-to-urban transition period in Western Society. The implication is that population can be distributed equally and that goods and services can be provided in central areas of predictable sizes. With hindsight we can now see that these early central place notions implicitly anticipated postindustrializing and ecumenopolizing trends. If municipalities, urban regions, megalopolis regions, and urbanized continents could all be planned as formal organizations, then efficiency in the rendering of goods and services could be improved.

Some urban planning at the national level is seen in the Netherlands, Great Britain, and Israel (Spiegel 1967; Osborn 1969; Merlin 1971). In all three, some implicit effort at conceptualizing urban development in terms of formal organization is manifest. Planners using the "urban hierarchy" and formal organization can develop structures to provide the distribution of goods and services with equity among urban populations. Rugged individualistic competition between and among urban center leaders is dysfunctional in a world with an urban population of more than 1.5 billion, and an expected urban population increase to some 3 billion by 2000 – with a continuing increase. Urbanized society involves a network of interactions between and among societal institutions. The big central places in the urban hierarchies and the large-scale multifunctional urban centers articulate on a worldwide basis for improving the quality of civilization, or they contribute negatively to "have" and "have not" conflicts.

The city by nature is communal. It is a sharing of functions and services to create a higher quality, more diversified social life than is possible at the nomadic or agrarian levels. Therefore, the Broadacre city model (Wright 1970) and the garden-city models are antiurban conceptions. But even with such planned low densities, urban services are still coordinated from city centers.

Central business district vs. the urban center

The importance of the city center becomes most recognized with the growth of the urban population associated with the industrial city. Accordingly, the concept of the central business district (CBD) was developed. The central business district, particularly when multifunctional, is a major sociophysical area of cities. The concept was named in 1937 by Proudfoot who pioneered in its analysis in Philadelphia. This original analysis focused on differential types of retail activity in the city. A few years later Olsson studied the central business district in Stockholm, Sweden. Olsson's analysis produced significant techniques for measuring the central business district with respect to multiple specializations like retail trade, wholesaling, government activities, and professional activities. For example, a shop rental index (the number of shops being rented in a building divided by the length of the building's frontage) was used to determine land use intensity. Further related refinements in delineating central business districts were developed by R.E. Murphy and J.E. Vance (Herbert 1973).

There has been and continues to be difficulty in identifying the precise boundary of a central business district. The differentiation between the CBD and the surrounding urban area is a matter of degree rather than of kind. Boundary distinctions are increasingly made on the basis of high land values and intensity of land use. Another boundary-measuring technique is based on residential population density. CBDs are characterized by a minimum of residents when hotel guests are subtracted from the computations. The day-night population differences in the CBDs are great.

The Central Business Index (CBI) is a measure of differential degree of function in the central business district as compared to peripheral areas. While this technique has been used with considerable reliability in municipalities in several places around the world, obtaining data for the index is complex and often involves more approximation than factual information. Accordingly, urban planners and administrators tend to rely on CBD delineation techniques which may have somewhat lower reliability but in the short run are more amenable to analysis.

In big cities with large central business districts, the anatomy of the CBD has some reasonably discernible characteristics. Particularly in the first half of the twentieth century, all of the activities carried out in the CBD were characterized by a distinct need for centrality. With rapid communication and rapid transportation in the latter part of the twentieth century, much but not all of the need for centrality is reduced. Nevertheless, the centermost node of large CBDs is still typically characterized by highly specialized services not duplicated in the fringe areas. Furthermore, in multistory buildings, street-level spaces are occupied by both services and retail activities requiring the highest amount of centrality. Office functions may vary by specialization, distance from the node, and number of stories above the street level. Financial districts, legal districts, corporate headquarters, and so forth also vary similarly. Retail shopping flows are frequently horizontal in the CBD, while corporate business, legal activities, and governmental business may be more vertical. Shopping malls, gallerias, street restaurants, plazas, pocket parks, and so forth are all typically located in the CBD with reference to the need for horizontal pedestrian movement. Subsurface utility and transportation rights and more recently air rights above streets, railroads, and easements are other measures of CBD intensities. Megastructures are built in CBDs as exemplified in Montreal, Canada, Vallingsby (satellite new town to Stockholm), and Cumbernauld (new town between Glasgow and Edinburgh). These multiservice buildings relate to subsurface activities, surface activities, air spaces, as well as to adjacent free-standing surface buildings.

Central business districts are living and moving spaces. Between 1906 and 1931 the San Francisco central business district moved both to the northwest and to the northeast, as the total municipal area grew. By the 1960s the famous Market Street in the original principal business district was in a state of decline. An underground subway transit was placed under the street so that by the 1970s the southern part of San Francisco's central business district was tied into a rapid transit system going throughout the city and also connecting it with surrounding municipalities.

Another way both to trace the movement and to identify the declining function of CBDs is to compare activities in a CBD and outside of it longitudinally over a period of years. The central business districts of New York, Los Angeles, and Chicago were studied comparatively for 1958 and 1963 using retail sales as an index. In 1958 CBD sales in New York were slightly larger than those outside of the CBD area. By contrast, Los Angeles had minimal CBD sales compared to outside area sales, and Chicago had slightly more than twice as much retail sale activity inside as outside its CBD area. By 1963 all three cities experienced more retail sales outside than inside their CBDs, but New York City continued to lead with a higher proportion of CBD sales than the other two cities. Similar patterns are found in San Diego, Los Angeles, and Houston, where automobile transportation dominates outside the central business districts so that sales in the CBDs were, respectively, 8 percent, 10 percent, and 15 percent. By contrast, in older eastern cities like New York, Philadelphia, and Boston, the central business district retail sales were, respectively, 41 percent, 32 percent, and 34 percent (Herbert 1973).

In cities like Boston, New York, and Philadelphia, at least through the middle of the twentieth century, residential population in the CBD areas retained some visibility — if not prestige and prominence. The multifunctionality of the districts further supported high rates of social interaction through cultural activities in art museums, symphony halls, sports arenas, and through religious activities. These multiple functions gave real urbanites a continuing reason to live in the central business districts for conveniences other than those related to economics.

Transitional areas, which became slums by the middle of the twentieth century, in some major American cities are being renewed and restored for real urbanite residential and multifunctional activities. These are exemplified by the restoration and upgrading of the Vieux Carré (French Quarter) in New Orleans, Georgetown in Washington, D.C., and the Coit Tower district in San Francisco. All of these areas have made an ecological shift from slum to fashionable area in the second half of the twentieth century. They continue to be inhabited by a considerable socioeconomic range of people. Services in the areas include residences, retail trades, restaurants, religious activities, schools, and a variety of historical sites of tourist interest.

Herbert Gans has identified another form of urbanite entrenchment in Boston's West End near the central business district area. In that reasonably low-income area, residents identify with families and friendships as well as with their physically deteriorating environment. There are satisfying qualities of life there which the urbanites revere and defend against invasion by urban renewal. Many urbanites from all social classes are manifesting a desire to be emancipated from homogeneous suburbs and reintegrated with the heterogeneous, multifunctional, stimulating urban culture near the central business districts. As much of the economic functioning of the central business district moves to smaller municipalities and suburbs with industrial parks, there are increasing opportunities for new-towns-in-town to provide residences for all socioeconomic classes of people in greater proximity to urban cultural activities.

Western World cities are again developing viable urban centers similar to those of earlier centuries and similar to those outside of major industrial areas. Urban centers are becoming the hub of Western cities for general social life rather than just for economic domination. As cities become large and societal, the development of urban centers, in sharp contrast with central business districts, will create the possibility for higher quality urban environment and for more social and less antisocial behavior. Urban centers replacing the central business districts will increase the stability and viability of large urban areas. The urban center is consistent with the trend toward the viewing of the city as a formal organization; the central business district is too narrow in focus.

Multifunctional centers

The multifunctional urban centers should be planned in direct relation to total social life needs. Such an urban core is more than a regional shopping center (Gruen 1973). The multifunctional center is not random. It is specifically planned to support and facilitate urban production and jobs (it is not just a white-collar ghetto); to support education and new undertakings (not only in formal schools but in continuing education, cultural programs, and so forth); to support health and welfare activities; to support government functions (including planned unit developments, property owner associations, municipal governments, special district governments, and metropolitan regional governments); to support recreation (both outdoor and indoor); to support institutions for religious meaning and social justice; and to support family life and housing needs. The multifunctional center is truly an urban core.

The multifunctional center does not deal equally with all institutional spaces. In small municipalities some institutions may not be dealt with at all. In others a multifunctional urban center may share the service of an institution with another municipality. But to the extent that a municipality is conceptualized as relatively free-standing, rather than as a satellite, the multifunctional center needs to provide services related to all societal institutions. Further, in order to render high-quality service, the multifunctional center must by plan and design articulate with other municipalities and with the society at large. Also in large municipalities the multifunctional center must by plan and design operate in cooperation with subcenters, community or neighborhood centers which are disbursed throughout the municipality. The multifunctional center has citywide and societal relevance.

Something like the multifunctional center "just happened" by gradual development in cities of the Middle Ages and the Renaissance. In municipalities in the last of the twentieth century, multifunctional centers will not just happen. The larger and more complex societies require systematic planning efforts carefully juxtaposing both private and public uses of space. Multifunctional centers can be achieved in societies adhering to the ideology of capitalism, the ideology of communism, or mixed ideologies. The multifunctional notion recognizes the character of urbanity to be much more than that of economics in business.

From a sociological point of view, the difference between multifunctional centers and unifunctional centers is sharp and clear (Gruen 1973). Sociologically the multifunctional center should provide for nonrevenue-producing areas like malls, courts, balconies, and lobbies as essential elements. The formal organization analysis suggests that the high-quality urban social environment, in contrast to the antisocial low-quality environment, involves the provision of spaces that have symbolic and prestige meaning even if they lack economic revenue-producing capacity. Conversely, the cost to business and governments, to say nothing of the cost to individuals, of antisocial behavior is part of the expense in protecting revenue-producing areas. A high-quality urban environment must produce social satisfaction as well as revenue.

Multifunctional centers involve complexities of high density and environmental recycling. A scientific mentality and advanced technology are parts of the multiurban center concept. Medieval and Renaissance cities were small by comparison and in fact were characterized only by pseudo multifunctional centers. Cities of that era were sharply different from their surrounding rural areas. Cities of the latter part of the twentieth century are socially large in terms of urban cultural plurality, and physically large in terms of sprawl. Moreover, they indirectly and directly control the production of food and fiber in the hinterlands around them. Although municipal governments may have virtually no control over rural land areas, elements within the multifunctional urban centers control the science and computers "down on the farm." The urban center may have a high population density. The built aspect of its environment may involve multiple stories below and above ground so that often the urban core is characterized by a skyscraper landscape and more recently by megastructures.

Advances in technology have made interior climate control possible. Stores, offices, residential areas, assembly halls, recreation areas, and so forth may be located in large buildings with few or no windows to the outside. In some cases this may even contribute to energy consumption efficiency. It may keep out dirt, noise, and other pollutants of the urban environment. In skyscrapers and megastructures, interior parks may reduce or eliminate the need for open space. High-speed elevators, people movers, computers, and cybernetics may all contribute to the smooth functioning of a complex multicenter.

The advantages of the multifunctional urban center are many. First, there is smooth functioning of primary and secondary social institutions due to physical proximity. Second, the multifunctional center implicitly, if not explicitly, reduces separation and facilitates cooperation among the heterogeneous urban population. Third, the multifunctional center, particularly if physically housed in a megastructure, supports recycling in the physical environment and the reduction of pollution problems. Fourth, the multifunctional center generates both a rational and an emotional identification with the city center — reducing loneliness, alienation, and anomie. Fifth, the multidimensional center has an opportunity to systematically interface with social life in the smaller segments of the municipality and the larger society outside the municipality. In effect, the multifunctional center is three dimensional — it is more than the sum of its parts. The multifunctional center may be viewed as a matrix, a total social organization. The old world character and "urban feel" of a municipality may be largely determined by the distribution and proportion of social and physical space allocated to each social institution in the urban center. In practical terms the amount of business, retail and other transactions, in the urban center may be directly influenced by the quality of total institutional life or the absence of total institutional life available there.

Many earlier-twentieth-century downtown areas have lost business heavily to peripheral shopping facilities. This is one serious liability of central business districts as compared to multipurpose urban centers. When there is little or no life in the city center other than business transactions, people move to new locations for business transactions when such alternatives prevail in other parts of the city, in suburbs, in satellite or adjacent cities. But when the city's center is a total expression of high-quality civilized environment, one retail business may move out, but the life of the center is not seriously jeopardized. The city's center is not a business, it is a range of social-institutional life-support systems.

The multi-institutional city center is beginning to emerge at various places throughout the big industrialized nations. In 1962 the Golden Gateway Center development was launched in San Francisco. It is multifunctional and ultimately will include some 2,600 residential units located primarily in high-rise structures, as well as retail stores, restaurants, office buildings, health facilities, and sports areas. This center serves family, economic, health, and recreational needs. It articulates with other social and geographic elements in the city of San Francisco and with societies around the world.

The Glatt Center in Zurich, Switzerland began development in the 1970s. It is located on a small site of thirteen acres in the heart of Zurich. It has excellent proximity to the national highway system, to a railroad system, and to residential areas. Pedestrian pathways and an electric minibus system are planned to facilitate horizontal people-movement. A base structure is landscaped as a pedestrian terrace as well as a location for restaurants, showrooms, sports facilities, health facilities, and some residences. High-rise office spaces project above the landscaped terrace. This center articulates with several social institutions within its own megastructure-like facility as well as throughout Zurich, and reaches to a systematic interfacing with the larger Swiss society through economic and cultural exchange.

In Montreal, Canada, Place Bonaventure was constructed in the 1960s on a six-acre site in the central business district. The multiple functions here relate to economics, recreation, and hotel residential space. The facility was systematically tied into underground transportation interchanges for the metropolitan area as well as to adjacent buildings in the downtown area.

The most far-reaching multi-institutional centers are proposed by Soleri in his arcology megastructures. The city centers are planned to interface with all social institutions in a recycled environment. Soleri argues that arcology megastructures, enormous as they would be, are distinctly human in scale; city centers in arcologies enable inhabitants to relate to a few kilometers rather than to hundreds of kilometers.

In urban sprawl, municipal residents are frustrated by time pressures, are overextended economically, and are fatigued from battling their way between suburbs and the city center. The arcology city center avoids these problems, preserves natural resources, reduces pollution, extends leisure, facilitates medical care, provides an environment for multiple kinds of education, is aesthetic, and is in proximity to residential spaces. In a physical three-dimensional sense and in a social organizational sense, arcologies are miniaturizations. They allow time and space for urban people to be urban. The arcology megastructure is said to make possible new heights in urban civilization. "With arcology," Soleri writes, "comes the possibility of leaping beyond the mechanical age into the cybernetic culture and thus the chance of averting the robotization of men, the blight of the environment, the slavery of the car, the starvation of culture, all scourges of our Western success story" (Soleri 1969, p. 31). The arcology city center is an urban node in relation to automated-cybernated industries, commercial facilities, residential areas, park spaces, culture centers, and air communication to other parts of the urbanized society.

Some new towns are planned with multi-institutional centers. However, most new towns are constructed on the garden-city model, and therefore many new-town urban centers are less successful from a multicenter point of view than they could be. Most new towns are planned for populations of 200,000 or less (Paris satellite new towns, aimed at approximately 500,000 each, are notable exceptions). Many of the garden-city new towns are more of a planned suburban illusion than real urban centers. Most of them are too small to support major libraries, science, museums, a symphony, athletic events, and hospital facilities. In essence most garden-city new towns are addressed to housing, jobs, and open-space needs. The town centers in these new towns relate more to urban regions and to ecumenopolizing trends than to balanced quality urban social life within the towns. Many of the smaller new towns offer much to improving the quality of residential life. But taken out of their regional context, they are as dysfunctional to urbanized society as were the unifunctional, economically oriented central business district substitutes for town centers in the early part of the twentieth century.

In sum, the multifunctional, multi-institutional urban center is the very heart of municipal life in the urbanized society. It is more than an alternative to suburban sprawl. The heterogeneous multi-institutional town center is compatible with and supportive of high-quality urbanized social organization involving multiple millions of people. Cities with multi-institutional centers can systematically and cooperatively interface with large numbers of homogeneous smaller satellite areas and suburban areas. Urbanized society will accommodate homogeneous suburbs and open-country wilderness life as long as major large multi-institutional urban centers are dispersed at semifrequent intervals throughout the ecumenopolizing channels.

PEDESTRIANS AND CITY CENTERS

In the comparatively brief 5,500 year history of cities, urban life has become a strong tradition at many different geographical locations on the planet Earth. Many cities have been built, plundered, and rebuilt multiple times. Natural disasters, pestilence, fire, and wars have plagued cities — even razed them — but seldom caused their demise. Some cities have died and new ones have been built adjacent to the old ruins. History instructs us that a city's central area may be unifunctional at one time and multifunctional at another time. A city's role in societal affairs may be dominating at one point in history, dominated at another point in history, and again expanded to domination.

This perspective on urban history is important to an analysis of urban centers in two ways. First, it means that circumstances beyond a particular municipality's control may force upon it an opportunity to rebuild its urban center along new social and physical principles. Traumas like a serious decline in pedestrian traffic and therefore in retail sales in central business districts — or catastrophes like war devastation — may precipitate moves for aggressive and systematic evaluation and planning of urban centers. Second, municipalities may on their own initiative study their social organization and quality of life, and initiate modifications and new directions for their centers.

The pedestrianization of several contemporary central business districts illustrates the case. Copenhagen, Denmark offers one outstanding example. By 1970 metropolitan Copenhagen had a population of 1,700,000. The city of Copenhagen had only 600,000 people (Lenberg 1974). The core of central Copenhagen was its central business district. Yet in terms of territory, that district was located at the physical site of the earlier medieval Copenhagen. Fires in the eighteenth century destroyed the medieval buildings. But in that industrially expansive era, a new city of Copenhagen was built with an essentially unifunctional central business district supporting local commerce as well as its competition in Western world industrialization. The streets for eighteenth- and nineteenth-century industrial Copenhagen followed the crooked and narrow earlier medieval pedestrian pattern. As the city moved into twentieth-century affluence and its citizens measured their accomplishment in the prestige of the automobile, working people relocated to the periphery of the city, and jobs followed. By the second half of the twentieth century, the central business district still had over 75,000 jobs but only 10,000 inhabitants. All of the CBD was served by electrified urban rail systems, and this plus the motorization of greater Copenhagen brought defeating congestion to the central business district. By the 1960s Copenhagen's city council developed and adopted a plan to ban vehicular and bicycle traffic (except emergency vehicles) from the major CDB streets. Between 1962 and 1967 pedestrian traffic increased between 35 percent and 45 percent on CBD streets. The future planning for the urban center of Copenhagen is multi-institutional. The functions will include retail trade, amusement-recreation, professional services, and government services. The historic character of the urban center will be retained. Newer, modern facilities will be constructed outside of the city center at a site known as "City West."

    The idea of pedestrianization for auto-free zones is expanding in many urban centers (Klein and Arensberg 1974). The motives for reducing or eliminating automobiles in central areas are many. In several places in the United States, more than 60 percent of the land is devoted to streets, parking lots, and other vehicular requirements. Noise pollution is reduced when automobile traffic is restricted or eliminated. Air pollution is also greatly reduced. For example, in 1970 when New York City experimented with closing Fifth Avenue to traffic, carbon monoxide in the air was reduced from thirty to five parts per million. In Vienna, a similar street closing brought a reduction of 70 percent. In Tokyo, removal of traffic from the Ginza caused a carbon monoxide reduction from fourteen to three parts per million.

    Removing automobiles is often good for retail trade. In numerous cities where pedestrian malls have been established in central areas, the retail sales have gone up, for example, from 14 percent to 35 percent in the American cities of Atchison, Kansas; Fresno and Pomona, California; Kalamazoo, Michigan; Providence, Rhode Island; and Minneapolis, Minnesota. Similarly, sales went up in Vienna, Austria from 25 percent to 50 percent, in Essen, Germany from 15 percent to 35 percent, and in Rouen, France from 10 percent to 15 percent. In the face of these successes, cities like Florence, Italy and Vienna are taking further steps to eliminate automobiles completely from their central areas. England is carrying out a systematic program of town expansion with pedestrian spaces being given a high priority (Hathaway 1974).

IMPLICATIONS

Trend evidence and projection make it clear that urban centers have an increased possibility of serving cities of different sizes at unifunctional and multifunctional levels. For small populations, some neighborhood areas with multiple functions are viable when they are planned to articulate with larger municipal areas and with urban regions. Some large urban cores can be specifically planned to service all social institutions. Medieval and Renaissance urban centers were often multifunctional. But it is only in the last of the twentieth century that large urban cores have both a possibility and a necessity of being multi-institutional in their design and service.

Many municipal areas are already societal in scale, and it appears that many more will reach a societal scale in the decades immediately ahead. While these municipal societies must interface with other governments and other municipalities, they may be systematically analyzed and planned as formal organizations. Many other organizations like hospitals, hotels, and welfare agencies have clear and distinct social-interactional relationships with the larger society around them. Municipalities in the 1970s often face near inundation with problems because there are so few systematic efforts to analyze needs and plan for services with organizational concepts.

Many municipalities in the last part of the twentieth century persist in being dominated by a single social institution or by a few social institutions. In some of these cases, central business districts may continue to be viable for the indefinite future when those central business districts are seen in systematic relation to the entirety of the municipality in which they are located and to their larger society.

In sum, urban planners, both social and physical, can identify the level and the complexity of urban centers. One model is insufficient. In some cases urban planners need to design shopping malls, in other cases regional shopping centers, in still different situations central business districts, and in many cities multi-institutional cores.

Large urban centers, particularly as contrasted with small town centers, have multi-institutional potential. They are societal apexes for hospitals, banks, libraries, museums, music halls, and stadiums. By considerable contrast, some important university centers, religious sites, governmental hubs, welfare facilities, and residential locations may be more in small town and suburban areas. Food and fiber production activities have historically been outside of urban centers. But even these activities in ecumenopolizing societies may be systematically planned for in relation to urban centers in order to achieve a high-quality social environment.

REFERENCES

BAILEY, J. (Ed.), *New Towns in America*. New York: Wiley, 1973.
BROADY, M. *Planning for People*. London: The Bedford Square Press, 1968.
BROADY, M. The Sociology of the Urban Environment. *Architectural Association Quarterly*, 1969, *1*, 65–71.
Building a city in the ocean. *The Futurist*, 1969, *3*, 66–69.
CAMPBELL, C. C. *New Towns*. Reston, Va.: Reston Publishing Co., Inc., 1976.
DANTZIG, G. B., & SAATY, T. L. *Compact City*. San Francisco: W. H. Freeman, 1973.
DOXIADIS, C. A. *Ekistics*. New York: Oxford University Press, 1968.
GRUEN, V. *Centers for the Urban Environment: Survival of the City*. New York: Van Nostrand Reinhold Co., 1973.
HATHWAY, A. Effects of town expansion on central areas in Denton. *Ekistics*, 1974, *219*, 110–13.
HERBERT, D. *Urban Geography*. New York: Praeger, 1973.
HOWARD, E. *Garden Cities of Tomorrow*. Cambridge: M.I.T. Press, 1965.
JENSEN, R. *High Density Living*. New York: Praeger, 1966.
JOHNSON, J. H. *Urban Geography*. Oxford: Pergamon Press, 1967.
KLEIN, N., & ARENSBERG, W. Auto-free zones: giving cities back to people. *Ekistics*, 1974, *38*, 122–25.
LE CORBUSIER. *The City of Tomorrow*. Cambridge: M.I.T. Press, 1929 and 1971.
LENBERG, K. Pedestrian streets in central Copenhagen. *Ekistics*, 1974, *38*, 129–33.
MERLIN, P. *New Towns*. London: Methuen, 1971.
MIELDS, H., JR. *Federally Assisted New Communities*. Washington, D.C.: Urban Land Institute, 1973.
Minnesota Experimental City: Socio-Cultural Aspects. Minneapolis: University of Minnesota, 1969.
MURPHY, R. E., & VANCE, J. E. Delimiting the CBD. *Economic Geography*, 1954, *30*, 189–222.
OLSSON. W. W. Stockholm: its structure and development. *Geographical Review*, 1940, *30*, 420–38.

OSBORN, F. J., & WHITTICK, A. *The New Towns.* Cambridge: M.I.T. Press, 1969.
PROUDFOOT, M. J. City retail structure. *Economic geography,* 1937, *13,* 425 – 28.
SADAO, S. Buckminster Fuller's floating city. *The Futurist,* 1969, *1,* 14 – 16.
SOLERI, P. *Arcology.* Cambridge: M.I.T. Press, 1969.
SPIEGEL, E. *New Towns in Israel.* New York: Praeger, 1967.
SPILHAUS, A. The experimental city. *Science,* 1968, *159,* 710 – 15.
WRIGHT, F. L. *The Living City.* New York: New American Library, 1970.

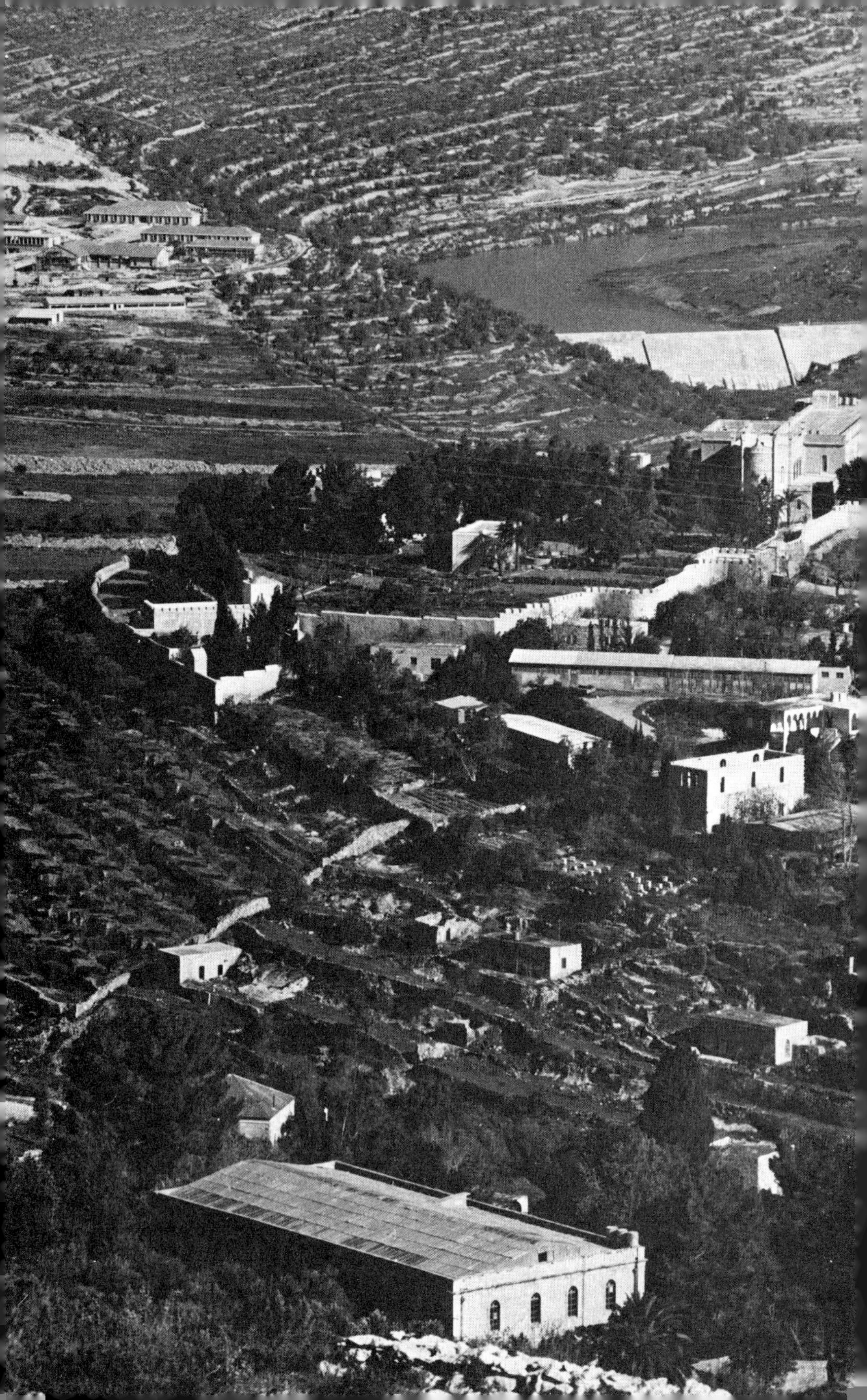

Urban Regions and Metropolitan Government   6

World population growth in the last one hundred years has contributed dramatically to the rise of urban regions. The world's 4 billion population in the 1970s is expected to nearly double by 2000. Most of the increase will be in urban regions (James 1966). Another perspective on urban regionalization is illustrated by data which report that only 2 percent of the world's population was in places of 20,000 or more in 1800. Some 20 percent of the world's population was in places of 20,000 or more by the middle of the twentieth century. It is expected that more than 50 percent of the world's population will be in places of 20,000 or more by 2000 (Bollens 1965).

The rapid growth of world city populations into urban regions involves more than the concentration of people in high densities. Profound structural changes occur. Most current societal structures were rural in origin. For example, most forms of government which dominate in the twentieth century have rural origins. Change in urban regions includes (1) the diminishing importance of the extended family; (2) the expansion of social institutions concerning government, health, welfare, science, and recreation; (3) the proliferation of both social and economic roles; (4) the creation of multiple new social, religious, political, and occupational associations; and (5) increases in social mobility (Fava 1968).

Government stands out as a problem of particular importance in urban regions. In the Soviet Union efforts are being made to decentralize control in urban regions. In the United States efforts are being

Metropolitan urban regions include open land in an Israeli desert. (Photo: Courtesy of World Health Organization.)

made to expand centralized control (Bollens 1965), though some aspects of revenue sharing have a decentralizing effect. In the U.S.S.R. the City Soviet is the local municipal government. From the 1930s to the 1970s, the Soviets built some eight hundred to one thousand new towns to contribute to the decentralization of their urban populations. In many cases the need for industrialization is also a strong reason for new-town development. Related to urban industrial expansion is the provision of public transportation, medical facilities, recreational areas, schools, and child care. Much of the planning for these amenities is decentralized to local areas although they are centrally financed (Tauban 1973).

In the United States there are 18,500 municipalities. The most recent census revealed that in the nation's fifteen largest Standard Metropolitan Statistical Areas, 50 percent of all workers were employed outside of the central cities. Furthermore, 72 percent of the persons living in suburbs worked in suburbs. Such data make dramatically clear the relation of the city to the urban region (*Municipal Yearbook 1974*).

Many metropolitan municipalities have grown together so much that citizens experience multiple city governments and special district governments daily. By 1972 the Census of Governments reported 576 Councils of Government. These are regional planning agencies, over 60 percent of whose members are local government elected officials. Almost every one of the nation's Standard Metropolitan Statistical Areas has a regional government. The Councils of Government are mechanisms for the bringing together of local governments.

Even the Councils of Government in the pluralistic American society appear to be inadequate to stimulate the amount of centralization needed to govern urban regions. For example, in 1969 a proposal was introduced into the California Legislature to create a Bay Area Home Rule Regional Government. The bill read in part,

> The Legislature further finds and declares that although existing regional organizations have made significant accomplishments within their respective functional responsibilities, the continued proliferation of special districts represents serious drawbacks: 1, there is no overall political process by which scarce regional resources can be allocated among conflicting demands in a balanced and coordinated approach to area wide governmental problems; 2, regional problems must reach a 'crisis' stage before agencies are authorized or created to attack them since there is no established pattern by which problems can be anticipated, planned for, and dealt with in an orderly fashion; 3, special purpose agencies tend to separate functions which produce revenue from those which do not, again making a balanced approach to total needs more difficult; 4, public interest in the operations of special purpose agencies is generally low and

may remove functions from control by officials who are politically responsible and responsive to overall Bay Area needs; and 5, the continued proliferation of special purpose agencies will diminish the importance of general purpose local government, reduce its vitality, and diminish its ability to attract the interest and support of its citizenry (California Legislature 1969).

This chapter focuses on the governments of urban regions as a challenge for innovation both for the present and the near future.

COMPONENTS OF REGIONAL PLANNING

Regional planning may take place at various levels. A central city and its suburbs may engage in regional planning. A district, province, or state in a nation may engage in regional planning. Regional planning may also exist at a national level, as exemplified particularly in the Netherlands and Israel.

The major components of regional planning include: (1) the balancing of population so that places of work and residence involve a minimum of daily commuting; (2) the development of regional transportational systems; (3) the delivery of major services on a regional basis; and (4) the designation of agricultural and nonagricultural land use in relation to people, services, and natural resources (Keeble 1972). The 1947 Town and Country Planning Act in Britain was an occasion of official Parliament endorsement of regional planning involving these basic principles.

The enumeration of components of a region and the endorsement of a scheme by a legislative authority, however, give few clues to the boundary delineation problem. An area that might be satisfactory for planning may vary in terms of employment, transportation, and services. Some have suggested that the physical extent of a region be sufficiently limited so that all parts may be reached in a single day. But such a delineation is largely unsatisfactory given rapid people-movement systems and long distance jet travel. Sociophysical considerations for boundary delineations are more satisfactory.

The importance of manipulating urban regions systematically can be illustrated in the case of the United Kingdom. The land area there is 94,000 square miles with a population of over 56 million. This is an average density of nearly 600 persons per square mile. By comparison, the United States has fewer than 60 persons per square mile. If one planned a region of 15 persons per acre, the entire population of England could be accommodated in an urban area around London with a radius of about forty-four miles (Keeble 1972). As one considers a possible doubling of population shortly after 2000 and an ecumenopolis development by 2150 with some 50 billion people, these regional planning densities are of great importance.

Within either the strip type suburbanization or new-town urbanization planning, the distribution of people related to places of employment and places for residence is complex. Cybernation and post-industrialization are variables of major significance related to place of work and place of residence. Transportation networks moving people to jobs vs. moving jobs to people must be evaluated both socially and economically. Strips and planned urban regions involve interface between "haves" and "have nots." Multiple-national industrialization becomes an element in eliminating both urban and national boundaries (Bagley 1975). The movement of urban people for services and profit throughout urban regions and across national boundaries becomes increasingly relevant both for planning and sociophysical reality.

The development and distribution of urban services have increasing regional visibility. Relative advantage and disadvantage become conspicuous. Moreover, disadvantage in some parts of an urban region increasingly becomes a cost to advantaged sociophysical places in the same region. Rioting and antisocial behavior in or near the core of a central city becomes a cost factor for citizens, businesses, and industries in suburban or fringe areas. Similarly, the high-energy-consuming urban regions of the world have by the 1980s become critically aware of the power of the less urban oil producing nations (Freedman and Berelson 1974).

Planning urban regions includes specific considerations for each of the following: (1) determination of a hierarchy of functional centers; (2) providing for an adequate people and goods movement system; (3) facilitating access to employment; and (4) the creation or restoration of identifying individuality within regions (Keeble 1972).

The concept of regional planning can be illustrated and better understood in Israel, the Netherlands, and Poland. Regional planning in Israel started promptly after the nation was established in 1947. The new nation had a small population of 600,000 Jews and 120,000 Arabs (Sarly 1974). In three years the national population more than doubled, and it has continued to grow. There has been enormous pressure to provide jobs and housing. In 1948 a policy was adopted which made new towns an appropriate technique for meeting political as well as socioeconomic needs. In the discussion that follows, we examine the Israeli new towns from the view of regional planning only. Many authors emphasize the shortcomings of Israeli new towns. No evaluation is implied here, either favorable or unfavorable, for individual new towns.

In a quarter of a century, thirty new towns have been started as elements of the nation's planning. By the middle 1970s, 20 percent of Israel's population lived in new towns. New towns are initiated and operated by a national planning department in the Ministry of Housing. (Small rural villages are administered through the Ministry of Interior.) The south and north parts of Israel received the highest proportion of new towns. The central coastal areas, with the already large population of Tel Aviv, received the fewest new towns. The early generation new towns were primarily oriented to physical production and the ideology of Zionism. They served, by intent, the needs of relatively poor immigrants. The latest generation of new towns is designed primarily to serve native-born Israelis who have experienced more of the affluence of the now larger urban environments. People who are unable to secure appropriate jobs, housing, and services in the larger urban areas now have an opportunity to migrate to recently developed new towns designed for target populations of some 50,000. They are intended to have a full complex of urban amenities.

The Israeli experience with regional planning uses new towns as a primary mechanism. The effort to see the nation as a total unit and to systematically distribute population, goods, and services by regional subunits is systematic. The Israeli experience illustrates the importance of operationalizing regional planning as if society were a formal organization. Specific goals are established, and specific means by which the goals are to be achieved are adopted. The major plan, or goals, are regularly reviewed so that the total planning effort can be continually corrected to focus on updated trajectories. Finally, a small nation like Israel must articulate its regional and national planning into the larger multinational ecumenopolizing trends.

The Netherlands constitutes another strong example of systematic regional planning. The 13.8 million Netherlands population is over three times that of Israel (Merlin 1971). On a world scale, however, both the Netherlands and Israel have small populations and high densities. Aside from population and density similarities, the planning history of the two nations is considerably different. Some national and regional planning in the Netherlands originated in the sixteenth century (Hall 1966). A new and more focused effort at modern city planning was initiated in 1901 with the passage of the Town Planning Act. In 1918 the polderbuilding was started in the Zuider Zee. Following World War II there was much rebuilding to be done, and subsequently the Planning Law of 1962 was adopted. The 1962 policy emphasized regional planning. Citizens, municipal authorities, and other local authorities are required to participate in local, regional, and national planning.

A 1966 national master plan was established. It not only dealt with goals but with means for achieving them. It specified cooperation of governmental units for planning housing, transportation, public works and water supply, finance and economic affairs, industry, agriculture, and sociocultural activities. Making corrections in the plans is illustrated in the case of the Randstad (a "ring city," or horseshoe-shaped area, from Amsterdam through the Hague to Rotterdam) as well as in the polder developments. In the case of the Randstad, new focus was placed on population containment by the use of linear green wedges rather than greenbelts. In the case of the polders, a new emphasis was placed on urbanization in contrast to the original emphasis on rural land development. Urban population in the polders will now relate directly to the Amsterdam conurbation. The Netherlands' regional and national planning is oriented to ecumenopolizing patterns in Europe.

Regional planning in Poland is instructive from a slightly different perspective from that in Israel and the Netherlands. The population is larger — by the 1970s over 34 million. At the end of World War II nearly 70 percent of the population was rural. New urban industrialization was planned in a major east-west and a major north-south axis (Merlin 1971). Planning was designed to encourage the growth of medium-size population centers for between 20,000 and 100,000 people. Regional planning emphasized the location of industry near raw materials. Services not dependent upon basic raw materials were located in the larger cities.

Poland was divided into seventeen regions for planning and development purposes. Upper Silesia is the nation's only conurbation, with a population in the magnitude of 2 million. In addition to an implicit formal planning organization, specific techniques for goal achievement were enumerated. New-town planning is a dominating technique. In some cases new towns are specified to promote decongestion in established areas. In other cases they are to stimulate the development of new industrial complexes. Few specific details are established for articulating the regional and national planning in Poland with the larger ecumenopolizing pattern in Western Europe. Communist Bloc political ideology orients the planning east toward other Communist Bloc countries and to the Soviet Union. The impact of Poland's urban regions extends beyond the nation.

From pedestrian cities to urban regions

In some circumstances urban regions have small walking or pedestrian-defined boundaries, and in other cases urban regions are metropolitan in scope and moving toward ecumenopolis. Questions of scale and experiences of urban overload have increasing importance in urbanized societies. As society reaches a near saturation point of urbanization, antisocial behavior accelerates. Anomie, alienation, and urban overload are widely expressed. Some individuals are challenged by and thrive in dense pedestrian centers in the core of megalopolis areas, while others reject the high rates of secondary social interaction there. One alternative is the garden-city model for new towns. This is a small scale, pedestrian, antiurban model. Most garden cities are planned regionally in proximity to larger and more densely established core cities. In the past twenty years in Poland and in Rumania, there has been regional planning to expand municipalities to populations of between 20,000 and 100,000. It is expected that urban overload will be reduced and pedestrian areas maximized in cities with these smaller populations.

The historic transition from a pedestrian-dominated city through suburbanization to an urban region is clearly seen in the case of Boston (Warner 1962). In 1850 Boston was still a pedestrian city with much of the population in a central two-mile radius area and some additional population in a peripheral three-mile radius. By 1900 the pedestrian city of Boston had succumbed to suburbanization, expanding to a ten-mile radius. The inner city continued to be the predominant place of work for most Bostonians, but a typical place of residence for only the low-income people. The suburban outer city became the bedroom for the middle and upper classes. In the late 1800s Boston was becoming a regional city. Its size had grown beyond the walking point to a place where the streetcar and the railroad were required to move people between places of work and places of residence. In Boston's urban transition the city grew from 200,000 persons in its pedestrian era in 1850 to more than 1 million people in its suburban and central core areas in 1900.

By 1970 the Boston Standard Metropolitan Statistical Area had grown to a population of 2 million. Furthermore, by 1970 Boston was the northern center for the eastern megalopolis area extending south through New York to Washington, D.C. Identification with Boston was submerged to the overarching scale of megalopolis. The urban region continued to grow west, connecting the eastern seaboard megalopolis with Chicago — all in an ecumenopolizing pattern. Pedestrian Boston became lost in an urban regional growth pattern similar to the municipal, regional, and national growth experience in the Netherlands as it is related to the ecumenopolizing adjacent areas in Western Europe.

The social history of London reveals over a longer period of time a city growing from a pedestrian nucleus through suburbanization to a massive urban region dominating a nation and playing a major role in the world (Bollens 1965). The medieval central core of London contains only a square mile of land and at night its population is less than 5,000. The area immediately around the medieval city, some ten square miles, has a daytime population of 1.5 million and a nighttime population of approximately 275,000. The next London ring is the location of the inner suburbs. This is a place of high-density housing extending out to the limits of the county of London. The high density results from the early development preceding electric trains and automobiles. Within the inner suburban ring there are some one hundred square miles with a population of 1.5 million. The next wave of population development extended out to the London greenbelt. This growth was facilitated by the automobile. All of the London area within the greenbelt contains a population totaling over 8 million in seven hundred square miles. It is this area inside the greenbelt which is referred to as the Greater London Conurbation.

Following World War II eight London ring new towns were established. They were started in 1947 and are beyond the greenbelt. They are planned to have individual populations of between 80,000 and 100,000. The London ring new towns now contain over 1 million population total. They have contributed to the stabilization of population growth inside the London greenbelt since the 1960s. They are designed primarily as pedestrian cities.

From the Roman pedestrian London village of the Middle Ages, the London urban region had grown to 10 million people. Since before World War II some 80 percent of the English population has been urban. Furthermore, approximately 40 percent of the English population is concentrated in London and other major urban areas in a megalopolis strip across the center of the main island.

The London urban region also illustrates the problem of government. As recently as the mid-1960s the London region had 118 local governments including 6 county and 16 special district governments. In 1963 Parliament passed a bill which provided for two-tier government. The overriding authority of government is the Greater London Council, under which are thirty-two boroughs and the medieval city of London. Most of the two-tier government is designed for a territory including six hundred square miles and 8 million people. The London region dominates the rest of the nation, and systematic planning efforts reflect that domination in airport locations, highway designs, and industrial sites. Only slightly less clear is the planning of London for its world role.

Both the Boston and the London experiences reflect urban regionalization which sharply separates place of residence from place of work. With megalopolizing urban regions there is in the latter part of the twentieth century a sociophysical planning effort to return a greater number of residential areas to the central core of the regions. This is partly illustrated by the new-town-in-town developments (Derthick 1972). While some programs for new-towns-in-town have failed, their significance for providing pedestrian-oriented residential space for the core of urban regions is important.

Other dimensions of in-town pedestrian development in major urban regions include preservation, renovation, and new construction combining residential, recreational, and commercial land uses in the same area. This is illustrated in Boston's waterfront (*Urban Waterfronts* 1975). The Boston waterfront area is designated as a 104-acre site under the direction of a redevelopment authority. It is being restored, and is allowing new high-rise construction. In one wharf area, 312 apartments have been constructed and/or renovated. In another wharf area, 95 condominiums have been built. Interspersed in wharf areas are commercial and residential facilities.

Subsidiary transportation is still another example of small-scale facilitation in larger urban regions. Subsidiary transportation systems are local in nature, designed to connect small areas with major metropolitan and urban regional transportation (Perloff 1975). Subsidiary transportation is an updating of past informal jitney systems, horse-pulled omnibuses, and the Latin American publicos. The subsidiary transportation in contemporary and future-oriented urban planning is generalized by group or function, and it is intercommunity rather than intracommunity. Specialized needs in the urban region include clientele who may not have regular access to automobiles, like the low-income people, physically handicapped persons, and the elderly. Special-interest groups need transportation to educational facilities, recreational facilities, and other special service areas.

The various responses to specific localized urban transportation needs include dial-a-ride buses, minibuses, vans, carpools, and other para-transit systems. Experiments with such systems are underway in old and new urban areas and in large and small urban areas, for example Ann Arbor, Michigan; Buffalo, New York; Columbia, Maryland; Kingston, Ontario; Regina, Saskatchewan; Rochester, New York; Toledo, Ohio, and Madison, Wisconsin. Variations on the subsidiary transportation system include subscription bus service in San Francisco, Los Angeles, Washington, D.C., and St. Louis. Company van pools are utilized in Minneapolis-St. Paul, Long Island, and New York-New Jersey. Car pool systems have been organized for the San Francisco Bay Area, Washington, D.C., St. Louis, and Los Angeles. Related subsidiary transportation systems are used in Europe.

From a social-organizational point of view there is considerable evidence that reduction of scale and pedestrianization of selected areas in major cities are both viable and desirable in the urbanized society. The pedestrian scale humanizes the city for large numbers of people (Fischer 1975).

Greenbelts

Greenbelts are regional planning instruments. They are intended to direct and even resist urban expansion through systematic development. They support multiple land use for recreation and agriculture. Greenbelts are expected to have a positive sociophysical environmental meaning in and for themselves (James 1966).

The greenbelt idea is not new. In Britain, Queen Elizabeth I encouraged the establishment of a greenbelt around London in 1580, but it failed then. In 1657 the British made another attempt to establish a London greenbelt (Thomas 1970). During the last decade of the nineteenth century and the first quarter of the twentieth century, open green space rather than greenbelts became an issue, and some was viably established. By this time there were some successful moves to establish green areas in the United States and other parts of Europe.

In 1938 the Green Belt Act was passed in Britain. Through this act some forty-four square miles of greenbelt have been preserved around London. The greenbelt includes farm land, wood land, downs, water, and some large country estates. Approximately 25 percent of the land is in full public open space, another 15 percent will eventually be designated for public open space, and some 60 percent is used primarily for agriculture (Thomas 1970). The total amount of greenbelt land and its specific boundaries continue to change slightly. For example, some local authority governments finance the acquisition of land for greenbelts. Following World War II there was more urban pressure to expand regional planning by strengthening the London Green Belt. Between 1954 and 1958 a greenbelt development plan was approved, and local community planning was articulated with it.

Since England was one of the first Western nations to experience intensive urbanization, preserving green space for amenity was an early concern not only in London but in cities like Birmingham, Leeds, and Sheffield. In the 1930s some of these cities were purchasing tracts of land beyond their boundaries. With the Town and Country Planning Act in 1947, local authorities took new initiatives in preserving green space. These early attempts focused more on town planning than on the greenbelts for their own sake. By the middle 1950s more attention was placed on greenbelts in and for themselves.

Eighteen greenbelts now exist in varying stages in England and Wales. In total they affect more than half the English and Welsh populations (James 1966). Their success is measured in different ways. Since 1950 the population outside the London greenbelt increased by more than 1 million in planned areas, including eight new towns. Within the greenbelt the London population lost 165,000 people and by the 1960s had become stabilized (Bollens 1965). Some observers look at this type of summary statistic and evaluate the greenbelt positively.

In other areas, and in the view of other planners, greenbelts are seen as excessively rigid—in fact as barriers to urban planning. In the

Netherlands the greenbelt idea is rejected in favor of green wedges. The implication is that urban sectors, more than concentric circles, support positive and flexible urban growth patterns. It is argued by some that the green wedges, more than the greenbelts, support urban regions growing into megalopolis patterns and ultimately toward ecumenopolis. Nevertheless, the greenbelt area around Moscow is planned in such a way that provision is made for population in new towns and other locations outside the greenbelt to commute into the center area of Moscow. Similarly, the greenbelt-type areas around Stockholm are planned to provide auto and mass transit commuting between the fringe new towns and the older central Stockholm areas.

In Copenhagen the greenbelt and the green wedges are integrated into the so-called "finger plan." In the Copenhagen plan, multiple-use green space is designated in wedge shapes between more intensely built up urban spaces, with the urban spaces moving toward the center and the green spaces toward the exterior, in a pattern similar to gears meshing together.

Sociologically green spaces or open spaces are mechanisms for providing density variations. They are also mechanisms for providing variation in amenity spaces. Furthermore, greenbelts and green spaces interface with environmental equilibrium and pollution reduction. Greenbelts, somewhat like new towns, are the subjects of much emotion as well as reason. Urban sociologists do not support greenbelts or new towns in and for themselves, but only as mechanisms in the planned environment which may further high-quality social life by reducing urban overload.

Standard Metropolitan Statistical Areas

Another major way of understanding urban regional development is to examine current census statistics. In 1970 there were 243 Standard Metropolitan Statistical Areas in the United States, plus four in Puerto Rico (see Figure 6–1). Since 1967 sixteen new SMSAs have been added. This indicates continued rapid urban regional growth.

In 1970, 126 of the SMSAs had a population of 250,000 or more. In every case more than half of the employed population living inside the central cities worked outside of them. Furthermore, it was typical for those persons living outside of the central city to work someplace in the SMSA other than in the central business district.

The expansiveness of the American SMSA is further expressed by minimal use of public transit and maximum use of private autos to place of work. The SMSAs in 1970 which had the largest proportion of public transportation uses were New York with 48 percent, Jersey City with 36 percent, Chicago with 23 percent, Philadelphia with 21 percent,

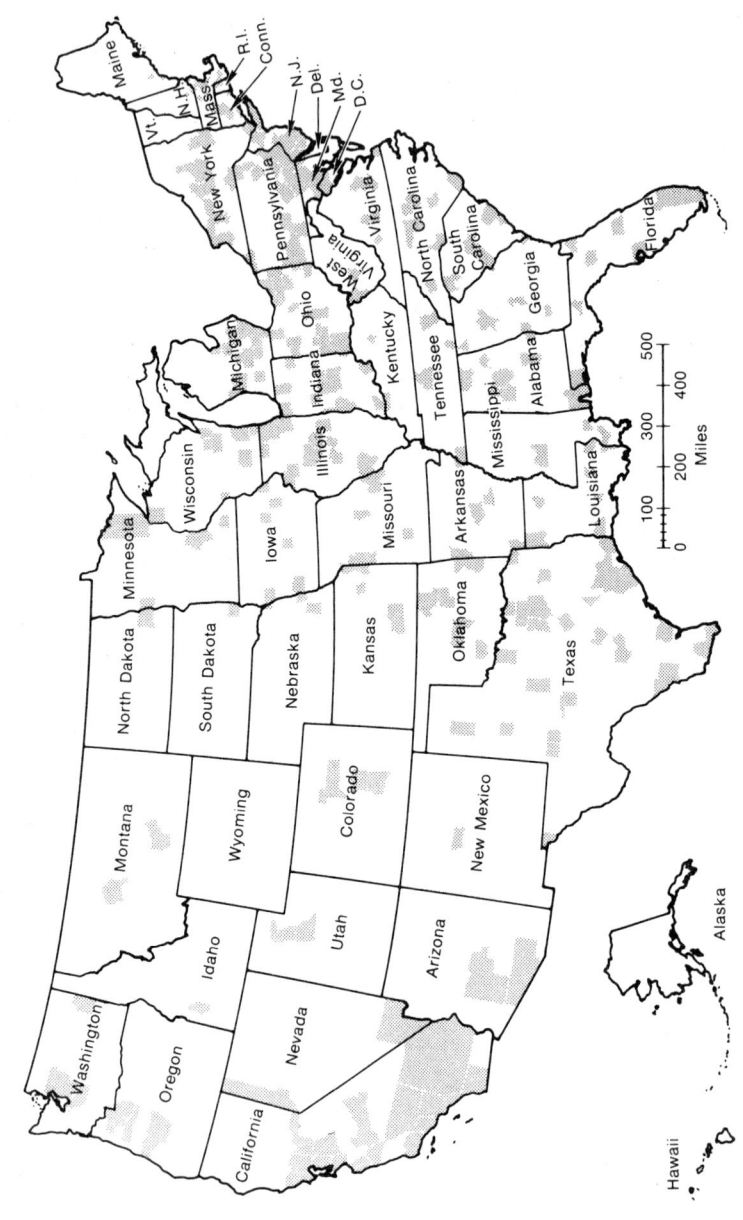

Figure 6-1 Standard Metropolitan Statistical Areas (Areas Defined by Office of Management and Budget, February 1971)

New Orleans with 20 percent, and Boston with 20 percent. At the other extreme were Anaheim-Santa Ana-Garden Grove, California, 0.4 percent; San Bernardino-Riverside-Ontario, California, 0.9 percent; Bakersfield, California, 1.1 percent; Flint, Michigan, 1.4 percent; Lansing, Michigan, 1.7 percent; and Phoenix, Arizona, 1.3 percent.

In America the SMSAs follow an ecumenopolizing pattern. A majority are located in the Northeast from Maryland to Massachusetts through New York to Illinois and Wisconsin. On the West Coast the SMSAs are continuous from San Diego through Los Angeles to San Francisco and Santa Rosa. In the Northwest the SMSAs are continuous from Eugene, Oregon through Portland to Seattle.

Megalopolis

The two most well known megalopolis areas are the American Northeast and Tokaido in Japan. In the United States this includes the area from Washington, D.C. through New York to Boston. In Japan the area includes Tokyo, Yokohama, Nagoya, Osaka, Kobe, and Kyoto (Gottmann 1961; Bell 1972). Both of these megalopolis areas have more population than many nations. The American megalopolis has over 60 million people and the Japanese megalopolis has an even larger population. Both are gigantic in scale. They are places of highly diverse and plural culture. These megalopolis areas include many of their respective nation's most highly educated persons. They are places of idea production and dynamic social change. Ecologically, they include large central-city populations, suburbs, satellite cities, some agricultural area, and some open green space. They are characterized by science, leisure, and long journeys to work. The physical environments of the megalopolis areas range from ugly to elegant. There is negative noise pollution from technology and positive noise pollution from symphonies. Air pollution in megalopolis areas contributes to extensive respiratory disorders.

The U.S.A. megalopolis is 600 miles long (740 kilometers), and the Japanese megalopolis is 400 miles in length (500 kilometers). Rail and auto movements are more numerous in Tokaido than in the eastern U.S.A. Airline movements are more numerous in megalopolis U.S.A. than in Tokaido. Communication by means of television and radio is characteristic of both megalopolis areas. The trend toward increased automobile ownership in Tokaido exacerbates the already critical transportation and pollution problems. A large proportion of housing units in Tokaido lack sanitary sewage hookups.

The experiences of massive daily movement and of cultural overload are found in megalopolis. Pockets of homogeneity and pedestrian neighborhoods are also frequent in megalopolis. In many respects the experience of megalopolis expresses opportunities for high-quality human civilization in spite of some short-range social problems.

From an urban sociology and planning point of view, megalopolis illustrates the opportunity to provide both heterogeneity and homogeneity. Megalopolis makes possible the stimulus of a plural culture juxtaposed with the tranquility of small neighborhoods, utilizing green spaces and Planned Unit Developments. In urbanized society megalopolis areas can be planned so that some people experience almost exclusively complex built environments while others experience nearly natural physical environments.

Megalopolis areas have large, nation-size populations. Accordingly, it is important that they be viewed and planned using organizational concepts. In megalopolis areas many different types of local communities and local governments may be sustained when their purposes are clearly enumerated and planned for as elements of larger systems.

METROPOLITAN GOVERNMENT AND SOCIAL ORGANIZATION

Between 1967 and 1972 the number of municipalities in the United States of America increased by nearly 500, or to a total of 18,516. By contrast, in Japan from the 1950s to the present the number of cities has been decreased from nearly 10,000 to fewer than 3,500 (Bollens 1965). Neither of these changes happened by chance. In Japan there are two levels of government below the central government: prefectures or provinces and municipalities. Recognizing the complexities of social organization in urbanized society, the central government offered financial inducements to local municipalities that would agree to merge. In the United States of America, there is a gradual but continual increase in the number of municipalities. Often this is to avoid annexation of smaller towns by larger cities. The smaller towns wish to preserve their image of independence.

In the London area of England the problem of governmental plurality has also necessitated change. The many local governments became so ineffective that in 1963 a two-tier government was established, namely, the Greater London Council.

Massive regionalization brings profound changes in social life. The larger megalopolis urban regions are societal in size and therefore must deal with social institutions related to family life, education, government, economics, religion, science, health, welfare, leisure, and the arts. Many large cities and urban regions are quasi city-states. Much inefficiency could be reduced by treating urban regions societally. They can be planned for socially, economically, and physically as societies, using mechanisms like the two-tier government to maximize local control and at the same time to achieve a broad efficiency.

Two-tier government

The two-level approach to metropolitan government is gaining recognition and viability (Bollens 1965). The two-tier form of government is a structure that provides for some services to be carried out regionally by local governments and for other services to be carried out regionally by special district governments. Most existing local governments continue to exist, but the two-tier system provides for areawide jurisdictions consistent with the needs of the urbanized society.

The two-tier government is a sharp contrast to annexation, which has enabled large, established municipalities to continue unilateral growth. Other techniques that have some viability in solving regional organizational problems include informal cooperation, service by contract, compact approaches, transfer of functions, extra-territorial jurisdictions, geographical consolidation, functional consolidation, and special districts (Martin 1971). The challenges and problems of urban regions in general and metropolitan government in particular are illustrated by this long list of techniques being used to cope with urban growth. The two-tier government appears to be among the most viable. Sometimes it takes the form of a metropolitan district. Such a district performs one service or a few services on a metropolitan-wide basis, while other local services continue to be provided by previously existing local governments. A second form of two-tier government is a comprehensive urban-county plan that calls for a transfer of services from counties to cities and/or from cities to counties so that the division of labor and the expanded territorial location facilitates the achievement of more efficiency and higher quality service. A third kind of two-tier government takes the form of a federation. In this case a new areawide government providing multiple functions may be established. This two-tier government structure is a compromise position between drastic obliteration of local governments and establishment of extensive new urban regional governments.

The first city-county consolidation in America occurred in 1805 when the city of New Orleans and Orleans Parish (county) were consolidated. In 1937 there was some consolidation of the city of Baton Rouge with East Baton Rouge Parish (county). By the 1970s there are some twenty-one city-county consolidation districts. The primary benefits from such consolidations of government are (1) greater efficiency in rendering services; (2) economy of scale and coordination; (3)

minimization of government fragmentation; (4) systematic combination of the resources of central cities with their surrounding areas; and (5) lessening of the need for special district governments. Two-tiered governments also make possible taxing at different levels by area of service (Taylor 1968).

The metropolitan district form of two-tier government is increasing in popularity and use. One-fourth of the SMSAs in America use some forms of metropolitan district government. These are often exemplified by port authorities, sewage disposal districts, airport and transit authorities, regional park authorities, public housing districts, and school districts. Devotion to a limited range of services or to a single service has contributed much to the achievements of these special district governments. Generally these governments have little or no taxing authority, and that contributes to their weakness. Special metropolitan district governments are also often accused of having insufficient accountability to local electorates.

The two-tier government is a strong recognition of regional needs. Nevertheless, it faces obstacles including a lack of state constitutional enabling legislation; opposition from local government officials who feel threatened; problems of how to elect or select officials; difficulty in determining how to assign which government specializations go to counties and which remain with the cities; and inadequate financial support from local governments.

The federated form of two-level government involves the creation of a new areawide government. This is but a slight variation on the two-tier theme. Theoretically, the federation gives stronger recognition to the realities of urban regions. However, a federated government is often viewed as being excessively removed from local people. Metropolitan Toronto is often cited as a strong example of federated regional government. The federation for the Toronto area came into existence in 1953. The new government had jurisdiction over a 240-square-mile area and a population of 1.2 million. Since its founding the federation has been enlarged to include law enforcement, air pollution, civil defense, and many aspects of licensing.

The continued use of various forms of two-tier governments is consistent with growth in urban regions. Questions are still raised concerning which functions of government should be assigned regionally and which ones maintained locally. But the strength of the two-tier government is sufficiently great that it warrants considerable attention.

Special districts

Special district governments may be both supportive of urban regional two-tier governments and threatening to them. In some cases a special district may achieve responsibility for rendering a particular service throughout a large area. An example is the Bay Conservation and Development Commission in the San Francisco Bay Area (Mogulof 1971). This conservation district must relate to a large number of other local governments as well as to other regional governments. In many respects its goals for conserving the bay are supportive to many other local and regional government services. In such a situation the Bay Conservation Development District is a systematic part of the formal organization of urban regional government in that area. It has clearly defined and potentially supportive roles.

Similarly, regional airport governments and regional transportation authorities may be more supportive of than competitive with local governments. Supportive special district governments can have highly visible and viable places in urban regional formal organization. Special district governments that are highly competitive, like those for sewage, irrigation, and police protection, may be vigorously attacked by other elements of local government in an urban region. In a social organizational sense, therefore, special district governments can offer most when their area of service is relatively unique, highly needed, and not easily duplicated on a small-unit basis by numerous local governments.

Citizen participation

In urban regions in general and in metropolitan government in particular, the maintenance of adequate means for citizen participation is difficult. In the Soviet Union large cities are divided into microrayons or neighborhood units. These microrayons have populations of between 6,000 and 12,000. They provide most of the convenience services for social life within the neighborhood units. Individuals from these local units have an opportunity to participate in the planning and government structure of the larger urbanized area (Fisher 1967).

Throughout the world the size of city councils varies, for example, from 15 in Los Angeles to 710 in Warsaw. Council size shows little relation to efforts to achieve citizen participation in urban government (Robson 1972).

In the United States since the middle 1950s the U.S. Department of Housing and Urban Development, particularly in Workable Program policies, has required citizen participation. By the 1970s the Workable Program requirements for citizen participation had become specifically detailed to identify proportions of minority citizens whose input would be required in decision making in many programs supported by federal funding.

Citizen participation in the federally supported Councils of Government is considerable. Some observe that Council of Government requirements for citizen participation are a compensation for the absence of minorities among elected officials. Citizen participation also may be a device for developing a constituency base. But the precise reasons for citizen participation are less critical to the thesis of this chapter than the fact of real citizen participation in regional planning.

Participation of citizens in the affairs of urban regions is normally at one of three levels: as persons being planned for; as individuals participating in the decision-making processes; and as group participants (Bodine 1967). But much citizen participation is more for emotional release than it is substantive. High civilization in large urban regions involves full recognition of the dignity and integrity of individual citizens. There is little to support the view, however, that even massive citizen participation will necessarily bring the best judgments and the highest quality decision making. If large urban regions can achieve more high quality civilization by being analyzed and organized as formal organizations, then citizen participants need to understand this organization. Alone neither professional planning elites nor rank-and-file citizen participants are adequate to insure high-quality urban regional life. Structures that provide for citizen participation and structures that support the training of urban regional planning professionals must both insure knowledge of organization on the part of participants.

Councils of Government

The American experience with Councils of Government is a special case illustrating the need to integrate urban regions from a systematic organizational point of view. Councils of Government came into existence in 1968 with Title IV of the Intergovernmental Cooperation Act. They were strengthened when they were given clearinghouse review authority over many local urban projects seeking federal funding. By the late 1970s there were over 570 Councils of Government. Over 60 percent of the Councils are made up primarily of elected officials from other local governments. The Councils are one of the major leadership attempts of the federal government to accelerate urban cooperation at regional levels. In effect Councils of Government are a form of social invention, operating at a low profile, for stimulating urban regional movement toward systematic planning.

URBAN REGIONAL PLANNING AND MANAGEMENT

Urban regions by definition are large — often societal in size. Increasingly, they are the realities of social life in the last of the twentieth century. They are part of a worldwide trend toward ecumenopolis.

Theoretically urban regions may be thought of and managed as formal organizations. But such a conception is new, and urban regional planning within the formal organizational model is still limited.

Japan has taken a major step to reduce the number of its municipalities by more than half in recent years. In the United States proposals are being introduced to reduce the number of governmental units also. Such reductions would contribute to the possibility of formal organizational management. Baldwin (1972) proposes reducing the number of coterminus states from forty-eight to fourteen. Two of these fourteen new states would in effect be city-states — New York and Chicago. Such a governmental organization could provide for three levels, national, state, and municipal.

Most of the world's urban regions are governmentally operating within social structures that originated in rural societies. The earliest shifts toward organized regional planning came in England in 1909. By the last of the nineteenth century England was the first nation of the world to become urbanized. In recognition of that change in ecology Parliament passed the Housing, Town, and Planning Act of 1909. In 1927 the Greater London Region Planning Committee was established. From World War II to the present, urban regional planning has accelerated in Britain (James 1966; Thomas 1970). Regional planning in Britain recognizes the lack of distinction between city and rural areas. Put another way, there is clear recognition that cities must be planned to deal with the total areas from which their resources come, the areas throughout which their services are extended, and the locations of the populations that utilize services both daily and over longer periods of time.

In the Soviet Union urban regions are increasingly planned and built in direct relationship to industrialization (Tauban 1973). Since 1926 the more than eight hundred new towns in the Soviet Union have been planned in relation to urban-industrial regional needs.

IMPLICATIONS

Israel, the Netherlands, and Poland all exemplify nations which increasingly plan urban growth and expansion regionally. In these and other areas, there is some emergence of urban regional planning based on formal organizational notions. From a sociological point of view, most of the formal organizational models, however, are still deficient in consideration of basic social institutions. As urban regions become societal in size, formal organizational planning models might explicitly provide for housing and family life, socialization in schools for all ages, jobs in economic production, government, explanation of human meaning through religion and civil rights, scientific development, health services, welfare programs, plus leisure, recreation, and the arts. In urbanized society, regions are more a matter of such institutional activity systems than of physical territory. All of those systems must be systematic parts of comprehensive regional planning if a high-quality urban civilization is to be achieved.

REFERENCES

BAGLEY, E. R. *Beyond the Conglomerates.* New York: AMACOM, 1975.

BALDWIN, L. *Reforming the Constitution.* Santa Barbara, California: American Bibliographical Center — Clio Press, 1972.

BELL, G., & TYRWHITT, J. (Eds.). *Human Identity in the Urban Environment.* London: Pelican Books, 1972.

BODINE, J. W. Citizen participation: the indispensable one hundredth of one percent. In H. W. Eldredge (Ed.), *Taming Metropolis.* New York: Doubleday Anchor Books, 1967.

BOLLENS, J. C., & SCHMIDT, H. J. *The Metropolis* (2nd Ed.). New York: Harper and Row, 1965.

California Legislature, Assembly Bill No. 1846, April 7, 1969.

DERTHICK, M. *New Towns in Town.* Washington, D.C.: The Urban Institute, 1972.

FAVA, S. F. (Ed.). *Urbanism in World Perspective.* New York: Crowell, 1968, 173–80.

FISCHER, C. S. Toward a subcultural theory of urbanism. *American Journal of Sociology,* 1975, *80,* 1319–41.

FISCHER, J. C. Urban planning in the Soviet Union and Eastern Europe. In H. W. Eldredge (Ed.), *Taming Megalopolis.* New York: Doubleday Anchor Books, 1967.

FREEDMAN, R., & BERELSON, B. The human population. *Scientific American,* 1974, *231,* 31–39.

GOTTMANN, J. *Megalopolis.* Cambridge: M.I.T. Press, 1961.

HALL, P. *The World Cities.* New York: McGraw-Hill, 1966.

JAMES, J. R. Regional planning in Britain. In S. B. Warner, Jr. (Ed.), *Planning for a Nation of Cities.* Cambridge: M.I.T. Press, 1966.

KEEBLE, L. *Principles and Practice of Town and Country Planning.* London: The Estates Gazette Ltd., 1972, 46–52.

MARTIN, R. C. Government adaption to metropolitan growth. In T. R. Dye & B. W. Hawkins (Eds.), *Politics in the Metropolis* (2nd ed.). New York: Charles E. Merrill Publishing Co., 1971.

MERLIN, P. *New Towns: Regional Planning and Development.* London: Methuen, 1971.

MOGULOF, M. B. *Governing Metropolitan Areas.* Washington, D.C.: The Urban Institute, 1971.

Municipal Yearbook, 1974. Washington, D.C.: National City Management Assoc., 1974.

PERLOFF, H. S., & CONNELL, K. M. Subsidiary transportation. *American Institute of Planners Journal,* 1975, *41,* 170–83.

ROBSON, W. A., & REGAN, D. E. *Great Cities of the World.* Beverly Hills, California: Sage Publications, 1972.

SARLY, R. Failure of the new towns. *Built Environment,* 1974, *8,* 612–16.

Standard Metropolitan Statistical Areas: 1967. Washington, D.C.: U.S. Government Printing Office, 1973.

TAUBAN, W. *Governing Soviet Cities.* New York: Praeger, 1973.

TAYLOR, L. *Urban-Rural Problems.* Los Angeles: Dickenson Publishing Co., Inc., 1968.

THOMAS, D. *London's Green Belt.* London: Faber and Faber, 1970.

U.S. Bureau of the Census. *Census of Population: 1970 Detail Characteristics,* Final Report, PC (1)-D1 United States Summary. Washington, D.C.: U.S. Government Printing Office, 1973.

Urban waterfronts design and planning. *Progressive Architecture,* 1975, *56,* 43–44.

WARNER, S. D., JR. *Streetcar Suburb.* Cambridge: Harvard University Press, 1962.

PART THREE
People and Space

Humans are social and culture-bearing animals. In the next two chapters we see that nowhere is this more clear than in people's efforts to inhabit and humanize urban space. Humans are adaptable and can accommodate themselves to many different types of architecture and built environments. Even more, people demonstrate remarkable ability to modify their natural and built environments to reflect and satisfy their urban values and needs.

Symbolic urban places and spaces go far beyond economics and architectural determinisms. Space for privacy and places for social livability vary greatly from one urban culture to another, and they vary through time.

Personal space, crowding, and territoriality all take on heightened importance in large and densely populated urbanized societies. Some spaces become psychically and socially satisfying and desirable while others become indefensible and terrifying. Quality of life is both strengthened and weakened in urbanization.

Chapter seven describes and presents some implications of space meaning and uses. In Chapter eight considerable attention is focused on details of sociophysical planning. Concepts and planning techniques are presented so that the reader is equipped as a professional and/or as a citizen participant to understand planning reports and to understand what goes on at planning and zoning meetings.

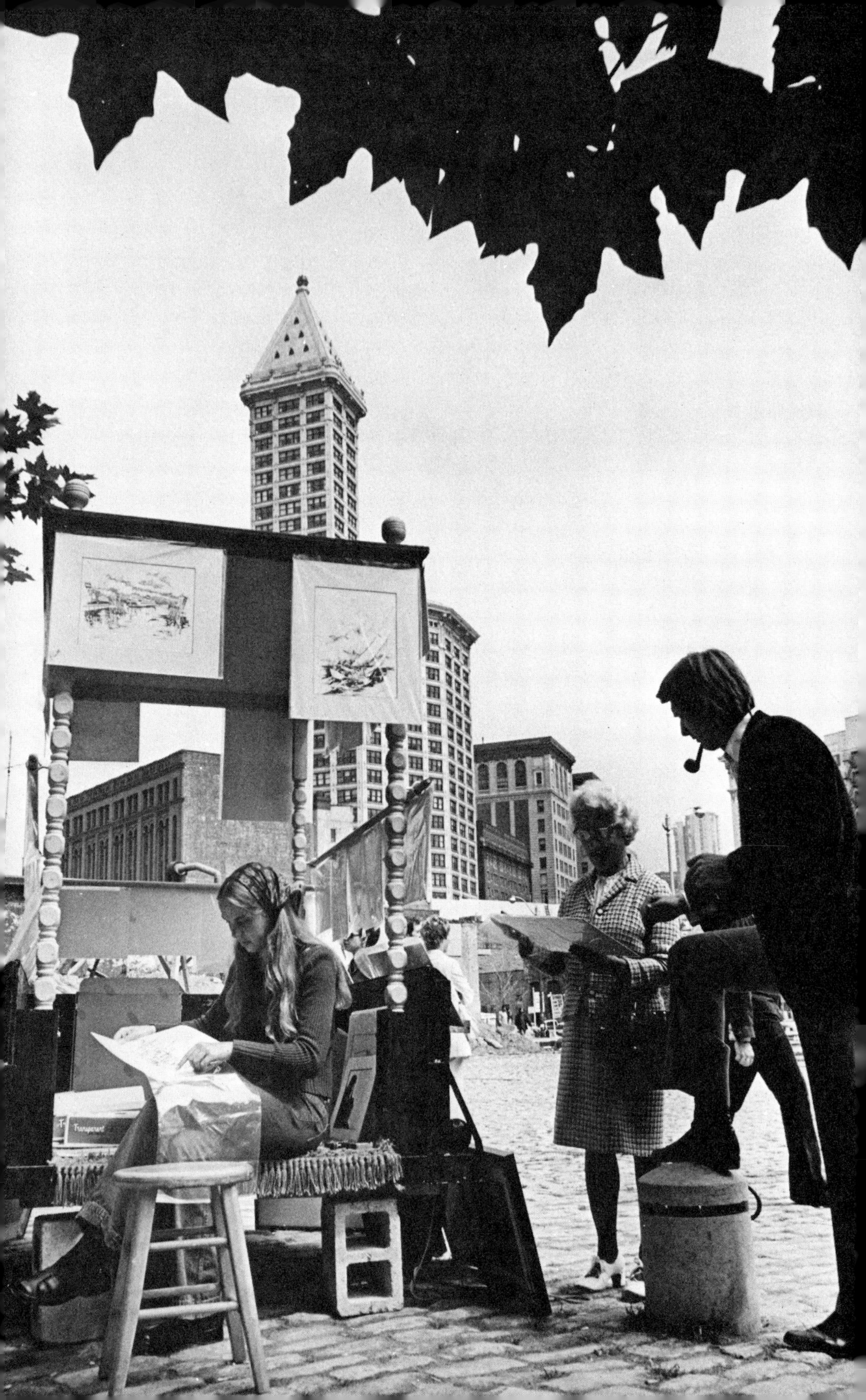

Space Meaning and Use

7

People and space issues are vastly important in a world of 4 billion persons, where population may double in thirty years and perhaps reach 50 billion by 2150. Many urban spaces are already characterized by high densities and crowding. In a nation like the United States, people in urban spaces produce over four-fifths of the society's total economic output (Wingo 1967).

Space problems are also important because they have contributed to wars. Living space was part of Germany's alleged reason for entering World War II. Outer space is a subject of scientific conquest for the U.S.A. and the U.S.S.R. Air space rights constitute critical legal and zoning issues in major world cities.

Some urban spaces are zoned for exclusive uses like manufacturing, commerce, and residences. Other spaces are specifically designated for multiple uses, as illustrated by school playgrounds being shared as park spaces or community play areas. Some spaces may be used with privacy, as frequently is the case in bathrooms and library study carrels. Spaces may be designated as public, as are parks and streets. Some spaces may have traditional use, as illustrated by the sacred worship areas in Kyoto, Japan; Jerusalem, Israel; and the Vatican City in Italy. There are traditional governmental space meanings associated with the Kremlin in Moscow, the United Nations in New York City, and Capitol Hill in Washington, D.C. In other cases urban spaces may change their meaning and use. In Boston, for example, wharf warehousing of the past is being renovated for condominium

Urban space may be used for people activities, as in this Seattle street scene. (Photo: Doug Wilson.)

apartments, restaurants, and museum uses. In San Francisco the Ghirardelli Square buildings, which were once a factory complex, now have become a posh novelty shop, restaurant, and tourist area.

In this chapter we examine the sociological meaning of spaces and the human use of spaces in order to increase understanding and to help plan higher quality urban environments.

SYMBOLIC SPACE MEANINGS

Social customs directly influence space allocation in buildings. For example, the Islamic Purdah tradition demands special spaces for female privacy. Accordingly, in a new town like Pakistan's Islamabad, kitchens and rear courts for residential areas need to be constructed so that there is no visibility for males from outside or above. By minimizing the use of multistory apartments and maximizing the use of high walls around rear patios, privacy is achieved for women. In sharp contrast is the neighboring new town of Chandigarh in India; with a predominantly Hindu population, there is less necessity for female privacy. The new town allows for multistory apartments and the use of fewer high-walled courts around kitchen areas (Lee 1967).

Another example of symbolic space meaning is illustrated in the case of the Boston Common (Firey 1947). This park-like land in central Boston symbolically expresses an open space available for the use of all citizens. Economically one might reason that such a piece of real estate is too valuable to be used only as a park. Many different types of multistory buildings that would be revenue producing could be placed on such a piece of land. But the Boston Common is vigorously defended against economic encroachment due to its symbolic meaning. Somewhat similar symbolic land use is found in New York City's Central Park, San Francisco's Golden Gate Park, Mexico City's Chapultepec Park, and London's Regency Park.

Amenity spaces in England, particularly in the form of greenbelts, are systematically preserved and defended against encroachment by destructive and polluting industries, transportation systems, and other uses that would reduce their size and aesthetic value (Thomas 1970). In very urbanized England, the symbol of open space as an amenity is a matter of critical importance. Howard Bracey, for example, explains in *Industry and the Countryside* (1963) that there are rigorous standards requiring unsightly industries to be screened by plantings in order to preserve the beauty and the integrity of the open spaces. The symbol as well as the fact of man in urbanized society in balance with nature is a critical issue in an area like the British Isles with more than 56 million people.

Symbolic meanings of residence spaces have been empirically measured in different ways. In 1928 Chapin developed a living-room scale consisting of items grouped into the following four categories: (1) fixed features like floors, floor coverings, and wall coverings; (2) built-in items like bookcases and window seats; (3) standard furniture like chairs and tables; and (4) cultural materials like furniture coverings, lamps, books, and musical instruments (Chapin 1935). Later the scale was refined to also measure the condition of the living room and its furnishings. By 1933 the instrument had become the Social Status Scale.

In the early 1940s Warner (1941) studied stratification including the symbolic meaning of residence. In his study of Newburyport, Massachusetts, he found that for the upper-upper class "houses themselves may be said to possess lineages of their own" (p. 8). The upper-upper class recognized that many houses may have more monetary value and even be more aesthetically beautiful than the lineage-possessing residences they occupied. Nevertheless, symbolic status was given a house that a distinguished family had occupied for multiple generations. Even specific rooms can take on ancestral significance. Furnishings can be endowed with symbolic meaning also. Warner found that among the lower-upper class some houses were remodeled and made "too much" like museum pieces, thereby reflecting a symbolically false image. The neighborhood location of a house and its yard care also both contribute to its symbolic meaning.

Contemporary American suburbanites place different symbolic meanings on residence (Werthman 1968). Werthman studying suburbs near San Francisco in the late 1960s found that extroverted, self-made business people tended to select ostentatious housing of a mock-colonial type. In contrast, in the same area it was found that the more inward looking professionals selected house types for their individual satisfaction. Often their houses were architecturally designed, but in any event they were constructed in such a way as to turn plain facades to the street and face principal rooms on patios or toward rear and protected yard areas. The symbolic meaning of these residences supported the different images of their successful business and successful professional occupants.

It has been found that the symbol of an ideal residence in areas like the United States, Australia, and England is the free-standing, detached, single-family unit with a yard (Michelson 1968). The high-rise, condominium, or apartment is rejected by most Americans as a place of residence because it does not symbolize a "proper home." Similarly, the mobile home is generally offensive to the American symbol of what a house should be. The converted truck or van for residential purposes expresses an even greater violation of residential symbolism. Houseboats as permanent residences are symbolically rejected as expressions of Bohemianism (Cooper 1974).

According to Kennedy (1953) and Hershberger (1970), the home is a female symbol, womb-like and warm in character. It has but one major masculine symbol, the chimney; vertical rigidity and flue heat make the chimney a phallic symbol.

The house may be symbolized in sacred — though generally not religious — terms. From ancient Roman times to the present the sanctity of the residential entrance is revered by the carrying of brides across the threshold, the removal of hats before entering, the wiping of shoes before the entrance, and in some Eastern areas the removing of shoes prior to entrance. In Orthodox Judaism the symbol of the house is interrelated with religion by the attaching of the Commandments on the doorpost in accordance with Deuteronomy, chapter 6:9, "And you shall write them on the door posts of your house and on your gates."

The symbolic meaning of the house is expressed by the hearth. This is the center of the home, the family, and perhaps the universe. Historically, one of the major female tasks has been to keep the hearth fire literally burning. Herbert Gans and others have found that in the contemporary culture of Boston's West End, the kitchen is a symbolic place for much family interaction.

Symbolically, the house may be for some a place of security, privacy, and tranquility. "A man's home is his castle" is a vernacular expression of such symbolism. But in many slum areas, safety, privacy, and tranquility are virtually unknown as home realities (Rainwater 1968).

The meaning of space may imply use control. For example, Morningside Park near Columbia University in New York City was designated as a building site for a gymnasium in the 1960s. It became a matter of controversy because it was the feeling of Black Harlemites that the park was theirs — their turf (Zeisel 1973). After demonstrations and conflict, the gymnasium was not built. The park continues as a symbol. The extent of turf symbolism might have been previously determined, and overt conflict avoided, if research had been done prior to the announced gymnasium building plans to determine the park's significance for the Harlem residents.

The symbolic meaning of the living room varies from culture to culture. Before architects can create a living space for improved social satisfaction, they should know its particular cultural meaning. In much of middle-class Western culture, the living room, if not a parlor, is special, almost sacred. Eating activities for many are to be removed from the living room, thereby making the living room-dining room combination unacceptable. Similarly when the living room takes on a high and nearly sacred status, direct entrance into it from the street is unacceptable, and an entry hall becomes a necessary addition (Zeisel 1973). The living room is also, for some, a museum-like space. It is a place decorated with the family's best furnishings and most prized possessions. For others the living room is a place more for group gatherings than for individual activities.

The social meaning of space largely determines human satisfaction or dissatisfaction with a built environment.

FROM NEIGHBORHOOD TO TOTAL LIFE SYSTEMS

In urbanized society the neighborhood and the city are being replaced by urban regions that are societal in scale. This involves providing high-quality life supports in environments that are large enough to fulfill all societal needs. Some express the view that we should no longer use the word "city," and that "the ordinary man and his family no longer live within a city but within a system of life processes which extend well beyond the city" (Bell 1972, p.241).

Still, most new towns and urban renewal planning utilize an outmoded neighborhood concept. Neighborhoods that are based on territoriality play limited roles in urbanized society. Only young children and elderly individuals now typically experience the neighborhood at a territorial level. Teenagers and young unmarrieds have much more of their social activity outside of territorial neighborhoods (Willis 1972). Urban economic production, recreational events, governmental supervision, health services, and the arts are all typically outside of residential neighborhoods. However, much religious participation still exists in parish or neighborhood churches. Neighborhood schools continue to be typical in many countries, but in the United States their validity is being seriously questioned in terms of racial integration and busing.

Architecture in its space design is gradually moving in the direction of becoming a social art. It may even become a sociophysical science (Canty 1974). In a few new towns the neighborhood as a core unit for sociophysical design is disregarded. Cumbernauld, Scotland for example is built around a megastructure core. It addresses all the institutional life support systems. It was not conceived as a formal organization, but it anticipates the possibility of urban areas becoming conceptualized as formal organizations.

Effrat (1974) notes that most new towns in Europe and America are still planned around neighborhoods with populations of 5,000 to 10,000 and with an elementary school and convenience shopping facilities. Much of the new-town failure is attributed to neighborhoods that are too small. Neighborhoods and communities, according to Effrat, are more matters of degree than kind. Both the neighborhood and the community are parts of larger urban social systems. Their territory is valid only insofar as it articulates with the larger social system or region.

Privacy

A satisfying quality of life in urbanized societies involves careful considerations for private spaces. Sociologists and physical planners are concerned with the impact of architectural design on group cohesion, worker morale, and neighborhood development (Schwartz 1972). People are by nature gregarious. In large urbanized societies they need spaces for both private and large group relationships. Husbands and wives, lovers, and clique groups need privacy spaces. Adolescents need to have small peer group privacy spaces. Confessional booths, library study carrels, and small tables in barrooms illustrate other privacy space needs. The culture further defines space separation and privacy by segregating many bathroom spaces by sex and often giving visual privacy for defecation.

The urban environment seeks to provide safety from spying, peeping toms, eavesdropping, and telephone wiretapping. The modern urban environment utilizes the buying and selling of privacy in hospital rooms, transportation facilities, hotel rooms, and theater boxes. Throughout the history of cities privacy has been a commodity of luxury. The higher social classes purchase more privacy, build more privacy into their places of residence, and arrange for more privacy in their places of work. Among the urban well-to-do, husbands, wives, and children have tended to have separate bathroom facilities and separate sleeping facilities. In slum areas multiple individuals — indeed multiple families — share toilet and sleeping facilities. Multiple children may share a bed. As American society shifted from rural to urban, there was a change from the multiple-hole outhouse to the solo-designed indoor "john." Some American middle-class spouses will knock at a bathroom door before entering to avoid invading privacy. By sharp contrast, in some places, like the army, bathrooms are so open that rows of toilets exist with no separation between them at all. Initially such openness is an invasion of privacy, but ultimately most adjust to a new definition of self. Physicians and chambermaids, for different reasons, have special societally approved "rights" to invade privacy not extended to most others in Western societies.

Urban privacy varies in the use of reading materials. In nineteenth century America one could read the Bible in public places with credibility. Sex books, if read at all, were used covertly in private ways. In late twentieth century America one reads the Bible privately and reads publicly magazines like *Playboy* and *Playgirl*.

Privacy satisfaction and complaints vary by social class. An early empirical study comparing lower-class families to middle-class families in New York showed that half of the lower-class families complained about lack of privacy compared to only 10 percent in the middle-class families (Cutler 1947). The lower classes complained about not having a single room for their personal use twice as frequently as persons in the middle class. At the other extreme, the middle class complained most about lack of outdoor privacy, insufficient rooms for special activities, lack of extra bathrooms, the absence of guest rooms, and the lack of live-in maid facilities. The middle classes and upper classes normally expect to have privacy spaces that the lower classes lack (Dahir 1950; Dean 1951). This indicates that high-quality urban environment in the industrial West must place a high priority on planning privacy spaces for multiple social classes for reading, study, aesthetic contemplation, and enjoyment. By definition the industrial and post-industrializing societies are "mind" societies. Accordingly, appropriate privacy spaces for mind edification can justify high priority.

In urban society privacy is socially defined for status. Major administrators may have private "executive washrooms" — in spite of the fact that biological elimination needs do not vary for kings, prime ministers, chief executives, athletes, or stock boys (Kira 1970). Stars in the theater may demand and get special dressing rooms with private bath facilities. Much urban transportation is divided into first and second class by the amount of space in bathroom facility provision. In many urban areas luxury, first class, and second class hotel facilities vary in size and bathroom privacy.

Solo privacy places like bathrooms may come to have use for emotional release unrelated to personal hygiene, namely, sulking, crying, daydreaming, or avoiding role responsibilities. Furthermore, bathrooms are places in which many suicides occur — possibly because individuals anticipate little intrusion.

Le Corbusier, Phillip Johnson, and other architects have designed residential quarters using the so-called "open" plan. In this architectural style there are few walls to give space separation, and most doors are omitted completely. Kitchens when not separate rooms do not eliminate the sight and smell of cooking. Dining and living rooms may be combined into one space. Bedrooms and living rooms may be combined. Only bathroom and closet space may be separated and closed with doors. Generally these open-type plans receive poor acceptance because they conflict with social notions of privacy.

Telephones may provide a type of privacy invasion. Some people turn to unlisted numbers, others to answering services, and some even refuse to answer the telephone except during specified hours (Kennedy 1953). Large plate glass windows may also produce privacy invasion. To counter this, frosted glass and/or one-way glass is used to protect certain entry halls and other privacy areas. Showers and bathing facilities may be screened with frosted glass or plastic rather than clear material. In contrast some large, clear glass windows provide security, allowing people in a residence to look out and know who approaches before a door is opened.

Livability

In the urbanized environment livability is important in residences, neighborhoods, communities, places of work, recreation areas — indeed in all life systems areas. Livability is the sum of the life support systems organized in such a way so that people can satisfy their needs and feel good about their environment. A primary sociophysical problem of livability, particularly in residential areas, is privacy (Rosow 1957). In residential areas most livability attention is focused on and desired by an intellectual-aesthetic minority, usually in the upper-middle and lower-upper classes. For these persons, housing livability is an extremely salient and sought-after value (Kennedy 1953). In middle- and lower-class housing, so little attention is paid to livability that frustration is widespread, particularly as it relates to privacy. The livability-privacy frustrations are greatest in relation to bedroom and bathroom facilities (Schorr 1970). When multiple persons must use the same bed for sleeping, relaxation, and sex, privacy invasions are frequent. The lack of privacy-livability in slum areas is a sexual stimulant. It is a factor that contributes to slum children's becoming sexually active at a very early age.

Mumford (1948) observes that with the proliferation of contraceptives, livability must accommodate the increased erotic possibilities of marriage. Mumford notes that there is little comparison concerning the sexual activity of married couples in the sixteenth century with that in the twentieth. In the last of the twentieth century, sexual intercourse, particularly for couples on the upper half of the social continuum, can take place nearly as often as desired with little or no fear of pregnancy. Taboos against sex play and nudity in bedrooms and bathrooms are reduced. Indeed, all parts of the residential environment must now be designed with a concern for increased sexual privacy. Such a livability consideration is insufficiently provided for in most lower income residential areas.

Architect Robert Woods Kennedy (1953) plans bedroom and bathroom areas for uses including dressing-undressing, storing clothes, washing, excreting, bathing, sleeping, sex, and child care. The amount and intensity of these activities vary by social class and from one urban culture to another. In some social classes nudity, even among the same sex, is viewed as a low-quality livability feature. Among others nudity between sexes may be considered acceptable or even desirable.

Sociologists find that individual physical livability features may be less significant than social satisfaction obtained in terms of the total environment. Festinger (1950) studied livability satisfactions among university students in prefabricated housing. Physically, the housing left much to be desired, even to the point of leaking roofs. The units were difficult to heat in the winter. Also at the time of the study, the ground area was not landscaped and was often muddy. Nevertheless, the students knew their duration in these residential quarters would be relatively short. Their social life with other students was adequate, indeed satisfying, and typically they reacted to the livability of their area by saying, "Oh yes, there are many things wrong with these houses, but we love it here and wouldn't want to move."

Livability satisfaction has been studied in the municipalities of Durham and Greensboro, North Carolina. Most of the respondents expressed general satisfaction with their respective communities. They were asked, for example, to rate "Durham as a place to live, taking everything into consideration." On a scale of "best possible," "very good," "good," "neither best nor worst," "bad," "very bad," "worst possible," the mode category was "good," 44.3 percent, and the second highest proportion responded "very good," 31.6 percent. Similarly, when asked about neighborhood satisfaction, over 70 percent responded "satisfied" or "very much satisfied." There was little difference in the high degree of satisfaction between the two municipalities. When social and physical elements of livability were studied, Durham respondents ranked the following items in order, listing "highly important" first and "least important" last: good roads, convenient transportation, good sidewalks, plenty of parks, schools close enough so that children can walk, shopping facilities not too far away, a city where people tend to their own business, low tax assessments, quietness, the right kind of people in the city, friends close by, a city that other persons in other communities think well of, a city of friendly people with whom you can talk on the street, a city where you can express yourself without worrying about what others think, and a city with a mixture of all types of people. A similar distribution of livability features was found for Greensboro respondents.

In 1975 the author conducted livability research in three Dallas-Fort Worth neighborhoods. Las Colinas is a planned new-town-type neighborhood in western Dallas. Its population is primarily upper-middle-class. In Forth Worth the Woodhaven neighborhood is a Planned Unit Development area. Its population is predominantly middle-middle- and upper-middle-class. And in central Dallas an upper-lower-class transitional neighborhood was studied. Over 90 percent of the residences were single-family-detached in the first two neighborhoods (although more apartments and condominiums were being built in these neighborhoods), and in the third location 56 percent of the residences were private apartments and another 40 percent public housing apartments. Most residents were White in the first two neighborhoods while there was a thorough mixture of Blacks, Browns, and Whites in the third area. In all three neighborhoods most residents had lived there less than two years.

In terms of livability, 91 percent of all residents responded that their location was satisfactory. Over half of the respondents in the two planned neighborhoods selected the location because they liked the environment, compared to only 6 percent making this response in the transitional-slum area. Twenty percent of the respondents in all three neighborhoods said they selected their location to be near their place of work. Twenty-one percent in the transitional area selected their residence because the cost was reasonable. No respondents in the planned areas gave reasonable cost as a reason for their satisfaction. Four percent of respondents in all three neighborhoods had selected their location to be near friends or relatives.

Life support systems like schools, shopping centers, and health facilities were more proximic to the transitional area than to the planned areas. There was more antisocial behavior in the transitional area, but space defensibility was considered a problem in all three areas.

Livability satisfaction is complex and difficult to research. Livability may be directly related to beliefs about housing and to the urban region (Schorr 1970). The market value of property may also affect livability satisfaction, ownership versus renting may affect satisfaction, space per person and/or number of persons per room may be an influential fact, and previous city residential experience may influence one's view of liability.

TOWN PLANNING, URBAN RENEWAL, AND NEIGHBORHOOD

Symbolic space meaning, privacy, and livability elements are all implicitly, and sometimes explicitly, manipulated in town planning and urban renewal projects. The purpose of the town planning exercise is to make the total urban environment more satisfactory (Wingo 1967). But sociophysical town planning for people and space is difficult. Changing human values must be carefully understood and new values anticipated. For example, the socio-psychological impact of the kibbutz in Israel relates to family physical space and to ethnocentric political ideology. In the U.S.S.R. the policy of placing children in communal nurseries and encouraging people of all ages to eat in communal dining halls directly impacts on physical planning for residential spaces in general and for kitchen-eating spaces in particular. Furthermore, socio-physical planners note the probability that people in the twenty-first century will spend longer periods of time in education and in retirement than did people in the first half of the twentieth century (Eversley 1968). Planners for the future carefully note that many family functions of the immediate past are being moved to the community at large. A different kind of built environment is necessary to accommodate these changed life styles and the ideologies that inform them.

Contemporary town planning accommodates increases in daily commuting and higher rates of mobility. One expression of this is uniformity in residential spaces, so that as people move from one geographic area to another it will be easier to accommodate to physical facilities and urban land use patterns that are generally familiar.

The superblock utilized in Radburn, New Jersey in 1929 illustrates new town planning related to space meaning and use ("Radburn Planning" 1960). The first superblock was an area of approximately 150 acres with an exterior road circling around the area and from which cul-de-sacs permeated toward the interior. The interior of the superblock is a neighborhood park on which houses face. The superblock separates foot traffic from auto traffic. Within the superblock a system of paths and walkways enable inhabitants to reach parks, schools, recreation facilities and a shopping area without crossing streets. The Radburn superblock idea is implicitly antiurban. It utilizes a low density with a large amount of green space. Critics of the superblock plan observe that there is a lack of privacy because houses front both on streets and on park lanes.

In a study of a New Orleans superblock area called Lake Vista, a high degree of satisfaction was found (Filipich 1971). Critics of the Radburn superblock argue that the location of shopping facilities in the center of the area, away from through streets, will be a failure. In Lake Vista, the interior shopping center has completely gone out of existence. The shops are now rented as offices, making them economically viable even though there was a failure in the original purpose.

The superblock innovation for town planning has been modified in the 1960s and 1970s to become a Planned Unit Development (PUD) or a Planned Development (PD). The Planned Unit Development in most cases is more explicitly urban than the superblock. It focuses primarily on residential units that are clustered, attached, or high-rise and on open recreational space. The PUD may also be designed to provide for convenience shopping, other service facilities, and employment.

Most new towns in Europe and the Americas are planned on the neighborhood concept even though many use neither the superblock nor the Planned Unit Development innovations. America's most widely publicized new towns, namely Reston and Columbia, south and north of Washington, D.C., respectively, are planned around neighborhood units with populations ranging between 7,000 and 10,000 each. Most of the British new towns, since the 1947 Town and Country Planning Act, are based on neighborhood units. In Runcorn, neighborhoods will have approximately 8,000 persons each. Britain's Washington New Town will have 4,500 persons in neighborhoods, and so forth. The general guidelines followed by the British new towns are those of the Dudley Report, which suggests that local neighborhoods should not exceed approximately 10,000 persons each (Willis 1972).

Even in far removed new towns like Brasilia, Brazil, and Chandigarh, India, variations on the neighborhood and superblock concepts are used. Implicitly, there is the assumption that the neighborhood unit is universally satisfactory in societies ranging from Europe to North America, to South America and to Asia. But the neighborhood is often found to be deficient in these cultures. In the early 1900s, when sociologist Cooley dealt with the neighborhood concept, he expressed the idea that it would contain some fifty to sixty adults primarily in face-to-face contact and mutual-aid relationships. Such a small social neighborhood would act as a factor in social control and social satisfaction (Cooley 1909). The smallness and the primariness of the neighborhood is lost in most new towns. Furthermore, we have already pointed out that in the dynamic urbanized social organization, large numbers of people experience few of their waking hours in a residential neighborhood territory. The social space of humans in large urban regions is of more importance than physical neighborhood space. University students, as research has shown, may express relatively high degrees of satisfaction with physically inadequate spaces because their social relationships are wide ranging and of a challenging order. In the Pruitt-Igoe Housing Project in St. Louis where most inhabitants were Black, with poor health, with low paying jobs or no jobs at all, a new physical environment was literally destroyed by eruptions of antisocial behavior.

Urban renewal, similar to new town planning, is often biased by physical-deterministic notions. There is a widespread belief that provision for a large number of livability factors is an improvement over a deteriorating physical environment in which social relations of long established durations are patterned. But students of the urban scene like Jane Jacobs and Herbert Gans submit that even in some slum conditions social and psychological livability factors are superior to those in new, well-designed buildings and in new neighborhoods. This is to say that even when urban renewal results in a new physical environment that is available to the original inhabitants, livability satisfaction may still be lower than in the previous slum environment.

Current planning of new towns and urban renewal projects is placing more emphasis on people and space relationships and less importance on the physical environment. Both old spaces and new spaces may have strong symbolic meaning. Ideological convictions in some urban areas may be intensely strong. High livability satisfaction is increased by providing physical space consistent with the ideology.

As municipal areas become large urban regions, sociophysical planners may achieve more by conceptualizing their plans in terms of societally sized organizations. Many failures in past sociophysical planning for municipalities and urban regions are due to their rural orientation. Futuristic people-space forms like megastructures, and specifically arcologies, may also fail if they are not explicitly planned in relation to societal-level organization.

Density

Sociophysical density is specifically related to the full range of questions concerning new towns, neighborhoods, livability, and privacy. Density concerns all aspects of the built environment. Most density research is based on subhuman animals or on institutional human populations, like autistic children, rather than on random samples of human populations (Calhoun 1962; Hutt 1966).

Extensive use of density concepts is found in the building of new towns and in urban renewal. City planners from the late nineteenth century to the present have often specified density statistics by gross acre. For example, Ebenezer Howard in 1898 suggested that ideal new towns would have eight to twelve units per gross acre. Le Corbusier in his 1924 work on *La Ville Contemporaine* suggested that there should be some 1,200 persons per gross acre. Accordingly, Le Corbusier saw vertical new towns having populations in the magnitude of 3 million whereas Ebenezer Howard saw horizontal, bucolic new towns having low densities and total populations of 30,000. In 1929 Clarence Perry called for an even lower density, namely five dwelling units per acre in neighborhoods of 5,000 to 9,000 persons. In 1932 Frank Lloyd Wright called for still lower densities, namely one dwelling unit per acre in his Broadacre City model. At the same time, Walter Gropius and M. Wagner were proposing four to ten dwelling units per acre. In 1947 Goodman and Goodman in their book *Communitas* proposed one hundred dwelling units per gross acre and an optimum population of 6 to 8 million (de Chiara 1975). By 1973 American new towns were being planned with densities ranging between twelve and twenty-five dwelling units per acre or between approximately 50 to 100 persons per acre (Bailey 1973).

Paolo Soleri's arcology megastructure model anticipates one of the strongest variations on the density concept that we know of, particularly as it combines with scale. His largest megastructure, Babelnoah, would have a population of 6 million people at a density of 333 per acre on a land surface of only 18,000 acres with a height of 800 feet. Babel-noah is designed to be constructed in a flat marshy area along a coastal plain. The megastructure new town would be built on stilts with the marshy plain under it becoming an open-air system of arteries and canals primarily for park use. On the stilts would stand a series of horizontal and vertical skyscraper units in which people would live, work, recreate, have hospital facilities, government facilities, educational facilities, and a full range of support activity systems for social living.

Asteromo is a space-capsule-type of urban arcology megastructure designed by Soleri for a population of 70,000 at a density of 162 persons per acre. The major diameter would be 1,400 meters and the maximum length 2,600 meters. In the interior there would be some 10 to 20 square meters of agriculture or garden space per inhabitant. In still other variations on the arcology megastructure model, as seen in the case of Arcbeam, a density as high as 58 persons per acre and a total of 65,000 individuals would be planned for. This kind of new town would be built above and into a ravine or canyon. In sum, Soleri's arcologies would range in density from 58 to nearly 1,000 persons per acre. In scale these megastructures would typically be many times larger than the Empire State Building in New York City.

Another variation on the high-density urban living theme is illustrated in the work of Leopold Gertsel in Israel (Gertsel 1966). Gertsel experiments primarily with mass clusters of housing in new towns. Some are built like ancient ziggurats with large solid masses broken by interior courts, light wells, and streets. In his "Elysian" housing project, residential structures are placed at the top of artificial clifflike stacks of offices, shops, factories, and auto parking. Residential quarters are elevated for good views and positions above noise.

We have looked at the impact of urbanized social organization on density, and we have examined new models for bucolic low densities and new models for high densities with large numbers of people in megastructures. In most respects these are consistent with recycled environments, with urban areas as formal organizations, and with the rapidly growing urbanized world population.

SOCIAL SPACE AND PERSONAL SPACE

Social space is open and public where people present themselves in daily living. Social space is where people engage in high rates of social interaction in homes, places of work, places of pleasure and recreation, etc. Personal space is private in the sense that it is around an individual's body. One may have personal space in a chair, with others near yet physically separated. Personal space is evidenced when two friends converse while standing close together yet carefully avoiding physical contact. Personal space may be intruded on in crowded elevators or in crowded halls. Bodily contact in these situations often engenders an "excuse me" or a "pardon me" statement (Lyman 1972). In the high-density urban environment, some specific physical spaces are planned and built to support personal space perceptions. With respect to both social spaces and personal spaces, sociologists and planners are concerned with territoriality, space invasion, and crowding.

Personal space invasion

According to Felipe and Sommer (1972), personal space is "an area with invisible boundaries surrounding a person's body into which no one may intrude" (p.54). Sociologically the concept originated with Simmel (1964) in the early 1900s, and it has been continuously investigated primarily in the tradition of social psychology. Personal space is associated with body language, conversational distance, the right to view and not to view, to touch and not to touch one's body, including such activities as masturbation and skin decoration (Lyman and Scott 1972).

Personal space considerations need to be noted critically in the design and use of libraries, art museums, and restrooms. In Hall's work on proximics, he differentiates distance-sets into categories like "intimate" and "casual-personal" (Hall 1972).

The expressing of personal space modification was found in the tradition of duelling scars among German students. Body manipulation by foundation garments, plastic surgery, ritualistic mutilation as found among Pre-Columbians who puncture the penis with thorns, tattooing the body, and among ancients and contemporaries piercing ears for decorative purposes are all dimensions of personal space expression.

Invasion of personal spaces in densely populated urban areas occurs frequently. In urban crowding, separate seating spaces are often designed to minimize, or even eliminate, one body touching another. When there is an invasion of body space by persons of the same sex, there may be the accusation of homosexuality. In other cases the urban environment may provide for love seats, or seducing niches, to facilitate intimacy between consenting members of the opposite sex. The act of rape is one of the clearest expressions of personal space invasion. Plays like *Oh Calcutta!* and *Hair* present other situations of personal space invasion that become legitimized. Striptease performances are examples of personal space invasion. In the play *Flower Drum Song*, the elderly Oriental parents who are distressed at a son's girlfriend's behavior complain that she entertains by dancing naked, allowing all to see what only a husband should see (Hammerstein 1958).

Personal space in some parts of the urbanized society is both sharply invaded and intensely protected. Physicians and nurses are generally given societal sanction to examine their clients' bodies, including the genital organs, which are sometimes colloquially referred to as "the privates." Affluent patients can often obtain more privacy than can poorer patients. Invasion of body space is generally a privilege assumed by attendants in correctional institutions, particularly at entry time, when anal and vaginal examinations are used for medical purposes, for drug detection, and for lowering the status of the subject. Personal space may be bought and sold, as in the case of prostitution. In the military and similar group living situations, personal space may be minimized but homosexual activity rigorously punished. Personal space may be enticingly decorated, as in sociobuilt environments like Playboy Clubs. Personal space may be scarcely recognizable at all due to clothing styles, as in religious orders where individuals are covered by habits, or in religious sects like the Amish where there are taboos against "suggestive" dress. Voyeuristic invasion of personal space is suggested and stimulated by bikinis and other scant dress on bathing beaches, while even exposing of the ankles in some cultures has been considered a "naughty" and indecent display of personal space. Researchers like Masters and Johnson have contributed to a redefinition of personal space by making it more socially acceptable to discuss human sexuality. Changing policies of separating or integrating athletic activities by sex reflect differing societal definitions of personal space.

As urbanized society becomes more and more crowded, social space and personal space become increasingly dependent on societal conditions rather than independent choices of individuals (Bechtel 1970; Horowitz 1970).

Crowding

Crowding in the urbanized environment is increasingly prevalent. There is much emotional rhetoric concerning it, but very little factual information at the human level. Numerous studies of lesser organisms have demonstrated antisocial behavior and even mutual destruction with high levels of crowding.

Crowding in Hong Kong, where there are some 3 million people in twelve square miles, has become an acceptable pattern of existence. The Hong Kong Housing Authority builds and operates low-income apartments providing only about thirty-five square feet — a six by six foot floor space — for an individual's living-sleeping arrangements. It is reported that if the space were doubled, people would sublet it (Sommer 1969). In densely crowded places like New York City's Manhattan Island the cavernously built high-rise environment is punctuated with many small, private gardens (McGrath 1974). There are roof gardens, balconies, and patios lushly planted with evergreens and flowers. Soleri's arcology megastructures would be similarly punctuated with patios, balconies, and other spaces for greenery. Crowding and urban forestry are complementary. Some high-rise housing units for New York's affluent have entire floors, sometimes at multiple levels, utilized as parks.

Adjustments to crowding and isolation are illustrated in the experience of man's built environment in Antarctica (Law 1960). Men in the isolated Antarctic stations learned to control emotions and to use social spaces for face-to-face interaction that would generate compatible results. There were no exits, outlets, or alternatives. Endurance in such isolation depends upon social behavior. Antisocial behavior can only be degenerative and destructive.

Restaurants and bar spaces are constructed to provide for compatible social interaction and money spending, while related reception and lobby areas may be intentionally inadequate and only moderately appealing. Hotel managers and restauranteurs build their environments for crowding and with high lighting and little soundproofing — all based on limited evidence that these will contribute to more money spending and higher rates of turnover (Sommer 1969).

The limited evidence on crowding concerning humans shows a remarkable capacity for accommodation to many different levels of density in limited physical space.

Territoriality

Lyman and Scott (1972) define territoriality as "the need of individuals and groups to claim some geographical area as their own." Specific environmental and spatial conditions may be viewed territorially. In a perceptual sense one may visualize an area as part of one's territory without physical attachment to it. International travelers may perceive a city in another part of the world from their current location as part of their territory.

Four types of territories are regularly identified: public territories, home territories, interactional territories, and body territories. In many streets, parks, and buildings, urbanites have only limited access. Some so-called public territories are owned as citizen domains and operated at taxpayer expense. Other quasi-public territories may be illustrated by elevators in private buildings. In both cases, access to and use of the territories may be more or less open and more or less restricted. Some parks and playgrounds may be unsafe at night. Streets may be lighted to provide increased safety, and elevators may be secured by closed circuit television monitor systems. In America, access to public bathrooms was once separated by race. In the last of the twentieth century public bathrooms are integrated by race but still segregated by sex. In another change of public territory use, bare-breasted women may be publicly viewed in San Francisco night clubs while prohibited from public view on streets. At some public beaches, nude swimming is tolerated and even protected by the police. Often in the same area, clothed voyeurists are prohibited from watching nude swimmers.

Home territories include residences as well as makeshift club-type spaces often used by young children, hobo and/or squatter areas, homosexual bars, and so forth. Territorially, home areas or turfs may be more than just residential. Nonresidential home territories may be places for social identity, as are clubs, or as are "gay bars" for homosexuals. They may be places of comfortable acquaintance, like hotel lobbies, airport terminals, baseball stadiums, and church sanctuaries — places often frequented on favorable terms. Business representatives may feel a "home territory" in several major hotel lobbies the world over due to extensive travel.

Interactional territories are places for social gatherings. They may include civic centers, auditorium lobbies, residential halls, and college quadrangles. A party is an interactional territory regardless of the particular design of its physical space. A discussion or recitation section for a university class is a social territory. Bars and restaurants are typically social territories, while libraries are typically nonsocial territories, and art museums may vary from social to nonsocial territorial spaces. Social territory may also be identified as the distance a child is free to move from its mother or a guardian. Social territory is also seen in the separation of male and female activity spaces. Kitchen areas in particular and interior residential areas more generally have tended to be female social spaces while exterior yard areas have been more male social spaces. Informal social territories may be characterized as places where persons might freely walk around dressed only in underclothing, like domestic residents' bedrooms or college dormitory rooms. Formal social territories may be places where individuals "present themselves," as in box seats or in dress circles at operas or plays and at formal receptions for dignitaries.

Territories may be designated by specific markers, like towels on poolside or deck chairs, "occupied" seat signs on airplanes, and "do not disturb" signs on hotel doors (Sommer 1969). Territorial encroachment and turf defense follow a number of cultural patterns. The untouchables in India's past caste system constituted a type of territorial separation. Isolation of persons who have communicable diseases like cholera, diphtheria, and chicken pox designates other types of territories. Orthodox Jews separate meat and milk dishes and may destroy them if they are mixed (Lewis 1975). Heterosexuals may quit patronizing a particular bar when their territory is invaded by homosexuals. In sum, social territories may have broad-ranging characteristics.

DEFENSIBLE SPACE

Some space utilization contributes to high-quality environment while other space use contributes to antisocial behavior. Oscar Newman's book *Defensible Space* (1972) is one critical summary of the situation in urban America.

Newman begins by observing that large numbers of one- and two-story buildings in or near central cities have been replaced by high-rise buildings. Land values have increased in some central city areas so that there is more use of high-rise than low-rise buildings. Most of the high-rise buildings constructed in the last quarter of a century are unifunctional. This is to say, most buildings are devoted primarily either to office space, manufacturing space, residential space, or administrative space. Several sociological consequences related to these changes are significant. In many unifunctional high-rise buildings, the number of persons in the building is directly related to hours of work, hours of recreation and leisure, or hours of sleeping and domestic residence activities. Some buildings are densely populated at certain hours and sparsely populated, or vacant, at other hours. Additionally, many buildings or groups of buildings may be occupied by several hundreds of people during certain peak periods. Most of the persons using the buildings will not be known to other users at all, while some will be known only as executives, janitors, or by other occupational categories.

Sociologically there may be many different primary group relationships in these large buildings and many persons may have limited use experiences during which they will have no primary group relationships. Accordingly, except in those instances where there are security checks, it is probable that most users of the high-rise buildings will be unknown or known to each other only on a limited basis. Informal social controls for high-quality environment, human decency, and personal and property protection are limited or lost. In earlier city developments with small buildings, many potential acts of antisocial behavior or building damage were discouraged or eliminated because intruders would be regularly recognized and apprehended. Many of the new high-rise buildings are greatly improved over earlier buildings for human comfort and amenities. Nevertheless, the buildings themselves are frequently abused and the human occupants too often mugged, raped, or in other ways victimized.

There is lack of clear definition concerning whose "turf" a building is. There is often a lack of definition concerning what kind of social interaction is intended and appropriate in the building's physical spaces. There may also be a lack of definition concerning personal space recognition and respect in buildings.

In order to overcome these problems, new high-rise buildings are increasingly being designed as megastructures. In such buildings many inhabitants will live, work, recreate, worship, and have facilities for many other services for their urban life needs. This establishes the possibility for more of the users of the building to become at least secondarily acquainted with each other in multiple roles. It may or may not contribute to more primary group relationships. It will, however, potentially contribute to social control and high-quality environment as people interact more with persons whose identities they know.

Newman cites specifically the physical design problem of the double-load corridor apartment buildings. This middle-to-highrise building with a central elevator shaft area and often with stairwells at opposite ends of a rectangular-shaped building theoretically provides an efficient movement of people from street level to place of residence. During work and recreation hours, the building may have a minimum population. During sleep and domestic hours, the population normally increases. In fact, most of the population in such a building has little or no knowledge of the other occupants. Therefore, an antisocial intruder may ride the elevator and walk the halls several times to ascertain the habits of coming and going of some residents. By such "casing of the situation" the intruder may learn that often he or she may be alone with a single building occupant in an elevator. If there is no electronic surveillance device, it is easy at knife or gun point for the intruder to require the other to step off the elevator into a hall that will have a high probability of being vacant and/or into an individual's apartment where there is "security" for subjecting the occupant to antisocial behavior.

Furthermore, Newman observes that many high-rise buildings are superior in part of their physical design but inferior in their total environmental relationship. Some middle-rise residential apartments, particularly designed for families with children, may have playground areas at the street level but no sanitary bathroom facilities at the playground level. Accordingly, service shafts, elevators, and hallways are used for urinating, becoming generally unacceptable for their intended use.

Newman further points out that even many middle- and low-rise buildings have few or no windows that face streets or entrance areas. It is difficult for an occupant to regularly and conveniently know who passes by the exterior of the building and/or who might be attempting entry. Furthermore, some high and solid patio walls, once scaled by persons oriented to antisocial behavior, provide security areas for the carrying out of their deviant or criminal acts (see also Jacobs).

Finally, outside of the built environment in park areas, Newman finds that in highly plural population areas, long narrow park spaces are more social and defensible than those that are deep. The latter cut off visual access and implicitly provide for seducing areas. The sociophysical solution to such problems is to provide restful park and green open spaces that have moderate visibility from passers-by in street areas and have moderate visual surveillance potential at all times from nearby building windows.

In a physically large building, sociodesign can facilitate high-quality civilized behavior by encouraging multiple functions, enabling users to become acquainted with each other in multiple roles, and increasing human social interaction surveillance that is natural in the course of daily activities.

IMPLICATIONS

The meaning and use of sociophysical space can be seen as a whole urban social system. Urban spaces have spiritual, economic, social, political, and recreational meanings. Uses vary from the highly individual and private to the highly social, visible, and public.

In urban systems many spaces may have multiple meanings and multiple uses in a single day, week, or at varying times. The built environment needs to be planned with a broad and aggressive acceptance of symbolic space meanings. The function of privacy and its relation to livability and status symbolism must necessarily become a part of the sociophysical planning matrix. Urban renewal and new-town densities which focus primarily on separated and segregated sociodesign function are antiurban. Unilateral segregating and separating of spaces exacerbate urban problems. Zoning and land use differences may only have strong viable integrity when established in terms of urban societal systems. Social territoriality, personal space, and crowding are variable conditions which can be used to support high-quality living. All social institutions must be overtly addressed in identifying space meaning and in planning space use.

REFERENCES

BAILEY, J. (Ed.). *New Towns in America.* New York: Wiley, 1973.
BECHTEL, R. B. Human movement and architecture. In H. M. Proshansky, W. H. Ittelson, & L. G. Rivlin (Eds.), *Environmental Psychology.* New York: Holt, Rinehart, and Winston, 1970.
BELL, C., & TYRWHITT, J. *Human Identity in the Urban Environment.* London: Pelican Books, 1972.

BRACEY, H. *Industry and Countryside.* London: Routledge & Kegan Paul, 1963.

CALHOUN, J. B. Population density and social pathology. *Scientific American,* 1962, *206,* 138 – 49.

CANTY, D. Using the social sciences to help make buildings both responsive and humane. *American Institute of Architects Journal,* 1974, *61,* 24 – 47.

CHAPIN, F. S. *Contemporary American Institutions.* New York: Harper and Brothers, 1935.

COOLEY, C. H. *Social Organization.* New York: Scribners, 1909.

COOPER, C. The house as a symbol of the self. In J. Lang (Ed.), *Designing for Human Behavior.* Stroudsberg, Pa.: Dowden, Hutchinson and Ross, 1974.

CUTLER, V. *Personal and Family Values in the Choice of a Home.* Ithaca, N.Y.: Cornell Agricultural Experiment Station, 1947.

DAHIR, J. *Communication for Better Living.* New York: Harper and Brothers, 1950.

DEAN, J. The ghosts of home ownership. *Journal of Social Issues,* 1951, *7,* nos. 1-2 (special housing issue).

DE CHIARA, J., & KOPPELMAN, L. *Planning Design Criteria.* New York: Van Nostrand, 1975.

EFFRAT, M. *The Community.* New York: Free Press, 1974, 1 – 34.

EVERSLEY, D. C. The shape of cities to come. *Town and Country Planning,* 1968, *36,* 53.

FELIPE, N. J., & SOMMER, R. Invasions of personal space. In R. Gutman (Ed.), *People and Buildings.* New York: Basic Books, 1972.

FESTINGER, L., SCHACTER, S. & BACK, K. *Social Pressures in Informal Groups.* New York: Harper & Brothers, 1950.

FILIPICH, J., & TAYLOR, L. *Lakefront New Orleans.* New Orleans: Urban Studies Institute, University of New Orleans, 1971.

FIREY, W. *Land Use in Central Boston.* Cambridge: Harvard University Press, 1947.

GERTSEL, L. High density living. *Architectural Design,* 1966, *33,* 93 – 94.

HALL, E. T. Silent assumptions in social communication. In R. Gutman (Ed.), *People and Buildings.* New York: Basic Books, 1972.

HAMMERSTEIN, O. *Flower Drum Song.* Columbia Masterworks, 1958.

HERSHBERGER, R. G. Architecture and meaning. *Journal of Aesthetic Education,* 1970, *4,* 37 – 55.

HOROWITZ, M. J., DUFF, D. F., & STRATTON, L. O. Personal space and the body buffer zone. In H. M. Proshansky (Ed.), *Environmental Psychology.* New York: Holt, Rinehart, and Winston, 1970.

HUTT, C., & VAIZEY, M. J. Differential effects of group density on social behavior. *Nature,* 1966, *209,* 1371 – 72.

JACOBS, J. *The Death and Life of Great American Cities.* New York: Random House, 1961.

KENNEDY, R. W. *The House.* New York: Reinhold Publishing Co., 1953.

KIRA, A. Privacy and the bathroom. In H. M. Proshansky, W. H. Ittelson, & L. G. Rivlin (Eds.), *Environmental Psychology.* New York: Holt, Rinehart, and Winston, 1970, 269 – 75.

LAW, P. Some psychological aspects of life at an Antarctic station. *Discovery,* 1960, *21,* 431 – 37.

LEE, M. Islamabad — the image. *Architectural Design,* 1967, *34,* 47 – 48.

LEWIS, S. The pious ones. *Planning: The ASPO Magazine,* 1975, *41,* 7 – 13.

LYMAN, S. M., & SCOTT, M. B. Territoriality: a neglected sociological dimension. In R. Gutman (Ed.). *People and Buildings*. New York: Basic Books, 1972.

MCGRATH, N. Manhattan's secret gardens. *New York Magazine*, 1974, 7, 48 – 57.

MICHELSON, W. Most people don't want what architects want. *Transaction*, 1968, 4, 37 – 43.

MUMFORD, L. *The Culture of Cities*. New York: Harcourt, Brace and Co., 1948, 431 – 2.

NEWMAN, O. *Defensible Space*. New York: Macmillan Co., 1972.

Radburn planning. *The Architect's Journal*, 1960, 132, 680 – 84.

RAINWATER, L. Fear and house-as-haven in the lower class. *Journal of American Institute of Planners*, 1968, 32, 23 – 31.

ROSOW, I. Specialists' perspectives and spurious validation in housing. *Marriage and Family Living*, 1957, 19, 187 – 96.

SCHORR, A. L. Housing and its effects. In H. M. Proshansky, W. H. Ittelson, & L. G. Rivlin (Eds.), *Environmental Psychology*. New York: Holt, Rinehart and Winston, 1970.

SCHWARTZ, B. The social psychology of privacy. In R. Gutman (Ed.), *People and Buildings*. New York: Basic Books, 1972, 152 – 69.

SIMMEL, G. The secret and the secret society. In K. Wolf (Ed.), *The Sociology of Georg Simmel*. New York: Free Press, 1964.

SOLERI, P. *Arcology*. Cambridge: M.I.T. Press, 1969.

SOMMER, R. *Personal Space*. Englewood Cliffs, N.J.: Prentice-Hall, 1969.

THOMAS, D. *London's Green Belt*. London: Faber and Faber, 1970.

WARNER, L., & LUNT, P. S. *The Social Life of a Modern Community*. New Haven: Yale University Press, 1941.

WERTHMANN, C. *The social meaning of the physical environment*. Unpublished doctoral dissertation, University of California at Berkeley, 1968.

WILLIS, M. Sociological aspects of urban structure. In G. Bell & J. Tyrwhitt (Eds.), *Human Identity in the Urban Environment*. London: Pelican, 1972.

WINGO, L. et al. *Cities and Space*. Baltimore: Johns Hopkins Press, 1967.

ZEISEL, J. Symbolic meaning of space and the physical dimension of social relations. In J. Walton & D. Carns (Eds.), *Cities in Change*. Boston: Allyn and Bacon, 1973.

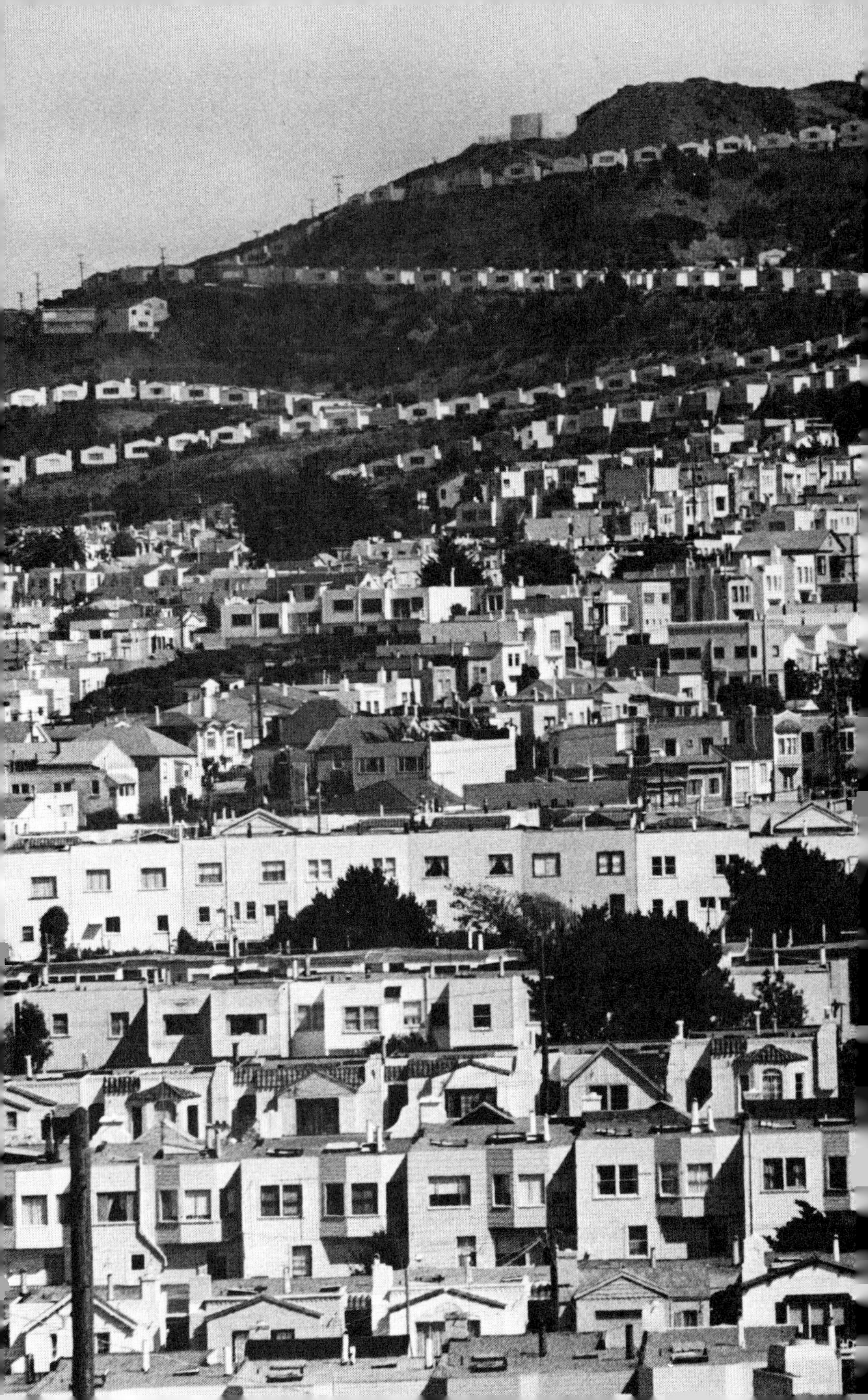

Land Use and Subdivision

8

In the most urbanized societies, 90 percent or more of the population live on less than 10 percent of the land. Land use in dense urban areas is, therefore, of considerable importance. In addition to surface use, air rights, view rights, and subsurface rights are increasingly of importance.

Urbanized societies use land outside of municipal areas for transportation systems that connect people, goods, and services between and among urban regions. Also, urbanized societies use open land areas for leisure and recreation purposes, even identifying some rural land preserves as wilderness areas.

Most food and fiber is still produced outside of the densely populated urban areas. However, in intensely urbanized societies like the Netherlands, England, and the United States, science and the cities control most food and fiber production.

One of the reasons that Soleri proposes an arcology megastructure for the urban built environment is to create what he calls a miniaturized city that will preserve maximum open-country space for food and fiber industry and for recreation. Similarly, Dantzig and Saaty (1973) propose a Compact City megastructure eliminating most auto traffic, facilitating climate control and recycling, and maximizing the use of open-country space for agriculture and recreation while avoiding urban sprawl. A third and somewhat similar megastructure model is proposed in the Minnesota Experimental City (*Minnesota Experimental City* 1969). It anticipates a similar open-space land dependency on the city values.

This scene shows subdivisions moving into open land near San Francisco. (Photo: Peter Menzel for Stock, Boston.)

As urbanized societies mature into the twenty-first century, their dominance over total land use needs to be carefully examined for purposes of planning high-quality urban environments. Accordingly, in this chapter we begin and end with broader views than traditional land use and subdivision concepts. These two major concepts are treated in detail and in broad societal perspective.

LAND USE CONCEPTS

A standard land-use coding manual is widely used in America (de Chiara and Koppelman 1975). It includes eight categories, namely: residential; manufacturing, trade, and agriculture; transportation, communication, and utilities; trade; services; cultural entertainment and recreation; food and fiber production; and undeveloped land and water. These physical planner urban-land-use codes correspond in part to social institutions. Residential land use provides physical space for family activities. Manufacturing, trade, and agricultural land use provide economic space. Educational and governmental spaces are provided for in the service category. The only institution that is conspicuously absent in this physical planner land-use code is religion. Yet in the physical planners' "color legend for land use categories," churches are designated. Unfortunately these physical planning land-use categories are out of priority for the operation of a high-quality urbanized environment. Too much physical and social space is allocated to economics and too little to religion and schools. Also in the post-industrializing urbanized societies, more sociophysical space needs to be designated in standard land use for hospitals, welfare services, and science. The space designated for transportation and parks is generally more sufficient.

In planning new towns, undertaking urban renewal projects, and extending existing municipalities, planners make projections for different types of land uses. For existing municipalities the process involves three steps. First, there is an analysis of the existing land use both within the municipality and in its adjacent areas. Second, space standards for each of the sociophysical urban activities are developed. More specifically, density standards are used for both residential and industrial areas. Traffic flow standards are used for transportation planning. Similar standards are used for determining the amount of retail business space and school space. Third, space requirements are balanced against the supply of available land.

The successful utilization of the above steps depends on an adequate understanding of social institutions. The operationalization of land use planning as explained by Chapin (1970) fundamentally involves the analysis of past experience. Industrial densities are defined as the number of manufacturing employees per gross industrial acre. Densities are usually differentiated in three categories: intensive, intermediate, and extensive. Floor space per employee is similarly analyzed for wholesaling and retailing. Square footage space requirements for central business districts, retail shopping centers, schools, and hospitals are projected largely on the basis of past experience. Chapin further recognizes that there is considerable variation in past experiences from one municipal area to another.

The Broady notion of conceptualizing the urban area as a formal organization offers the possibility of systematically relating land use projections to social institutions. It also offers the possibility of varying projections by differing amounts of cybernation and/or post-industrialization.

Private versus public ownership ideology

In the United States in particular and much of the industrial West in general, there is a strong — if not rugged individualistic — ideology for private urban land ownership. Title to land ideologically frees the owner from governmental service and regulatory controls. But near the end of the twentieth century, very little urban land in America is owned and utilized beyond the regulatory limits of urban ordinances, particularly those dealing with fire safety, sanitation, and health. Nevertheless, the private ownership of land is so extensive that laws of eminent domain are required in order to assemble land even for public use.

Most new-town development in existing municipalities, or adjacent to them, is enormously frustrated by the inability of builders to accumulate land without exploitive speculation. England and Sweden have governmental authority at the national and municipal levels respectively for facilitating urban developers in the process of land acquisition. In the Soviet Union land is held by the state, thereby eliminating major problems in designating it for new development.

Actual land uses do not vary greatly whether the land is held publicly or privately. The significance of land ownership for urban planning lies primarily in the recognition that urbanized social organization by nature involves a considerable amount of cooperation. Urbanized societies are oriented to professional and service activities. Such societies can be operated with either a maximum or a minimum of private land ownership. The planning and organization of such societies, however, is facilitated by more public land ownership (Doxiadis 1974).

URBAN LAND USE PLANNING

In the preindustrial city, the classic land use trilogy was for the castle, market, and temple. With industrialism these three grew and expanded into urban land use focusing on production, business, government, housing, a host of services, and most recently on recreation. In effect, by the middle of the twentieth century the significance of the temple in the central city had been replaced by the central business district, and that is now being replaced by recreation areas (Gottmann 1975). As urban societies move toward post-industrialization, transportation, communication, health, and welfare facilities all constitute added dimensions to land use. In Japan some planners are referring sociologically to this land use condition as the "information society" (Gottmann 1975). In America this author has referred to this condition as the "mind society"(Taylor 1975).

Comprehensive plans and zoning

Comprehensive planning and zoning are the techniques currently most used to bring some order into land use. Both comprehensive urban plans and urban zoning ordinances are twentieth-century developments. Chronologically zoning preceded comprehensive planning. Early in the twentieth century courts in the United States began to uphold zoning ordinances. Soon the courts required a justification for zoning, and this stimulated the development of comprehensive planning (Gallion and Eisner 1963; Rody and Smith 1968; de Chiara and Koppelman 1975).

The comprehensive plan is also sometimes called the urban general plan or the master plan. By definition it is a long-range projection for orderly urban growth to be administratively coordinated by government. The comprehensive plan is a guide, and in many respects a process. Urban areas are complex organizations. Therefore the comprehensive plan must be regularly reviewed and updated. The basic elements of a comprehensive plan are physical, economic, and social.

Comprehensive plans designate land use areas into residential, commercial, industrial, and open spaces. More specifically comprehensive plans specify land for conservation (including identification of flood plains), for subdivisions, for flood control, for open spaces, and for agriculture. Residential land is normally divided into low density, meaning one to six families per net acre; medium density, meaning seven to fifteen families per net acre; high density, meaning sixteen to twenty-five families per net acre; and trailer park designations, normally with ten to thirteen families per net acre. Commercial land use is normally divided into central business districts, community shopping centers, neighborhood centers, and office-institutional areas. Industrial land is bifurcated into light and heavy industrial areas. Recreation land uses are divided into neighborhood parks, community parks, regional parks, and wilderness areas. Public facility lands are designated for civic centers, fire stations, libraries, police stations, and schools. Street and highway land uses are divided into freeways, major highways, secondary highways, and collector streets. Transportation land uses differentiate auto, rail, water, and air. Finally there may be a quasi-public land use designation for institutions like hospitals and penal facilities (Gallion and Eisner 1963). Large municipalities and large urban regions require that all the social institutions must be specifically identified in the comprehensive plan. Furthermore, comprehensive plans for an urban area must articulate with the other plans in an urban region.

The comprehensive planning process

Urban comprehensive plans typically project optimum private and public land use for ten to twenty years. Provision is made for regular review and updating of the plans. Step one in the planning process involves the development of a statement of goals and objectives. Currently there is considerable difference of opinion concerning the degree to which the goals and objectives should be established by planning professionals rather than by citizen groups. Increasingly planning professionals attempt to utilize techniques whereby citizens can participate with them in setting the initial goals and objectives (Taylor and Busam 1976).

The second planning stage involves basic studies. A base map is developed, a land use map is developed, economic studies are made, and population projections are made. The third stage of comprehensive planning involves the reevaluation of goals and objectives in light of this new and systematic evidence. The fourth stage is the actual writing of the plan. The plan will have chapters or sections dealing with land use, transportation, and community facilities. Urban renewal and historic preservation often become specific parts of a master plan.

Implementation of the comprehensive plan is carried out through capital improvement programs and by social initiative, both private and public. The police power of the urban government is also used in plan implementation. Urban police power is embodied in zoning ordinances, subdivision regulations, building and housing codes, and health and welfare requirements. With each phase of implementation it is desirable to reevaluate the comprehensive plan (de Chiara and Koppelman 1975).

A more detailed examination of the elements of the comprehensive plan is necessary. The urban base maps identify features such as the street system, railroads, rivers, and parks. A major outgrowth of the base maps is a second set of maps showing existing land use facilities in the municipality. A third set of maps shows the topology of the area with special emphasis on subsoil properties and flood plain areas. From a sociobehavioral point of view, cognitive mapping needs to be added at this point. Physical map information is insufficient without a social map identifying the symbolic meanings and importance of the physical features on the landscape.

Land use maps increasingly designate subsurface uses, surface uses, and air rights or visual uses. As megastructures increase in importance in the urban environment, land use above and below the surface also increases in importance.

Population studies generally have focused projections indicating anticipated growth in the number of people in urban areas. In recent years, however, some older central cities have experienced decreases in population. Population studies need to be related to cognitive mapping and land use. It is now important that population studies and demographic maps identify the number of people in an area, like a census tract, by variation in a twenty-four-hour period, showing day by day variation and weekday-weekend differences. Some transportation arteries will be "overpopulated" during early morning and late afternoon hours and underutilized at other times. A central business district may be "overpopulated" during the midday hours of the working week and underutilized during evening hours and weekends. Similarly, residential areas may be "overpopulated" during evening hours and "underpopulated" during working hours. The social and economic cost of building urban areas that have over- and under-population at varying times in the day or the week is great. Some patterns of antisocial behavior increase during hours of underpopulation. Other patterns of antisocial behavior obtain most in hours of overpopulation. Both types of antisocial behavior could be greatly reduced by establishing comprehensive planning goals and implementation techniques to reduce the amount of movement of large populations diurnally between places of work, residence, commerce, and recreation. Megastructures are one alternative in the organization of cities for the integration of sociophysical spaces for high-quality living.

Economic studies traditionally are concerned with the number of jobs that are generated by commerce, industry, and government for urban inhabitants. These studies are highly deficient. Most frequently municipalities are adjacent to other municipalities in large urban regions. Furthermore, as many Western societies move in a post-industrializing direction and increasingly utilize cybernation, the economics of people and jobs become more complex. Additionally, as birth rates and familism decline, more women are available for positions in the labor force. High-quality urban environments must therefore create satisfactory alternatives for women. Health and longevity also increase; accordingly more economic provisions are needed for the older populations.

The "community facilities plan" is one of the most critical for achieving a high-quality environment. This is the part of the comprehensive plan that deals most with schools and general socialization. It specifies educational and cultural facilities, locating schools, colleges, museums, and so forth. Still, this component of the plan deals only implicitly with science, relating it primarily to universities. Comprehensive urban planning in the last of the twentieth century is done in mind societies where information is largely based on science. A comprehensive plan to maximize positive social relationships needs to focus specifically on the location of scientific institutions. Science is too important an element for modern urban life to be implicitly rather than explicitly planned.

Medical facilities are another component of the community facilities plan. In addition to hospitals, these facilities now specify nursing homes, clinics, etc. There is still generally insufficient explicit planning for social welfare beyond health needs. Rehabilitation facilities are important dimensions of urban life, and they too need to be specified.

Government and all public buildings are other components of the community facilities plan. Here there is a detailed specification of the location of fire departments, police stations, jails, public markets, civic auditoriums, and related facilities.

Churches and related religious facilities identified in this part of the plan are generally given minimal or insufficient attention.

Open spaces and/or parks are a favorite subject of planners. There has been a bias favoring parks. There is little hard evidence indicating the extent to which park facilities necessarily improve the quality of the urban environment. Indeed Newman (1972) observes that some kinds of large parks are places that harbor antisocial behavior. Moreover there is little exploration of the development of parklike spaces in megastructures. In the Compact City plan, open park space would be built on top of and into the megastructure building. Similarly, in Soleri's arcology plans, open parklike spaces are integrated into the built environment.

Environment is the last major element of the community facilities plan. Here attention is given to items like water supply, water treatment, and water storage. Solid waste facilities and sanitary landfills are specified. Air pollution and flood control are further items for planning attention. Through all of this, there is a limited discussion of recycled environments.

Transportation planning

The transportation plan tends to be dominated by projections for street systems. This is related to land use densities. In the newer industrial cities of the Western world, low densities prevail. From the middle of the twentieth century to the present, low densities have been greatly facilitated by the availability of private automobiles. From the thirties to the sixties, the large automobile was a matter of status. More recently, it becomes an object of inconvenience — of traffic congestion, high purchase cost, and high operating cost. The lower residential and low industrial densities exacerbate the problem of developing mass transit systems. Large numbers of riders are needed to support transit corridors. With low-density land use, many people are beyond reasonable walking distances to mass transit stops. Dial-a-bus and minibus systems have not yet been demonstrated to be viable alternatives.

Highways are generally classified into express systems, major arterial systems, collector street systems, and local street systems. Expressways with limited access have average user trip lengths of over three miles. They are generally spaced about three miles apart, and they constitute up to 8 percent of an urban area's street system. Major arterial streets have average trip lengths of over one mile. Collector streets have average trip lengths of under one mile. The major arterial and the collector streets together constitute between 20 and 35 percent of the street systems in American municipalities. Local streets are primarily related to access and only secondarily related to movement. Average trip length is under one-half mile. These local streets constitute 65 to 80 percent of America's urban roadways (de Chiara and Koppelman, 1975).

Open space planning

Urban open spaces are identified throughout the course of urban history. Many open spaces in Babylon and Rome were private (Dober 1969). In the Middle Ages and Renaissance, forests, green spaces and other open spaces were associated with manor houses and castles. At the end of the nineteenth century, particularly in England, some paternal industrialists designed cities in a utopian-like manner with considerable open green space. The founding of Port Sunlight in England in 1889 illustrates this type of development. Ebenezer Howard's garden city movement illustrates a further emphasis on the open space and park ideology. In America, landscape architect Olmstead and others gave specific leadership to the design and development of parks. New York's Central Park, San Francisco's Golden Gate Park, Chicago's Lake Front Park, and the New Orleans City Park are all examples of this emphasis. In the 1930s Frank Lloyd Wright developed the concept of Broadacre City. This low-density development would have a maximum green space. In the same year Le Corbusier's *La Ville Radieuse* showed how a high-density vertical development could provide for large amounts of urban green space. The preservation of greenbelts around municipal areas is an old idea that became firmly implemented in the twentieth century, particularly in England.

Outdoor recreation, particularly participated in by urbanites, began to increase in the 1920s and continues in a growth trend. Therefore, planning for regional parks and wilderness areas has expanded. The Outdoor Recreation Resources Review Commission was endorsed by the American Congress. That commission developed projections for leisure time and outdoor recreation through the year 2000. The commission reported its findings in 1962, and partly as a result of its work the Bureau of Outdoor Recreation was established in the U.S. Department of the Interior.

One of the most far-reaching developments for the creation of urban open spaces is the use of clustering in subdivisions. Often clustering is achieved in Planned Developments. A smaller acreage may be used for dwelling units, but the number of units may also be increased. Similarly, there is an economy or reduction in linear street footage. The reduction in overall acres for building sites may be used to increase open space for recreation amenity.

The sharing of common open spaces is the key to this Planned Development design. In the continental United States there were ten acres of land per person at midcentury, but that will decrease to six acres per person by the year 2000. Clustering can continue to insure optimum open space for the larger population.

Both in Hawaii and in California, open-space planning confronts the preservation of views. For example the Manoa District in Hawaii extends from the mountains to Waikiki Beach. The height of structures is specifically regulated to preserve views both to the mountains and to the sea. The entire area is tied together by a linear park system. In the new town of Irvine in southern California, building heights, particularly in the foothills, are regulated for the preservation of views (*Interim Policy Plan of the City of Irvine*).

SUBDIVISIONS

In modern urban history the building of cities has been primarily a matter of surface subdivision of land. There has been only limited subsurface building and limited vertical megastructure building involving considerable air rights use. There are a few examples of subsurface developments, particularly in China, and an increasing number of high-rise vertical developments that are megastructures or near megastructures, for example, the John Hancock and Marina Towers buildings in Chicago.

In most cases the surface subdivision of land is legally guided by municipal subdivision ordinances. The specifics are carried out by the municipality's planning board using techniques for hearings and approvals. Subdivision involves the development of streets and intersections; the provision of off-street parking; the grading of lots; the location of utilities and utility rights-of-way; the development of dead end or cul-de-sac streets; the development of street numbering systems; the location of driveways, sidewalks, and houses; in some cases the location of cluster and/or planned unit developments; and determinations of density (de Chiara and Koppelman 1975). City builders, particularly new-town developers, designate land for residences, industry, commerce, offices, town centers, schools, churches, hospitals, streets, and utilities.

Subdivision planning is old, but its contemporary form in America dates from 1928. At that time the Standard City Planning Enabling Act was published by the United States Department of Commerce. This Act made subdivision regulation a part of comprehensive planning in American cities. Previously fragmented subdivision regulations were transferred from city engineers and surveyors to city planning departments or commissions. From a physical planning point of view, the subdivision regulations of the twentieth century have contributed somewhat to orderly growth and development (Goodman and Freund 1968). Subdivision regulations are normally controlled through plat approval procedures. Planning commissions approve or reject plat maps. Subdivision proposals are reviewed by health officers. This review is to insure that there will be safe water and an adequate sewage disposal system. From the tax official's point of view, subdivision regulations are required to insure adequate land titles. From the city engineer's view, the subdivision regulations make possible the enforcement of safe street design and adequate utility systems. Similarly from the fire chief's view, subdivision regulations make possible the insuring of adequate fire protection along with streets that are large enough for the maneuvering of fire-fighting equipment. School and park officials also review subdivision plans to insure adequate space for these two land-use activities. To the lot purchaser, the subdivision plan assures a buildable site with appropriate orientation and drainage. These elements of subdivision review relate to urban institutions and to the concept of the city as a formal organization.

Subdivision ordinances and enforcement

Subdivision ordinances are legal documents and in effect part of the "police power" of municipalities (Goodman and Freund 1968). They are modifications of the private ownership ideology in America. The Standard City Planning and Enabling Act defines subdivision as "the division of a lot, tract, or parcel of land into two or more lots, plats, sites, or other divisions of land for the purpose, whether immediate or future, of sale or building development." Frequently small subdivisions involving only two or three lots are exempt from this definition.

The Standard Act applies not only to the area within the city limits, but generally enables municipalities to have some regulatory power for a distance of five miles beyond their limits. This is done on the assumption that much land immediately beyond a municipality's political limits will in the future become annexed into the municipality.

It is typical for the municipality's planning agency to be designated as the authority to approve plans. However, a major street plan must normally be approved before the balance of the development plan can be accepted. Accordingly street planning in America becomes one of the most powerful dimensions in city planning. In many respects this exacerbates the economic and social cost for people movement in urban areas. The probability of putting a primary emphasis on pedestrian movement is minimal.

The enforcement provisions of the Standard Act include (1) making the sale of land without an approved plat subject to criminal penalty; (2) authorizing cities to prohibit the sale of unplatted land; (3) making it unlawful to officially record unapproved plans; (4) prohibiting improvements on unapproved subdivisions; and (5) refusing a building permit for unapproved areas (Goodman and Freund 1968). The courts have upheld the constitutionality of subdivision regulations and enforcement provisions.

Subdivision regulations to be most effective must be used in consort with comprehensive plans, official municipal maps, zoning ordinances, and other statements of municipal policies concerning growth, expansion, and redevelopment. Official maps, for example, designate street dimensions with which new subdivisions must ordinarily conform. Zoning ordinances specify minimum lot areas and frontages. Increasingly health and pollution ordinances also specify measures for upgrading subdivisions.

It should be noted that restrictive covenants or deed restrictions are generally not part of the regulatory power of municipalities. Typically they are private forms of contracts specified and entered into by citizens and property owners beneath the level of subdivision regulations and other municipal ordinances. They may specify in greater detail the use of land areas as long as they do not prohibit access to specific categories of people, such as racial minorities.

Subdivision designs are normally executed by a developer preparing a preapplication. These may be sketches showing only the most general details. Next, the preliminary plat is the first official step required of the developer seeking approval. Ordinances specify in considerable detail what is to be shown in a preliminary plat and in more detail what is to be shown on a final plat. Engineering detail and land titles may be shown on the final plat. Unfortunately, the final plat shows little or no direct relationship to social institutions. Social planning is weak to nonexistent in subdivision plan development and often in street design as well. Recently designers of major highways and thoroughfares have been required to address social impact questions, but subdivision plat developers remain exempt from such a planning input.

Subdivision ordinances normally prohibit building in flood plains, where soil and subsoil conditions are unsatisfactory to support structures and/or where there are recognizable dangers for health and safety. Many municipalities require that proposed subdivisions be in general compliance with the municipality's or the region's comprehensive plan. There are frequent requirements specifying that subdivisions must be coordinated with neighboring areas, particularly as these concern street connections, utilities, drain facilities, and open spaces. Conspicuously absent are requirements related to social interaction, schools, social welfare, health, and jobs.

Subdivisions normally specify in great detail the names of streets, drives, lanes, circles, places, ways, avenues, and courts. Subdivision regulations normally specify lot size and setbacks in detail. By the second half of the twentieth century normal minimum lot frontages varied between 60 and 70 feet with a minimum area of 6,000 square feet per single family. During earlier periods lot sizes were considerably smaller. The increased lot size tends to depedestrianize urban areas, increase the need for private transportation, and accelerate greatly the cost of public transportation.

Subdivision regulations further specify the amount of time that can lapse for improvements to be made. Improvement schedules include items like grading lots and roads, providing storm drainage facilities, providing water supply and fire hydrants, providing municipal sanitary sewage, road surfacing, sidewalk building, curb-guttering, street light installation, provision of recreation facilities, providing off-street parking, and landscaping. Again, elements of social consideration and social planning are conspicuously absent in typical subdivision time schedules. In some cases the city planning commission may persuade subdivision developers to dedicate land for school sites, parks, playgrounds, or other related social facilities.

Many types of land use are intended to be regulated in subdivision development but seldom in fact are. Among these are cemeteries, where subdivision regulations are grossly inadequate. Cemetery developments are frequently even exempt from plan approvals. Many commercial subdivisions, industrial subdivisions, mobile home subdivisions, hillside subdivisions, and waterfront subdivisions may be largely exempt from rigorous planning board scrutiny. In other words, subdivision regulations are ineffectively organized to deal with unconventional layouts of land use. All of this underscores the inadequacy of subdivision regulations.

Due to the rapid increase in the mobile home industry in the 1950s and 1960s in America, special subdivision attention had to be directed to design sites for their location. After some investigation it was determined, for example, that the layout of mobile homes on angled lots, rather than on lots perpendicular to streets, gave occupants the most favorable views (Bair and Bartley 1960). Less attention has been given to planning mobile home parks in clusters so that small, intimate groupings might be provided, particularly for convenience in child care. A major problem facing subdivision layouts for mobile homes continues to be their lack of public acceptance. Often the greater amount of attention continues to be focused on the designation of buffer areas between mobile home locations and other more conventional land uses.

The hillside subdivision has increased in prestige and importance since the 1950s in the United States. By definition a hillside subdivision is considered to be in a location with an average drop of fifteen feet or more in one hundred feet. This kind of subdivision is particularly prevalent in places like California where there has been concerted pressure brought against urban growth in the flat, fertile agricultural valley areas like Santa Clara (Taylor 1969). There has also been a prestige demand for the dramatic setting and views provided from the mountainsides. Nevertheless the problems of street collapse and residential failures are notable. Landslides due to erosion, fills, different soil types, and so forth all become major problems. The provision of water and sewage is problematic and costly in some hillside subdivisions. To overcome many of these problems, regulations demand that lot sizes vary significantly with the slope of the hill, the amount of landfilling, and the type of soil. As always, the major subdivision issues tend to be physical rather than social.

On balance one may summarize the impact of subdivision ordinances as being more important in theory than in fact. Often they are combined with overzoning, spot zoning, variances, exceptions, lax administration, and limited inspections. When all of these are combined with the inadequate focus on social planning, the subdivision often becomes at best a physical designer's proposal for residential prestige (Haar and Wingo 1963).

Planned Unit Developments

The Planned Unit Development (or Planned Development) is an outgrowth of a garden-city movement following World War II. By definition the PUD is a project including the following characteristics: residential units are grouped in clusters to maximize open space; different types of residential areas are involved (usually townhouses, apartments, and detached units); higher densities are planned than in single-family projects; frequently part of the land use is for nonresidential purposes, particularly convenience shopping and recreational spaces.

The Planned Unit Development is a major modification of previous zoning and subdivision regulations to which specified lot sizes, setbacks from streets, side setbacks, and rear setbacks were applied. The Planned Unit Development makes possible zero lot lines and the moving of structures to one side of a lot, thereby maximizing the use of physical land on the remaining sides of the structure. Cul-de-sacs are often incorporated into the physical planning of PUDs. More emphasis is placed on pedestrian ways, and the separation of pedestrian paths from auto traffic. PUD land uses reduce the miles of streets to be constructed, as well as the amount of sewage lines, water lines, and other utility hookups. PUD land developments can be high-rise, middle-rise, or single-story developments (*Planned Unit Developments* 1969). Theoretically PUDs are cheaper for builders, and should be cheaper for buyers as well. Planned Unit Developments are amenable to new towns, suburbs, and urban renewal alike.

The cluster development is closely related to the PUD. It has similar advantages in shorter streets and shorter utility lines. It maximizes the open spaces or green space available for pedestrian ways and parks. Cluster development is used for high-rise residential units as well as for single-story ones.

The major problems associated with the Planned Unit Development and its variation, the cluster development, have to do with management and maintenance of open spaces. PUDs and their variant forms require some kind of property owner association involving regular monthly charges for maintenance. They are a fundamental deviation from the ideology of private land ownership. They have the social organizational advantages, however, of combining higher densities with open spaces. They support communal living and social interaction. PUDs and cluster developments in effect facilitate the feasibility of public transit systems and sociophysical developments.

NEW TOWN LAND USE

New town land use categories follow a clear pattern. The types of land use generally include residential, open space, commercial, industrial, institutional, and roadway (Bailey 1972; Mields 1973). American new-town land use patterns are similar to those in Europe (Osborn and

Whittick 1969; von Hertzen and Spreiregen 1973). They generally follow the garden-city model, which is low-density, with maximum green space, and implicitly antiurban.

Many new towns on both sides of the Atlantic have demonstrated remarkable innovation in using Planned Unit Developments, clustering, and superblocks. Many new towns have designed their land use to provide for small neighborhoods clustered into large communities and several communities combined to constitute the total new town. At the neighborhood level emphasis is placed on high degrees of social interaction and maximization of pedestrian traffic, particularly to schools, convenience shopping centers, churches, and related facilities. In the European new towns, considerable land use planning is directed to public transit as a primary means of moving people. This is particularly illustrated in Runcorn, England, where the public transit system is designed to bisect most communities so that citizens will have a convenient walking distance between the transit stops and their places of residence. By sharp contrast, in America most new towns have either no public transit or minimized public transit. Some have attempted innovative dial-a-bus programs. Nevertheless, the general low densities and convenient street provisions for automobiles tend to reduce the effect of innovative bus systems. Children and adult walking trip distance calculations are nevertheless a part of new-town land use planning (Bailey 1972).

In American new towns, the percentage of land devoted to the several land uses varies considerably (see Table 8–1). Approximately 25 percent of the land area is devoted to parks and open space. Nearly 40 percent is devoted to residential use. Other uses vary widely, and religious use is specified only once.

New towns in the past twenty-five years have tended to be highly systematic in growth by stages. Land use development is systematically planned to increase every four to five years so that the new towns will normally be completed in a twenty-year period. Finally it must be observed that land use planning in new towns, more than in subdivisions, is oriented to formal social organization. For example, more emphasis is placed on land for health facilities, for educational institutions, for cultural and entertainment facilities, for indoor and outdoor recreation spaces, for religious buildings, as well as for law enforcement and public safety. Land use is systematically planned in relation to social institutions.

IMPLICATIONS

Land use and subdivision regulations are influenced by ideologies of

TABLE 8—1   Land Use in Selected United States New Towns

Land Use Categories	Cedar-Riverside	Flower Mound	Jonathan	San Antonio Ranch
Residential	25%	50%	29%	45%
Commercial	3	6		2
Industrial		9	24	13
Cultural	2	2		
Parks	17	21	28	24
Streets	19	5	6	7
Educational		5	4	4
Institutional	34			
Religious			1	
Other		2	8	5
	100	100	100	100

public ownership and private ownership. In spite of these ideologies, social institutions need to be systematically provided for in the land use of large urbanized areas.

Comprehensive planning and zoning are essentially new experiences in large metropolitan areas and are even newer on a regional basis. Increasingly municipalities and metropolitan regions are societal in size. Effective land use therefore can be enhanced when it is planned and managed at a societal level.

Subdivision of land in small spaces within municipalities can facilitate social interaction. To date most subdivisions are based on physical design with only minimal social and behavioral consideration. Accordingly, most subdivision regulations of the past twenty-five years have contributed little to the systematic growth of urban areas as formal organizations.

The land-use experience in new towns is closest to a viable perception of urban development along formal organizational lines. To date, however, most new towns have been small, indeed satellites to larger metropolitan areas. They are subsocietal. To that extent they are greatly dependent on the larger and older urban populations near them. Nevertheless, the new-town model is very useful for understanding urban areas in their organizational context. Land-use planning generated along the lines of the larger new-town developments is instructive for high-quality urban environments.

REFERENCES

BAILEY, J. (Ed.), *New Towns in America*. New York: Wiley, 1972.
BAIR, F. H., JR., & BARTLEY, E. *Mobile Home Parks in Comprehensive Community Planning*. Gainesville, Fla.: University of Florida, 1960.
CHAPIN, S. *Urban Land Use Planning*. Urbana: University of Illinois Press, 1970.
DANTZIG, G. B., & SAATY, T. L. *Compact City*. San Francisco: W. H. Freeman, 1973.
DE CHIARA, J., & KOPPELMAN, L. *Urban Planning and Design Criteria*. New York: Van Nostrand, 1975.
DOBER, R. P. *Environmental Design*. New York: Van Nostrand, 1969.
DOXIADIS, C. A. The great urban crimes we permit by law. *Ekistics*, 1974, *38*, 85–88.
GALLION, A. B., & EISNER, S. *The Urban Pattern*. New York: Van Nostrand, 1963.
GOODMAN, W., & FREUND, E. *Principles and Practice of Urban Planning*. Washington, D.C.: International City Managers Association, 1968.
GOTTMANN, J. The evolution of urban centrality. *Ekistics*, 1975, *39*, 220–27.
HAAR, C. M., & WINGO, L., JR., *Cities and Space*. Baltimore: Johns Hopkins University Press, 1963.
HUNTOON, M. C., JR. *PUD: A Better Way for the Suburbs*. Washington, D.C.: The Urban Land Institute, 1971.
Interim Policy Plan of the City of Irvine. Tustin, Calif.: Haworth and Anderson, n.d.
MIELDS, H., JR. *Federally Assisted New Communities*. Washington, D.C.: Urban Land Institute, 1973.
Minnesota Experimental City. Minneapolis: University of Minnesota, Experimental City Project, 1969.
NEWMAN, O. *Defensible Space*. New York: Macmillan Co., 1972.
OSBORN, F. J., & WHITTICK, A. *The New Towns*. Cambridge: M.I.T. Press, 1969.
Planned Unit Development. New York: New York City Planning Department, 1969.
RODY, M. J., & SMITH, H. H. *Zoning Primer*. West Trenton, N.J.: Chandler-Davis Publishing Co., 1968.
SOLERI, P. *Arcology*. Cambridge: M.I.T. Press, 1969.
TAYLOR, L. *Idea People*. Chicago: Nelson-Hall, 1975.
TAYLOR, L. *Urban-Rural Problems*. Los Angeles: Dickenson Publishing Co., 1969.
TAYLOR, L., & BUSAM, T. Farm land and planned urban areas: a socio-physical planning model. Paper read at the Fourth World Congress for Rural Sociology, Torun, Poland, August, 1976.
U.S. Bureau of the Census. *Census of Population: 1970, Detailed Characteristics*. Final Report PC(1)-D1, U.S. Summary. Washington, D.C.: U.S. Government Printing Office, 1973, 723.
VON HERTZEN, H., & SPREIREGEN, P. D. *Tapiola: Finland's New Garden City*. Cambridge: M.I.T. Press, 1973.

PART FOUR

Urban Problems and Institutions

In this section urban problems are examined with a special view toward their amelioration. Urbanization is a very new social experience. It is still very much in the process of development, and is characterized by swift and far-reaching changes. Problems abound but so do prospects.

Many urban problems exist because large numbers of people still have a small, subsocietal view of cities. Moreover, many adult urban residents were socialized in their early life in small towns or rural areas. Problems of longer life and very large populations impact heavily on urban areas. Cities have an aura of glamour and delight, yet for many people a reality of squalor and poverty.

Most of the world's large urban areas are societal in size. Yet the only real notion of city-states we have is historic — from Greece, when cities were of subsocietal size. Chapters nine through twelve examine problems of housing, jobs, transportation, education, religion, art, recreation, health, welfare, and crime — each at an urban societal level. The reader is encouraged to consider possible problem solutions in this broad perspective.

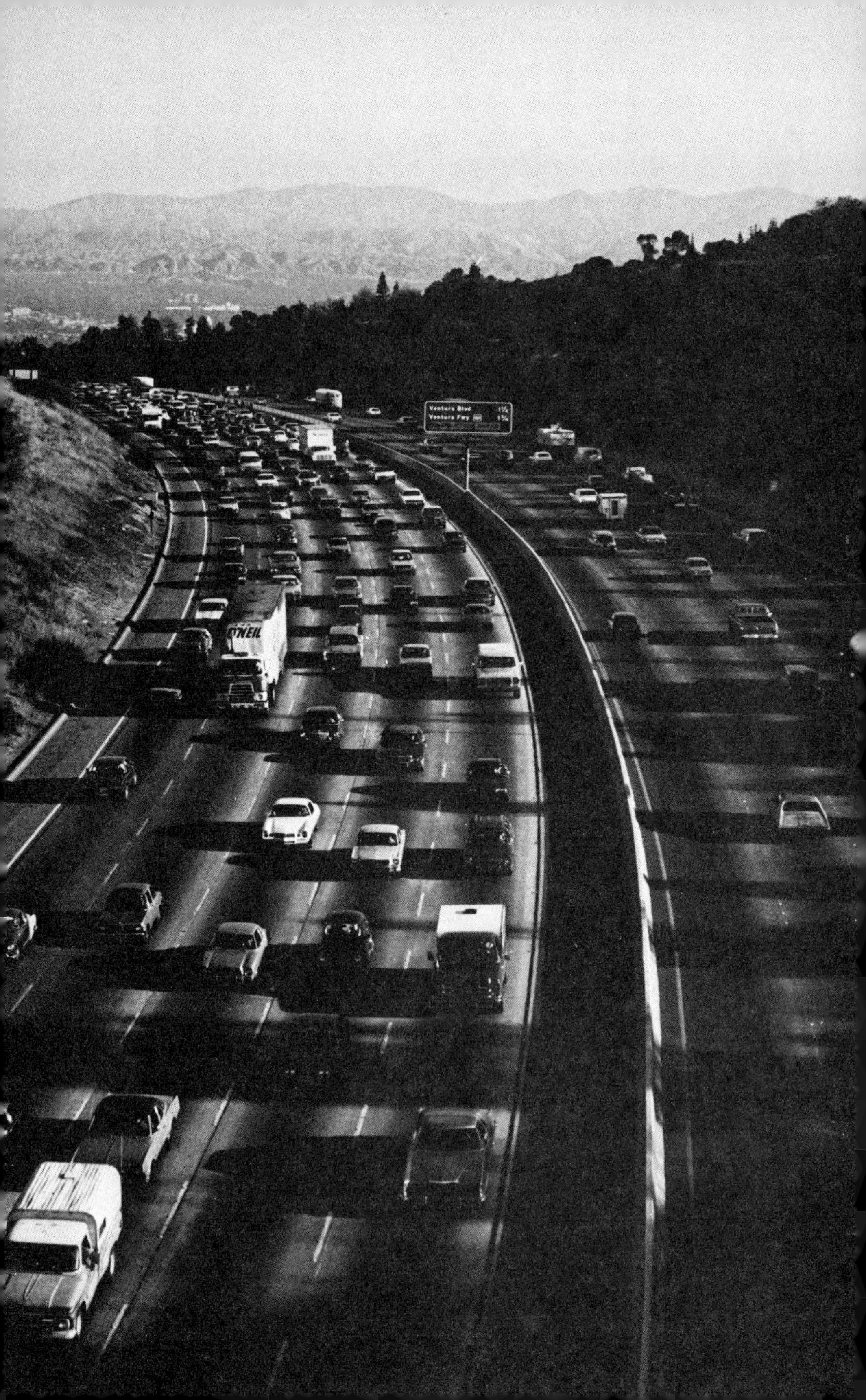
Ventura Blvd
Ventura Fwy
O'NEIL

Housing, Jobs, and Transportation

9

In urbanized and post-industrializing nations, housing, jobs, and transportation all constitute problems. They are urban activity systems that need to be planned more on a regional basis in order to achieve the highest quality environment for a maximum number of people. These were not major problems in early cities, but they have become critical issues with urbanization.

ISSUES

By the end of the twentieth century, in the world's urbanized nations most people will reside in large urban places. In the capitalist nations, only a small proportion of the urban population will live in government-owned housing. The national governments, more than the municipal governments, subsidize public housing. In the case of the United States, the U.S. Department of Housing and Urban Development requires most large municipalities to have a low-income housing plan in order to qualify for many different types of federal financial assistance. All such housing, however, accommodates but a small fraction of urban residents. America also indirectly subsidizes much middle-income housing by tax laws that allow mortgage interest tax deductions and by interstate highway programs. In the noncapitalist countries, housing is massively provided by the government, but more housing planning is national than municipal (Di Maio 1974). In effect, cities as such provide little housing.

Superhighways represent both urban prospects and problems. (Photo: Peter O'Brien for The Stockmarket.)

By the 1970s most people worked at jobs in or near municipalities. But municipalities are not organized to plan for jobs. In both capitalist and noncapitalist nations, municipalities employ a minority of the urban labor force. This situation is illustrated in the case of the United States. There are over 87 million Americans in the labor force. Less than 2 million of them are employed by municipalities. In 1960 when the nation had 68 million people in its labor force, only 1.4 million were municipal employees (*Municipal Yearbook, 1974*).

Municipalities universally provide street systems. Only a minority provide public transportation systems, and these transit systems move a minority of the urban population. Moreover, urban transportation systems that carry a municipality's name may not be owned and/or controlled by the municipality.

Housing and residential meanings

Adequate housing for urban populations is one of the indexes of a high-quality environment — indeed of civilization itself. With the rapid urbanization of the past one hundred years, the task of building housing has lagged behind population growth. It constitutes one of the basic urban problems. In a formal sense a few municipalities control a little housing, and most control none at all. It is typical for municipalities to pass ordinances governing new building standards and specifying conditions for occupancy. But municipal regulations have done little to upgrade substandard residential units, although some effort has been made in this regard. Even more critically, municipalities can do little to stimulate the construction of new housing.

Municipal officials in general, and urban planners in particular, have attempted to give leadership direction to housing densities. Nevertheless, residential densities remain largely related to social values like prestige, to the general affluence of municipal areas, and to the transportation systems. Accordingly, in urban areas where people value separating place of work from place of residence and value low density, expensive commuting patterns are generated. This has meant that as the old industrial and urbanized nations move toward suburbanization and post-industrialization, deteriorating and less prestigeful residential areas are found in central cities while new, expensive, and prestige residential areas are found in suburbs.

Urban renewal is a worldwide technique for reducing the imbalance of central city and suburban housing quality. Often urban renewal involves national subsidizing of residential construction and occupancy. When the amortization of residential units is tied to the ability to earn, and when city revenues are largely tied to property taxes, then the urban social system is thrust out of balance. Low-income populations grow in increasing proportions in the subsidized housing of big cities, while the affluent move to the suburbs. Theoretically at least, the more affluent suburban population in the more expensive property generates a reasonably adequate tax base for providing suburban services. In the older central cities, much of the subsidized housing is removed from tax roles. The earning power of its occupants is low. Forrester points out in *Urban Dynamics* (1968) that there is little possibility for satisfactorily operating the large and old central cities when the housing generates an increase in low-income and ghetto populations and accelerates the movement of professional and affluent people to suburbs. Viewing world housing as a whole, Abrams (1968) writes that by 2000 it is a safe bet that most people will live in slums.

Sociophysical planners confront two major issues concerning housing. First is the question of separating or integrating places of work and places of residence. Both urban populations and urban planners lack agreement concerning whether separation of places of work and residence creates a higher quality environment than their integration. If a society or an urban region is sufficiently affluent in time and in commuting technology (as well as in the energy resources needed to operate cars of the commuting transportation system), then it is a question of time and motion planning efficiency. Without this affluence, significant amounts of housing integrated with other urban service areas will contribute to a higher quality social life.

The second issue concerns an adequate distribution of social and occupational classes of people throughout an urbanized area to operate an optimally high-quality environment for most citizens. Some of the specific norms concerning this last issue are expressed in the language of open housing rights, technological breakthroughs for constructing higher quality housing at lower costs, and the provision of privacy and security in places of residence. In major cities over much of the urbanized world, access to high prestige, to high paying jobs, to affluency for transportation systems, and to opportunities for education (neighborhood schools versus integrated schools) are a few of the conflict situations which have segregated urban people into big-city slums and affluent suburbs. If municipalities and urbanized regions are to be effective systems, then residential units must be interfaced with the total urban fabric and distributed throughout urban areas.

Even with rapidly growing world population, urban planning can continue to provide for some degree of citizen choice between high-density and low-density living. Moreover, systematic urban planning can facilitate choice between high- and low-density living by age cycles. Residential neighborhoods based on territoriality are more significant for youngsters under age ten and for persons over age sixty than for people in the middle years. As both male and female adults enter the labor force, most nonsleeping hours are spent outside of residential neighborhoods, particularly where they are separated from places of work, commerce, and recreation.

The meaning of residential spaces varies considerably. Among the more affluent, residence serves largely for status. Square footage per person is high. Much provision is made for privacy, personal cleanliness, food preparation, and leisure. Many of these spaces may receive little or no use during many hours in a typical day or many days in a typical week.

Among the lower socioeconomic urban classes, Gans (1962) and Rainwater (1966) report that security and privacy are primary values. Gans particularly focuses on differential male-female uses of interior residential spaces. Among the upper-lower classes from Boston, he finds that females want large kitchen areas, which are used as much for social gatherings as for food preparation. Males want an adjacent but separate living-room-type area for social relaxation.

Different types of exterior spaces are desired adjacent to residences. In Boston's West End, Gans reports that teenage girls want to be where they can view teenage boys for conversational purposes, but otherwise be spacially separated. For the lower class, particularly in the St. Louis, Missouri Pruitt-Igoe housing project, Rainwater discovered that play areas for very young children must be proximic to the mother's supervision (McCue 1973). Play areas for slightly older children may be somewhat removed, but need to be outfitted with recreational equipment and toilets.

Exterior residential spaces can contribute to social or antisocial behavior. Newman (1972) found that long, windowless halls (called "double-load" halls) in high-rise buildings reduce sociability and increase indefensibleness. Wood (1961) submits that middle-rise residential units with large exterior hallways can provide places for infant care, for children to interact in small play groups, and for adults to come to know each other in social rather than antisocial ways. Also cul-de-sac and superblock designs contribute to positive social behavior for persons who want to identify with territorial neighborhoods.

Social and physical planners need to design spaces for residences in accordance with the age structure of their anticipated occupants.

Jobs and income distribution

Much employment and unemployment data are produced for municipal areas. If employment is high it reflects well on the municipality and is used by Chamber-of-Commerce-type organizations to bring positive recognition. When unemployment is high there is a negative reflection cast upon the municipality.

Urban employment problems are exacerbated by the increasing maldistribution of jobs. High paying and more professional jobs are proliferating most in suburban areas, and low paying manual jobs remain or increase in the core areas of large central cities. In other cases the maldistribution of jobs is made worse by commuting. A disproportion of highly trained professional and service workers may reside in suburban areas and commute to the best jobs in the central city. Few of the central city blue-collar and low-income workers commute to suburbs.

The distribution of jobs between central cities and suburban areas is a matter of conflict. As an attempted solution, some city planners and new town planners have tried to design adequate space in their land use planning for industrial and business areas to generate jobs sufficient for the population expected. In some countries like England, Japan, and the Soviet Union, industrial location as well as industrial expansion and contraction are extensively controlled for adequate job distribution.

In the United States the need for equitable job distribution in urban areas became so critical in the 1970s that the U.S. Department of Labor provided funding to municipal governments and regional governments for manpower planning. This planning is direct manipulation of part of the urban social system. But the American record of achievement in urban manpower planning is limited because municipalities and manpower agencies have no authority over industrial, governmental, and business expansion and contraction.

Unemployment rates for minorities, youth, the aged, and other disadvantaged persons remain higher in the big central cities than in the newer surrounding suburban areas. Municipal officials now offer charismatic leadership in attempts to stimulate job expansion. If the municipalities or metropolitan regions were in fact to become formal organizations, they would have significantly more input related to job creation.

Training is still another issue which must be confronted by municipalities and urban regions if they are to adequately plan for manpower. Most job-training schools and programs are located in cities. However, municipalities typically have little or no input related to training programs even when they utilize the city's name. Further, municipalities regulate neither the age of entry nor the age of retirement from jobs. Child labor laws, equal employment opportunity laws, and retirement rules are promulgated at state and national levels.

Other critical issues in planning for jobs in urban areas concern the type of work, the hours of work, and the amount of pay. For example, planning consultants to Flower Mound New Town (in the Dallas, Texas metropolitan area) confronted these matters in a post-industrializing framework. Several elements in the planning of that new town were manipulated. Considering the possibility of cybernation, planning consultants to Flower Mound recommended the anticipation of a shortened work week, more females in the labor force, more hours for recreation, more families with fewer children, and more married couples with no children. They also anticipated a commuting distance of approximately twenty-five miles daily. Finally the Flower Mound consultants recommended planning for the professional and clean industrial jobs which will be characteristic of mind societies.

British urban planners have a more controlled social system within which they can plan jobs. To a considerable extent industrial location, expansion and contraction are all regulated by the central government in London. However, in most urbanized nations industrial-business planners face no directives to interface their plans with job training programs and vice versa. Municipalities and urbanized regions fall far short of being a formal organization in which planners can maximize people's opportunities by integrating the major elements of the labor force system. This would necessitate urban sociophysical planners' being able to recommend not only industrial-business sites and school sites, but also amounts and types of job training. Particularly on the urban regional level, planning recommendations for job training at secondary, college, and professional levels must be made if the highest quality environment is to be achieved. Related projections must also be made for on-the-job training.

In most urbanized areas, jobs constitute the mechanism by which society distributes the goods and services for human survival. Jobs are critically related to urban ecology and to social class. This is significantly illustrated by data which show that family income inequality is greater in large urban areas, defined as Standard Metropolitan Statistical Areas, than in non-SMSA counties (Foley 1977). In many urbanized societies young people are expected to take entry-level jobs at low prestige and low pay. As they progress chronologically through their lives they are expected to compete for higher paying and higher prestige levels of work.

As urbanized societies move in a post-industrializing direction, occupations will become less diversified and more aggregated into professional and/or mind type work (Taylor and Sutaria 1975). In the urbanized mind societies, there is growing evidence that the body of knowledge used in an occupational lifetime does not totally exist in what has been the typical training period, namely from ages fourteen to twenty-two. Given this situation, urban planners must reject the old manpower model, which was to train for the first eighteen to twenty-two years, work for the next forty to forty-five years, and retire for the last ten to fifteen years. A new manpower training model must emphasize job training for those aged fourteen to twenty-eight and a mixture of work, job training, and education for persons ages seventeen to fifty, plus a longer period of retirement (Taylor 1976) (see Figures 9–1 and 9–2). Specifically this means that urban planners must anticipate a shorter work week with more workers who will be off the job and in training one day a week, one week a month, or one month a year — as appropriate to their skill level. Between 1990 and 2000, urban planners should project larger populations to fill industrial and business jobs. Also, larger populations should be anticipated in job training because of a societally accelerated system of sabbatic type retraining or upgrading experiences. And with possible trends toward zero population growth, urban planners should anticipate more females in the labor force.

Figure 9–1 Traditional Manpower Model

Train 4 to 8 years	Work 40 to 45 years	Retire 10 to 15 years

Figure 9–2 A New Manpower Model

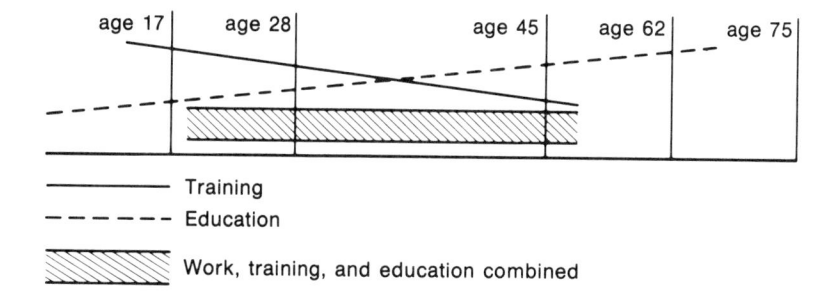

———— Training
– – – – – Education
▨▨▨▨ Work, training, and education combined

Transportation and movement

In less than two hundred years the impact of transportation on cities has been revolutionary. The first locomotive was used at the beginning of the nineteenth century and the first automobile at the end of that century. Trains, cars, and planes have transformed human settlements. In pedestrian cities people could cover distances of about two miles or the equivalent of walking for about thirty minutes. With mass transit and jet travel, it is possible for the world to be one large urban system (Wedgwood 1966; Doxiadis 1970).

Super roadways have become a worldwide phenomenon in the second half of the twentieth century (Larson 1964). A worldwide network of super highways facilitates the growing ecumenopolis — worldwide city. The massive highway systems stimulate strip urban growth.

In 1882 Arturo Soria y Mata proposed the development of a linear city along the transportation and service core. A small model of the Cuidad Lineal was built in suburban Madrid. However, at about the same time, Ebenezer Howard proposed the more circular and traditional garden city, and it has attained worldwide acceptance since the middle 1940s. Nevertheless, with international highway development, the prospects for linear cities now increase.

Transportation, like housing and jobs, is a major urban activity system. Even prior to the energy crisis of the middle 1970s the interface of roads with housing and the social environment of cities increased in importance. In planning new towns, in suburbanization, and in urban renewal, statistics concerning population densities in transportation channels determine the feasibility of mass transit. Improved transportation is a major component for high-quality environment in the future.

Housing, jobs, and transportation all interface as social problem issues and as social prospects in an urbanizing world.

HOUSING AND ACTIVITY SYSTEMS

Housing is a major activity system, the primary purpose of which is to provide adequate residences for urban citizens, places for child rearing, and spaces for family social interaction. Housing is also designed to provide some space for food preparation, sleeping, and health care. From another perspective, housing is an activity system for employing construction and maintenance workers.

In the West in general and in America in particular, the housing system is dominated by a private property land ownership ideology. A person's house is viewed as a "castle." People want unrestricted rights to use housing and to dispose of it at their will. Accordingly, private ownership of housing ranges as follows: 77 percent in Yugoslavia, 62 percent in Hungary, 61 percent in the United States, 60 percent in Finland, 60 percent in Ireland, 53 percent in Norway, and 50 percent in Czechoslovakia, Italy, and Belgium. By contrast, low housing ownership in the West is found in the Netherlands, 29 percent; West Germany, 35 percent; Sweden, 36 percent; and Switzerland, 44 percent (*HUD International Brief* 1971).

There is increasing pressure on national and municipal governments to improve housing quality where private capital fails in the task (Abrams 1968). Indeed in the Soviet Union one of the first decisive actions after the 1917 Revolution was the nationalization of housing. The physical property was transmitted to the City Soviets for distribution. There was also a banning of private real estate transactions (Pawley 1971).

There are two major conditions that confound systematic efforts in planning for high-quality housing. First, the physical units are generally built to last between forty and sixty years, or for two to three generations. In that long a time period, technology related to housing construction changes considerably. New housing units may be more feasible than renovating or updating old units. Sociologically there are also many changes in family structure in a two-to-three-generational period. Housing needs now are different from those of three generations ago. This is illustrated in the case of the United States by the birth rate plunge from over twenty-five per one thousand in the 1950s to under fifteen in the 1970s. The number of bedrooms needed for child rearing is reduced. During the 1950s four-bedroom and larger housing was desired, and by the 1970s such units had become too large. Some imaginative housing design efforts have been developed to allow for adding on bedrooms and removing them at different stages in the life cycle, but none of these have become widely accepted. In addition to changes in birth rates, there are ongoing changes in family systems. Some suggest that by 1990 the "parenthood is fun" myth will be dead, and that in fact most married couples will have no children at all. A few marrieds will have large families, and their primary contribution to society will be that of procreating and rearing children. Most people will need small residential units, and the childrearing families large ones (Davids 1971).

Second, some observe that in capitalistic economies the subsidizing of low-cost housing for low-income people confounds systematic efforts to improve the quality of the environment. The subsidized housing programs may, on the surface, be viewed as "gifts" to the city from larger governments. In effect, the low-income subsidized housing is occupied disproportionately by persons who are unemployed and who have low education, poor health, and high birth rates. These individuals are the least likely to be able to support a large number of children. Their lifestyle becomes a drain on municipal services. The subsidized housing is in effect pronatal. It is seldom accompanied with adequate health care, job provision, and remedial education (Forrester 1968).

Housing activity systems must be viewed as an integral part of national societal systems. In America, for example, the housing industry alone provides for over a million on-site jobs annually. This is a large single category of workers (Meyerson 1962). In the last two decades American new housing starts have been in the magnitude of two million annually. Residential areas provide 50 percent of the local tax revenue and are the largest single item in local capital improvements.

Old housing far outweighs the importance of new housing in total residential units. In America older housing constitutes 97 percent of the supply in any one year. Some dilapidated housing is removed, particularly from older cities, and replaced with new housing. However, most new housing is largely of the single-family detached type and is located in new suburban areas where childrearing is a major consideration for middle-income people. By the 1970s America's stock of housing units totaled over sixty million. Most were in cities and suburbs. The proportion of farm residences is small. Second homes for vacation purposes are still few but are increasing in number. Home ownership and single-family detached units still dominate in America.

Typically, American homes are constructed by small builders who erect fewer than twenty-five houses per year. But all of this is changing. Apartments, cluster homes, and condominiums are increasing. Large-scale residential building and prefabrication are increasing. Technology for large-scale building is advanced. Trade unions and outdated building codes contribute major barriers to significant mass production of housing units.

There is an increase in the trend toward megastructures. In Chicago, Illinois the John Hancock Center and the Marina Towers have important megastructure characteristics. New York's Olympic Tower is another example of the developing megastructure idea.

The systems for housing in urbanized society are in their infancy. Their prospects for change and improvement in support of high-quality human environment are many.

Housing conditions

Housing conditions can provide support for or detract from health, education, work, and family stability. The housing condition in the last quarter of the twentieth century in most of the world's large urban areas is substandard. Many people have abysmal slum housing. Large numbers of inhabitants in cities like Calcutta and Delhi are street people with absolutely no residential space (Mayur 1975). If evidence records that the first famine occurred in Egypt nearly fifty-five-hundred years ago, and if one compares the housing squalor in modern Cairo, the record of human progress is negligible (Pfeiffer 1975).

When Charles Abrams was asked to address the question of the probable condition of housing by the year 2000, he opened his discussion by observing that "there is no sure way of predicting the outcome of the battle between pills and passions or the vagaries of man's capacities for building or destroying" (Abrams 1968, p. 209). Beyond this disclaimer he went on to report that a quarter of the population of the United States of America lives in slums. Moreover, throughout the less developed nations of the world people still build what they call housing with their hands, similar to the processes used some five thousand years ago. In much of Asia, Africa, and Latin America, populations are expected to reach several times their present magnitude by 2000. Building industries there are currently inadequate to meet more than a fraction of residential housing needs. Abrams glumly asserts that in less than three decades most of the world's human population will live in slums, be street sleepers, or live in squatments. Beyond this gloomy prediction, for the twenty-first century there are some more optimistic outlooks. The experience of urbanization is new. The technology for residential unit construction in many respects is rapidly expanding. In the short run, labor union organization and family ideology inhibit the utilization of much of the available technology. In the long run that will change. Densely populated urbanized societies will achieve residential flexibility and environmental recycling to bring the quality of the human environment to new apexes.

For America Abrams suggests a new federal Urban Land-Space Agency. NASA is the model proposed for the new agency. The land-space agency would be empowered to purchase land and to release it for the sytematic extension of urban development. The agency would also have the authority to acquire land in existing cities for planning and redevelopment into relating housing, commerce, industry, and recreation.

As recently as the 1930s local property taxes collected by municipalities were more than the taxes of the national and state governments combined in America. They have dropped to under 10 percent of the total, and now more than 70 percent of the national population lives in cities. This is another way of saying that housing is a societal matter more than it is a municipal or individual problem.

Never before have so many human beings lived together in such high urban densities. During early city development, places of residence and places of work were in proximity. With industrial advances in the West, places of work and residence have become separated. Trains, automobiles, zoning ordinances, communication, and prestige differentials have all contributed to the separation. As one views urban areas organizationally, it becomes clear that the separation of place of work and place of residence is contradictory to the highest quality environment for the largest number of people. Clustering, planned unit development, and megastructures are promising alternatives for improving world urban residential conditions.

Residential use and design

Residential use is insufficiently studied by social scientists. The literature that does exist is biased disproportionately toward middle-class Western family life styles (Riemer 1947). There is an emphasis on privacy. This means for both apartments and detached housing units that there should be separate rooms for bathing, sleeping, food preparation, recreation, and study. From another view, privacy is aimed at reducing overcrowded conditions — often defined as the use of one bedroom by children of the opposite sex beyond the age of ten (Pawley 1971).

Growing out of the crowded tenement condition associated with the new industrial cities in the late nineteenth and early twentieth centuries was a reform movement. This movement proceeded to explore several utopian plans for housing, and finally by the middle of the twentieth century the most widely accepted plan was the garden-city-type development. It implies low densities and maximum open space. In these developments there has been an upper-class bias and a family bias. In the last of the twentieth century as urbanized society moves to a new stage of stability, it is increasingly apparent that many residential units will not be used for family formation purposes — particularly if by that is meant child procreation and rearing. Many husband and wife teams will have no children at all. Many adults will live out longer periods of their life as singles. Many families will send children at an early age to daycare and related centers for much of their socialization and training. Many oldsters will be provided for in retirement communities and other facilities which offer custodial care. For increasingly significant numbers of the urbanized population, residential units will be used primarily for sleeping and personal care more than for child-rearing, social gathering, and food preparation. The extent to which residential units will be used for prestige remains unclear.

Even for that housing which will be used by the most traditional type families, there is a need to provide a built environment that is more supportive of family social interaction. Wood (1961) suggests that even in high-rise housing, people need active exercise, need sunshine and fresh air, need to get "out," need to go somewhere — to shops, to churches, to movies — and need to take care of some household chores like washing cars and repairing bikes. Wood's point is that the physical design of housing should provide for these needs. Newcomers and strangers should be aggregated rather than separated by the design of buildings. Mothers in high rise buildings should be able to observe children at play easily. Exterior balcony corridors may replace the isolating and indefensible interior corridors. This makes possible interaction between mothers and children and also increases the possibility of neighboring. Such exterior corridors are referred to as "sidewalks in the sky" or "backyards in the sky." Design for visibility and social interaction also supports social control. Strangers are integrated into the local activities when they are readily visible.

Loitering is a widespread human activity. It is particularly a part of teenage culture. The physical design even of high-rise buildings can make possible acceptable places for loitering where informal social controls are possible. When no acceptable places for loitering are physically accommodated, unacceptable places are created. Physical design for loitering and recreation at multiple ages is consistent with positive neighborhood building and with building strong informal social control.

Accommodation of human aggregates needs to be considered more in the design of residential structures. Overemphasis is placed on privacy. Urban people are by nature social types. For example, in upper-income housing units, recreation facilities regularly include swimming pools, tennis courts, and cocktail lounges. In lower income and in public housing units, swimming pool and tennis court facilities are among the first items subtracted in a budget crunch. Generally, provision of places for beer drinking is considered culturally unacceptable. Variations on the theme of the English pub are not provided in lower income housing.

Residential design in urban areas must be plural. Many different types of accommodations ranging from high-rise through middle-rise to single detached units are necessary. Subcultures of people will have greater and lesser needs for social interaction in their residential areas. Many persons will have residential needs that vary sharply with different stages in the life cycle.

The physical technology for residential building is often primitive or out of date (Meyerson 1962). In the early 1970s a direct frontal attack was launched by the U.S. Department of Housing and Urban Development to improve residential building technology (Villecco and Dixon 1970). America faces the need to provide nearly three million housing units per year. Its housing construction industry is traditional and small-scale. Accordingly, HUD's Operation Breakthrough was oriented toward the designing and testing of new prototype systems, experimenting with the newly designed systems on selected sites throughout the nation, and moving those that are evaluated as successful into mass production. Over twenty firms were selected to participate in the Breakthrough program. They utilized design teams of engineers, sociologists, management experts, and architects. The prototypes confronted urban renewal needs, high-rise construction, middle-rise construction, and new low-density development areas.

Local building codes and zoning ordinances are major barriers to new housing construction innovation. In order for municipalities to be selected as sites for the prototype development, their governments were required to waive local zoning ordinances and code restrictions. Operation Breakthrough was successful in technological innovation. The techniques, unfortunately, are still only minimally accepted by municipal governments and labor unions. Furthermore, insufficient attention was directed to social changes in life styles. Most of the new residential unit designs anticipated reasonably isolated family social systems in the process of rearing children and other traditional homemaking details.

Residential satisfaction and social class

Residential satisfaction is higher among the upper classes than among the lower classes. Careful analysis reveals that in fact this is influenced most by the ability of the upper classes to have larger activity systems, to travel widely, and to experience many aspects of social life more fully than persons in the lower classes (Popenoe 1973).

Local neighborhoods are important for social control and for the support of child socialization. Particularly for those individuals with the least amount of mobility, physical designs, like cul-de-sacs for example, may increase positive social interaction. Furthermore, physical designs of high-density living which have six or eight residential units sharing common entrance and exit stairwells increase the possibility of security and for help when needed even though they often do not increase regular daily social interaction.

Popenoe (1973) asserts that social class is the most important single variable in understanding residential differences. The lower classes have few choices. The upper classes may obtain homes with low density and rooms for specialty activities. The upper classes may select housing for prestige. Their social interaction is more often on a person-to-person level than on a family-to-family level. Older and more established individuals tend to participate more in social life beyond the neighborhood than do younger persons and new arrivals.

Social class homogeneity, particularly among the lower classes, tends to increase neighboring (Dennis 1963). Working-class neighborhoods are characterized by higher rates of proximic social interaction than middle- and upper-class neighborhoods. This is true on both sides of the Atlantic.

As one moves down in the social class hierarchy, housing satisfaction is increased where there is adequate security. Rainwater (1966) finds that lower class people interact more behind the security of locked doors. They have few complaints about the physical spaces in which they feel secure. There is a high preference for balcony or court spaces directly attached to the residence so that there is a safe opportunity to take the open air. The lower classes prefer to have residential units with six or eight entrance ways and a common hall. This enables people to feel that they can get mutual aid or assistance when necessary. Similar findings are reported for moderate-income housing projects in San Francisco (Cooper 1971). A study of residents in three-story buildings in the center of San Francisco in the St. Francis Square project reveals high satisfaction because buildings are designed around a superblock providing safe play areas for children and conversation spaces for adults. The units are grouped in sixes and use common entrance-exit stairwells. This facilitates acquaintances. More than three-fourths of the families in the units of six knew five other families well enough to call them in an emergency. Also satisfaction was increased in this housing development because it was immediately adjacent to a school. Children even in a big city could walk safely to school. The St. Francis Square Housing Project provided community, parking, laundries, garbage collection, and adjacent school facilities. It received high marks in terms of resident satisfaction.

By contrast the Pruitt-Igoe Project in St. Louis, Missouri was a massive failure. It opened in 1954 – 55 with thirty-three eleven-story buildings. Its 2,700 units were designed to provide housing for 10,000 people. From a social-institutional point of view, the project was incomplete. The living-dining-kitchen areas in the four-bedroom apartments were the same size as those in the two-bedroom apartments. This provided inadequate space for the larger number of inhabitants. There were no balcony spaces for open-air access. Long interior isolating double-load corridor halls were used. These became places for antisocial behavior. There were no toilet facilities provided at the street-level playground areas. Accordingly, entry stairwells were used for bathroom purposes and soon became undesirable spaces.

Condominiums

The condominium as a type of residence is old, dating from ancient Egypt (Berman 1968). In the first century B.C. the Romans established enabling legislation for condominium construction on a large scale (Laney 1970).

The condominium has been extensively used in the Paris area since World War II. There, over 90 percent of new residential development is in condominium units. In Brazil more than half of the office building in recent years has been in condominiums. Prior to the Housing Act of 1960 there was little use of the condominium in the United States of America. But by the middle 1970s some residential condominium development was found in most metropolitan areas. Recently, commercial condominiums have been gradually developing in the United States of America.

Condominiums and cooperatives are similar but different. In condominiums, individual apartment- or unit-owners hold title to their separate spaces and have a share of ownership in a common property. In cooperatives, all occupants have a stock ownership in the total project and no individual unit ownership. In condominiums, individuals have a vote proportionate to the amount of their individual ownership. In cooperatives, each stockholder has one vote regardless of the size or value of his unit. In condominiums, individuals pay property taxes on their own units; in cooperatives, shareholders pay a part of the tax on the entire project. In condominiums, individuals may or may not have a mortgage, while in cooperatives, if there is a mortgage, it is on the entire unit and all individuals are liable for that payment.

Condominiums in the United States are controlled by states rather than by municipalities or the federal government. There is general similarity in the enabling legislation following the Housing Act of 1961, so we illustrate the state laws with a single example. In 1963 the legislature of the state of Texas passed the "Condominium Act" (Hemingway 1966). The Texas condominium form of ownership follows that used more than two thousand years ago. It is also a form which is widely used in Europe and South America currently. The Condominium Act provides for ownership allowing equity growth, interest deductions, depreciation for tax purposes, and theoretically lower costs due to the elimination of landlord profits. In Texas the basic document is a "Declaration of Condominium Regime." The Declaration of Condominium Regime includes: (1) a definition and description of the physical property and its built units; (2) a precise description of the property to be owned by the individual purchaser; (3) a prohibition against waiver of partition of the common facility; (4) a provision for cross-easements; (5) a provision for operation and maintenance upkeep by a council of co-owners; (6) a detailed statement of restriction to maintain the land as a harmonious environment; (7) a provision for collection of expenses for maintenance and upkeep; (8) an enforcement provision due to the failure of property owners to pay proportionate shares of charges; and (9) governing rules regulating by-laws.

From a sociophysical planning point of view, the condominium land use can contribute to curbing urban sprawl and to the achievement of a higher quality urban environment (Kean and Sanders 1963). The condominium property ownership combines the elements of private ownership with cooperative planning and maintenance of common elements like halls, stairways, entrances, exits, basements, yards, gardens, parking areas, storage spaces, elevators, commercial facilities, and recreational facilities (Ashby and Bailey 1970). The condominium type of property organization is consistent with the view of urban areas as formal organizations. There continue to be problems, however, as condominium ownership is worked into a formal organization pattern. For example, many states still do not make possible the legal incorporation of the management associations. Also there are many significant problems concerning tort and liability insurance. It appears that each unit property owner may share in liability for negligence in the common property, like halls, stairways, and elevators and for insufficient supervision in recreation areas like pools, playgrounds, and golf courses. Adjustments in these regards need to be made.

As citizens in major urbanized societies increasingly expect governments to assume more leadership responsibility in providing decent housing for all people, a condominium for lower income groups increases as a significant possibility. Well planned and well managed condominiums and cooperatives can be cheaper in initial cost and continual maintenance than individually owned detached units (Hick 1970). Both condominiums and cooperatives are feasible for low-income occupants. They can provide the possibility for dignity in ownership which would otherwise be unavailable to low-income ghetto people ("What Housing Cooperatives Do" 1968). There are both economic and social advantages in cooperative and condominium developments for low-income people. Costs can be reduced in cooperative management of properties. There may also be cooperative food dispensaries related to the housing units. Social advantages include group identity and group participation in the management process. There is a democratic selection of management bodies. The democratically organized management bodies may additionally develop nurseries, daycare centers, summer camps, and recreational programs. In these and many other respects condominium and cooperative ownership interface well with the formal organization of densely populated urban areas.

Condominium property organization is being systematically used to provide residential amenities of high quality so that population may remain in cities ("Professional Condo Merchandizing Helps to Keep 'em in the Cities" 1970). Some condominium units are especially designed and managed to provide residential and recreational space for middle-income families. High-rise developments can provide open space for adequate parking, swimming pools, wading pools, sunbathing, putting greens, tennis courts, shuffleboard courts, and other amenities. As a part of urban renewal programs, small and orderly apartment units may be systematically converted to condominium developments (Miller 1971). The condominium is also a form of property organization suitable for vacation or second homes (Romney 1967; Green 1970).

The condominium residential unit may be a social system in miniature. With a little imaginative planning it can provide not only for residences but for recreation, food service, nursery care, and other types of services.

High-rise

The high-rise physical structures for residences, offices, and related uses are consistent with the urbanizing built environment (Le

Corbusier 1971). The idea of built heights is as old as cities themselves. The Tower of Babel exemplifies this in the early city. Height in cities has often been used to demonstrate religious exaltation. Height in city buildings is often also used for aesthetic purposes. Height in cities is used for ethnocentric symbolic designations as illustrated by the Tower of the Americas in Mexico City (Aregger and Glaus 1967). As urban populations have grown, residential buildings have become increasingly anonymous; builders are unknown, designers are unknown, and house names are replaced by numbers. Some believe that high-rise buildings will increase even more the anonymity of urban life. But some buildings are middle-rise and high-rise "shells" into which individuals may place highly unique and originally designed residences. Isolated examples of high-rise building started both in Europe and America prior to World War II. In New York City, legend has it that department store magnate John Wanamaker built an early high-rise structure to demonstrate that his economic power towered above his competitors' (Aregger and Glaus 1967). Similarly, the Chicago Tribune Building is associated with economic power. Some high-rise building took place in Dusseldorf in 1924 and in Rotterdam in 1929. But in the main, high-rise building did not become a widespread phenomenon until after World War II.

Following the middle 1940s, two opposite directions in residential development were pursued in Europe. One was the garden-city model. More recently, and not promoted by any systematic movement, high-rise residential structures have become widely used. There were social motivations to improve housing quality. The implicit belief was in architectural determinism to improve the environment for human residences. The row housing and subsequent tenement blocks were deteriorating into slums in the face of a growing urban population. Sociological studies determined that migrants to the complex urban environment could adjust and were willing to adjust to densities above those known in agricultural villages, particularly when a high-quality sociophysical environment is provided. The high-rise building seemed justified. Advantages in early high-rises were for single individuals or couples without children. Gradually it was learned how to construct high-rise buildings with facilities adequate for childrearing and family socialization. Moreover, families in large cities tended to be small and thereby capable of accommodating to the advantages of carefully planned high-rise buildings.

The cost of high-rise buildings continues to be higher than that of low-rise buildings. Nevertheless, the reduction in transportation costs for daily movement may outweigh the additional construction cost. Special play areas in the form of roof gardens and platform green space may be provided for children and other persons in high-rise units.

High-rise units are provided for both low-income and high-income people. Much public housing in an area like New York is middle-rise and high-rise, thereby making available green play space for children. Upper-class high-rise buildings are dramatically illustrated in the case of New York's Olympic Tower. There, one-bedroom units start at a purchase price of $122,000 plus a large monthly maintenance charge. Larger eight- and nine-room units typically sell for over $500,000 with monthly charges in the magnitude of an additional $1,000. Out of the world's approximate 4 billion population, it is estimated that only 88,000 people could afford to live in Olympic Tower. Among the amenities in this building are a block-long interior park, a multistory waterfall, and two floors of plush shops. Adequate parking and extensive security are provided as part of the building's amenity package.

The high-rise built environment continues to move in a megastructure direction. A megastructure by definition is a building in which multiple social institutions are provided. The John Hancock Center in Chicago, Illinois is a leading example. This is a 100-story building in which there are some 700 apartments. They range in size from efficiencies to four-bedroom luxury units. Some 800,000 square feet of office space is also available for large and small tenants. Commercial space and lobbies total 300,000 square feet. Additional amenities are restaurants, health clubs, swimming pools, and ice skating rinks. So many services are provided in this megastructure that many residents can spend multiple days or even weeks of their lives there without ever exiting the building. The megastructure, even more than the high-rise in general, articulates well with the planning of urban areas as formal organizations.

Housing in the last of the twentieth century is more than residence. It is an activity system in construction, use, maintenance, and support for total life.

JOBS AND ACTIVITY SYSTEMS

It now appears that by the end of the twentieth century half of the world's population will both work and live in cities. Some five thousand years ago when cities were invented, few people regularly worked and lived in them. In the urban social system of work, cities as such employ but a small proportion of the labor force. For example, in the United States only .02 percent of the labor force was employed by municipalities in 1970. The full-time employees were less than half of this percentage. Municipal employees serve primarily in police protection, fire protection, sanitation work, and education. Nevertheless, the point is that cities as such can do little to create jobs for urban citizens.

Job opportunities in urban areas are primarily controlled by private capital or governmental units much larger than municipalities. Cities are greatly handicapped by a lack of formal direction over job creation and over migration of persons in and out of their corporate limits.

As some large industrial societies become increasingly urbanized, as in the case of the United States, there are dramatic shifts in the location of the labor force. Between 1960 and 1970 both people and jobs moved from central cities to suburban areas. According to the *Manpower Report of the President* 1974,

> By 1970, seventy-two percent of employed suburban residents in the fifteen largest SMSAs worked in suburbs. Moreover, according to the research reports issued by the Commission on Population Growth and the American Future, employment in thirty-nine suburban areas grew from 3.7 million persons in 1948 to 8.1 million in 1967, while employment in the neighboring central cities expanded from 8.9 million to 9.7 million. In other words, the suburban rings absorb eighty-five percent of the new job opportunities in these metropolitan areas. Central cities in the same thirty-nine SMSAs experienced a seventeen percent drop in jobs for production workers between 1948 and 1967, while employment in the suburbs expanded by 1.1 million jobs for fifty-eight percent.

Now it is found that nearly 60 percent of the individuals who live in the suburbs also work in the suburbs.

In addition to population and job shifts from central cities to suburbs there is an imbalance in the type of jobs being shifted. The older central cities retain a disproportionate residue of the relatively unskilled and low-paying jobs. Middle jobs and high-quality jobs are both found in suburbs (Goldsmith and Stockwell 1969).

Urban planning is addressed to both job creation and the nature of jobs. The concern for job creation is illustrated in the case of Calcutta (Lubell 1973). Calcutta is a major industrial, banking, and general economic center for India. Some authorities argue, however, that since before World War II, Calcutta has been a city in great decline. Its large jute-processing industries, metal working shops, engineering industries, and major port activites have all grown and expanded — but insufficiently to meet the need of migrants from rural areas of India and from what was East Pakistan. Additionally, Calcutta is faced with a seasonal migration of rural workers during the periods of the year when agricultural jobs are reduced. Calcutta has a large educated middle class. Analysis of persons who seek employment indicates that 31 percent already hold full-time jobs, but are underemployed. Sixty percent are totally unemployed, and 9 percent of the job seekers have only part-time work. Another element that influences the social system of providing jobs is the absence of adequate transportation. When places of residence and places of work are separated and means of transportation to jobs are inadequate, the unemployment situation is intensified.

Urban social planners analyzing the institutional elements of jobs, residence, education, and transportation can systematically develop models and project techniques for balancing urban populations and jobs. In the planning of a new-town area near Dallas, Texas, planners focused extensively on postindustrializing society trends as they relate to jobs, residence, and transportation (Dykman 1971). Residence, industrial sites, and transportation were projected in view of the declining industrial share of the area's total employment since 1920. Since the 1940s, most manufacturing jobs have been defense related. By 1980 it is anticipated that service and professional jobs will employ more than twice as many workers as goods-producing jobs. Accordingly, for a new-town development that was anticipated for completion by 1990 a disproportionate number of service-professional jobs were anticipated. Furthermore this analysis pointed to the development of multinational corporations and to automation and cybernation which will influence job development in the Dallas-Fort Worth world-oriented metropolitan area. Both job creation and residential life styles in such a new-town area must anticipate a maximum of professional mind-oriented people and a minimum of blue-collar and/or manual-oriented workers with their accompanying life style.

These job-planning assumptions not only relate to urbanization, but also implicitly support megalopolis and ecumenopolis urban patterns as well. Indeed, current urban planning models suggest that human beings will continue to work as a means for obtaining their goods and services for survival. Quality of life in urban areas must, therefore, depend on job adequacy for urban citizens to achieve the means of satisfactory existence.

TRANSPORTATION AND ACTIVITY SYSTEMS

Transportation in urbanized society needs to be considered at two levels. One is the gigantic task of moving mass numbers of people rapidly and efficiently within urbanized areas as well as around the crust of the planet Earth from one urbanized area to another. The second consideration focuses on the pedestrian, on movement in a human scale where foot transit is separated from mechanical transit. It addresses the issues of providing streets for casual walking and for social life, and foot paths and byways for aesthetic amenity and safety. Such pedestrian ways are considered in urban renewal plans, garden-city new towns, and megastructures.

We start with the consideration of massive transportation systems that are suprahuman in scale. Urbanization is said to have developed within the last one hundred years. The urbanized form of human settlements is largely a product of transportation innovation. In the nineteenth century the train and the car were introduced. These two, along with the plane, became massively normative for large-scale people movement in the twentieth century. Initially they seemed to defeat the pedestrian city while generating megalopolis areas and urban regions, and contributing to ecumenopolis. Following World War II, the automobile was supported by the building of a large-scale, worldwide freeway system. Freeways accelerated suburbanization and strip-city development (Larson 1964). The freeway transportation system is a significant step toward the achievement of ecumenopolis. Most auto speeds were slow prior to World War II. Roads were narrow and inadequate even when cars were built for higher speeds. By the middle 1950s the United States passed a National Highway act. This interstate highway system in a decade and a half produced over forty thousand miles of new super roadway networks. This is the most significant single development in urban planning in the United States to date. This North American interstate urbanizing highway system connects with the Pan American highway system. In Europe a continental urbanizing highway system is under development by the direction of a United Nations Economic Commission. The European modern roadway system will encompass thirty thousand miles. Similar United Nations highway initiatives are being planned for Asia, the Middle East, and Africa. Strip urbanization is accelerating along these highway systems. In scope and magnitude today's super highways diminish the significance of those produced by ancient Rome and the early Incas.

With massive intercontinental highway systems, the prospect for the linear city is heightened. Mass transit systems, in consort with intercontinental highway systems and in consort with vertical people movement systems in megastructures, can be combined to achieve high-quality living for urbanites. One of the problems in current transportation planning is that excessive calculations are based on existing transportation technologies rather than on new ones. Freeways can be incorporated into buildings and new urban forms (Halprin 1966). Freeway interchanges can be designed to create a parklike atmosphere while at the same time providing elevation separation for pedestrian and traffic movement. In this sense the roadway itself becomes a part of the built architectural environment of urbanization. Along the freeway there can be green linear parks. While freeways are designed for rapid movement, studies in California suggest that the average distance traveled on them is only six miles. This suggests that freeways are more directly related to their immediate metropolitan area than to connecting major metropolitan areas. Parking design is also related to highway planning (Delvin 1975). Finally, there is federal legislation in the United States which requires that social impact studies be done concerning the site selection and development of highways (*Social and Economic Effect of Highways* 1974).

Pedestrian ways and human scale movements are increasingly being designed in conjunction with major highway systems (Wedgwood 1966). While human beings on foot can no longer cover the distance of the world's great cities, humanized cities still have spaces where pedestrians can interact. This human scale design is physically built in such a way that a half-mile to a mile-and-a-half becomes a pedestrian social life space. Another index is to design urban spaces so that city residents may within a thirty-minute walk reach jobs, theaters, markets, and schools. This is often done by juxtaposing superblocks between and among major highway or transit systems. In this kind of planning, urban residents have the advantages of both rapid movement over multiple mile distances and slow interactional movement in walking spaces.

The pedestrian scale for urban design is accented in megastructure towns like Cumbernauld, Scotland. Rapid transit and the major highway systems connect the new town of Cumbernauld to Glasgow and Edinburgh. Within the town center itself, the megastructure design makes it possible for most residents on a day-to-day basis to satisfy their life needs by walking. Superblocks as a component of urban design are used in such suprahuman-scaled cities as Brasilia and Chandigarh, enabling walking spaces to prevail for many activities.

In other examples of humanizing transit scale, one may cite the funicular as used to move people up and down the hillsides in cities like Bergen, Norway. From the waterfront to the hilltops, the Bergen funiculars give residents a human and breathtaking view. Mall development in major cities, as illustrated by the closing of traffic on Minneapolis' Nicollet Avenue and on Copenhagen's main commercial streets, show pedestrian scales interfaced with major metropolitan areas. Additionally shopping centers and specialty centers are being built around pedestrian enclosed areas with automobiles relegated to peripheral parking lots. These are exemplified in San Francisco's Ghirardelli Square and the Cannery. Here walks, pathways, stairways, ramps, and elevators displace the automobile and dignify the pedestrian in cities connected by freeways and rapid transits.

Transportation as an activity system in a hundred years has become a dominant element in transforming the city into an urbanized area. Transportation, like housing, is a significant component of the institutional space in society. The construction and maintenance of highways and people-moving systems provide jobs. Transportation systems sometimes interface with urbanized areas negatively as they produce noise pollution and air pollution. Transportation systems may interface positively with urbanized areas as they free people to utilize and experience the resources of regional and continental areas and move urbanization toward ecumenopolis.

IMPLICATIONS

In urbanized society, planning for housing, jobs, and transportation must be related to institutions. Housing is a part of procreation, recreation, and economics. Jobs are components of economics and socialization. Transportation is both a technical system and a social system whereby people in urbanized places relate to each other on secondary levels and also on primary levels. Mass transit brings people into a large societal network. Pedestrian movement facilitates primary and interpersonal social relationships.

Conceptualizing the city as a formal organization clarifies the nature of planning for housing, jobs, and transportation.

REFERENCES

ABRAMS, C. Housing in the year 2000. In W. R. Ewald (Ed.), *Environment and Policy.* Bloomington: University of Indiana Press, 1968.

AREGGER, H., & GLAUS, O. *Highrise Buildings and Urban Design.* New York: Praeger, 1967.

ASHBY, L. C., & BAILEY, J. H., III. Condominiums: incorporation of common elements — a proposal. *Vanderbilt Law Review,* 1970, 23, 321–68.

BERMAN, D. S. Condominiums — opportunity and pitfalls. *Building,* 1968, 14, 48–50.

COOPER, C. St. Francis Square: attitudes of the residents. *American Institute of Architects Journal,* 1971, 60, 22–27.

DAVIDS, L. North American marriage: 1990. *The Futurist,* 1971, 5, 190–94.

DENNIS, N. Who needs neighbors? *New Society,* 1963, 2, 8–11.

DEVLIN, G. A. New directions in parking design. *Urban Land,* 1975, 34, 3–9.

DI MAIO, A. J., JR. *Soviet Urban Housing.* New York: Praeger, 1974.

DOXIADIS, C. A. The role of transportation in the cities of the future. *Traffic Engineering and Control,* 1970, 18, 18–29.

DYKMAN, J. Manpower. *Flower Mound Background Papers.* Dallas: Flower Mound Corporation, 1971.

FOLEY, J. W. Trends, determinants, and policy implications of income inequality in U.S. counties. *Sociology and Social Research,* 1977, 61, 441–61.

FORRESTER, J. W. *Urban Dynamics.* Cambridge: M.I.T. Press, 1968.

GANS, H. J. *The Urban Villagers.* New York: Free Press, 1962.

GOLDSMITH, H. F., & STOCKWELL, E. G. Inter-relationship of occupational selectivity patterns among city, suburban and fringe areas of major metropolitan centers. *Land Economics,* 1969, 45, 194–205.

GREEN, D. New way to afford a second home. *Mechanics Illustrated,* 1970, 66, 65–67.

HALPRIN, L. *Freeways.* New York: Reinhold Publishing Co., 1966.

HEMINGWAY, R. W. Condominium and the Texas Act. *Texas Bar Journal,* 1966, 29, 731–44.

HICK, R. K. Lower income housing: condominium vs. cooperative. *Illinois Bar Journal*, 1970, *59*, 62 – 71.
"HUD International Brief." Washington, D.C.: U.S. Department of Housing and Urban Development, 1971.
KEAN, M. B., & SANDERS, A. A. Property — condominium in Pennsylvania — panacea or Pandora's box? *Villanova Law Review*, 1963, *8*, 538 – 53.
LANEY, T. D. Condominiums. *Skyscraper Management*, 1970, *55*, 10 – 13.
LARSON, C. T. The motor road: forerunner of the universal city. *Traffic Quarterly*, 1964, *23*, 459 – 90.
LE CORBUSIER. *The City of Tomorrow and Its Planning*. Cambridge: M.I.T. Press, 1924 and 1971.
LUBELL, H. Urban development and employment in Calcutta. *Ekistics*, 1973, *36*, 434 – 39.
Manpower Report of the President. Washington, D.C.: U.S. Department of Labor, 1974, 80 – 81.
MAYUR, R. The coming Third World crisis: runaway growth of large cities. *The Futurist*, 1975, *9*, 168 – 74.
MEYERSON, M. *Housing, People, and Cities*. New York: McGraw-Hill, 1962.
MCCUE, G. $57,000,000 later: an interdisciplinary effort is being made to put Pruitt-Igoe together again. *Ekistics*, 1973, *36*, 322 – 24.
MILLER, H. L. Converting a small apartment building to a condominium. *Journal of Property Management*, 1971, *36*, 29 – 44.
NEWMAN, O. *Defensible Space*. New York: Macmillan, 1972.
PAPAIOANNOU, J. G. Future urbanization patterns: a long-range, world-wide view. *Ekistics*, 1970, *29*, 368 – 81.
PAWLEY, M. *Architecture vs. Housing*. New York: Praeger, 1971.
PFEIFFER, J. Hunger and history. *Horizon*, 1975, *17*, 31 – 47.
POPENOE, D. Urban residential differentiation. *Ekistics*, 1973, *36*, 365 – 73.
Professional condo merchandising helps to keep 'em in the cities. *Apartment Construction News*, December 1970, 9 – 11, 13.
RAINWATER, L. Fear and the house-as-haven in the lower class. *Journal of the American Institute of Planners*, 1965, *32*, 23 – 31.
RIEMER, S. Sociological perspective in home planning. *American Sociological Review*, 1947, *12*, 155 – 59.
ROMNEY, K. B. Take a second look at the vacation condominium. *Journal of Home Building*, 1967, *4*, 50 – 53.
Social and Economic Effects of Highways. Washington, D.C.: U.S. Department of Transportation, 1974.
TAYLOR, L. *Ideal People*. Chicago: Nelson-Hall, 1976.
TAYLOR, L., & SUTARIA, T. People and job matching in post-industrializing society. Paper read at the Meeting of the American Sociological Association, San Francisco, 1975.
VILLECCO, M., & DIXON, J. Breakthrough? *Architectural Forum*, 1970, *132*, 50 – 61.
WEDGWOOD, R. Doxiadis' contribution to the pedestrian view of the city. In D. Lewis (Ed.), *Pedestrian in the City*. Princeton, N.J.: D. Van Nostrand Co., 1966.
What housing cooperatives do. *Cooperative Housing*, 1968, *7*, 8 – 14.
WOOD, E. *Housing Design: A Social Theory*. New York: Citizens Housing and Planning Council of New York, Inc., 1961.

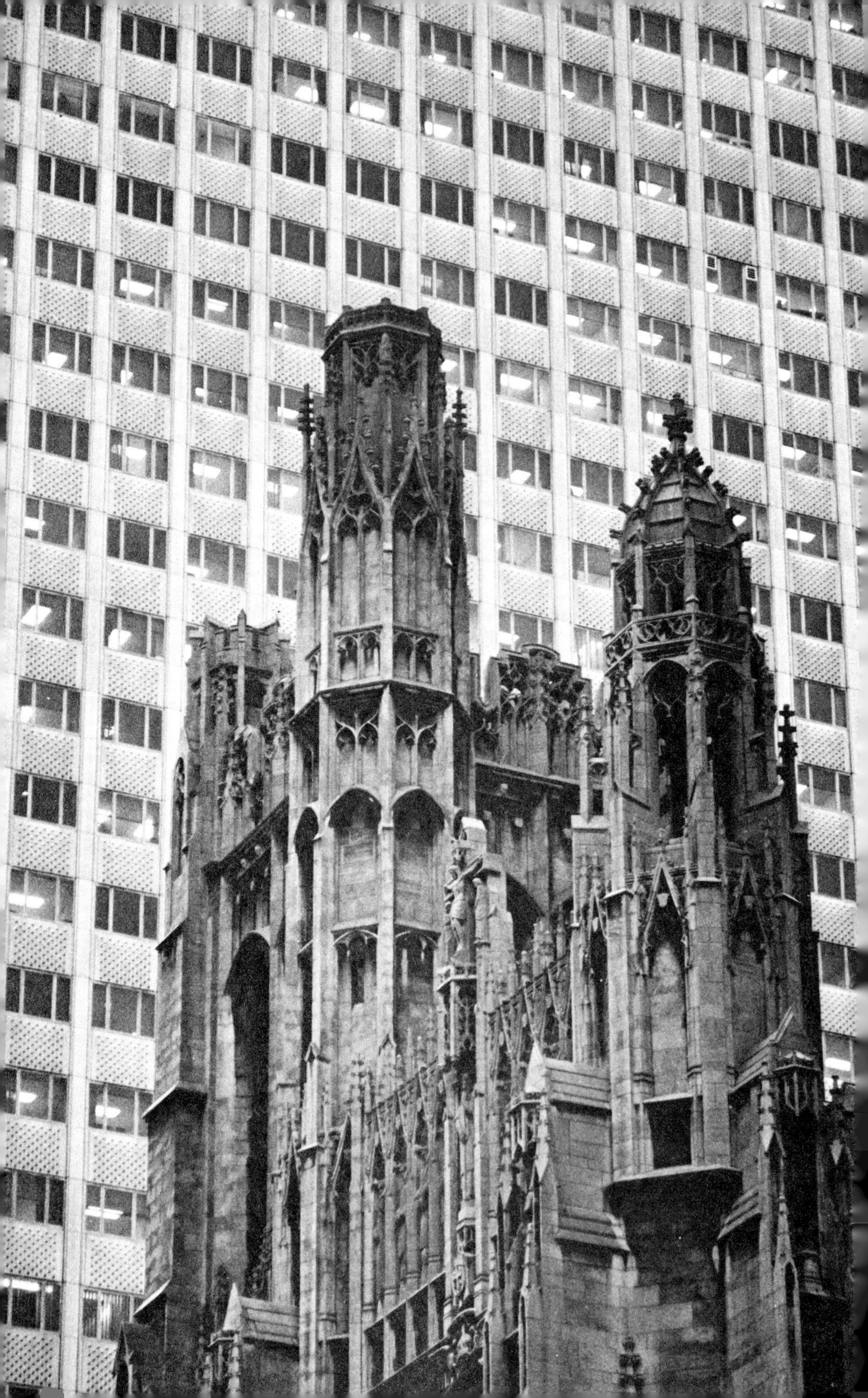

Education and Religion

10

Religion and education both in different ways contribute to the socialization of people. Both are means by which societies transmit their knowledge from one generation to the next.

Religions attempt to explain the meaning of human existence. They support humaneness and civilization. They have not always supported city life although their pageantry and liturgy have reached apexes in cities.

When people invented cities, religion played a prominent role in them. Much early city development in the Near East involved theocracy, with priestly and governmental functions often being carried out by the same persons. The large and most prestigeful edifices were for religious activities. Ziggurats are an example. Acropolis developments like that in Athens, Greece were places where early urbanites erected buildings showing homage to their gods. For hundreds of years in Christian societies, through the Middle Ages and the Renaissance, cathedrals and other churches were the tallest and most dominating buildings in cities.

In industrial cities, the physical form of the church was greatly surpassed in size by commercial and manufacturing buildings. Also with the rise of industrialism, knowledge generation and transmission became more elaborate in cities. Schools and universities expanded rapidly. Their physical space in cities in the last quarter of the twentieth century is greater than that for churches.

This large, urban church is dwarfed by a New York skyscraper. (Photo: Mike Mazzaschi for Stock, Boston.)

The once nearly dominant religious expression in early cities is now very small, indeed nearly absent, in some large urban areas. Urban expansion in the nineteenth and twentieth centuries often has been excessively dominated by economic institutions and work considerations. Schools and educational activities have grown particularly because they support job training and related vocational instruction.

The power of knowledge is clear. Urbanized societies cannot operate without it. Schools are not a matter of choice, as many people regard religious participation. Nevertheless, society in general and educators in particular continue to be unable to demonstrate in rigorous cost-benefit terms the value of education. Data show that in the United States in recent years, over $50 billion has been spent annually to educate children from the kindergarten to the twelfth grade. Additionally there is a large cost for higher education and continuing education. (There is more difficulty in estimating the dollar cost for operating institutionalized religion in America, due to its division into some 260 bodies.)

Sociophysical planners are concerned with educational and religious programs. They plan for the building of schools and churches. Still, planning for these important institutions remains inadequate.

In the contemporary city much education, in the form of basic socialization, takes place informally in streets, factories, parks, museums, and other places. Similarly, much human orientation to religion takes place in family settings and in small study gatherings, often in locations other than religious buildings. Robert Bellah (1968) goes so far as to suggest that there is a civil religion in America. He suggests that civil rights legislation, for example, might be the real content of an urban society's expression of religion or spiritual values.

In this chapter we explore the issues involved in projecting space for high-quality educational and religious expression in urbanized society.

EDUCATION IN URBANIZED SOCIETY

In Medieval cities, much education was of a craft guild type. One learned by doing under the direct tutelage of a master craftsman. Even through much of the Renaissance city era, professions were learned by working with a practitioner more than by studying in the universities. The body of specialized and scientific knowledge expanded steadily as a corresponding necessity to growing industrialization, to advances in food and fiber production, and to refinements in health care. Schools as such gradually became normative. Many early schools were private and/or church related. From early urban times through the eighteenth century, religious organizations produced and supported much of the body of knowledge on which cities prospered. But as science and mind-based urban societies matured, both more basic and more specialized training became so generally needed that education grew into a large separate enterprise.

In nineteenth century America it was argued that the urbanizing nation could not afford universal education. The objections were overcome. Elementary and secondary education were established as matters of states' rights rather than put under national or municipal control. With hindsight that may have been a poor decision. From the time small rural schools were established, they have been increasingly consolidated into urban school systems. By the 1970s public school systems totaled only 17,000 in the United States — down from 108,000 in the 1940s. Generally, school system boundaries are not the same as municipal boundaries, but often provide for surrounding rural people.

In an organizational sense public school systems are a socialized industry with a near monopoly. Although private schools exist, most urban people obtain their education in public schools. Public education is frequently supplemented by private efforts. Docents from museums may provide enriched art training for students. Science museums may offer special courses for school-aged children, sometimes free and sometimes on a fee basis. Little League Baseball programs and related athletic programs may provide recreational education that supplements physical education in schools. Numerous other aspects of urban life supplement education.

The social system of education is highly visible. This makes somewhat easier the task of planning spaces in which education might take place under optimum conditions. There remain, however, complex questions concerning which human social mixes, in various types of physical environments, produce the richest and most qualitative learning experiences.

Urban purposes of educational socialization

Schools from day-care centers through university professional training exist to disseminate from one generation to the next the knowledge base for high-quality urbanized society and for individual social satisfaction. In industrial nations, states, provinces, and municipalities, there is often fierce competition for high-talent manpower. From time to time this is viewed as a "brain-drain" from one area to another. Progressive and aggressive municipal leaders often study carefully the educational attainment level of their citizens on a citywide basis as well as in local neighborhoods. Municipalities may be ranked on the basis of their quality of educational opportunities. Municipal government leaders and Chamber of Commerce leaders may support educational innovation for excellence. They often use as an inducement in recruiting new industry the high quality of schools and universities in their urban area.

The ability of schools to pass on knowledge from one generation to another is influenced by the genetic inheritance of students; the home environment, particularly in early years; components of the school system like teachers, buildings, equipment, and the socioeconomic mix of students; plus the nonhome and nonschool environment — the neighborhood. This means that schools should be planned in relation to the total urban environment. It is inadequate for physical planners to assert, for example, that schoolrooms and schoolyards must have a specific number of square feet per child in order to achieve educational excellence. The success of schools must be seen in relation to a wide range of urban institutions including the family, the church, health care, recreation, and jobs.

Professional educator-planners recognize that the function of learning may be achieved in some subject areas more out of schools than in them. Distributive education is most effective when carried out in stores and in shops. Significant amounts of medical education are received through hospital internships. Internships are widely used in many kinds of advanced and craft work also. Accordingly, some educational spaces and facilities need to be provided for "on location."

Many employees learn more about their specific work on the job than in schools. We acknowledge this on-the-job learning. However, the tasks of sociophysical planners are most related to the provision of classrooms, laboratories, and other physical spaces for formal learning (Downs 1976).

Expanding childhood-to-adult educational programs

There is wide agreement in urbanized societies that youngsters can begin systematic education at age six. The expansion of the urbanized body of knowledge has become so extensive that twelve years of classroom study is now normal — perhaps optimal — for disseminating the basic skills needed to serve society and to achieve self-satisfaction. Indeed persons having less than five years of formal education are viewed as functional illiterates for urbanized society. At the upper end of the continuum, some 25 percent of the industrial urban populations are educated for professional and executive work. These individuals spend between sixteen and twenty years (or more) of their lives in formal education and training. Such highly trained persons are in the middle to the late twenties before they enter the world of work on a full-time basis.

It is not the primary task of the sociophysical planners to determine whether it takes five or more years of education to be above the functionally illiterate level or twenty years of education, more or less, to be appropriately trained for professional or managerial work. We only want to plan for educational facilities given societal notions of how much education will be required. But the societal definitions are not always clear, and they change through time. For example, early childcare centers, preschool nurseries, and kindergartens all are increasingly appended to the educational facilities needed in the last few years. At the other extreme, continuing adult education and special short courses are increasing. A third new requirement area is for remedial training facilities for the physically and socially handicapped. The urbanized society operates on a seven-day-a-week basis and around the clock. Accordingly there are increasing demands to provide specialized education at nights, on weekends, and in the summer. Educational planners are called upon to design sociophysical facilities for internship and continuing adult education in hospitals, factories, and related locations outside of school buildings.

Sociophysical education planning

Public education dominates in urbanized societies. In effect the systems of education are highly centralized. Most urbanites live in large urban areas where they are required to utilize the services of one educational system rather than select among competing systems. This enables planners to build to the specifications of a specific school board. But as the population moves, sometimes rapidly, from central cities to suburban areas, there obtains an oversupply of educational spaces in the depopulated central city and an inadequate supply in the growing suburbs. Economist Milton Friedman (1962) has suggested that one possibility for correction of the maldistribution of educational facilities would be to provide for profit-motivated competitive educational firms. In such a case, publicly financed vouchers of a fixed sum per individual could be used to buy their desired educational services from an "approved" supplier at any location acceptable to the purchaser.

Physical planning for education is directed by some established guidelines. The most widely established principle is to construct neighborhood schools. Physical planners assert that nurseries should be located in residential areas, with a one-eighth- to one-fourth-mile walking distance. Elementary schools in residential areas should have a one-half-mile walking distance. Junior high schools should be located so that there is a maximum three-fourths-mile walking distance. Senior high schools are ideally located when there is a maximum walking distance of one mile. It is expected that nursery schools should serve populations between one and two thousand. Elementary schools should serve populations of up to seven thousand. Junior high schools may serve populations between ten and twenty thousand while senior high schools may serve populations of over thirty thousand. The norm for public school classrooms varies from thirty to thirty-five pupils. Nursery schools may average as few as seven pupils while senior high school classes may average a high of fifty.

Similar physical planning specifications are enumerated for school playing fields and neighborhood play lots. For example, the American Association for Health and Physical Education suggests that a neighborhood park-school area should be twenty acres. The division of land should be as follows: school buildings, two acres; parking, one acre; playlot, one acre; hard-surface game courts, two and one-half acres; turf field-game areas, five and one-half acres; park area, including space for drama and quiet activities, five and one-half acres; buffer zones and circulation areas, two acres; recreation service buildings, .2 acres; and senior citizen area, .3 acres (de Chiara and Koppelman 1974; *School Sites — Selection, Development, and Utilization*, n.d.).

In nations like the United States fundamental societal questions are being raised concerning the adequacy of neighborhood elementary and secondary schools. Questions increasingly raised concern the possibility of the multiple use of educational facilities for children and adults during the day, in the evenings, and during summer. Some efforts are also made to provide multiple use of parks and recreational facilities with school district facilities.

Social planning for education involves relating people at all ages to the growing and changing knowledge base. Moreover, education must interface with other social systems. This is illustrated in part by the greater attention given in recent years to group care for young children in day-care centers and nurseries. Some of these facilities are operated by churches, by voluntary associations, and by private entrepreneurs as well as by schools. Planning must be done with all of these types of operating agencies accordingly. At the adult end of the continuum, educational planning must focus more on continuing education opportunities and specific retraining courses. Educational planning is also done by science museums, theatre groups, and art museums, where educational departments and educational staff are being expanded. Specific retraining programs may be provided in conjunction with employment. Some retraining facilities are planned in hospitals and in industries, where large numbers of technical specialists are employed. For several decades universities, junior colleges, and high schools have offered night courses and other special courses for adult continuing education and retraining. Specific physical spaces need to be provided for these training programs.

Planning for education is also aided by a body of research which reports how space is used in libraries, dormitories, and classrooms. At library study tables, people prefer to leave a vacant chair on either side of them and/or to work at opposite ends or opposite sides of a table. These are, in effect, places for study rather than social interaction. High-rise dormitories appear to be more isolating and less satisfactory than lower buildings unless special efforts are made to stimulate student acquaintances and social interaction. Hard, straight-back chairs in dormitory rooms are found to be more desirable for study purposes than are soft, upholstered ones. Many classrooms are dehumanized by drab colors and hard-surfaced chairs that are fastened to the floor. Indeed, dormitory lounges and school classrooms may be rendered largely dysfunctional when excessive amounts of furnishings are built-in (Sommer 1974).

Questions are also raised by social planners concerning the possibility of using modern church educational facilities for continuing adult education and for nursery school space. But churches in many societies are highly autonomous and are divided into multiple denominations. Where planning authority is weak, and must be generated by persuasion, possibilities of cooperation between social institutions and agencies are reduced.

Most sociophysical educational planners work for one specific agency — usually a local school board. But total social system educational planning is cheaper for taxpayers and more effective for contributing to a high-quality urban environment. Therefore, planners must seek opportunities to develop educational spaces in multiple institutions.

Neighborhood schools and educational park facilities

In urbanized society, schools have the possibility of being multifunctional and thereby related to neighborhoods as total learning centers. For young children there is a sociophysical advantage in locating schools within walking distance of their homes. Even more ideally, school children might not have to cross streets. But both of these conditions increasingly fail as more detached housing becomes larger and is situated in the center of lots that are six thousand square feet or more. That physical design of residential areas negates the possibility of walking to school for most children. The goal of walking to schools is inconsistent with the status value of large, detached homes on large, high-prestige lots. Planned Unit Developments or superblock physical layouts constitute major alternatives. These alternatives in effect subtract much of the narrow side strips of yards from large lots by clustering homes, while retaining large open spaces that are available for multiple recreational facilities to be used by schools and as neighborhood parks. Neighborhood learning centers can have facilities used for education and leisure for all people in the area, not just those in kindergarten through the twelfth grade.

A neighborhood's interest in its learning center is illustrated in the case of the Watts area of Los Angeles. An old school facility there dating back to 1906 needed to be replaced by a new building to accommodate sixteen hundred persons. The site was limited in size. Planners and the school board interviewed teachers, pupils, recent alumni, and other neighborhood adults before building the new facility. Many assumptions were found to be false. Officials implicitly assumed that the neighborhood was highly mobile. In fact they found that the average length of residence was nearly ten years. It was assumed that residents had little concern with lawlessness at the school facility. In fact it was discovered that a high priority was placed on having a school where vandalism would be controlled and where discipline and good citizenship were highly significant parts of the training. It was assumed that ethnic people wanted ethnic teachers. It was found that in fact they wanted outstanding teachers regardless of ethnicity. It was assumed that ethnic people wanted ethnic culture taught. This was found to be true. It was assumed that if you were to ask neighborhood adults what they wanted in a school, their requests would be unreasonable. This was found to be false. Rather than wanting carpeting, artificial-grass playing fields, and separate toilets for all classrooms, what they wanted was better educationally equipped classrooms, a resource center, and after-school study facilities ("Big, Complicated City," 1970).

There is slowly increasing some integration of school board policy and municipal ordinances which make possible the use of school facilities as general neighborhood facilities. When school policies and municipal ordinances intermesh in a cooperative system, neighborhood schools may become neighborhood centers for twelve months in the year, seven days in the week, and fourteen to sixteen hours in the day. Increasingly, well planned urban learning centers, churches, shopping facilities, health facilities, recreational facilities, and residential units all interface in a systematic way for complementary trade-offs, avoiding much wasteful duplication and eliminating many security problems.

An alternative to the neighborhood school is the "educational park." In those situations where physical neighborhoods are greatly decentralized and physically separated or where there is excessive homogeneity, educational parks offer positive alternatives. In the large urbanized society, some specialized facilities are clustered to render a more high-quality service. In some cases there are regional parks with special educational facilities that cannot be provided at smaller locations. Similarly, there are regional medical facilities and regional shopping facilities. The educational park is sociologically broader than the neighborhood. It may offer diversity and in-depth specialization of training — possibly for both children and adults. In large urbanized societies high-quality environment can be achieved most by juxtaposing some neighborhood educational centers and some regional educational centers. Social organizationally there should be more validity in the educational center than in the school. The concept "school" is too restrictive and implies a single function. The "educational center" may offer activities for senior citizens, for preschool youngsters, for voluntary groups like Little League, Boy Scouts, and Garden Clubs. The educational center may supplement its services by serving breakfasts, lunches, and even dinners. The larger halls may be used for special community lectures and cultural events (Dye 1968).

Educational facilities in new towns

In the garden city new town model, educational buildings tend to be facilities that are closely related to neighborhoods as a total social system (Tennenbaum 1965; Merlin 1971; Mields 1973). We illustrate the situation with the "neighborhood schools" in the new town of Columbia, Maryland. There each of the neighborhoods will have its own elementary school and each of the villages a secondary school. The schools are located in relation to other neighborhood and village services. They are near the shopping facilities, and they are intended to be used for adult education programs as well as for community activities. Libraries are in proximity so that they can receive maximum use by both school children and adults. Schools are supplemented with day-care facilities and multipurpose meeting rooms. The sociophysical planning recognizes the place-boundness of both young children and mothers. Accordingly, the schools become central elements in the neighborhood focus rather than isolated, single function facilities. On a much larger scale, in the new town of Brasilia the residential superblocks are designed to interface convenience shopping, churches, health facilities, education, and recreation. In new towns there are unique opportunities for schools to become significant parts of the total urban life social system rather than to remain isolated, single functional facilities in residential areas.

Learning environments and other urban systems

Urban social planners increasingly demonstrate that the city itself, the total urban environment, is a learning center. Sociologists, physical planners, and professional educators recognize that the environment of learning far exceeds the physical premises of the school (Downs 1976). Isolated unifunctional neighborhood schools can at best make a limited impact on people's learning. With the possible exception of boarding schools, most people spend more hours of their day in nonschool than in school environments. Excellent teachers with excellent facilities have a limited probability of success unless their efforts and facilities are reinforced by a positive sociocultural environment. The body of knowledge and skills needed for quality survival in urban life is learned both in schools and outside of schools. Therefore planning for high-quality urban learning environments necessitates that planners examine proposed school facilities in specific relationship to all other urban systems.

RELIGION IN URBANIZED SOCIETY

From the origin of cities to the present, apexes of religions have been expressed in them. Juxtaposed to these pinnacles of worship have been abysses of despair. Most urbanized people exist between these religious extremes. Indeed so lukewarm is the orientation of the current urban masses to things religious that civil religion, at least in the U.S.A. and the U.S.S.R., is widely characteristic. In the Soviet Union, China, and many Communist Bloc countries, participation in organized religions is officially discouraged.

In the Middle Ages and the early Renaissance great churches and cathedrals physically dominated the urban landscape. In Western urban areas, where Roman Catholicism has dominated, the parish church in addition to the cathedral has been conspicuous on the physical and social landscape. But today in most new towns, churches are conspicuous in their absence (Lewis 1966; Bailey 1973).

The city in the urbanized twentieth century continues to be the place where human beings express the pinnacles of civilization. The world's major places of worship, operas, athletic events, art museums, educational institutions, and stock markets are found in densely urbanized places. The masses of population now live in the world's big cities or in their suburban fringe areas. We are concerned with how sociophysical planning in cities, suburbs, and fringe urban areas can facilitate the population's understanding of the meaning of human existence through religion.

Purposes of religion

In societal terms religion assists human beings in knowing who they are and why they exist. Satisfactory meaning reduces alienation and anomie, increases satisfaction in living, and supports a high morality. There is much evidence that in urbanized parts of the world alienation and anomie are widespread. One might observe that the traditionally organized forms of major world religions are failing to achieve a satisfactory communication of the meaning of existence to urban man. There is some suggestion that today storefront-type churches or sects are growing more rapidly than older church religions. This growth may be an expression of the perceived irrelevance of some forms of the large churches. It may also be a manifestation of frustration with the so-called "social gospel" and its failure to achieve social justice.

The concept of civil religion is not new. It was used by Jean Rousseau in the eighteenth century. The powerful expression of civil religion in the twentieth century, however, needs careful scrutiny. It suggests the borrowing of belief symbols from a major religion, in this case Christianity, for their expression in political and economic activities. In the case of civil religion in America, we follow for example Bellah's citing of Lyndon Johnson's presidency. On March 15, 1965, Mr. Johnson went before the United States Congress to press his case for a strong voting rights bill. He suggested that the power of America could defeat enemies, double the nation's wealth, and conquer outer space; but if we failed in extending voting rights to Blacks, he said, the country would have to face the religious charge, "What is a man profited, if he shall gain the whole world, and lose his own soul?" And he went on further to point out that the Great Seal of the United States says, in Latin, "God has favored our undertakings." Mr. Johnson charged that God would not continue to favor everything that we do, and that we must divine his will. The implication was that his will favored strong civil rights (*U.S. Congressional Record* 1965).

We might push beyond the Johnson example and suggest that religious expression in a nation like America is more overtly seen in a full range of efforts to achieve civil rights than in specific worship practices in churches, synagogues, and other places of religion. Nevertheless in a sociophysical planning sense such civil religion expressions are deficient. There is a sacred dimension to many forms of human activity. Urbanized society may from time to time elevate the New York Stock Exchange, a Monet painting, or a baseball hall of fame to sacred levels. While such expressions may bring dignity and respect to specific elements of urban culture, they do not ultimately explain the meaning of human existence.

The urbanized society, like cities over five thousand years ago, needs a sociophysical environment in which humans can interact specifically for the purpose of examining the meaning of existence. This is similar to providing a sociophysical space in which social interaction can take place for economic activities, health and welfare maintenance or education.

Sociophysical planning for religion

Sanctuaries for worship, altars for expressions of commitment, libraries for study, and chapels for contemplation are all parts of the urban built environment which can support man's search for the meaning of existence. Humans live in societies that survive on signs and symbols. This differentiates human society from other societies. Accordingly the signs and symbols, both social and physical, of the meaning of urban man's existence are as essential as those signs and symbols which support his economics, government, and health. Urban planners need to designate more adequate space for religious signs, symbols, and activities.

New-town planners invariably designate space for residences, commerce, industry, schools, and health facilities. Often neglected is space designated for religious activities (Bailey 1973; Mields 1973). De Chiara and Koppelman's book *Urban Planning and Design Criteria* is essentially a volume of standards used by physical planners. In its six hundred pages there is a one-page entry concerning churches. The sources for the one page of standards are twenty years old. The standards suggest that a population of 5,000 persons could support three churches. No adequate reference is made to the problem of multiple denominations. Moreover this assumes that in America some 60 percent of the population will affiliate with churches. The optimum size for a congregation is reported by many churchmen to be about 500 people. Downtown churches, however, may need 1,500 to 2,000 or more members to support their diverse programs. In terms of physical space it is suggested that one acre is adequate for a church anticipating 400 members or fewer, and that four acres is appropriate for a church expecting 1200 members. One writer indicates that five to six acres is optimal for a 600-member church in order to provide 150 parking spaces. Additionally, it is suggested that eight acres is optimal for a church that will also have a parochial school.

The above standards are overly precise for the American situation where there are more than 260 religious bodies. By contrast sociophysical planners normally have to work with only one school board, one health agency, one welfare agency, and one park board per municipality. There is no central clearing house agency for the many religious bodies. Nevertheless planners can consult local Councils of Churches in urban areas to facilitate their determining of site designations.

It is noteworthy that in the monumental urban planning megastructure innovation of Soleri (1969), religion or churches as such are not specifically mentioned. Soleri summarizes thirty-seven major elements for human existence in a high-quality megastructure environment. Element number twenty-four is titled "Arcology and the Sacred." He writes, "Limitless energies in limitless space for limitless time are the scattered ingredients by which nature works. For man to succeed, he must make tight bundles of that minimal proportion of them allowed to him so that his own infinity — the infinite complexity of his compassionate and aesthetic universe — can blossom" (p. 31). Such an expression is hardly a guide for sociophysical planners to use in siting religious facilities. Similarly, in the imaginative plan for the *Compact City* megastructure for 250,000 people, there is only a one-word reference to churches (Dantzig and Saaty 1973). On page forty-three in *Compact City* there is a drawing indicating locations for research space, high school and university space, stadium and auditorium areas, manufacturing facilities, hotels, shops, residences, churches, and hospitals.

This limited concern in sociophysical planning for religious expression is widespread. It is the thesis of this author that a high-quality urbanized environment must provide appropriate spaces for human social interaction related to meaningful religious expression. It is not the job of urban planners to define what kinds of religious expression should be made. However we can examine some of the types of sociophysical spaces used for religious purposes and plan for them.

Neighborhood and new-town churches

Many forms of religious expression are closely related to dyads, as illustrated by a priest and a parishioner in confession; others involve small groups in prayer; others involve individual contemplation. Large-scale religious drama and pageantry are also known. Wide ranges of forms of religious expression are accommodated in urbanized society. As urban areas expand in an ecumenopolizing direction, suburbs and fringe areas grow more rapidly than central cities, and neighborhood churches have expansive potentials. Neighborhood places of worship, like neighborhood schools and convenience shopping centers, have a distinct opportunity to play significant and positive roles related to other institutional aspects of life, so physical planners may locate shops, schools, and churches in groups. Some religious bodies support these efforts by suggesting that their facilities may be shared among multiple denominations, with social welfare service groups, and with education (Houda 1974). Some religious bodies indicate that neighborhood churches should be modest in scale, suggesting a "servant theology" in contrast to monumental and grandiose cathedral-type buildings. House-type structures may serve well as churches in some expanding suburban areas.

In new towns the neighborhood church may be specifically sited. In some cases it may be a multipurpose church (Bishop 1969). In England there is a New Town's Minister's Association. It is specifically concerned that old social and physical church patterns not be forced artificially into new towns. The Association encourages research that will facilitate worship practices and physical facilities serving wider needs.

There is an effort to encourage greater teamwork or interdenominational cooperation in new-town church programs. In some cases the religious facility is referred to as a pastoral care center. Multipurpose physical facilities are being designed to serve both social and worship needs. Ministers, priests, and rabbis increase dialogue and cooperative utilization of worship facilities in new towns (Sherrard and Murry 1968; Schaller 1972). Churches and social services become increasingly integrated and increasingly professionalized. Some worship centers become places where people are instructed for greater civil rights involvement. In juxtaposition, in some new towns in suburban areas church membership is growing rapidly but is not always easily distinguishable from country-club-type activity. Indeed all of the sharing of church facilities is not an index of ecumenicalism, but in some cases is an index of reduced human concern with religion.

The physical design for neighborhood and new-town churches is specified ("Congregation Churches" 1958). In England new-town churches are planned for seating capacities, youth halls, multipurpose auditoriums, and parking spaces. These specifications are similar to the sociophysical planning standards reported in the book by de Chiara and Koppelman.

Churches in large urban centers

The major city church may be a cathedral-type in form or, more recently, megastructurelike. Historically the principal church in a major Western city was cathedral-like, if not a cathedral in fact. Whether a temple, mosque, or church, the principal religious edifice in large cities has been physically grand in scale. For example the new St. Mary's Cathedral in San Francisco has a seating capacity for 2,400 people plus standing room for another 2,000 worshipers. Many small cities in the world have fewer than 4,400 people. Major forms of religious pageantry are often associated with such central-city churches. Frequently these downtown churches have great "voices" from their pulpits and from their choirs.

Still more recent responses of churches to the needs of central cities are illustrated by the eleven-story community use building constructed by Presbyterians in an urban renewal area of Winnipeg, Canada ("New Projects of Interest" 1975). This high-rise community building provides space for a permanent interdenominational chapel, senior citizen housing, a comprehensive health clinic, a food cooperative, and multipurpose areas for community functions. Central-city churches also develop specialized programs like rescue missions, Salvation Army facilities, "Junkie Priest" and "Jazz Priest" orientations, along with community action programs.

Religious centers in urban areas have multiple voices—subtle and poignant articulation for the mighty and powerful, humble and compassionate articulation for small groups in neighborhoods, along with social action strategies to reduce poverty, help the lame, and care for the infirm.

IMPLICATIONS

Both education and religion are significant social systems in urbanized society. Education is fundamental in providing the knowledge base on which urbanized society operates. A comparable fundamental role for religion is less clear. In societies like the Soviet Union and China, religious expression is minimal and must struggle for survival. In the urbanized U.S.A. expressions of civil religion appear to be gaining strength and possibly outweighing the impact of organized churches.

In this chapter we have been concerned with social planning and with physical planning for educational and religious facilities. The implications are that both need to be planned with overt recognition of their interface with other urban institutions. If school and church planning were viewed as elements of formal urban organization, their physical spaces would serve better the social needs of their programs. Multipurpose facilities related to multiple urban institutions are needed for educational centers and pastoral centers in the urbanizing society.

REFERENCES

BAILEY, J. (Ed.). *New Towns in America*. New York: Wiley, 1973.
BELLAH, R. N. Civil religion in America. In W. G. McLoughlin & R. N. Bellah (Eds.), *Religion in America*. Boston: Houghton-Mifflin, 1968.
Big, complicated city: simple, easy approach and a neighborhood picks the school it wants. *American School Board Journal*, 1970, 43, 25–28.
BISHOP, D. New towns and the church. *Architect and Building News*, 1969, 2, 63–67.
Congregation churches. *Architect's Journal*, 1958, 128, 825–34.
DANTZIG, G. B., & SAATY, T. L. *Compact City*. San Francisco: W. H. Freeman, 1973.
DE CHIARA, J., & KOPPELMAN, L. *Urban Planning and Design Criteria*. New York: Van Nostrand, 1974.
DOWNS, A. *Urban Problems and Prospects*. Chicago: Rand McNally, 1976.
DYE, T. R. Urban school segregation. *Urban Affairs Quarterly*, 1968, 24, 141–61.
FRIEDMAN, M. *Capitalism and Freedom*. Chicago: University of Chicago Press, 1962, 85–107.
HOUDA, R. W. Let's share our church buildings. *Cutting Edges*, 1974, 3, 1–2.
KINCHELOE, S. Churches and cities change together. In H. Hughes (Ed.), *Cities and City Life*. Boston: Allyn and Bacon, 1970.
LEWIS, D. (Ed.), *Pedestrian in the City*. Princeton, N.J.: D. Van Nostrand, 1966.
MERLIN, P. *New Towns*. London: Methuen, 1971.
MIELDS, H., JR. *Federally Assisted New Communities*. Washington, D.C.: Urban Land Institute, 1973.
Municipal Yearbook, 1974. Washington, D.C.: International City Management Assoc., 1974.
New projects of interest. *Faith and Form – Journal of the Guild for Religious Architecture*, 1975, 8, 1–3.
SCHALLER, L. E. *Church Planning in New Towns*. Naperville, Ill.: Yokefellow Institute, 1972.
School Sites: Selection, Development, and Utilization. Washington, D.C.: Department of Health, Education, and Welfare, n.d.
SHERRARD, T. D., & MURRY, R. C. The church and neighborhood community organization. In B. J. Frieden & R. Morris (Eds.), *Urban Planning and Social Policy*. New York: Basic Books, 1968.
SOLERI, P. *Arcology*. Cambridge: M.I.T. Press, 1969.

SOMMER, R. *Personal Space*. Englewood Cliffs, N.J.: Prentice-Hall, 1969.
SOMMER, R. *Tight Spaces*. Englewood Cliffs, N.J.: Prentice-Hall, 1974.
TENNENBAUM, R. Planning determinants for Columbia. *Urban Land*, 1965, 24, 3–8.
U.S. Congressional Record, House of Representatives, 15 March 1965, pp. 4924–26.

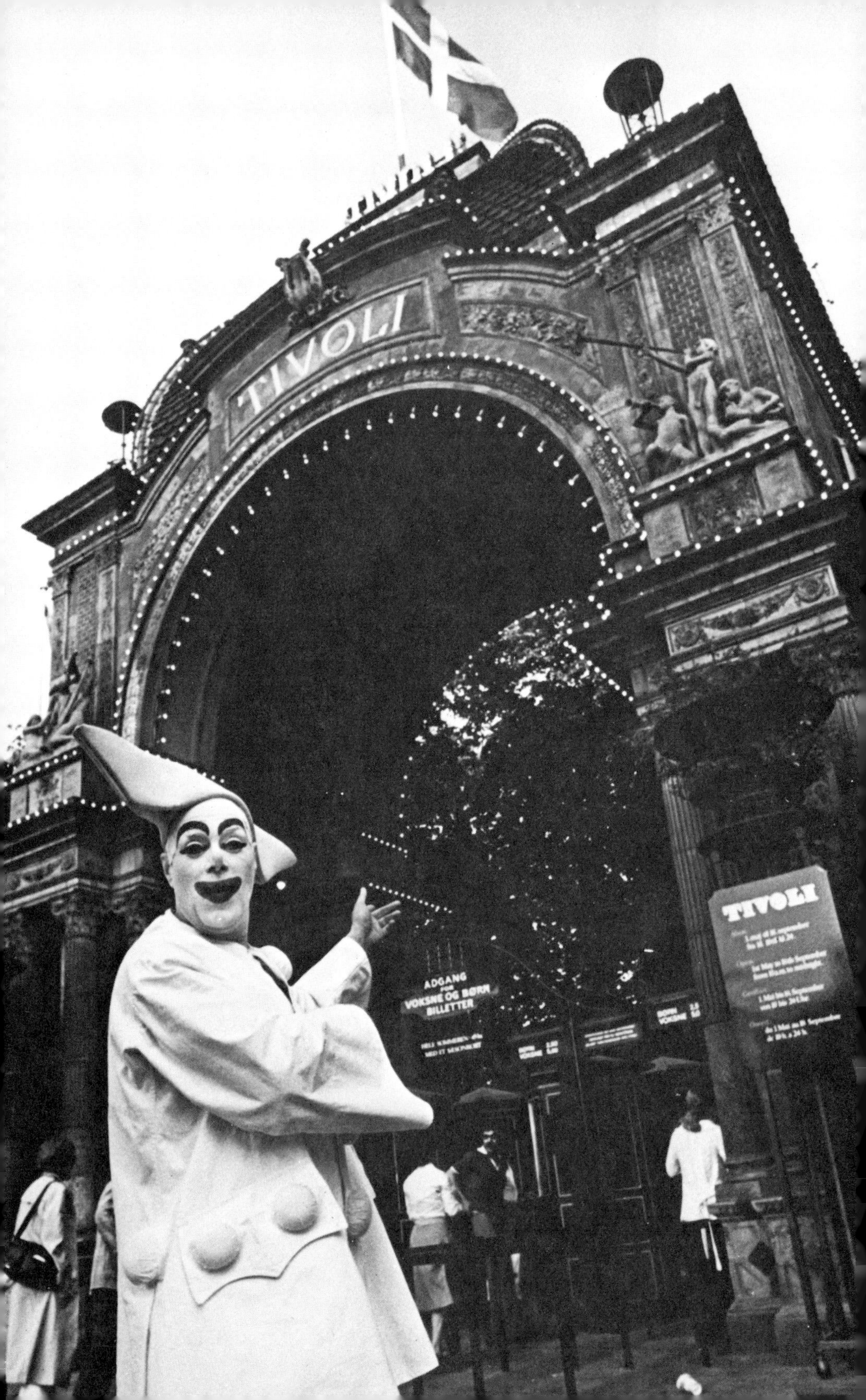
TIVOLI
ADGANG
VOKSNE OG BØRN
BILLETTER
TIVOLI

The Arts and Recreation

11

Anthropological evidence indicates that artistic expression and recreational-leisure activities are found in all societies. However, in preliterate and ruralized societies the arts and recreation are minimal — at a folk level. It is in the high culture of cities that the arts and recreation flourish and become highly organized in their own right (Boaz 1955; Hauser 1957).

When the arts and recreation become institutional in scope, sociophysical spaces are specifically utilized by them and need to be designed for them. Urban plans for the arts and for recreation are the subject of this chapter.

THE ARTS AT THE APEX OF URBAN CIVILIZATION

Arnold Hauser (1957) writes that "the country is, in contrast to the town, unsuitable for the practice of art — above all, for the fine arts which have a more than purely decorative function. In the country there are no proper tasks for art, no public, and none of the necessary means" (p.149). In large urbanized areas there are tasks, publics, and means for many art forms including dance, film, music, opera, painting, sculpture, theatre, and writing. For each of these art expressions there is an accompanying need for physical space designed as auditoriums, conservatories, libraries, movie houses, museums, performance halls, schools, and so forth. This is in no way to suggest that all

Commercial parks, such as Tivoli in Denmark, are modern urban pleasure gardens. (Photo: Courtesy of Danish National Tourist Office.)

art expressions are found in these spaces. In urban areas there are street arts, supergraphics on buildings, "happenings" in parks, as well as paintings, sculpture, and chamber music in residences. Buildings like hotels, banks, shopping centers, and schools are places where various forms of art are from time to time exhibited and performed. Nevertheless the highly developed arts do most often thrive in specialized physical settings (Taylor 1960; Albrecht 1970).

Additionally, the forms of urban spaces and the character of the urban built environment may themselves be part of the urban aesthetic expression. Baroque or city-magnificent designs have a special aesthetic quality. A major expression of urban art is found in architecture. Sometimes the architectural forms themselves become the aesthetic character of an urban environment.

The arts in cities

Lincoln Center for the Performing Arts in New York City is but one of many examples of a sociophysical environment for the arts at the apex. William Schuman, the center's president in 1963, said, "It is an idea rooted in the belief that the role of the arts is to give more than pleasure: that music, drama and dance provide enrichment beyond understanding. Through these arts we encounter qualities of perfection, nobility and splendor which engage the heart, the spirit and the intellect. To the extent that this enrichment is provided, we create more civilized communities — not only locally but nationally and internationally as well" (*Lincoln Center for the Performing Arts* 1964, pp. 7-8). Lincoln center was designed with sufficient physical space to provide for audiences totaling 3,200,000 persons a year, plus additional millions through radio and television. All of the halls together have a total seating capacity of 13,000. Many municipalities in the world have fewer persons than Lincoln Center has seats. Some nations have fewer people than Lincoln Center has for its total annual audience.

Lincoln Center is in the heart of the American eastern megalopolis. Its site is fourteen acres on Manhattan's upper west side. In the mid-1950s the Lincoln Square area was scheduled for urban renewal. In the Lincoln Center planning process, a committee visited cultural institutions in London, Paris, Vienna, Milan, Strasbourg, and Cologne. Engineers and architects were called to design buildings and project costs. By the mid-1960s Lincoln Center costs were estimated to be over $160 million. Ground was ceremonially broken by the then President Dwight Eisenhower. In 1962 Philharmonic Hall opened its doors for the first performance in the new center. It was subsequently followed by the Vivian Beaumont Theatre, Library, and Museum; by the Metropolitan Opera House; and by the Juilliard School of Music. Also included were the New York State Theatre, the Damrosch Park, and the Guggenheim Band Shell.

In order to get people to and from this performing arts center, subway access was planned as well as the construction of an underground parking garage. Parking spaces for 721 cars, concourses and escalators, and wheelchair accommodations all add to the center's accessibility. The parking garage is owned by the City of New York and operated on a concession basis.

The Lincoln Center buildings were planned and designed by internationally famous architects. In themselves the buildings are works of art — a type of the city-magnificent. They articulate together to make the total site a place of beauty for intensive cultural life.

Lincoln Center expresses one strategy for sociophysical planning in the area of the arts. It was built by individuals, foundations, and corporations with help from the city government, the state government, the federal government, and foreign governments. Gifts came from most of America's fifty states, from labor unions, college groups, and music societies. From around the world gifts included, for example, $2.5 million for the Metropolitan Opera House from the Federal Republic of Germany, and chandeliers for the opera house from the Austrian government. Other gifts came from Japan, New Zealand, and the Congo. Performances from Lincoln Center are sent throughout the nation and tour internationally as well. Paintings and sculpture adorn the buildings, lobbies, and park areas.

Another example of sociophysical planning for the arts is found in Minneapolis, Minnesota. As with Lincoln Center, the Minneapolis Arts Complex is located downtown. The new 2,600-seat Minnesota Orchestra Hall is located adjacent to the city's well known Niccollet Mall. It is at the downtown end of a greenway through which pedestrians may walk to Loring Park and beyond to the adjacent Walker Arts Center and the Guthrie Theatre (see Figure 11–1).

The new Hirshhorn Museum and Sculpture Garden in Washington, D.C. is a significant example of sociophysical planning. The Museum is prominently situated on a 4.4-acre site on the south side of the Capitol Mall. It was designed in the 1960s. The facility articulates with the original 1791 Pierre L'Enfant design for Washington, D.C., and the 1902 McMillan Commission's update for the Mall. The building's stark, plain, round exterior is intended to complement the eighteenth-century brick Smithsonian building on one side and the mid-twentieth-century concrete boxlike Air and Space Museum on the other side. Within this site the building, like many along Washington's Mall, was designed to be imposing, prominent, and easily identified.

Architect Gordon Bunschaft reasoned that the Museum must accommodate large crowds of people. Accordingly its circulation patterns are simple. The building has a minimum of interior and exterior detail. Its purpose is to exhibit art and sculpture to large numbers of people

Figure 11-1 Minneapolis Orchestra Hall to Guthrie Theater

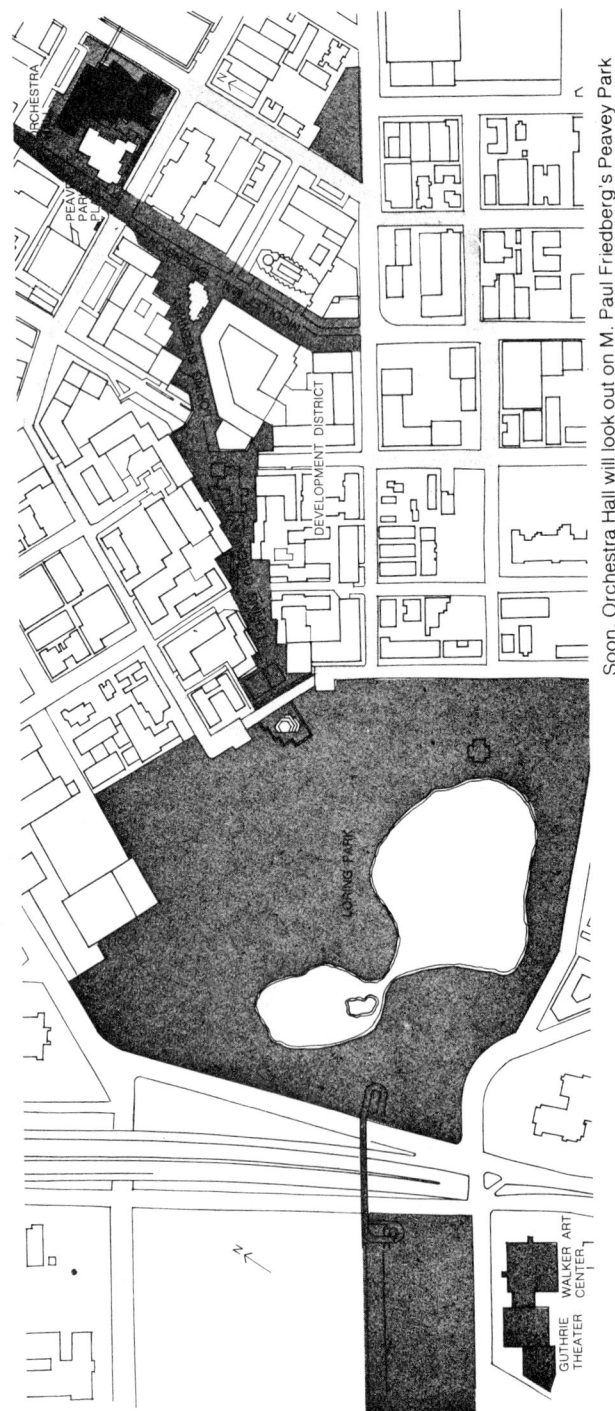

Soon, Orchestra Hall will look out on M. Paul Friedberg's Peavey Park Plaza and the Nicollet Mall extension. Eventually, Loring Greenway will tie it to Loring Park, to Walker Art Center, and the Guthrie Theater.

Source: Reprinted from the February 1975 issue of Progressive Architecture, copyright 1975, Reinhold Publishing Company.

who will be active in different ways. In many respects the building and its collection are products of the culture of a brash young society seeking a brand of mass civilization. The contents of the building embody a $25 million collection of 4,000 paintings and 1,600 pieces of sculpture. The large collection and massive numbers of people interface so that visitors "participate in the act of consuming culture quickly and efficiently" ("Museum as Monument" 1975). In terms of sociophysical planning, the building of the Hirshhorn Museum and Sculpture Garden is typical. The donor, Joseph Hirshhorn, and the federal government, represented by the Director of the Smithsonian Institution, held the real decision-making power concerning site and building form. The users of the museum, the public, were only considered as the architect, donor, and government officials became their advocates.

Museums are generally sociophysical environments that grow and change through generations. Minnesota's Minneapolis Institute of Arts facilities expansion is typical in illustrating growth and change over many years. A 1915 classic-eclectic building was expanded, adding more space for a children's theatre company, the Minneapolis College of Design, and a parking ramp. The entire complex utilizes a four-acre site in an older residential area of Minneapolis. Most of the residences are two story and have considerable yard space plus arborial growth around them. Fitting a museum and other related arts buildings into this environment is difficult. But the Society of Fine Arts in Minneapolis, which is the administrative operating organization, in 1965 had research done involving interviews with staff and the community. The research showed that the arts complex should be a regional center for scholarly activities as well as a community center. There was also a desire specified on the part of the Society of Fine Arts to change the museum's image from a stuffy, austere, and static place to a dynamic educational center. An internationally known Japanese architect, Kenzo Tange, was selected to design the expansion. Although the architectural quality of the new structure is controversial, in regard to the pattern of total sociophysical planning, the complex gets high marks because of the client's direct efforts at assessing user needs both in the community and in the urban region.

In Fort Worth, Texas, three art facilities have been expanded in the 1960s and 1970s. They are the Amon Carter Museum of Western Art, The Fort Worth Art Center, and the Kimbell Art Museum. Each is in a parklike setting within visual and easy walking distance of the other. A considerable degree of cooperation concerning acquisition and program emphasis is also followed by these museums. The Amon Carter has a high-quality collection and hangs first-class exhibitions of American Western art. The Fort Worth Art Center specializes in twentieth-century art. The Kimbell Art Museum has a more traditional collection, emphasizing European art and pre-twentieth-century art. The three art facilities have a variety of lecture, concert, and film programs. They also have specific educational programs, particularly for school children. In addition the museums are proximic to a large coliseum, a science museum, and two legitimate theaters. Major roadways facilitate the area's population's getting to this cultural center. To a great extent parking lot facilities are shared, particularly as people often visit more than one of the facilities at a time. The parking lots easily accommodate school buses. Collectively these cultural facilities constitute an example of presenting the arts and sciences in dynamic programs primarily by bringing audiences into their buildings.

In the 1950s the Louisiana Foundation was established to run the Louisiana Museum located just north of Copenhagen, Denmark. The site is a magnificent grounds and house that had belonged to a Danish nobleman. The name Louisiana was selected in recognition of the nobleman's wife Louise. The sociophysical plan called for bringing together architecture, landscape gardening, painting, sculpture, graphic art, and handicrafts, and a music program. The hundred-year-old house is retained primarily as an entrance and office space. To the house is attached a large modern building with ample glass window space to enable visitors to see the landscape and the sculpture on the grounds, as well as large walls for interior exhibition. Additionally, this museum has a studio in which children may participate in painting and other art activities while their parents view the exhibitions. Dining facilities are also provided. Some 200,000 persons per year visit the museum. The Louisiana Club has 5,000 members who participate in evening musical events, lectures, and film showings. Louisiana is a living museum environment with dynamic programs for all ages (*Louisiana*, n.d.).

Art museums have become major components of cities in the last one hundred and fifty years. Historically their origin dates in antiquity, but their widespread existence is a nineteenth- and twentieth-century urban phenomenon. In 1972 the National Council on the Arts and the National Endowment for the Arts combined efforts to carry out the first major national museum survey in America (McGrath 1971; *Museums USA*, 1974). In order to qualify as a museum for the survey, institutions had to meet six criteria: (1) they must have had a permanent facility open to the general public on a regular schedule; (2) the facility had to be open at least three months a year and twenty-five hours a week; (3) it must have had an annual operating budget of $12,000 or more; (4) it must have owned at least part of the material it exhibited; (5) it must have had at least one full-time, professionally trained employee; and (6) it must have been nonprofit and tax-exempt. By these criteria, 1,281 museums were identified in the fifty states and the District of Columbia. The types of museums were: art (19 percent), history (37 percent), science (16 percent), art history (10 percent), and others (18 percent). The annual operating budgets were under $50,000 for 831 of the museums. Only 5 percent had an annual budget over $1 million. Most museums were found to be in cities, but only 16 percent of them were municipally governed. Similarly, only 18 percent of the museum-operating revenues came from municipalities. Indeed, only 37 percent of the museum income came from government while 63 percent was private. A total of 308,205,000 visits were made to the survey museums in 1971–1972.

Museums are used by children and adults of all ages. They range from being treasure houses preserving *objets d'art* from past ages, to exhibitions concerning the future. Some museums are quiet in mood, employ conservators, and provide laboratories for tedious restoration work. Museums may also be dynamic educational institutions, even with extension programs which arrange exhibitions to be sent as traveling road shows. Museums also have docents give lectures to visitors.

The arts, particularly painting and sculpture, are predominantly seen in great cities where they are intermeshed with architecture and with commerce. For example there is a fifty-foot-high Picasso steel sculpture piece at the base of a skyscraper in Chicago's Civic Center. Similarly, there is a large Calder sculpture piece at the base of the Fort Worth Bank Building in Texas. Toronto International Airport in Canada is elegantly refined with large primitive Eskimo carvings, an eight-by-twenty-foot sculptured brass screen, and a nine-by-sixteen-foot mural (Redstone 1968). The Eugene City Hall in Oregon has a sixteen-foot-by-four-foot wood sculpture in its garden, plus an eight-foot-high metal sculpture.

Churches and synagogues in effect become significant art museums in many of the world's great cities. Shopping centers, particularly with enclosed climate-conditioned malls, utilize extensive amounts of sculpture. Some of the sculpture is specifically designed so that children may climb on it, sit on it, and otherwise interact with it. Commercial buildings, particularly bank buildings, use large amounts of art work in their public spaces. Some of them, like the Chase Manhattan Bank in New York, become patrons of the arts. Government buildings, like the United Nations Headquarters, are enriched with works of art.

Some great metropolitan areas, like Mexico City and Guatemala City, are outstanding for their use and display of art. In both of these cities there are numerous examples of government and private buildings with entire facades decorated in bas relief sculpture and/or mosaics.

The city as an art form

Beauty in cities is found from their origin to the present. Planning which is specifically intended to beautify the city as a whole, however, is essentially a nineteenth- and twentieth-century phenomenon. The nineteenth-century building of Washington, D.C. in accordance with L'Enfant's 1791 plan illustrates the use of wide baroque avenues as an aesthetic form. In the 1860s Haussmann did much to open up the city of Paris with wide avenues and places for large-scale parades and promenades in an aesthetic baroque street style. In Brazil's new capital also the streets are laid out in a suprahuman or baroque aesthetic style. (Only the street design, and not the architecture, is baroque in Brasilia.) Much of the intent for this large-scale or suprahuman aesthetic design of cities is related to the desire to increase green space in them.

The desire to develop more open green space in cities was a response to two motives, namely, to improve the social welfare of people in densely populated centers, and to improve the urban aesthetics. The aesthetic motive is clearly seen in what has become known as the city-beautiful movement. In the 1890s, ideas of urban beautification were being crystallized by architects and landscape architects. This was seen most clearly at the World's Columbian Exposition of 1893 in Chicago (Scott 1969; Tunnard 1970). Buildings at this World's Fair soon became widely known as the "White City." They spawned the city-beautiful planning movement. There was an interfacing of rugged individualism with civic art, and a Greek revival in architectural style. Wide streets and park spaces were characteristic of the city-beautiful movement.

Edmund Bacon (1974) calls beauty in the city an "act of will." Beautiful cities have a total scale and a satisfying scale as viewed by human beings in them. Vallingsby, a new town near Stockholm, Sweden, illustrates this. Bacon argues that Vallingsby was an effective model, but he feels it is disappointing in reality when individuals interact with it. The town center is too large to have a personal quality about it and too small to have a grand or suprahuman scale. By sharp contrast, Brasilia has a suprahuman scale both in its governmental building areas and in its residential superblock areas; the definition of scale is clear. In Chandigarh, India, the scale is grand and suprahuman in the governmental building area, but small and specifically human in the residential superblock areas. The point is that neither the design nor the scale of a beautiful city can be left to chance. Beautiful cities are a matter of plan—acts of aesthetic will.

The mass arts of cities

In the last of the twentieth century, radio, television, and stereo records have technologically made it possible to develop a mass music and mass drama experience. Over one hundred sixty million dollars are spent for hi-fi equipment and over forty million dollars for concert recordings in America annually. Over half a billion dollars are spent annually for concert tickets (Kaplan 1960). At mid-century, Beethoven's Ninth Symphony had sold over one hundred fifty thousand recordings. America had but ten symphony orchestras in 1900 and more than a thousand by the last quarter of the century. Similarly, the number of opera companies is now about one thousand, and there are more than five thousand community theatre groups. In the visual arts many so-called limited edition copies are being made of various types of original paintings. They are widely purchased at modest prices. Also numerous art magazines with high-quality reproductions have substantial circulation in urbanized nations. Toffler (1965) reports that 85 percent of all American symphony contributions are in amounts less than one hundred dollars. These are indexes demonstrating mass interest rather than limited elitist interest in the arts. The art mobile is a technique being used by some museums to bring parts of their collections and exhibitions out of their premises and into places where people are located. Similarly, some museums are setting up temporary exhibitions in places like factory lunch rooms. These are efforts to put art in daily living-working environments.

There is a new mass patronage of the arts in America. Typical collectors in the second half of the twentieth century are middle-income professionals. They are individuals who devote both money and time to orchestras, museums, and theatres as well. Increasingly, large urban churches support amateur and professional theatrical and music groups of their own. Some municipalities utilize tax money to subsidize the arts. For example, the city of San Francisco has a 3 percent tax on hotel rooms, part of which is used to support the arts.

Planning for the arts

There are no universal or even widely accepted planning standards for art museums, theatres, or music halls. There is even a minimum of technical information concerning lighting and acoustics. Although there are museum associations and theatre guilds, most physical plants are the result of private gifts. As apexes of urban civilization, these facilities are limited and unique. Until the second part of the twentieth century they have been elitist — planned for the classes and not for the masses. In the past five to seven decades, many museums have been opened to the general public, often free of charge. Many museums are totally inadequate for the large crowds of people who inundate them, particularly on holidays.

There are several major variables for consideration when planning for the arts. Theatres are to be planned differently for different types of performances. Theatre-in-the-round is suitable for intimate plays and small audiences. Auditorium-type theatres are needed for large productions that are intended to be seen primarily from only one angle.

Orchestra pits are needed for musical productions. Set storage and revolving stages facilitate most productions. Large lobbies and refreshment areas supplement the style of theatre-going—places for members of the audience to see and be seen while players have rest periods and time for set and costume changes. Adequate public transit and parking facilities are essential for the smooth movement of several hundred to several thousands of people with dispatch prior to and immediately following performances

Museums need to be planned to articulate with their city environment and with the type of materials to be presented in them. Most museums need more storage and vault space than exhibition space because only a small proportion of the objets d'art are expected to be on view and available for study at a given time. Galleries need to be sized in accordance with the type of materials to be exhibited. Some galleries may be small in order to house miniatures, and others extremely large. Large halls and service elevators must be provided. Museums usually need large lecture halls as well as small, intimate study and studio spaces. With excessively large peak audiences, special designs must be used to insure maximum protection of art from damage and from theft. Many art objects require climate control for protection against deterioration. Museums require galleries for changing exhibitions, particularly for exhibitions loaned from other museums.

Library and restaurant facilities support both the style of life associated with museum-going and study activities sponsored by museums.

Most theaters, museums, and music halls have regular and predictable peak use periods. Therefore, clustered and shared spaces often facilitate both art participants and staffs. Parking lots, transportation access, libraries, restaurants, and ticket lobbies can all be shared, or partly shared, when art complexes are systematically designed (Hopkins 1972).

RECREATION AND URBANIZATION

Recreation in urban areas, like the arts, is extensive and diverse. The most outstanding performers and teams come to major urban stadiums. Moreover, in areas of the world where post-industrial society is developing, opportunities for urban recreation accelerate (Riesman 1958). Mass recreation and leisure are now typical as the work week shortens from sixty hours in the previous century to under forty hours in the 1970s.

Dumazedier (1967) puts it another way by observing that in the United States of America an hour and a half per day is sufficient for a housewife to complete housework. By contrast the French housewife spends five hours in the same home care tasks. The difference is due to the amount of mechanization and household appliances. The reduction in time spent in housework may increase leisure time and change women's urban life styles.

The sociology of housing reveals special types of residence-centered recreation in the urban environment. More priority is placed on domestic family rooms and specific residential leisure facilities. Residences are places where people come for television viewing, music playing, parlor games, and so forth. Most leisure reading is done in homes. Urban man now has as much time for recreation and leisure as for sleeping. Accordingly, the sociophysical environment which supports recreation both in the home and out of it justifiably receives an intensified planning effort.

Vacation trips are taken mostly by urbanites. They are particularly popular among affluent classes who can flee crowded urban areas from time to time by plane, recreation vehicle, or camper. Tourist accommodations both within big cities and in remote open areas are now developed internationally.

Open space for recreation

Open space for urban recreation ranges from remote wilderness areas to small central-city pocket parks, from balconies and patios to playing fields and stadiums (Taylor and Jones 1964). Wilderness users are disproportionately urban people. They are from small suburbs and large cities. They tend to be in their middle thirties, disproportionately male, and mostly from the higher occupations and professions. Municipalities have no authority over the wilderness areas. Wilderness land preserves are normally controlled by provincial governments or national governments. Next in remoteness and size to the wilderness areas are the metropolitan regional parks. They may be operated by special district governments or by some other intermediate-level government, but seldom by one single municipality (Shomon 1971). Some regional park boards are given tax authority to support their programs. Regional parks may be large enough to provide for ecological balance, for camping, for participator sports, and for nature walks.

A variation on the regional park theme is the greenbelt. This is the preservation of a strip of land around a major urban area to provide open space as well as ecological balance. The greenbelt may have some multiple use in that part of the land; it may be cultivated for agriculture and tree farming. The greenbelt around the city of London is the most famous example of this type of open space. Numerous other municipalities have also adopted greenbelt strategies to achieve a higher quality recreational environment.

At the other extreme is the pocket park. This is the development of a small piece of open land in a large city into a space for leisure and recreation. One of the most notable of these is New York's Paley Park. It was opened in 1967 on Manhattan Island at 53rd Street just off Fifth Avenue. Its total area is only 2,520 square feet. It is planted with deciduous trees that are watered from underground so that paving can be within a few inches of the trunks. At the back of the park is a manmade waterfall with a pool at its base. Walls are planted with kudzu and English ivy to provide a cool cover. Chairs and small tables are clustered under the trees. The park is opened daily at 8:00 A.M. and has attendants on duty continually through the early night hours. Between two and three thousand people use the park regularly on sunny days (Shomon 1971).

Balconies, patios, and playing fields are regularly found in cities. Balconies and patios may provide quiet, contemplative leisure space for individuals and for small group activities. Playing fields are larger and provide primarily for active participation sports. Some playing fields are aggregated to provide for large numbers of games simultaneously. This aggregation of playing sites is used extensively in Mexico City and in Brasilia. Playing fields are usually neighborhood or village facilities while recreational balconies and patios are primarily extensions of individual residential spaces.

Parks are for people. They are usually designed for multiple uses (Rutledge 1971). As Tom Hoving observed when he was head of the New York City Parks Department, "They are neither open-air gymnasiums nor botanical gardens. But many large well organized parks can adapt to different uses at different times" ("Parkitecture" 1973). Flexibility in park use was a principle that guided Frederick Law Olmstead when in the 1850s he designed the now famous New York Central Park. For more than a century, urban parks have continually expanded in area and in use. They are usually designed by landscape architects, managed by professionally trained recreationists, and under policy direction of citizen park boards. There are also parks that charge fees and/or operate for profit, like Copenhagen's Tivoli and Southern California's Disneyland.

In sociophysical planning, parks, like other parts of the environment, are viewed as parts of a larger urban social system. Planners start with the assumption that parks are for people. Therefore, access must be easily available. Special and compatible areas must be arranged. For example, children's play areas need to be located so that adults can supervise unobtrusively. In other cases, spaces may be provided for individual contemplation — that is, quiet activities separated from group participation activities. For example, benches may be arranged in groups to facilitate people's facing each other for conversation, or they may be arranged back-to-back or even with some kind of buffer planting between them to provide for quiet isolation space. Often parks must provide for separating automobile and foot traffic and in some cases even must provide separate lanes and paths for bicycle and horse traffic. Overpasses and underpasses may facilitate these separations.

Specific standards are followed for various games and recreational areas. For example, physical planners design totlots to have between 2,400 and 5,000 square feet of surface area. In addition to this basic size, they must be fitted carefully into an environment for their unique use. They may require additional space to be used as a buffer zone between the totlot and the nearby street or other incompatible land use (Rutledge 1971).

Standards for recreational activities may be found in books like de Chiara and Koppelman's *Urban Planning and Design Criteria.* In the case of some recreation areas, such as those for tennis and swimming, the physical dimensions are specified by the rules of the game, whereas others, such as those for picnicking and fishing, are determined more by attitudes and value judgments. In the case of picnic sites, research findings show that between ten and fifteen per acre, or between 3,900 and 4,300 square feet per each picnic area, is desirable. Certain game activities should have playing areas designed systematically in terms of the direction of the sun and the prevailing wind. Tennis courts should be perpendicular to the sun's course, baseball diamonds should be laid out so that the sun is not in the batter's or viewers' eyes. Plantings may contribute to the general aesthetic quality of a park and also provide buffers to minimize noise, avoid unattractive views, reduce wind, and retard soil erosion. Detailed specifications for playing fields are laid out in rule books. Once the rules of the game are accepted, the land area needed will vary only by physical features of the site and access to it.

Standards for hiking, nature trails, and fishing are more complex. Nature trails, for example, are specified in length by miles and width by feet with number of persons maximum per mile. Similarly, hiking and riding trails are determined in terms of mile lengths. It is recommended that rest stops be established every three to five miles and overnight campsites every ten to twenty miles. Width of trails varies considerably, but emphasis should also be placed on providing maximum views.

The design of campsites constitutes a challenge to provide for privacy, utilities, and sanitation. Campsite variations include squares and circles with electricity, water, and sanitary facilities located centrally. Buffer planting for privacy, utility service cores in the center, and ample access roadways are designed according to terrain. Fourplex arrangements provide for approximately 2,400 square feet of camping area per unit, and circular designs provide approximately 1,850 square feet per campsite.

Planning for winter sports is newer. We illustrate the need to accommodate urbanites who exodus to snow slopes by only one example, namely ski areas. Space and slope areas are divided into three categories for beginners, advanced, and experts. Studies reveal that an average skier utilizes 8,000 feet of skiing area per day. This may be accomplished by making four trips on a slope with a 2,000-foot drop or sixteen trips on a slope with a 500-foot drop.

Multipurpose recreation areas

Multipurpose land use areas can provide various types of recreation and leisure advantages for urbanites. Neighborhood parks and school recreation facilities can often be combined into one facility. Flood plains that are unsuitable for industrial, commercial, and residential structures may often be utilized satisfactorily as park and recreation areas. Some types of agricultural land may also be effectively utilized for urban recreation. This is specifically illustrated in the case of hunting fowl along the periphery of some cultivated land areas. Agricultural land and greenbelt land may be used also for hiking and birdwatching. Open-country recreational land in urban areas may provide additional functions like noise abatement and pollution reduction.

An example of a flood-plain area becoming developed into an immensely successful urban recreational linear park is found in the American River territory as it flows through the city and county of Sacramento, California (Shomon 1971). The county has remained constant in land size since it was established. The city, on the other hand, has grown rapidly in population and in territory. In 1960 the Standard Metropolitan Statistical Area had 625,000 people and in 1970 its population totaled over 800,000; by 1980 it is expected to be more than 1 million. Green space for recreation and for pollution control was rapidly shrinking. In 1962 a group of citizens organized the Save the American River Association. They were effective in having five thousand acres along twenty-three miles of flood plain designated as the American River Parkway. Now the recreational facilities along this parkway include an eighteen-hole golf course, twenty miles of recreational trails, and a fishing and boating area. Other recreational activities provided for in the American River Parkway include picnicking areas, overnight and day camping sites, livery stables, and swimming and archery areas. Boy Scout and Camp Fire Girls facilities are provided also.

New towns constitute another important example of large amounts of green space designated for multiple purposes. As a general rule, new towns, in the garden-city model, attempt to designate about 30 percent of their land area for open space and recreational use. One of the most well known examples of favorable achievement in this regard is that of Reston, Virginia. This new town is designed to accommodate 75,000 people by 1980 on a wooded, rolling site of 6,800 acres. The location is eighteen miles west of Washington, D.C., four miles east of the Dulles International Airport. The residential areas are divided into seven villages around two lakes. Also industrial locations are designated. But the emphasis at Reston is on public open space, much of which is owned and maintained by a property owner's association. Specific recreational facilities include walkways, bridle paths, areas for swimming, boating, and fishing, and five golf courses. Other garden-city new towns tend to approximate the amount and range of recreational activities found in Reston (Seeley 1973; Barasch 1974).

Planning for recreation

Several sets of planning standards exist for recreation. All of them lack widespread adoption except for playing-space sizes related to specific game rules. Recreation is more active than contemplative, just the reverse of the situation with the arts. Therefore, it is by degree at least easier to plan for recreation. In many municipalities one parks-and-recreation board has decision-making and management responsibility for most outdoor recreation. Planners can deal primarily with one agency or board.

Outdoor recreation planning needs to emphasize ecology, especially related to user populations. Some plant types are more resilient than others in the face of large populations. Some soil types quickly disintegrate under intensive trail use. In addition, some water areas become quickly polluted when use is overly intensive.

Access must be systematically planned for people, camping gear, boating equipment, and other recreational support materials. Meals, training, comfort stations, and first-aid facilities are important elements of the outdoor recreation environment. Sheltered protection against inclement weather is also a desireable addition to planned recreational areas.

Outdoor recreation space needs to be systematically planned to interface with the arts, schools, and health and welfare programs. Also a recreational planning matrix needs to consider different ages and both sexes, and provide for both active and passive participation.

IMPLICATIONS

In terms of sociophysical planning, the arts and recreation should be expressions of human heights in civilization. Provision must be made to record past achievements as well as to provide for high-quality current participation. Physically some 30 percent or more of urban land area may be productively utilized for the arts and recreation if a high-quality environment is to be obtained. The arts and recreation express wide-ranging differences. The reading of a poem or a novel may be supported by quiet and solitude. A big city's pocket park may be smaller than a suburban lot. Art facilities, like New York's Lincoln Center, may have a total seating capacity larger than the population of many small towns. Some urban regional park systems and wilderness areas may encompass an acreage greater than that of many municipalities.

With people enjoying longer lives and shorter work periods, planning for the arts and recreation needs a higher priority for the future than it has been given in the past. Specific standards need to be developed and their adoption utilized in the expansion of existing cities and the development of new urban areas.

Finally, recreation and the arts need to be planned in relation to education, health, welfare, and transportation.

REFERENCES

ALBRECHT, M. C., BARNETT, J. H., & GRIFF, M. *The Sociology of Art and Literature.* New York: Praeger, 1970.

BACON, E. N. *Design of Cities.* New York: Viking Press, 1974.

BARASCH, S. B. *Recreational Planning for New Communities.* New York: An Exposition-University Book, 1974.

BOAS, F. *Primitive Art.* New York: Dover Publications, 1955.

DE CHIARA, J., & KOPPELMAN, L. *Urban Planning and Design Criteria.* New York: Van Nostrand, 1975.

DUMAZEDIER, J. *Toward a Society of Leisure.* New York: Free Press, 1967.

Evolution of a museum. *Art in America,* 1965, 53, 28–32.

GREEN, H. & HOLZMAN, H. Orchestra hall. *Progressive Architecture,* 1975, 56, 50–53.

HAUSER, A. *The Social History of Art.* New York: Vintage Books, 1957.

HOPKINS, H. Ft. Worth siblings. *Art in America,* 1972, 60, 49.

KAPLAN, M. *Leisure in America.* New York: Wiley, 1960.

LERMAN, L. *The Museum.* New York: Viking Press, 1969.

Lincoln Center for the Performing Arts. New York: Lincoln Center for the Performing Arts, Inc., 1964.

Louisiana. Humlebaek, Denmark: The Louisiana Foundation, n.d.

MCGRATH, K. M. *1971 Financial and Salary Survey.* New York: American Association of Museums, 1971.

MARGOLIES, J. S. Three new theaters. *Art in America,* 1970, 58, 88–93.

Museums. *Progressive Architecture,* 1975, 56 (special issue).

Museums and the Environment. New York: Arcville Press, 1971.

Museums as monuments. *Progressive Architecture,* 1975, 56, 42–47.

Museums U.S.A.: Highlights. Washington, D.C.: National Endowment for the Arts, 1974.

Parkitecture. *Progressive Architecture,* 1973, 54 (special issue).

REDSTONE, L. G. *Art in Architecture*. New York: McGraw-Hill, 1968.
RIESMAN, D. Leisure at work in post-industrial society. In E. Larrabee & R. Meyersohn (Eds.), *Mass Leisure*. New York: Free Press, 1958.
ROUSSEAU, J. J. *The Social Contract*. Translated by E. Barker. London: J. M. Dent and Sons, 1913.
RUTLEDGE, A. J. *Anatomy of a Park*. New York: McGraw-Hill, 1971.
SCOTT, M. *American City Planning Since 1890*. Berkeley: University of California Press, 1969.
SEELEY, I. H. *Outdoor Recreation and the Urban Environment*. London: Macmillan, 1973.
SELZ, P., & KOSTOF, S. Three new museums. *Art in America*, 1968, 56, 104–07.
SHOMON, J. J. *Open Land for Urban America*. Baltimore: Johns Hopkins Press, 1971.
TAYLOR, L. Participation in the art world by town and country people. *Journal of Home Economics*, 1960, 52, 421–24.
TAYLOR, L., & JONES, A. R. *Rural Life and Urbanized Society*. New York: Oxford University Press, 1964. (See especially chapter 7, "Vacationing Itinerants in Rural Areas.")
TOFFLER, A. *The Culture Consumers*. Baltimore: Penguin Books, 1965.
TUNNARD, C. *The City of Man*. New York: Charles Scribner's Sons, 1970.

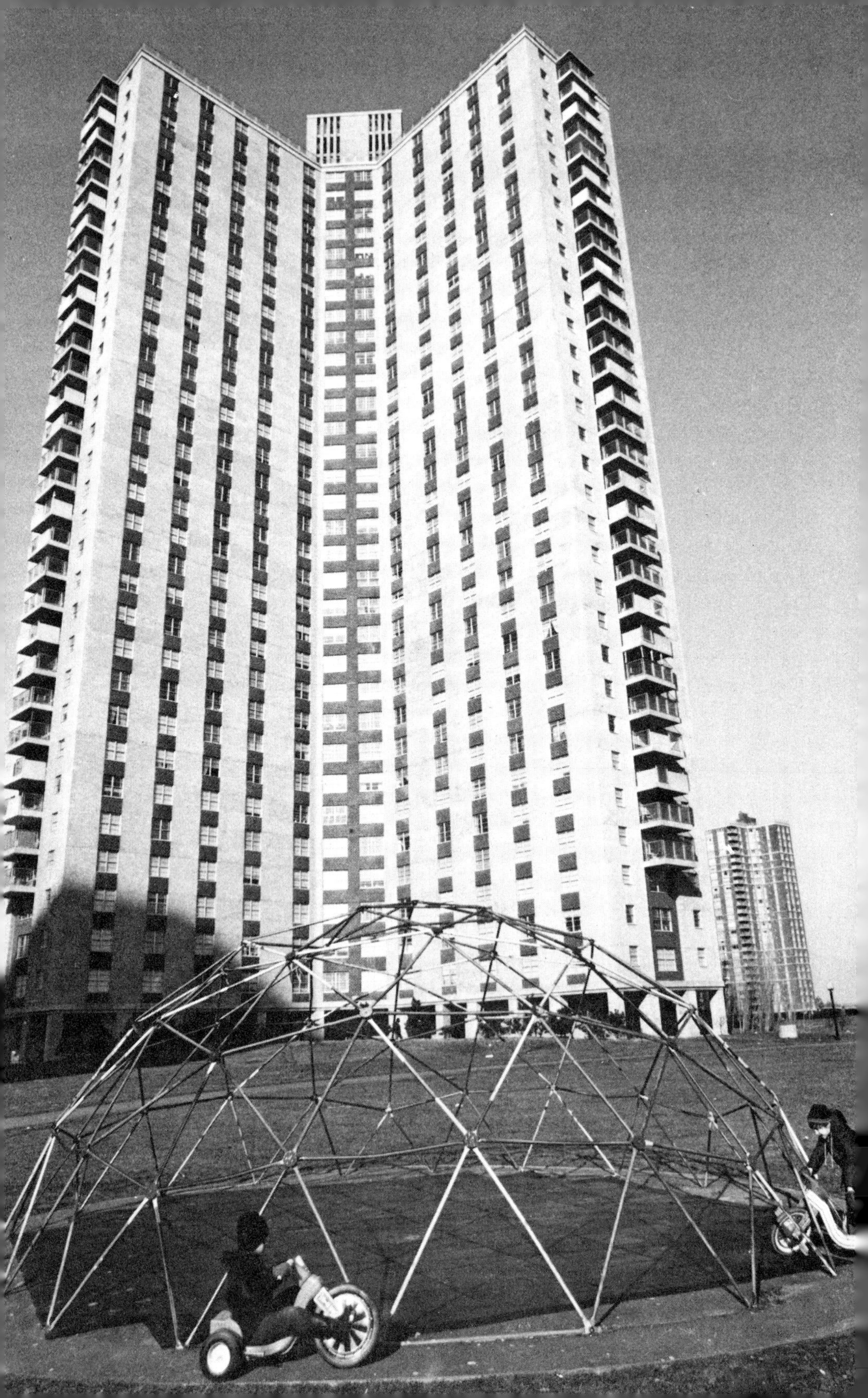

Health, Welfare, and Crime Deterrents

12

The advantages of urban life are many, but they are sharply punctuated by problems of health, welfare, and crime. Urban data show a high correlation between these problems and large urban populations that are densely settled. There are some exceptions to the large urban populations and the antisocial behavior correlations. Moreover urban environments can be built to reduce disease, provide for high-quality welfare, and deter crime. Humans by nature are gregarious animals and potentially well suited to urban life. Health advantages, the delivery of welfare services, and the attainment of safety are all potential major urban amenities.

City planning grew out of the desire to ameliorate urban social problems (Goodman and Freund 1968). Ebenezer Howard's classic book explaining the garden-city new-town model was subtitled "Nothing Gained from Overcrowding" (Howard 1965). But in spite of these views and correlations, there is little conclusive evidence concerning urban density and social problems. The concept of "urban overload" is increasingly heard, and people's techniques for dealing with it are clear (Milgram 1970; Palen 1975). Additionally, urban social structures may be created so that individuals can avoid overload problems. Urban health departments and urban welfare departments, for example, may become substitutes for individual concerns for health and welfare.

From a positive view, large urban environments support superior research hospitals and provide a range of welfare services far surpass-

Large urban developments, such as this New York City cooperative, provide play spaces for small children. (Photo: Fredrik D. Bodin for Stock, Boston.)

ing anything known in rural societies. Techniques for delivering health and welfare services to urbanites are continually refined and updated. Certainly urban people come to expect a wide range of quality health and welfare services. Preventive medical practices are an example. These may include inoculation against certain diseases in order to enter schools and/or the requirement of physical examinations in order to obtain certain jobs. Some segments of urban populations view these requirements as invasions of personal rights and freedoms. Still other subsets of urban populations, particularly the disadvantaged poor, may argue that their access to health and welfare services is insufficient. Such insufficiencies stimulate demonstrations and antisocial behavior — increasing crimes against both persons and property in cities. In effect the urban environment sets in operation a spiraling rise in expectations. When the design of cities contributes to the inadequacy of meeting health and welfare expectations, antisocial behavior is one result.

The goal of this chapter is to examine planned social and physical organizations for reducing disease, facilitating the delivery of welfare services, and decreasing crime.

HEALTH AND URBAN PLANNING

Health is a biosocial phenomenon. According to the World Health Organization health is defined as "a state of complete physical, mental, and social well being and not merely the absence of disease and infirmity" (Jus 1973, p. 125). Urban people may be primary causers of disease, transmitters of disease, or targets of disease. Humans cause disease by misuse of the natural environment, by creating malfunctioning built environments, by overpopulation, and by using malfunctioning technologies (Cappon 1974). Humans transmit diseases through both social and physical interaction. Urban people are the targets of some diseases because in biological terms they are "living hosts." Natural hazards target urban populations with some epidemics.

Part of the urbanization experience of humans in the last one hundred years is an advancing medical technology which has nurtured population growth and the doubling of the length of life. These medical advances have been supported by urban scientific contributions to nutritional and food production achievements.

In science-dominated urbanized societies, disease is viewed as a challenge to be eradicated. Accordingly, the preservation of health becomes an expanded urban activity system.

Health care as an urban social system

The elements of the health social system include, first, people — healthy people, sick people, research people, and health-care people. Hospitals and out-patient clinics are sociophysical elements of the health system. Increasingly we recognize air pollution, water pollution, sound pollution, and crime as components in the health environment. More recently, particularly for psychiatric disorders, we recognize urban social interaction in work, commuting, families, and small groups as elements in the health activity system. No less important are issues concerning the economics of health. The costs of medicine and hospital services to individuals are a major social problem. High costs contribute to demands for socialized medicine. The accumulated cost to society of illness in work absenteeism, socialized medical care, and antisocial behavior is astronomical.

An examination of urban medical systems in the United States, the Soviet Union, and China is instructive. While these are not mutually exclusive examples, ideologies and levels of urbanization are sufficiently different to demonstrate variations in planning.

American urban health systems

From a macrosociological viewpoint, America's health system in the 1970s is relatively "open." Its boundaries are permeated by Medicare. The linkage between the medical system and the society at large is poignantly illustrated by the annual loss of 540,000 man years due to heart disease alone. Half of the individuals rejected for military service in the United States are disqualified for medical reasons. While most advances in medicine are biological, urban America experiences a situation in which half of all hospital beds are utilized for psychiatric care (Field 1970).

The United States attempts to respond to medical care needs using a supermarket-type hospital. The supermarket hospital is impersonal. Medical specialists backed by a large supporting staff treat a heart, a kidney, a lung, an eye, or an ear more than a total individual. The role of the general practitioner or the family physician is largely replaced by specialists (Field 1970). The technology developed to support expanding medical knowledge is usually available only in the supermarket hospitals. Biological persons are well cared for by this system, but sociological persons and psychological persons are cared for poorly. There is an increasing need for family physicians. The planning of space for medicine in urban society needs to facilitate more health generalists' being able to treat whole persons.

As the urban medical social system expands, health personnel grow in numbers and in type. Medical specialists are at the apex. Beneath them are the general practitioners. The next lower categories are persons in allied health occupations like nurses, technicians, and therapists. At the bottom of the hierarchy are support staff like stenographers, repairmen, laundry and cleaning workers, ambulance drivers, and cooks. Table 12 – 1 shows the expansion of health and allied personnel from 1900 to 1970. In seven decades the number of physicians has doubled. The number of dentists has more than doubled. Professional nurses have increased from less than one thousand to over half a million. Additionally there are significant expansions among biological scientists, biostatisticians, clinical psychologists, dental hygienists, dieticians, health educators, medical laboratory technologists, medical records librarians, optometrists, pharmacists, rehabilitation counselors, social workers, and therapists. As health care expectations increase, many kinds of professionals and nonprofessionals become integral parts of medical teams. Yet while the medical teams expand in large hospitals, many patients fail to cope with the "highly confusing and disturbing labyrinth, a Kafka-like medical maze, often what we might call the 'medicine of the absurd' technological sophistication and the dehumanized handling of recipients of the sophistication" (Field 1970, pp. 171-172). Urban planners are challenged to provide for sophisticated and advanced practices by placing them more in the context of the whole person.

TABLE 12—1 Persons Employed in Selected Health Professions in the United States, 1900–1970

Year	Physicians	Dentists	Professional Nurses
1900	123,500	29,700	640
1910	152,400	40,000	50,500
1920	151,300	56,200	103,900
1930	162,700	71,100	214,300
1940	174,500	71,000	284,200
1950	199,900	75,900	375,000
1960	242,500	87,000	504,000
1970	284,000	91,000	629,000

Source: U.S. Public Health Service, Chart Book on Health Status and Health Manpower *(Washington, D.C., 1961) and U.S. Census of Population,* General Characteristics, 1970, *Vol. 1, Part 1, Section 2, Table 221 U.S. Summary (Washington, D.C., 1970).*

Soviet urban health systems

The social system of medicine in the Soviet Union involves centralized five-year planning for the number of hospital beds, the number of physicians, sanitoria bed capacities, the training of medical personnel, and the amount of medical facility construction. At lower administrative levels, planning and programming is carried out for specific needs. The Soviet Union is divided into fifteen constituent republics for administrative organization. Each of the republics is divided into *oblasts*, and each *oblast* is further subdivided into *rayons*. *Oblast* populations usually range between one-half million and several million people. At the *rayon* level, particularly in rural areas, populations may be a few thousand; the largest are in Moscow with populations of one-half million. For health planning purposes, each *rayon* is divided into *ucastoks* or medical districts. The various kinds of *ucastoks* include therapeutic communities for adult populations up to two thousand people, pediatric medical districts for between eight hundred and one thousand children, obstetrical and gynecology medical districts for about two thousand persons, and industrial *ucastoks* for about two thousand factory workers each (Popov 1971).

The principles for health planning in the U.S.S.R. include a balance of objectives, flexibility, efficient resource use, and projection of manpower requirements. Health planning is done comprehensively. Hospital care, outpatient care, and health resorts are all planned simultaneously. The purposes of the planning are highly specific. For example, from 1966 to 1970 the goals of Soviet health-care planning focused on the reduction of both morbidity and mortality primarily among children, the reduction and/or eradication of communicable diseases, overall improvement in medical care standards, improved medical research and utilization of research personnel, increased quality in medical training and placement, improvement in the technology of health services, and improved working and living conditions for health personnel (Popov 1971).

Out-patient care in the U.S.S.R. is far greater in proportion than hospital care. Recently the differential has run as high as forty-two out-patient contacts for every one hospitalized patient. In urban areas out-patient care is provided for by "poly" clinics, out-patient clinics, follow-up centers, and children's and women's clinics. Rural areas still have significantly less medical care.

In the U.S.S.R. hospitals tend to have more beds than in the U.S.A. In America there are more support personnel for physicians and accordingly fewer physicians per ten thousand population than in the U.S.S.R. The point is that while there are real differences in the content of the health social systems in these two nations, the fact of

Chinese urban health systems

The health-care systems in China that we consider here date from 1939 (Liang 1974). When the Chinese People's Republic came into power there were 10,000 so-called modern physicians and some 500,000 traditional healers for a population of 600 million. Both disease and poverty were rampant. Prior to the communist regime the occupation of physician was held in low prestige — not fit for a gentleman and comparable to a tradesman or an artisan. There were early attempts to substitute modern medicine for traditional medicine but they had all failed. At the communist takeover in 1949 modern medicine was available only for government officials and for a small fraction of the population living in cities. By 1954 the Mao government had brought about the integration of modern medicine and traditional medicine. New institutes were opened for the study of traditional medicine, and research was carried out to ascertain its points of validity. Traditional medicine was used for practical and ethnocentric reasons, but scientific medicine was introduced into the training and practice.

The People's Republic initiated a Patriotic Health Campaign early on in a fight against flies, rats, sparrows, mosquitoes, and syphilis. Working against these health hazards were birth control specialists, barefoot doctors, and factory doctors. China approached the health systems with realism. It stressed that which could actually be done by its delivery system, which was dominated by traditionalism. It avoided Western health care methods which are capital-intensive and hospital-specialist based. Between 1949 and the 1970s four principles guided the regime's medical social system: "One, serve workers, peasants, and soldiers; two, regard prevention as the principal activity; three, unite Western and Chinese traditional doctors; four, combine public health with mass movements" (Liang 1974, p. 209).

The medical system in China still has direct concerns for sanitary projects, community latrines, and general health education programs. The achievements are many. Nevertheless, differences in quality and quantity of health care for the 20 percent urban population and the 80 percent rural population are significant. The urban population is enormously advantaged in health care, but systematic efforts are continually being made to narrow the gap.

China's health ministry is urban oriented, but efforts are being made to broaden its focus. Medical education reforms are in progress which require students to practice while continuing their study. The central government is in charge of medical hospitals and equipment.

Drug production and health workers' salaries are matters determined at local levels. Since the Cultural Revolution, medical teams have been widely dispersed. Their goals are to spread preventative medicine and therapeutic services. Accordingly, efforts are being made to train auxiliary medical personnel from villages. Ultimately this means one peasant doctor for each 1,500 people, and one volunteer sanitary worker for each 200 people, plus one midwife for each village.

A continuing high priority is placed on the party's planned parenthood programs. Patriotic health programs continued to be expanded during the "great leap forward." At the elementary level the barefoot rural doctors are said to meet a minimum of only three years of elementary school. Their counterparts in the cities are the Red Guard doctors, and in the factories the worker doctors. Their functions are primarily environmental sanitation, health education, immunization, first aid, and simple primary medical care.

In the Chinese health-care system the ultimate goal is to make medical service available free to all people. Currently all persons except government and factory workers pay for medical services.

The cases of the U.S.A., the U.S.S.R., and China illustrate health social systems that are ideologically dominated by local control in the case of America and by centralized control in the case of the U.S.S.R. and China. But regardless of this ideology, as human societies urbanize, the elements of health care are increasingly seen in social systems terms. Even when physicians engage in private practice for fees, the requirements of modern medicine necessitate their participation in the hospital system and their utilization of large numbers of semiprofessionals and lower support staff. In China the system of health care is most particularly visible at the environmental level, where it is aimed at improved sanitation.

World health planning — an alternative

In 1970 the World Health Organization focused attention on environmental health and its relation to the total health care system (Haffen 1972). With increased numbers of people in densely populated urban areas, the relationships of health to water pollution, air pollution, and noise pollution became more critical. Pesticides, for example, may become health hazards in food. Air pollution has several devastating impacts on human health, particularly involving the respiratory system. Water pollution has a broad range of negative impacts on health. Noise and radiation pollution impact negatively on urban man's health. The polluting impact of people on people at high densities is far less understood but nevertheless recognized as part of the environmental health social system complex.

Wolstenholme (1969) presses the view that individual nations should not attempt solutions to their own health problems as if they were in a vacuum. The further assertion is made that health service should become a "pilot plan" for world society. We must order a sociophysical environment which will provide for improved individual health, and through that strategy, contribute to sustaining healthy societies. Indeed Maxmen (1976) asserts that "Doctors will be obsolete in fifty years, replaced by computers and a new type of health care professional" (see also Herber 1962). From the World Health Organization view, as the planet's population increases, as mobility accelerates, and as multinational industries expand, the health or nonhealth of people on one part of the planet impacts on those in all other parts. Nevertheless, barriers to world health strategies are deeply rooted in different value systems. In the urbanized-industrial parts of the world, disease control is largely a matter of biology and scientific management of the environment. In ruralized parts of the world, health may be regarded as more a matter of fate and explained by religions rather than by science. The Norwegian health specialist Evang (1969) puts it succinctly: "our world at present is deep-frozen in an unhealthy medium of national and political interests and tradition, made even more unappetizing by the generous addition of racial and religious prejudices" (p. 167). In Buckminster Fuller's "World Game," man must be returned to a condition of comprehensiveness at a world level (Fuller 1970). Fuller views health as man's ability to cope effectively with the environment through organization rather than by monetary means.

Both nationally and internationally, basic questions concerning health planning for the year 2000 include whether or not access to health service should be free or prorated on a financial need basis. If total health care is to be provided, it becomes in fact a type of income redistribution system.

Both nationally and internationally, planned reform of medical delivery systems are questions to be considered if high-quality urban societies are to exist. Already in Great Britain the geographic distribution of specialists is generally controlled by government-owned hospitals that control staffing patterns in terms of delivery system needs (Burns 1973).

Sociophysical health planning: some alternatives

Health planning is multifaceted. Here we discuss only three aspects of health planning: sociophysical health system elements; health-promoting social structures as alternatives to disease-control structures; and world health plans. In the case of health care, planning is designed for the deliberate intervention of change in an operating social system (Rosenthal 1970). The planning model involves first the definition of the system, second the specification of the objectives, third the statement of policies, and fourth a system of evaluation. Planning personnel may include physicians and other members of allied health medical organizations but should not be dominated by them. In the past much of what has been called health care planning has in fact been partial hospital planning dominated by medical practitioners. In the case of social systems planning, participants must include consumers of health services, general community members, government officials, and health practitioners. By the nature of the case the system is defined at a societal rather than an individual practitioner level. The objectives of the system planning are to bring equity among consumers, producers, practitioners, and the society at large. Viewed in this larger perspective, the policies for operating the system must interface with the general level of service desired by the total society. One society might desire to make medical services free, another to make only selected services free, and still another to operate medicine on a pay-as-you-go system. The general policy for operating the medical social system may vary also concerning the number and roles of specialists and the number and roles of general practitioners. One system may call for a maximum number of general practitioners and a maximum number of support staff while another system may call for a maximum number of specialists and fewer support staff. Real constraints may be thrust on policy choices by resource limitations, political limitations, and informational limitations.

Subsystems may be defined in the planning model. These may deal with specialized services like dental care and eye care. The operation of a general systems planning model is also utilized at the subsystems level.

Health-promoting social systems, sometimes referred to as healthing systems, may be specifically articulated as an alternative in medical planning. Healthing employs the general social systems model. Its specific content, however, is unique. Most health systems are disease-epidemic-crisis oriented. By contrast, healthing is a positive model. It seeks to describe healthy behavior and to enforce that behavior. Hoke (1974) suggests that to implement a healthing model we need two complementary medical cadres, one a disease profession and the second a health profession. The former would concentrate on treating disease while the latter would focus on improving health situations. The social system for the health profession would emphasize activities in schools, factories, and other places where large numbers of people are found and could be made receptive to health-care information. In effect environmental and educational manipulation would be used to stimulate and maintain positive healthing. The healthing systems model involves reinforcement and sociocultural pressure. To date in urbanized society, we have established more sick roles than health roles. Indeed, the few health roles we have defined such as the "health nut," the "food faddist," or the "super athlete," frequently have negative images.

The social system for the healthing environment can be rationally planned. Sociophysically this is already seen by the use of architectural psychology in the construction of some new schools and hospitals using color, space, and sound to ameliorate the environment. Other subunits of the healthing environment are exemplified in Alcoholics Anonymous, groups for the aged, and programs for the deaf and blind.

From a biological point of view it is probable that people will never solve disease problems completely. From a sociophysical point of view it is entirely possible that healthing situations can characterize large urban environments. Soleri refers to his arcology megastructure designs in healthing environment terms. Certainly in social system planning, the arcology is an example of the potential healthing environment.

As urbanization rapidly becomes a worldwide phenomenon, the health social system must increasingly be articulated on a world scale. Ultimately the sociophysical medical planning suggested here involves a conscious social systems approach recognizing that energy and money spent for disease control and for health must be balanced with resources for education, industrial production, and other societal needs. As both the values and needs for improved health maintenance increase in urbanized society, the importance of national and international healthing environments is accelerated. Social structures that support preventative medicine deserve greater planning priority.

WELFARE AND URBAN PLANNING

In the last one hundred years as many societies have moved toward a saturated urbanization, welfare needs have increased. Much of the physical city planning movement is a direct outgrowth of poverty conditions in major urban areas. Physical planners have sought to improve the built environment, and thereby hoped to ameliorate the welfare of urban people.

In rural societies welfare was largely taken care of in families or kinship groups. Populations were typically small and low-density. These factors tended to reduce both real and apparent social welfare needs. In large, densely populated urban areas, secondary social structures are developed to offset urban overload problems and to fill voids in reduced kinship and family structures. Much of the early craft union movement was welfare-oriented.

By the 1970s more than 6 percent of the U.S.A. population received monetary payment under public assistance programs (*Public Assistance Statistics* 1970). In America public assistance programs have grown as the society has urbanized, even in the prosperous mid-twentieth century.

A basic welfare policy question, similar to that in health, concerns whether or not welfare is a right or a privilege (Sternlieb 1973). Some major welfare needs that are widespread in urban areas include aid to dependent children, old age assistance, aid to the blind and disabled, and home relief. Some of these major welfare needs are the residue of societies that have recently and rapidly experienced a transition from rural to urban. In such transitional stages, significant proportions of citizens may be poorly prepared to serve themselves or society. This is to say that some welfare needs may in fact be ephemeral, since urbanization is such a recent phenomenon. On the other hand, many urban conditions of life produce overload and alienation. Unless urban societies can develop sociophysical mechanisms to reduce urban overload, they will in fact continue to generate large numbers of people in need of welfare. Also, to the extent that urbanized societies continue to use individual jobs as a mechanism for distributing the means of subsistence, unemployment will be a serious social welfare problem. Guaranteeing annual income, used with population control, is an alternative.

Welfare and urban social organization

Social welfare becomes institutionalized in urbanized societies in their early stages of development. We examine the developing phenomena of welfare and urbanization in the U.S.A. and the U.S.S.R. In the American experience the first half of the national period was predominantly rural. From the 1860s to the present there has been rapid urbanization. In 1920 the U.S. Census of Population reported more people residing in urban than in rural areas for the first time. A decade and a half later, the first Social Security Act was passed. Each year since, the federal Congress has in some way extended the benefits of social security. Such legislation makes normative the urbanized society's commitment to a decent standard of living for all people, to antipoverty programs, and to economic opportunities. Many voluntary social welfare programs carry out vital functions in urban areas. Municipalities and states also provide welfare services, but the federal government's welfare programs are increasingly dominant.

In America social welfare programs fall far short of being a viable social system. There is no overall planning (Pumphrey 1966). Between 1935 and the 1970s, the annual number of recipients of some form of welfare dependency allowance in the U.S. has grown to over 14 million persons (*Bureau of Labor Statistics Report 375* 1973). Cycles of poverty are growing. In the American patchwork welfare system, insufficient recognition is given, for example, to the fact that family space needs are greater before families reach their high earning power (Goodman and Freund 1968). There is a similar lack of facing up to the relationship between birth control and social welfare.

In both urban renewal and new-town planning, heterogeneous population mix is supported over homogeneity. Yet in the Pruitt-Igoe Housing Project in St. Louis, Missouri and in Boston's West End, Rainwater and Gans, respectively, empirically identified social discontent as people grieved for lost homes and familiar homogeneous neighborhoods. The greatest proportions of people with welfare needs are generally found distributed in slum areas adjacent to central business districts.

In the Soviet Union urbanization and social welfare needs have been addressed by dramatically new techniques in the last sixty years. Under the Czars, poor laws were vague and resources scarce (Madison 1968). The Ministry of Interior administered the welfare program as a charity operation before 1917. Little progress was made. By the end of the czarist regime, Russian welfare programs were behind those of other industrializing countries in Europe. Under the Soviets, urbanized welfare is based on citizens' legal rights to comprehensive assistance. There is a movement toward a state-guaranteed minimum income. Provisions for expectant mothers and for child allowance are being expanded. Similarly, services are expanded for the physically disabled, the emotionally disturbed, and the aged.

Soviet welfare programs are being decentralized in their administration. This is in an effort both to decrease alienation and to encourage young adults to seek careers in the welfare bureaucracy. While the Soviet social welfare program more approximates a social system than that in America, it faces many practical short-run problems. Most local agencies are only partially staffed by professional social workers. They are frequently overworked and undertrained. Problems for the Soviet system are still exacerbated by the residue of population who were stunned and left homeless by years of war and social upheaval from 1917 through World War II. More than a generation of unsupervised children now complicate welfare needs. Welfare benefits are not yet uniformly available throughout the U.S.S.R. More importantly, social insurance benefits are frequently inadequate.

The Soviets, more than the Americans, place a high priority on making the welfare system function properly. In America priority emphasis is on rehabilitation, and in the Soviet Union emphasis is on sustaining persons who need assistance (Madison 1968).

Social welfare planning: some alternatives

Welfare planning may be viewed as more social than physical. This is to say that fewer specifically designed physical spaces are required to support high-quality social welfare institutions than is the case for other urban activity systems related to hospitals, schools, and recreation. Gerontological facilities, day-care centers, and counseling offices exemplify some specific social welfare spaces. But in the main, social welfare is more related to employment opportunities and to family structures. Yet physical design of urban spaces may increase security or decrease it, increase aesthetics or decrease them, increase access to services or decrease it, and so forth.

Dykman (1966) has suggested that social planning may be articulated at three different levels: societal-level planning; evaluation of specific action programs; and local community planning. These are not mutually exclusive levels of planning. Instead they suggest that clarity concerning the level at which planning is being done be observed. Furthermore, the comparative examination of American and Soviet welfare planning illustrates the importance of differentiating precisely between efforts at short-range rehabilitation and efforts to alter circumstances that generate the need for welfare assistance in the long run. While Americans have put priority on short-range rehabilitation, the Soviets have put priority on long-range modification of the social system. Social planning suggests that both rehabilitation and changes in the system are needed. Planning for them must not be confused. Social organizational theory indicates that in the dynamic urbanized society with high rates of social interaction, some people will not be able to cope with the system. They will need continuing sustaining support. In other cases national, regional, and local social welfare planning should be interfaced. Such integrated planning can facilitate a reduction of urban overload and minimize alienation. Planning social welfare from a societal view can sustain comprehensiveness, enabling maximum numbers of people to be achievers for themselves and for society.

Planned Unit Developments and megastructures are two types of societal-local planning in which welfare systems may be in harmony with other urban systems. Sociophysical planning for welfare also involves ecological balance. In sum, social welfare in urbanized society is a matter of access to the multiple institutions of the society.

CRIME DETERRENTS AND URBAN PLANNING

Crime rates, based on acts of antisocial behavior reported to the police, tend to be highest in central-city areas and lowest on the urban fringes. Closer examination of the ecological distribution of crime also shows direct relationships with poor health, unemployment, limited education, broken families, minimal religious participation, and high use of welfare services. These general relationships are reported from the 1930s to the present for urban areas, particularly in the Western industrial nations (Harries 1974).

Urban ecology and antisocial behavior

Acts of antisocial behavior against both persons and property are most frequent and severe (1) among people in the lower classes, (2) among ethnic minorities, (3) in the early dark hours of the morning, and (4) on Fridays, Saturdays, and Sundays. Male youths and young adults are the most frequent offenders (Shaw 1929; McClintock 1963; Wallis 1967; Palen 1975). Harries has studied reports of antisocial behavior in Belgrade, Yugoslavia; Birmingham, England; London, England; and Seattle, Chicago, and Washington, D.C., United States. Data are from the 1920s to the 1960s. With the exception of Belgrade, a generally high correlation was found between high crime rates and nearness to the Central Business District. There were more common social characteristics than there was common ecology. The Belgrade data revealed that the highest rates of delinquency were not those in the districts most proximic to the central business area, but in an area of some 2,000 residential structures that had been built illegally. Furthermore, there was a substantial proportion of unregistered subtenants and much heterogeneity of population. Families in the area were large. Social pathologies including prostitution, gambling, alcoholism, begging, and fortune telling were typical. There was an absence of open recreational space.

In Seattle, crime was found to be most concentrated in skid-row areas where unemployment was high and there was a disproportion of unmarried males. Ethnic homogeneity was also high. In Washington, D.C.'s high crime areas there also was ethnic homogeneity — a dominance of blacks. Crime areas were in general characterized by low incomes, low education, poor health, and overcrowding.

Urban antisocial behavior is extensively related to inadequate access to and utilization of urban social services including health facilities, educational opportunities, housing, and jobs. The challenge of urban sociology and physical planning is, therefore, to organize and build sociophysical environments that will optimize people's opportunities for positive integration into the plural society, particularly in the early years of life.

Crime deterrents planning — some alternatives

Systematically planned defensible environments are possible. For example in densely settled urban residential areas, low-rise apartments can be planned so that multiple units have windows overlooking common entrance areas. On one hand, this makes it possible for persons to be under surveillance in entrance areas. This also facilitates neighbors' coming to recognize each other and to distinguish strangers. In high-rise units, interior hallways can be made defensible by making them large enough to qualify as social interaction areas. Indefensible double-load hallways can be redesigned to make them social gathering places (Newman 1972). In some cases hallways may be made exterior to buildings and widened as balconies so that passers-by will be under surveillance from apartment windows. Such widened balcony hallways may become places for communal babysitting and other neighborly social interaction. Linear parks may be designed so that persons passing by from streets and sidewalks will be able to look through parks, deterring crime in the process. Playground and other recreational facilities at the base of and/or on the roofs of buildings need to be accompanied by toy storage areas and by restroom facilities. These additions can deter theft and reduce antisocial behavior.

These sociophysical plans are consistent with the gregarious nature of man. They stimulate positive social interaction rather than create a police-type environment. Superblocks and Planned Unit Developments are further examples of sociophysical design for stimulating social behavior and reducing criminal acts. Comprehensive planning that integrates jobs, recreation, residences, commercial areas, and church sites facilitates social rather than antisocial behavior.

The study of crime deterrents is necessarily shorter than the study of health and welfare. Crime deterrents are a matter of sociophysical design. Health and welfare, by contrast, are both types of social service desired by urban people. We do not discuss here the design of jails and penal type facilities. Ideally a well planned urban environment should stimulate so much positive social behavior and negate antisocial behavior to such a degree that the systematic planning of penal institutions would be minimized. The few that would be needed would be oriented to sufficiently unique needs as to put them beyond generalized planning.

IMPLICATIONS

Health, welfare, and crime deterrents are each examined in this chapter from the point of view of social organization. Traditionally, health and welfare have been planned as if they were services to be delivered to an urban population in a vacuum. The implication here is that when these health and welfare delivery systems fail, crime rises. Data referenced in this chapter indicate that superior health facilities and superior welfare facilities, particularly in their physical forms, alone will do little to upgrade the quality of urban life. Ultimately one observes that in the changing urbanized ecology, suburbs which by default have more access to most of the social institutions also have the highest quality of life. There is much variation within the suburban areas. It is the balance of social systems in the general area and not the suburbs per se which are related to high-quality life styles. For example in Washington, D.C., which is predominantly Black in many areas, there are pronounced differences between areas where Whites live (predominantly on the west side of Rock Creek Park) and where Blacks live (on the opposite side). Where the affluent Whites even in a predominantly Black city are able to interact with all of the social systems of urbanized existence, quality of life is high. Older suburban areas are reporting increases in antisocial behavior as they experience physical deterioration, population shifts, and disequilibrium in their institutional urban activity systems.

Healthing environments are integrally related to the total social system of urban areas. The ideology of the healthing environment, in a social systems sense, leaves for the welfare programs the core of those individuals who for reasons of age and disability are unable to participate fully in the plural urban environment. This is in sharp contrast to the welfare structures in America since the 1930s, which have been disproportionately focused on rehabilitation. Much of the rehabilitation is focused on persons under age forty, for whom the social system of the urbanized society initially malfunctioned. Methods of rehabilitation are economically expensive for the society at large and have little possibility for success when the urban social system that originally malfunctioned continues in conflict. The cost to the individuals involved is even more critical than the economic cost to the society.

Health, welfare, and crime need to be viewed as parts of the larger urbanized society rather than as independent social structures demonstrating failure and conflict.

REFERENCES

Bureau of Labor Statistics Report, 375. Washington D.C.: C.P.S. Series P – 23, No. 29, 1973.
BURNS, E. *Health Services for Tomorrow.* New York: Dunellen Publishing Co., 1973.
CAPPON, D. Priorities in environmental health. *Ekistics,* 1974, *37,* 160 – 68.

DYKMAN, J. Social planning, social planners, and planned societies. *Journal of the American Institute of Planners*, 1966, *32*, 70 – 71.

EVANG, K. Political, national, and traditional limits to health control. In *Health of Mankind*. Boston: Little, Brown and Co., 1969.

FIELD, M. The medical system and industrial society. In A. Sheldon, F. Baker, & C. P. McLaughlin (Eds.), *Systems and Medical Care*. Cambridge: M.I.T. Press, 1970.

FULLER, R. B. *Operating Manual for Spaceship Earth*. New York: Pocket Books, 1970.

GOODMAN, W., & FREUND, E. *Principles and Practice of Urban Planning*. Washington, D.C.: International City Managers Association, 1968.

HAFFEN, B. (Ed.) *Man, Health, and Environment*. Minneapolis: Burgess Publishing Co., 1972.

HARRIES, K. *The Geography of Crime and Justice*. New York: McGraw-Hill, 1974.

HERBER, L. *Our Synthetic Environment*. New York: Alfred Knopf, 1962.

HOKE, B. Healths and healthing. *Ekistics*, 1974, *37*, 169 – 72.

HOWARD, E. *Garden Cities of Tomorrow*. Cambridge: M.I.T. Press, 1965.

JUS, A. Social systems and the criteria of health as defined by the World Health Organization. *American Journal of Psychiatry*, 1973, *130*, 125 – 31.

LIANG, M. et al., Chinese health care. *Ekistics*, 1974, *37*, 206 – 11.

MCCLINTOCK, F. H. *Crimes of Violence*. London: Macmillan, 1963.

MADISON, B. *Social Welfare in the Soviet Union*. Stanford: Stanford University Press, 1968.

MAXMEN, J. S. *The Post-Physician Era*. New York: Wiley 1976.

MILGRAM, S. The experience of living in cities. *Science*, 1970, *167*, 1461 – 68.

NEWMAN, O. *Defensible Space*. New York: Macmillan Co., 1972.

PALEN, J. *The Urban World*. New York: McGraw-Hill, 1975.

POPOV, G. A. *Principles of Health Planning in the U.S.S.R.* Geneva: World Health Organization, 1971.

Public Assistance Statistics. Washington, D.C.: Department of Health, Education, and Welfare, 1970.

PUMPHREY, R. The reinstitutionalization of social welfare. In S. B. Warner, Jr. (Ed.), *Planning for a Nation of Cities*. Cambridge: M.I.T. Press, 1966.

ROSENTHAL, G. Planning in the health care system. In A. Sheldon (Ed.), *Systems and Medical Care*. Cambridge: M.I.T. Press, 1970.

ST. PIERRE, C. Health planning in R. Buckminster Fuller's world game. *Ekistics*, 1974, *37*, 180 – 83.

SHAW, C. & MCKAY, H. D. *Delinquency Areas*. Chicago: University of Chicago Press, 1929.

STERNLIEB, G. *The Ecology of Welfare*. New Brunswick: Transaction Books, 1973.

WALLIS, C. P., & MALIPHANT, R. Delinquent areas in the county of London. *British Journal of Criminology*, 1967, *7*, 254.

WOLSTENHOLME, G. E. W. Outlines of a world health service as a step toward man's well-being and toward a world society. In *Health of Mankind*. Boston: Little, Brown & Co., 1969.

PART FIVE

Planning and Urban Prospects

Sociological inquiry into urban life styles is older than the discipline of city and regional planning. But sociologists have studied the city more for description and theory than for planning. Much of the discussion of the previous sections adheres closely to the traditions of urban sociology. Much of the information in the following section aims at interfacing urban sociology with city and regional planning.

Chapter thirteen deals with the societal context of planning and its relation of institutions to a planned high-quality life. The major elements of physical urban planning are related to specific people systems. Citizen participation and multisocietal planning are also discussed.

In Chapter fourteen the renewal of urban environments is discussed in social context. The focus is worldwide.

Chapter fifteen explores the prospects and problems of several different new-town models for higher quality urban environments. New towns are often viewed as spectacular. This may or may not be warranted. They are a worldwide experience, but they involve very few people as residents. To date, new-town projects implicitly interface with suburbanization, metropolitan regions, and the trend toward ecumenopolis.

In Chapter sixteen, a positive look is taken at the difficult subject of urban policy. The focus is at once on regional, national, and world urban policies.

le centre commercial
flandre est ouvert
DÈS MAINTENANT VOUS Y TROUVEZ...
BOULANGERIE PATISSERIE
TRAITEUR COMESTIBLES
RESTAURANT
MEUBLES
• PARFUMERIE ESTHÉTIQUE
• CONFECTION • CHAUSSURES ENFANTS
• MERCERIE
• SUPERMARCHÉ CASINO
DES LOCAUX SONT ENCORE DISPONIBLES
enseignements :
9, rue nationale 75640 paris cedex 13
éphone: 584.14.21 poste 649
FFF

Urban Activity Systems and Comprehensive Planning

13

Systematic comprehensive planning is a major challenge of urbanized society. The need is new and urgent. Most of human history has been rural. The invention of the city is an alternative to rural life. And in the last one hundred years, many societies have gone beyond the alternative of the city to become urbanized. This means that the rural way of life has been absorbed into a city-dominated culture. Urban and rural ecology are no longer separated but are integrated into one. In effect in this urbanized condition there is no such thing as city planning. Instead, comprehensive societal planning is needed. The remains of city planning and of rural planning become elements in comprehensive urbanized planning.

Until the twentieth century, even the so-called great cities of the world have been small. Their populations have been greatly dependent upon the ruralized society surrounding them. But by the second half of the twentieth century, the balance of power shifted to urbanization. Urbanized society in many parts of the world now dominates even food and fiber production, distribution, and consumption. Until recently most people were born in rural areas, socialized in rural areas, and sustained their economic life in rural areas. With industrialization and urbanization, most people in many societies are born in urban areas, socialized in urban areas, obtain their economic subsistence in urban areas, maintain their health in urban areas, and experience their leisure in urban areas. In the twentieth century, urban life has become

French comprehensive planning includes housing, restaurants, markets, furniture stores, and recreational facilities, as seen in this urban complex. (Photo: Owen Franken for Stock, Boston.)

a total societal environment for most people in Europe, North America, and many other areas of the world.

Early cities needed little or no planning. They were not intended to support the totality of societal life for the majority of people in their areas. Well into the twentieth century, many cities have been little more than street departments, fire departments, police departments, and sewage departments. Even these limited facilities were primarily designed to support only commercial and governmental activities. With almost lightninglike change, by the mid-twentieth century, cities in Europe and North America were being confronted with deterioration, slums, and social disorder. They were becoming societal environments, and they were not prepared for it.

Nineteenth- and early-twentieth-century planners were generally physical determinists. By training or intellectual orientation, they were landscape architects, engineers, or architects (Scott 1969). Accordingly, they went about attempting to make cities beautiful, often by establishing parks and large thoroughfares to improve safety, sanitation, and residential habitation. The quality of life in cities continued to deteriorate. Rural-urban migration exacerbated slum social problems. Settlement houses and a myriad of both voluntary and public social welfare agencies were introduced and experimented with to improve the welfare of urbanites. As physical determinisms in urban planning increasingly failed, social planning and urban welfare expanded. But it was only after World War II that serious efforts in the systematic integration of physical and social planning began to expand. Still, there is limited real comprehensive sociophysical planning.

THE SOCIETAL CONTEXT OF PLANNING

Societal planning focuses primarily on people. It is concerned with their need for schools, housing, health, welfare, jobs, and recreation (Broady 1968). Social welfare planning became a massive concern in the urbanized western nations in the 1930s. Initially welfare planning was a unilateral effort. The first welfare programs were designed to assist people temporarily until they could work out of the depression and back into the economic mainstream of their society. Social welfare legislation in the 1930s was characteristically national in scope. Municipalities neither controlled it nor had much interest in it. Public and private social welfare agencies had virtually no authority over municipalities. Accordingly, urban planning and social welfare planning had no systematic interface.

During the crises of the World War II years, urban areas had some reprieve from the conflicts and malfunctionings of their social life. The labor force shortage meant jobs were available for all able-bodied citizens. Welfare problems were temporarily ameliorated for masses of urbanites. During this era, housing and transportation were the most malfunctioning elements of urban living. In the postwar years of the 1950s, housing shortages, job shortages, inadequate health facilities, and insufficient gerontological programs combined to expand crimes against people and property.

Throughout the 1950s, in an almost determined effort to avoid comprehensive societal planning, nations passed legislation like the United States' 1954 Housing Act and 1956 Civil Defense Highway Act. Both of these examples of central government initiative show segmentation rather than comprehensiveness. Similarly, in response to the malfunctioning educational institutions, the American Supreme Court in 1954 handed down a decision for school ethnic integration. This decision was also segmental. This is to say, housing, transportation, and education were treated as if they were separate urban problems.

By contrast there followed some timid moves toward comprehensiveness. In 1954 the U.S. Department of Housing and Urban Development began requiring a so-called Workable Program from municipalities if they were to obtain most types of federal funding assistance. Workable Programs were intended to help city planners and decision makers see specific proposals in relation to the total city. During the same time, 701 Comprehensive Planning came into being. Implicit in the government's 701 Comprehensive Planning was the view of municipalities as formal organizations. But even this so-called comprehensive planning, where it was used at all, had little authority over welfare programs, educational programs, health programs, and industrial locations. Kaplan (1973) argues that during the 1950s and 1960s, urban planning was more a cosmetic fiction than a social reality (see also Norton 1960).

While the 1950s and 1960s were years of struggle and limited accomplishment for urban planners, they were a time when sociologists and architects expanded dialogue. By the end of the 1960s, a viable conceptual base for comprehensive sociophysical planning was being developed on both sides of the Atlantic (Erber 1970; Bell and Tyrwhitt 1972; Deasy 1974; Forbes 1974). The American Institute of Architects had a research committee actively considering the interface between anthropology, sociology, and psychology as these social and behavioral sciences relate to the built environment. Growing out of this kind of experience, some architectural firms now employ or retain the services of sociologists. Positive primary social interaction is recognized as one type of deterrent against crime and one technique for making the built environment defensible. Architects are becoming more willing to conceptualize cities as social organizations. There is increasing recognition that social satisfaction is determined more by social relationships than by the physical environment.

The sociology, architecture, and planning interface is bringing a keen awareness of people's desire to participate in decisions that affect them personally in their living environment. Sociophysical planning studies make it clear that where people do not come into contact, they do not make friendships. Similarly such studies make it clear that friendships are not forced by the built environment, but are in fact a result of shared values and interests which are sustained by social interaction. Accordingly, superblocks or Planned Unit Developments alone are insufficient to develop a high-quality environment if the people who inhabit these spaces share few values and interests in common. Sociophysical planning study illustrates, for example, that functional distance is more crucial than physical distance in planned environments. This is illustrated by six-foot-high fences between backyards and sideyards, particularly when visibility is limited. Under such conditions there may be more interaction across streets than between people whose yards are adjacent but separated by high and dense fences. Sociophysical profiles are increasingly used in planning (Deasy 1974). Sociobehavioral science design teams are used both for urban renewal and for new town planning.

The societal context of planning is further illustrated by surveys and social problem studies conducted by sociologists. Investigations reveal critical disruption of social interaction networks in urban renewal programs in American cities. Extensive resettlement planning is needed (Gans 1959; Schorr 1963). In England it has been found that working-class people who are forced to move to middle-class residential areas in urban renewal projects and new towns try not to adopt middle-class lifestyles but only to adjust themselves to their new environment (Young and Wilmott 1957). Gans (1961) recommends that sociophysical planning use block homogeneity and community heterogeneity to improve social integration and social satisfaction.

Social isolation is separately identified from physical isolation in planning. Young mothers, young children, and senior citizens may often be socially isolated while physically proximic to other people. This can be sharply reduced by recognition of the problem early on in site planning. Increased recognition of primary relationships is important in planning local neighborhoods as well as larger scale urbanized areas (Buttimer 1974).

SOCIAL ACTIVITY SYSTEMS AND PLANNING

Urbanized societies are large and are societal in scope and character. Accordingly, urban areas must facilitate the full range of social activity systems related to modern living if they are to be high-quality environments. Social institutions are by definition sets of social norms which guide human behavior in areas of activity required for human existence or which are highly valued in a particular society. For example, societies have integrated sets of social norms related to family life, primarily to regulate procreation. There are sets of social norms related to production and distribution of goods and services, primarily to insure orderly economic activities. Urbanized societies have sets of norms related to science, for knowledge production and use. Also, urbanized societies have developed institutional sets of norms related to recreation and leisure. The meetings, values, objectives, and ideologies of urbanized societies are expressed in the total confirmation of their social institutions.

Urbanized societies have become so complex that it is typical to identify in them social activity systems for family life, economics, government, education, religion, science, health, welfare, art, and recreation (Williams 1970; Chapin 1974). The first five of these activity systems are found in all societies, rural as well as urban. Anthropological study reveals that even preliterate rural societies have some minimal forms of art and recreation, but they are not institutionalized. They remain essentially individual or small group acts of expression. Also in ruralized societies health and welfare activities are subsumed into family and religious activities. By the middle of the twentieth century, societal values for health and welfare were so greatly expanded that each of these had become a separate social activity system in urbanized areas. From the Renaissance through the Industrial Revolution into the early twentieth century, ideas of science were growing rapidly, but remained essentially a matter of independent exploration and invention. Science was considerably nurtured and supported in the educational space. Following World War I in Western urbanized societies, it became clear that industry, schools, and government were all utilizing science and scientists to such an extensive degree that the scientific knowledge base became a power in its own right. In effect, a set of social norms supported by values and sanctions now make science a free-standing and powerful activity system. Modern cities are in effect scientific laboratories, storehouses of scientific knowledge, and places for the intellectual life of scientists. The ideas of science and the roles played by scientists are of importance in the operation of large cities and urbanized areas. Urban renewal, planned garden cities, and proposals for megastructure environments are all making greater demands on science. The comprehensively planned environments of the Minnesota Experimental City, of Soleri's arcologies, of Buckminster Fuller's ocean cities, and of Dantzig and Saaty's Compact City utilize automation, cybernation, and other science-based notions.

In urbanized environments, disease control has expanded rapidly. Early industrial cities experienced population losses due to pestilence — a condition largely unknown to urbanites in the second half of the twentieth century. While urban areas are far from achieving healthing environments, the institutions of health have reduced the death rate and extended longevity. As a result, urbanized environments in the last of the twentieth century devote a smaller proportion of the sociophysical space to procreative and family activities. Some of the space is now transferred to health and welfare activities. Similarly, by the 1970s the scientific knowledge base, largely through automation and some cybernation, has made possible the shortening of the work week from more than sixty hours to less than forty hours. Indications are that the work week will experience much more shortening in the decades ahead. This reduction in the amount of time spent working in urbanized economic institutions is related to the expansion of art and of recreational events.

It must be reiterated that there is a proliferation of institutional activities in complex urbanized societies. Comprehensive planning must address all of the institutional activities and be societal in scope. Specifically, when city government leaders present their constituents with bond issues, there needs to be a direct and clear explanation of the way each item is related to the social activities in the city and to the region of which it is a part. In the absence of such clear delineation, power brokers like the late Robert Moses in New York City and Georges-Eugene Haussmann in Paris will continue to create social disorganization and conflict due to their use of unilateral plans (Saalman 1971; Caro 1975). In essence, planners like Moses and Haussmann cannot successfully develop highways and transportation facilities as if they were in vacuums. The institutionalization of city activity systems gives stability to the urban society.

Some large cities become characterized as government centers, industrial centers, educational centers, or religious centers. This is to say that in some places one or a few urban activity systems may be emphasized more, although not at the expense of others. The contrast between Rio de Janeiro and São Paulo, for example, is largely a matter of a different distribution of urban activity space. The former city has a larger leisure-recreational institutional space and the second a larger commercial-industrial institutional space. Vatican City in Italy and Togliatta in the Soviet Union are different because the former has a primary focus on the religious life and the latter a primary focus on industrial space. The difference between Acapulco in Mexico and Oxford in England is largely explained by the large recreational space in the former and the large educational space in the latter. The point is that planners in particular and citizens in general must be cognizant of the fact that different social activity systems will change the quality and quantity of urban life styles. Even more important is the need to recognize that certain urban activities are required if urban areas are to survive.

On a very small scale, the garden city new town model comes close to addressing the need for a balance of social activity spaces. Also the garden-city model, particularly as expressed by Ebenezer Howard, and as extensively utilized in England since 1946, interfaces the city with its agricultural hinterland especially in economic and in recreation space. While the garden-city model is more antiurban in its total conformation than the megastructure model, which also implicitly addresses institutional relationships, it is sufficiently compatible with the late twentieth-century value system to be accepted, while most megastructures are so innovatively advanced they tend to be rejected as science fictional or utopian ideas.

Sociophysical changes in urbanized areas are inseparable from urban social activity changes. The relationships between urban activity systems constitute social organization or social disorganization. Antisocial behavior and indefensible spaces are matters of social control, values, education, and opportunity. Translated into sociophysical planning terminology, this means that if religious values suggest that one knows "who one is" by work and occupations, urban activity systems must make rewarding jobs available or recognize that the possibility of antisocial behavior will increase. Similarly the institutional relationships between health, education, and economics must be planned for in relation to other social activity systems in order to reduce antisocial behavior. Urban planning that does not interface all social activity systems in the boundary of a city is deficient from a comprehensive point of view.

Planning is also usually less than comprehensive because the scope is too limited. The social activity systems that operate in a city are also influenced by the surrounding region, nation, and often multiple nations. Cities and metropolitan regions, particularly in urbanized societies, do not exist in vacuums. Even when local cities or urban regions carefully and systematically develop plans addressed to all social activity systems, they still do not control the probability for high-quality environment. For example, the economic institutions of a city or urban region may depend upon energy, raw materials, and sales from other cities in urban regions. In the early 1970s the extensive scientific and economic institutions of the Tokaido megalopolis in Japan were temporarily thrust into crisis when the oil-producing Arab countries refused to sell sufficient oil to operate Japanese factories. Similarly the interrelationships of one urban region's institutions with those of a larger multinational area are seen in the "common market" developments in Europe and in Latin America. In both continental areas, the economic institutions of cities are directly influenced by decisions made outside of their political limits. Indeed, for most large urbanized areas of the world, the problem of controlling jobs in particular and the economic activity space in general is exacerbated by the ascendancy of multinational corporations.

In the educational and the science activity spaces, the phenomenon of "brain drain" further illustrates the interdependence of urban areas. In the United States, educational institutions in the eastern megalopolis area and in the Midwest have disproportionately trained scientists who have been "bought" by urban areas in the far West. Similarly, United States universities have provided professional and technical training to many international students. Often these persons want to remain in America, draining their home nations of their potential contributions. In the 1950s and 1960s, national and continental highway systems were developed which connect major urban areas around much of the world. Until the crisis of the gasoline shortage became sufficiently great, cities directly connected by autobahns or freeways had distinct advantages. Forrester (1969) demonstrated in the case of Boston that a city which greatly expands its social welfare supports and low-income housing creates family problems, government problems, and social disorganization. This social disorganization was increased because the poor who came to occupy Boston's low-income housing paid little or no tax and thereby reduced the tax base for operating other city social activity systems. Such a condition precipitates the now well documented "middle-class white flight." Freeway systems and communication systems break the boundaries of cities and urban areas. One result is to leave older central cities with a residue of low-income population with poor health, limited education, and few job opportunities, while the highly educated and advantaged population migrates to suburbs and returns to the central city only to selectively use recreational, artistic, and economic institutions. When there is an insufficient population base to support these activity systems, both the suburban cities and the central cities decline in their human environmental quality.

COMPREHENSIVE PLANNING

Comprehensive planning involves close specification of goals for each social activity system plus regional, national, and multinational interface recognition.

Traditionally, comprehensive planning has meant physical planning. Physical planners have been concerned with land use, utilities, transportation, and urban design. Such planners have asserted that their purposes are to improve the health, welfare, safety, and convenience of urban areas (Gallion and Eisner 1963). There has been an implicit physical determinism, which is inconsistent with social reality. In effect the model has been to plan first the sewage systems and streets, and then to consider social relationships related to housing, health, social welfare, and so forth.

Comprehensive planning is by nature long-range. Typically, projections are made for ten to twenty years in the future with provisions for regular review and update. With the reality of review and update, planning becomes more a process than a finished product.

Critics of comprehensive urban planning are caustic in their negative evaluations and assertions of shortcomings (Kaplan 1973). Without defending comprehensive planning practices of the past, we observe that cities are new, urbanization newer, and comprehensive planning the newest — it is still in its infancy. Only in the first quarter of the twentieth century did courts begin upholding the right of cities to zone land. In implementing zoning, comprehensive planning resulted. In rapid-fire succession in the nations of England, the Netherlands, and the United States, city growth became the dominating national feature. World War II did not terminate urban comprehensive planning — in some ways it accelerated it — but it further modified its nature. In the Netherlands, urban planning was more directly interfaced with national planning. In England, London-guided urban plans were directly interfaced with regions. In the more laissez faire America, the government in Washington, D.C. gave increasing support to urban comprehensive planning while leaving its origin and focus essentially to a local government.

In the United States the Housing Act of 1954 specifically approved Workable Program certification for municipalities if they were to obtain many types of federal funding for urban community improvement. The Workable Programs were to be recertified each two years. This visibly accelerated the importance of comprehensive planning. The Housing Act of 1954 included Section 701 on Comprehensive Planning Assistance Programs. This legislation was designed for funding to come one-third from local municipalities, one-third from state governments, and one-third from the federal government. Social organizationally this was a step, no matter how tentative, in the direction of interfacing local municipal plans with state development and with federal development. Subsequently the Congress furthered its stimulus for planning in America by passing enabling legislation for regional Councils of Government. The Councils of Government have been essentially coordinative, lacking basic authority to implement planning. By the mid-1970s these types of support for comprehensive planning in the United States are being phased down.

Major comprehensive planning elements

Traditional planning elements include mapping, land use analysis, population studies, economic studies, community facilities, transportation, housing, central business district projections, parks and recreation plans, public facilities plans, industrial development plans, and public utilities plans (de Chiara and Koppelman 1975). More recently urban renewal and historic preservation elements have been added to physical planning.

Base maps include the location of the street systems, railroads, rivers, parks, and other community facilities. Data for base maps come from the highway department and from municipal, state, and federal agencies. The land use analysis plan designates residential areas divided into high and low densities, commercial areas for central business purposes, plus neighborhood shopping facilities and highway-oriented commerce. Industrial land use is divided into sites for light and heavy manufacturing. Other items include open areas for parks and recreation, school sites, locations for government buildings, and areas for cultural facilities like libraries, museums, and theatres. Base maps also show the locations for fire and police facilities, medical service facilities, and utility facilities. Land use analysis indicates places where there is potential conflict in land development.

The population analysis shows present and projected demographic characteristics. Population studies show changes in ecological areas by socioeconomic characteristics. The economic studies focus on the way residents of an urban area make a living. Such an analysis includes the number of jobs in industry, retail sales, services, and agriculture. These analyses show current distribution plus projections for the future.

The community facilities plans relate to goals expressed in the urban area. Generally they are closely related to transportation planning and include items like parks, golf courses, and greenbelts. More specifically the facilities plan locates playgrounds, swimming pools, and gymnasiums as well as spaces for larger spectator sports. Educational and cultural facilities along with hospitals and nursing homes are planned. Locations for churches and their related facilities are noted. Public buildings like municipal offices, police stations, jails, public markets, civic auditoriums, and so forth are cited. Environmental facilities for water and sewage treatment, flood control, pollution control, and so on conclude the major items in the community facilities plan.

The transportation or thoroughfare plans concern roadways, railroads, waterways and harbors, and airports. The highway system is traditionally divided into local streets, major streets, and limited access routes. More recently, social impact studies and environmental impact studies are required in transportation planning.

The housing study in a comprehensive plan shows the location of different types of housing, from detached to multiple-unit. Housing densities, the age of housing, and the condition of housing are also typical subelements in the planning. Housing codes and housing renewal areas have recently received expanded attention.

Commercial development plans on base maps show gross floor area, classify commercial use by areas, show parking and loading facilities, and specify the distribution of employees by peak periods. Basic data for these plans come from tax records, utility companies, the U.S. Census, and the Chamber of Commerce. Employment and wage analysis are typical subcomponents. The central business district plan is highlighted. Number of stores, salaries, gross sales, profits, and wages, along with parking facilities, commuter origin and destination studies, and traffic circulation studies are parts of the central business district analysis.

The public facilities plans show locations for administrative centers related to activities like police, fire, public works, health, recreation, and schools. The analysis of these locations is intended to reveal any deficiencies in the rendering of services along with recommendations for overcoming the deficiencies related to future population projections for the area.

Industrial development planning shows the location of industries, their age, their expansion and/or contraction potential, and so forth. Tax records, utility company records, Bureau of the Census data, and Chamber of Commerce data are all utilized in industrial development planning. Diversified industrial development is desired to give a spread in the types of jobs available to people in the urban area.

The public utilities plans show electric lines and easements, telephone lines and easements, water lines, sewage locations and easements, gas service locations and easements, and drainage facilities and easements. Analysis of these locations is related to population growth.

Urban renewal is a newer element in comprehensive planning. An analysis is made of the need to update existing facilities or to replace them. Some attention, though usually asserted to be insufficient, is given to the relocation of individuals while urban renewal takes place. Urban renewal planning sometimes involves the changing of the land use for an area and sometimes involves the updating or replacing of physical facilities for a continuation of the existing type land use.

In some respects historic preservation, also a new element in physical planning, is related to urban renewal. Buildings of architectural quality may be preserved even if their use is changed. Historic preservation may also be specifically planned to give people in an urban area a sense of its history as well as to provide stability of meaning. This is sharply brought into focus in Warsaw, Poland, where the old city was totally devastated during World War II. It is now replaced in a faithful reconstruction of its centuries-old tradition. Surrounding the old city are miles of new buildings in new styles.

Social activity systems are indirectly addressed in these planning elements. But they are divided in such a way that the comprehensive plan, even within municipal limits, is not articulated as a social system, much less as a formal organization. The focus of the so-called comprehensive plan is physical and is oriented toward one municipality, as if it existed in a vacuum. Councils of Government may facilitate the interfacing of one municipality's comprehensive plan with that of another, but to date in most places of the urbanized world, regional and multiregional comprehensive planning is limited to nonexistent.

Isadore Candeub (1970) presses the view that planners in the 1970s are still attempting to use techniques developed in 1910. Furthermore, he asserts that citizen education is one of the most significant contributions of current comprehensive planning. There is no implication that it is bad. In contrast, the implication is that the comprehensive planning, at best, is a coordinating effort and is sharply deficient in action. Comprehensive plans are frequently large undertakings that last from two to three years. In the view of this considerable effort, there remains much confusion concerning the real purpose of such plans. Governmental forces larger than municipalities have pressed for Workable Programs, Community Renewal Plans, and Community Action Plans. Action techniques that have been introduced include the Planned Unit Development and the Code Enforcement Area. In spite of these, there remains an urgent need to vastly restructure the planning process to emphasize first social, second economic, and third physical needs. When social and economic needs are not addressed with priority, physical planning fails or, as in the case of the Pruitt-Igoe Housing Project in St. Louis, has a short life as originally constructed.

Citizen participation and advocacy planning

Citizen participation and advocacy planning surfaced in the 1950s and 1960s with some strength. By 1970 the Workable Program requirements included a statement on citizen involvement as follows: "The establishment of programs designed to achieve meaningful involvement of citizens, including poor and minority groups, in planning and carrying out HUD-assisted programs related to the Workable Program" (*Workable Program for Community Improvement: A HUD Handbook* 1970). The 1970 Workable Program Handbook further specified in considerable detail that citizens often feel cut off from government by traditional methods of participation, namely voting, attendance at meetings, and letters to congressmen. Accordingly, new forms of interaction between citizens and local governments are required. The Workable Program, which had to be renewed each two years, required the demonstration of continuous efforts to bring citizens — particularly the poor and minority categories — into satisfying and rewarding participation efforts. New forms of community-wide advisory committees were being recommended. But by the end of the 1970s the Workable Program itself was being phased down.

Advocacy planning, in addition to citizen participation, has grown since the 1950s (Kaplan 1973). Although city plans and city planners have had but the most minimal impact on the decision-making process, some have recently manifested considerable consciousness and willingness to advocate the position of poor clients. The advocacy concept is borrowed from law. Planners attempt to defend the interests of their clients. Advocacy in some cases becomes a form of technical assistance. Indeed, when it is less than technical assistance, there is often an implicit elitist characteristic. Most planners listen very little to the public and attempt to make most recommendations from the top down.

Another serious problem with either citizen participation or advocacy planning is the disparity between the physical lifespan of the built environment and the knowledgeable lifespan of citizens. Typically, buildings have a lifespan of between two and one-half and three generations, or upwards of sixty years. Most citizens spend their first twenty to twenty-five years in school and related training activities in complex urban societies. Accordingly, they have an active mature life in preretirement years far shorter than the lifespan of buildings. In effect, then, citizen participation in planning is characterized by one generation of citizens planning for the succeeding generation.

Behavioral and physical data

With assertions increasingly being made that more sociophysical planning should be carried out, we examine now some of the techniques for obtaining sociobehavioral data related to the physical and built environments. Surveys, questionnaires, and interviews are the most widely used techniques (Lang 1974). Additionally, social and behavioral data are obtained by sociometric techniques, content analysis, the use of semantic differential scales, and unobtrusive measures like physical traces and archival records (Webb 1966).

The semantic differential scale is used to compare different environments. This method, along with unobtrusive measures, may be strongly combined with survey and interview data for building a sociophysical theory interfacing sociology, psychology, architecture, and planning. More social and behavioral science data input are going to be essential if comprehensive planning is to become a reality.

National and multinational urban planning

The urbanized sociophysical environment is increasingly national and multinational. Accordingly, comprehensive planning, even for local municipalities, to be effective must specify articulation at a societal level. This is clearly seen in the case of the United States when in 1957, for the first time, the nation consumed more oil than it produced ("Energy and Society" 1975). From that time to the present, urban planning in the United States which does not address the source of energy is in effect less than comprehensive (Freedman 1974). By the last of the twentieth century the urbanized nations of the world have made it clear that events which take place on one part of the earth's land potentially affect all of its 190 million square miles (Blumenfeld 1970). Food production, water resources, air pollution, and energy are all critically essential to the densely populated urbanized areas of the world. The world's urban population is expected to exceed its rural population by 2000. Indeed the world's population is expected, by some, to reach thirty to fifty billion by 2150. Comprehensive sociophysical urban planning will be necessary on a world scale long before the population reaches such a large number.

IMPLICATIONS

It is widely observed that urban comprehensive plans receive little use in terms of actual implementation. It is also observed that they are generally more comprehensive in name than in fact. Therefore, in effect the unused "advice" of the less than comprehensive plans may be a blessing in disguise. In 1953 President Eisenhower established the Advisory Commission on Intergovernmental Relations (Scott 1969). In 1961 the Commission recommended that state-level metropolitan affairs units of government be established. The intent was to bring some coordinated urban planning at the statewide level. Some fifteen years later little has been accomplished regarding this recommendation.

Regional planning is identified in the San Francisco Bay Area, the Toronto Area, and the Miami Area. Most of the planning efforts in these kinds of examples are, however, segmental rather than comprehensive. The Bay Area Rapid Transit system, to be specific, is far more developed than many other related sociophysical concerns in that region. In Toronto and Miami, federated and two-level government planning is far more extensive than other elements of comprehensive planning. There are many examples of special district governments on a regional basis. Nevertheless, the major characteristics of government in urbanized areas originated in the nineteenth century. Local autonomy prevails more forcefully than the professional planning experience.

In Britain, regional planning is developed extensively (James 1966). The density of population in England has brought planners and the citizenry to recognize that central cities cannot be separated from life in their regional hinterlands. Accordingly, higher priority efforts are being placed on sociophysical plans that directly interface urban and rural areas. In Britain, greenbelts are widely used as one technique for preserving an equitable balance between densely built environments and multiple-use open spaces. New towns are related to larger older existing urban areas and to greenbelts as well as to other amenity areas.

Satisfaction with life styles and amenities is tolerably high in those areas where comprehensive plans address most social activity systems as well as regional and national relationships.

REFERENCES

BELL, G. & TYRWHITT, J. *Human Identity in the Urban Environment*. New York: Penguin Books, 1972.
BLUMENFELD, H. The rational use of urban space as a national policy. In E. Erber (Ed.), *Urban Planning and Transition*. New York: Grossman, 1970.
BROADY, M. *Planning for People*. London: Bedford Square Press, 1968.
BUTTIMER, A. Sociology and planning. In J. Forbes (Ed.), *Studies in Social Science and Planning*. New York: Wiley, 1974.
CANDEUB, I. New techniques in making the general plan. In E. Erber (Ed.), *Urban Planning and Transition*. New York: Grossman, 1970.
CARO, R. *The Power Broker*. New York: Vintage Press, 1975.
CHAPIN, F. S. *Human Activity Patterns in the City*. New York: Wiley, 1974.
DEASY, C. M. *Design for Human Affairs*. New York: Wiley, 1974.
DE CHIARA, J., & KOPPELMAN, L. *Urban Planning and Design Criteria*. New York: Van Nostrand, 1975.
Energy and society. *The Addendum*, No. 5 (November, 1975).
ERBER, E. (Ed.) *Urban Planning in Transition*. New York: Grossman, 1970.
FORBES, J. (Ed.) *Studies in Social Science and Planning*. New York: Wiley, 1974.
FORRESTER, J. W. *Urban Dynamics*. Cambridge: M.I.T. Press, 1969.
FREEMAN R., & FREEMAN, B. *Human Population*. San Francisco: W. H. Freeman, 1974.
GALLION, A. B., & EISNER, S. *The Urban Pattern: City Planning and Design*. New York: Van Nostrand, 1963.
GANS, H. J. The balanced community: homogeneity and heterogeneity in residential areas. *Journal of the American Institute of Planners*, 1961, 27, 176–84.
GANS, H. J. The human implications of current redevelopment and relocation planning. *Journal of the American Institute of Planners*, 1959, 25, 15–25.
JAMES, J. R. Regional planning in Britain. In S. B. Warner (Ed.), *Planning for a Nation of Cities*. Cambridge: M.I.T. Press, 1966.
KAPLAN, M. *Urban Planning in the 1960s: A Design for Irrelevance*. Cambridge: M.I.T. Press, 1973.
LANG, J. et al. (Eds.) *Designing for Human Behavior: Architecture and the Behavioral Sciences*. Stroudsburg, Pa.: Dowden, 1974.
NORTON, P. L. (Ed.) *Bair Facts*. West Trenton, N.J.: Chandler-Davis Publishing Co., 1960.
SAALMAN, H. *Haussmann: Paris Transformed*. New York: George Braziller, 1971.
SCHORR, A. L. *Slums and Social Insecurity*. Washington, D.C.: U.S. Department of Health, Education, and Welfare, 1963.
SCOTT, M. *American City Planning Since 1890*. Berkeley: University of California Press, 1969.
WARNER, S. B., JR. (Ed.) *Planning for a Nation of Cities*. Cambridge: M.I.T. Press, 1966.
WEBB, E. et al. *Unobtrusive Measures*. Skokie, Ill.: Rand-McNally, 1966.
WILLIAMS, R. M., JR. *American Society*. New York: Alfred A. Knopf, 1970.
Workable Program for Community Improvement: A HUD Handbook. Washington, D.C.: U.S. Dept. of Housing and Urban Development, 1970.
YOUNG, M., & WILMOTT, T. *Family Kinship in East London*. London: Routledge, 1957.

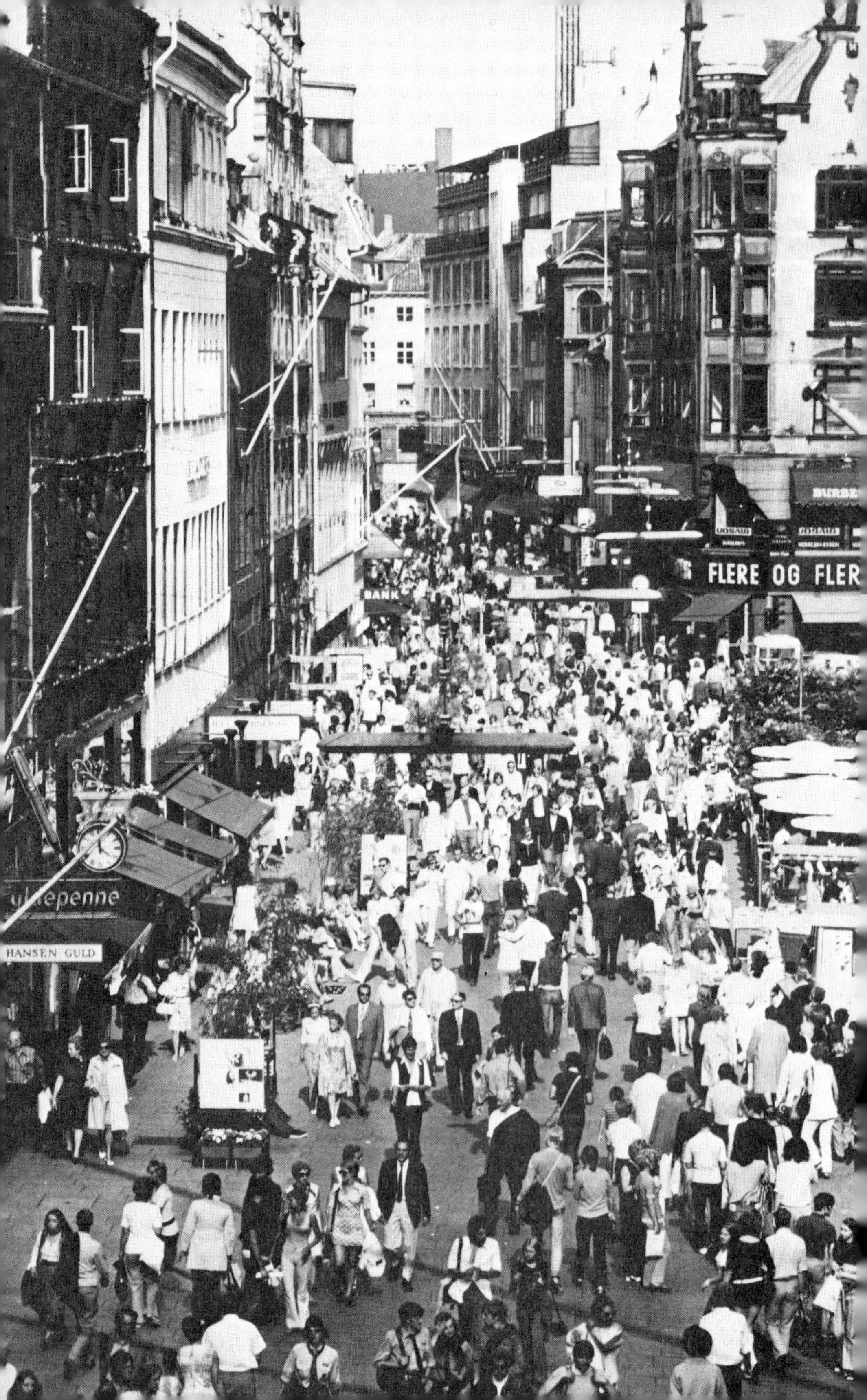
FLERE OG FLER
BANK
HANSEN GULD

Urban Renewal   14

Urban renewal, new towns, and policies for future urban growth are closely related. The urban environment has been a part of the human story long enough for a few cities to have had multiple renewal experiences. Some have been destroyed and rebuilt several times. From Haussmann's rebuilding of Paris between 1852 and 1870 to the present, a specific concept of urban renewal has been growing. In the last quarter of a century, numerous governmental urban renewal programs have been developed. In this chapter we focus on concepts and programs for urban renewal.

THE NEED FOR URBAN RENEWAL

From one point of view, urban renewal is an old process. In a natural way it is the mechanism by which cities have lived over hundreds, and in a few cases thousands, of years (Doxiadis 1966).

Most urbanization has taken place in the last one hundred years. Most of the buildings in this recent period have had a life expectancy of fifty years or less. Accordingly, the problem of keeping the urban area renewed is enormous now and will shortly become even greater (Clawson 1968). By the last of the twentieth century the entire world is urbanizing at a more rapid rate than ever before (Duggar 1965). For the United States in particular, the rapidity of urban growth was clearly expressed by Lyndon Johnson in 1965 when he called upon Congress to

Revitalized Copenhagen has removed cars and returned people to the downtown streets. (Photo: Courtesy of Danish National Tourist Office.)

establish the Department of Housing and Urban Development. He said, "In the remainder of this century — in less than forty years — urban population will double, city land will double, and we will have to build in our cities as much as all that we have built since the first colonists arrived on these shores. It is as if we had forty years to rebuild the entire urban United States" (Adde 1969).

Urban renewal is now a regular part of the experience of rapid worldwide urban growth. Demographers project that by the year 2000 more than half of the world's population will be urban. In other words, we anticipate an urban population in 2000 approximately equal to the world's total population in the 1970s. In the face of this demographic change, some question whether the building of new towns rather than the renovation of existing towns is not where efforts should be directed (Grebler 1964). Here we examine the potential validity of both urban renewal and new-town building as cooperative, rather than mutually exclusive, contributions to the urban environment.

The character of older urban environments may add quality and meaning to life. Their residents may identify strongly with the established environment. Some parts of the urban built environment may, with both social and economic feasibility, be shifted to new uses. This is illustrated by novelty centers like the Cannery in San Francisco, which changed from a factory to a fashionable shopping center, and by the warehouses in Boston, which changed to apartment and condominium use. Cities that have needed to be renewed following the devastation of war have approached renewal in sharply different ways, as illustrated in Warsaw, Poland and in Rotterdam, the Netherlands. In the case of Warsaw, most of the old city has been rebuilt with faithful architectural adherence to its prewar character. In Rotterdam, renewal buildings are modern in architectural style and designed to support a new kind of social life. In many cases, urban renewal involves historic preservation to facilitate human identity with the past, while much else in the urban environment facilitates a quest for the future.

In some neighborhoods of big cities both in America and in Europe, good maintenance along with neighborhood renewal programs are socially and economically viable. This is in no way to suggest that urban renewal is limited to blight removal and slum clearance. Nevertheless, it may facilitate both of these.

Urban renewal concepts

In this book "urban renewal" is used broadly to mean planned change in the urban environment for present and future aspects of the total social system. Clearly it refers to more than slum clearance, although it often utilizes slum clearance as a major effort. As a concept urban renewal is new, and the term is often used variantly and inconsistently. In other language areas in the world urban renewal may be referred to as *renovation urbanie* or *stadterneuerung*. It includes nonresidential renewal as well as residential renewal. Urban renewal is needed in both the public and the private sectors. In capitalist nations where citizens have extensive freedom in ownership and use of land, renewal is frequently confounded by property acquisition problems. Often government intervention in the form of eminent domain, condemnation, code enforcement, and so forth are required. Indeed as Grebler (1964) writes, "The ingredients of governmental initiative and financial support, planning, and large-scale enterprise distinguish urban renewal from the piecemeal replacement of structures, building by building, that has been going on for centuries."

Scott Greer (1965) refers to urban renewal as a "theory." By this he means that it is an overt effort at controlled social change. Urban renewal is based on assumptions concerning how change can be achieved and concerning desired or improved needs. Theoretically the concept includes improved human welfare, innovation of a rational order, and sound standards of design for community integration.

Small urban renewal projects, for example the often-cited experience of block-by-block residential clearance for new low-income housing, may produce negative and unintended results (Forrester 1969). The strategy and scope of urban renewal must systematically interface with comprehensive regional planning and with urban activity systems. Doxiadis (1966) writes, "The larger the area to which policies and programs pertain, the greater are the chances for implementation. On the basis of this principle, we should start with national programs and proceed to state programs, to metropolitan area programs, to local area programs, and only then to project programs" (p.156). Another urban renewal principle, according to Doxiadis, is simultaneous development of all dimensions of the renewal program.

Elements of renewal must include, first, realism. Identification of a realistic program involves a consideration of economic, social, political, technical, and cultural environments. Second, an urban renewal program should be designed to encompass the longest possible time. Programs that are constricted to short time periods and limited geographical areas have greater probabilities of failure. Third, before renewal can proceed effectively, all programs within the renewal area need to be classified according to their importance. The classification should address the question of the number of people who would be affected by the plan, and the cost of the plan in total and on a per capita basis. Fourth, urban renewal should only proceed after goals have been clearly specified. Fifth, specific details of a program can only be articulated within a general policy framework. Finally, urban renewal should proceed on a basis of continual study, evaluation, and reappraisal.

Formulating the urban renewal concept in the above manner makes it clear that much urban redevelopment in the past and much current slum clearance fall outside of this definition. Conceptually we are now confronting urban renewal as a process — a regular part of the life and nature of the urban environment. It is more than just the replacement or updating of single buildings.

URBAN RENEWAL IN THE UNITED STATES

America from an urban point of view is very new. In the United States there are no ancient cities, no medieval walled towns, and only a few Romanesque- and Renaissance-styled buildings. Most of America's urban growth has been based on the ideas and technology of industrialism, plus widespread use of transportation and communication. Many of its urban edifices are intended to be only temporary. Those designed to last a little longer usually have a life expectancy of fifty years or less. America's new urban experience and its short-lived physical structures have been, in effect, largely consistent with the plural and dynamic urbanization of society. Therefore in the United States, more than in many older nations, city building has been coterminous with urban renewal from the point of origin. As Grebler (1964) writes, "It is not much of an exaggeration to say that the evolution of an articulate national program for the renewal of its cities and towns since 1949 has placed the United States in a position of leadership. Most of the Western countries of the European continent are only now [1964] on the threshold of national renewal programs" (p. 11).

America's specific urban renewal programming may be said to have started with the Housing Act of 1937. In terms of the principles enumerated above, urban renewal started in America as a program with national legislative support. It had two broad objectives, namely, pump priming of the depression economy and improving housing. This renewal program of the 1930s took two forms. Mortgage money was provided for individuals who with assistance could afford to buy single-family detached homes. For those who could not afford to purchase even with assistance, slums were cleared and publicly subsidized low-income housing was rented.

Much of America's urban renewal image is associated with housing, but in fact from its inception the goals and purposes have been broader and more all-inclusive. During World War II most urban renewal projects were temporarily put aside. Cities changed much during the war years, but generally not as a result of specifically planned urban renewal. During the war years dilapidated housing and urban slums grew. After considerable congressional debate the Housing Act of 1949 was passed. It was more oriented toward slum clearance than

toward support for public housing. The Housing Act was amended in 1954. With this amended legislation, a bona fide urban renewal program was instituted. Its major innovative mechanism was the Workable Program. The policy of the new program was designed to increase involvement from the private sector, expand the responsibility of local governments, require specific citizen participation by neighborhoods, and relate renewal to comprehensive planning (Greer 1965).

Urban renewal programs were expanded again with the Housing Act of 1961. At that time a new emphasis was placed on nonresidential redevelopment. More particularly the new legislation required a comprehensive renewal program embracing an entire city and its plan for the future. Renewal of central business districts gained support under the 1961 legislation. Urban renewal has now become a large-scale program aimed at all aspects of the city's core.

The major urban renewal emphasis in America from the 1930s through the 1950s was physical more than social (Anderson 1964; Doxiadis 1966). Since the 1960s, Community Renewal Programs are becoming more comprehensive in scope and more people-oriented in goals. Community Renewal Programs are in effect a social counterpart to physical renewal programs.

In spite of the above national legislation programs, urban renewal in America is slow and insufficient. It is still far from a systematically conceived process. It is anticipated that there will be a continuous dynamic change in America's cities and that urban renewal will have to be modified to reflect future changes. Changing social structures in cities will require new and different types of land use and also different population densities. More and larger areas of short-physical-duration buildings will become dilapidated and will need to be upgraded or removed — both of which will require urban renewal.

Suburbanization is a major new dynamic dimension of urbanized America which is variously impacting on the need for urban renewal. Suburbanization creates a redistribution of population, new scales, and new densities, and leaves a vacuum in many older central cities to be filled by poor people or not filled at all. As suburbanization becomes more mature, the balance of population is located in the suburbs, as indicated in America by the 1970 Census. In one sense what was a suburb becomes a new city or a substitute city. When there is a new or substitute city, one must question the economic and social viability of urban renewal (Gottman 1961). What are the goals, needs, and purposes of urban renewal in old cities if the populations have evacuated to the suburbs? When cities and suburbs intermesh and form megalopolis areas, the urban renewal process becomes in effect part of the metabolism — an element in the life of urbanized areas.

A balanced city life and growth require a dynamic and continuing process of urban renewal. Urban renewal in America first focused on housing, later on central business districts, and more recently on the full range of social institutions for urban man's existence (Adde 1969). Downtown urban renewal programs have been interpreted broadly. They are both private and public and involve substantial land use changes. For example, in New York City a large convention auditorium was added in one previously deteriorating residential area, and nearby the Lincoln Center for the Performing Arts stands magnificently on a site also previously occupied by deteriorating housing. In Minneapolis the new symphony auditorium in the downtown area is proximic to major new banking buildings and a new-town-in-town, and also connects with a linear park moving from the downtown area to a cultural center. In Fort Worth, Texas, a water garden, convention center, and city hall complex illustrate both private and public urban renewal of deteriorating commercial buildings. Universities and other related institutional facilities are also expanded via the mechanism of urban renewal. Renewed downtown church sites may take the form of multiuse high-rise buildings, providing housing for the elderly, medical facilities, and worship facilities in a single building. Central-city urban renewal in Washington, D.C.'s Georgetown and in New Orleans' Vieux Carre involve historic restoration and preservation.

America's urban renewal programs in the 1970s involve all of the major social institutional spaces concerning families, economics, schools, governments, and churches. Additionally, some urban renewal programs involve social activity systems like health, recreation, art, welfare, and science. American sociophysical planners still lack a strong theory of urban renewal. Nevertheless, the experience is increasing, the concept is becoming more clear, and we move ever closer to the possibility of an urban renewal theory.

WORLD URBAN RENEWAL EXPERIENCES

Immediate factors pressing for urban renewal in European cities are in several respects sharply different from those in America. Physical destruction from World War II was a major urban renewal factor in Warsaw, Rotterdam, London, Leningrad, Berlin, and many other European cities. Above and beyond war damage is the invasion of European cities by motorized traffic, especially the automobile (Grebler 1964). Additionally many European cities experience pressure for expanded downtown conveniences. Most of the above are juxtaposed with pressures for conservation or historic preservation. Many contemporary European cities have experienced some five hundred or more years of continual physical existence. In France, for example, two-thirds of the nearly 14 million dwellings are over fifty years old and one-third are over one hundred years old. "Even more than the age of the dwellings, it is their unsuitability to the requirements of modern urban life that makes urban renewal a vital necessity" (Duggar 1965).

Population redistribution in European cities is generally less than that in New World cities. Nevertheless the physical environment of European cities is more adversely affected by traffic congestion, particularly in their old centers. Streets are small, narrow, and often follow grade elevations that are either inadequate for or prohibitive of large amounts of traffic. Often the traffic congestion problems in European cities are exacerbated by age-old traditions, like urban workers' returning home for their midday meals. Related to the automobile are parking problems. Many of the beautiful and once-pedestrian areas in Europe's plazas and squares are now overrun with parked cars. Some renewal programs to counteract the traffic problem are plans to eliminate all traffic, or traffic during many day hours. The return to pedestrianization of central Copenhagen is such an example. Surburbanization in Europe is less widely known than in America except for new population centers in planned satellite new towns as illustrated by those around London, Stockholm, Paris, and Moscow.

Peripherally constructed ring roads are an increasingly significant part of urban renewal. Expansion of public transit is another widely used technique for urban renewal in and around many European cities. Since 1946, the so-called London Ring new towns have been specifically planned to accommodate a total way of life within their physical location, thereby minimizing the need for commuting into London or to other cities. In sharpest contrast to London's new towns, the new towns around Stockholm are connected to the city's large central business district by high-quality highways and by mass transit. People in these new-town urban renewal environments can opt to commute daily into Stockholm or to obtain jobs and other goods and services in the new-town areas, making a trip to Stockholm the exception rather than the rule.

European cities are experiencing some population shift. In order to utilize this shift for the highest quality urban environment possible, the French, for example, have developed a square footage space tax that is levied against both new and expanded office and industrial developments in Paris. Parallel to this tax are financial subsidies paid for similar expansion and development in selected provincial cities (Duggar 1965).

Some European cities have housed universities for multiple centuries. Generally they have been small and physically scattered. In the last half of the twentieth century, the explosive growth of idea power is much a part of European culture and urban life. Accordingly, places like the University of London, the University of Amsterdam, and many others are being greatly expanded through urban renewal programs. Other European urban renewal expansion is related to health facilities, welfare facilities, industrial expansion, and the opening of green spaces along with the creation of greenbelts.

In the mid-1960s Duggar completed an empirical study of urban renewal in thirty-one countries, including five in Africa, nine in Asia, ten in Europe, three in North America, and four in Latin America. Much of the character of worldwide urban renewal can be understood by examining summaries of his findings. For example, it is reported that 80 percent of the study countries are involved in urban renewal because their older buildings are at a lower efficiency scale than that demanded by late-twentieth-century urban quality of life standards. Further it is reported that urban renewal is a typical response to overcrowding in buildings. Seventy-five percent of the study areas reported providing for governmental, educational, and sports facilities in their urban renewal projects. Over 80 percent of the study urban areas plan to improve central business and/or industrial areas. In sharp contrast, only 33 percent of the study areas attempt to find ways for sculptors and other artists to contribute. More than 66 percent of the world's urban renewal projects involve improved streets, sewers, utilities, public buildings, and public lands.

Most of the world's urban renewal programs involve systematic regulations for controlling unsanitary building conditions. Moreover 60 percent of the urban renewal projects require maintenance of public utilities. In considerable contrast, only 25 percent of the urban renewal projects help property owners and occupants to support good physical conditions. Less than 40 percent of the projects provide financial aid or organizational advice and assistance to individual owners and occupants for improvement. Over 75 percent of the programs are designed to improve traffic and transportation systems. Some 70 percent of the programs attempt to restructure towns to accommodate more vehicles. Sixty percent of urban renewal projects include improved access between towns and their regions. Viewed from several different perspectives, world urban renewal programs are broadly confronting large population movements, particularly as they relate to transportation systems and associated needs.

Few world urban renewal programs, less than 30 percent, place importance on systematically comparing renewal plans with new town plans. A similar low percentage place emphasis on encouraging populations to remain in villages or smaller urban centers. An even smaller proportion of the urban renewal plans are directly related to regional planning as a whole. Also, slightly less than 50 percent of the programs are supported by policy development for whole regions. Less than 25 percent of the urban renewal projects place priority on low-income housing. A similarly low proportion of the programs are concerned with relocation of the poor. Similarly, a low priority, 25 percent, was placed on low-income housing for disadvantaged and minority groups, meaning the elderly, refugees, religious minorities, and racial minorities. Over 50 percent of the world's urban renewal programs place priority on solving health and educational problems. Typically under 40 percent of the programs use local manpower in self-help improvement programs. Less than 25 percent of the renewal programs attempt to free women from household duties. Only 35 percent of the renewal programs attempt to reduce the journey to work. This is related to less than 25 percent of the renewal programs which are aimed at lowering unemployment.

Finally, Duggar found that some 75 percent of the world's urban renewal programs had the power to acquire land by compulsory appropriation, usually known as eminent domain. Moreover, approximately 60 percent of the programs had authority to take possession of land while a tribunal was determining the appropriate price for the land. In overview, one must observe that world urban renewal tends to be more physical than social. Moreover, world urban renewal programs tend to be localized rather than integrated into regional systems of planning. Although some urban renewal is dominated from central national governments down, this is generally not interfaced with requirements for regional planning. In effect, systematic urban renewal is still conceptually in its infancy. It is far from being a part of the dynamic functioning of the social organizational life of an urban area.

SOCIAL ORGANIZATION AND URBAN RENEWAL

There is a need for urban renewal conceptual clarification. There is much criticism of urban renewal projects. Some of the criticism is warranted, and some is unjustifiable. In essence the weight of the criticism asserts that urban renewal is essentially a bricks-and-mortar matter with insufficient concern for people (Anderson 1964). Additionally there is considerable criticism asserting the view that urban renewal is too project-oriented and lacks sufficient comprehensiveness (Montgomery 1965). Indeed we have seen that some urban renewal projects and policies are essentially slum clearance in orientation. But when urban renewal is examined more extensively on a worldwide basis, it becomes apparent that it is of massive importance. In the past, urbanization has been small and has been disproportionately limited to a few countries in Europe and North America. In the last of the twentieth century, urbanization is large and is expanding worldwide. It is in this sense that urban renewal is more important now than in the past.

We can now say that urban renewal needs to be conceived as a continuing process. Furthermore the urban renewal process must be both social and physical. It may be carried by governmental organizations, by private capital, or by both in varying degrees of cooperation. In order to achieve maximum benefit, it must not be random or the result of unilateral decision-making.

Cities are changing social organizations. In urbanized society, large city and megalopolis regions embrace all of the needs of social life. Therefore urban renewal plans must be examined in terms of their interfacing with family life, educational activities, jobs in economic systems, religion, government, health, welfare, the arts, recreation, and science — the urban social activity systems. In addition to physical environmental impact, urban renewal must be examined for total social organizational impact.

Units of urban renewal may be satisfactorily carried out in a project-like manner when they are clearly related to the society as a whole. They must not, however, be limited projects in the sense of unilateral design or single goals, as if in a vacuum. For example, the folly of low-income housing in Boston, as detailed in Forrester's book *Urban Dynamics*, or the failure of the Pruitt-Igoe Housing Project in St. Louis, Missouri, can be largely attributed to incomplete consideration of urban activity systems. In the case of Boston's low-income housing, the Forrester analysis indicates that living standards are ultimately lowered when provision is made only for housing and not simultaneously for jobs, education, health, and so forth. Most individuals who are incapable of providing their own housing have additional handicaps or other needs. This was similarly seen in the St. Louis Pruitt-Igoe Housing Project where deteriorated slum housing was removed and replaced by new housing units. These apartment complexes soon became centers for antisocial behavior because their homogeneously lower income inhabitants needed jobs, day-care facilities, recreation facilities, educational assistance, special health care, and so forth.

The life of urbanized man does not exist just in housing projects. The life of a dynamic twentieth-century city is not supported just by people in low-income housing projects. The process of urban renewal must extend over multiple decades and itself be designed to accommodate sociophysical change. Doxiadis (1966) put it this way: "The entire urban organisms must be reconstructed. . . . In order to be successful in such an effort, we need a national ekistic program [i.e., a program that takes into account urban activity systems] that is as long term as possible; and until we prepare it, we should have an interim program for the transitional period. Partial programs for urban renewal, or housing, or community facilities only, even if they encompass the whole nation, will lead nowhere" (p. 169).

IMPLICATIONS

Urban renewal must be the result of a continuing comprehensive planning process. It must reflect the broadest possible urbanized societal view. Urban renewal requests may proceed from the bottom up or from the top down. The initiation of requests for urban renewal may, accordingly, vary sharply between democratic societal ideologies and communistic societal ideologies. But the end result of the urban renewal process must be highly similar in its contribution to the achievement of high-quality environment for urbanized people. Citizen participation must be an overt and explicit part of the process whether it is ideologically initiated from the bottom up or the top down. Moreover, local citizen input needs to be systematically interfaced with professional, regional, and societywide citizen input.

Urbanized societies are large-scale and dynamic. Accordingly, the urban renewal process must be societal in scope and plan while the implementation may be systematically subdivided into small units which can be carried out on a project-by-project basis. In the urban renewal process, projects must be integrated rather than treated as if they were in a vacuum.

REFERENCES

ADDE, L. *Nine Cities: The Anatomy of Downtown Renewal.* Washington, D.C.: The Urban Land Institute, 1969.

ANDERSON, M. *The Federal Bulldozer.* Cambridge: M.I.T. Press, 1964.

CLAWSON, M. Urban renewal in 2000. *American Institute of Planners Journal*, 1968, 34, 173–79.

DOXIADIS, C. A. *Urban Renewal and the Future of the American City.* Chicago: Public Administration Service, 1966.

DUGGAR, G. S. *Renewal of Town and Village: A Worldwide Survey of Local Government Experience.* The Hague: International Union of Local Authorities, 1965.

FORRESTER, J. *Urban Dynamics.* Cambridge: M.I.T. Press, 1969.

GOTTMAN, J. *Megalopolis.* Cambridge: M.I.T. Press, 1961.

GREBLER, L. *Urban Renewal in European Countries.* Philadelphia: University of Pennsylvania Press, 1964.

GREER, S. *Urban Renewal and American Cities.* New York: Bobbs-Merrill, 1965.

MONTGOMERY, R. Improving the design process in urban renewal. *Journal of the American Institute of Planners*, 1965, 31, 7–20.

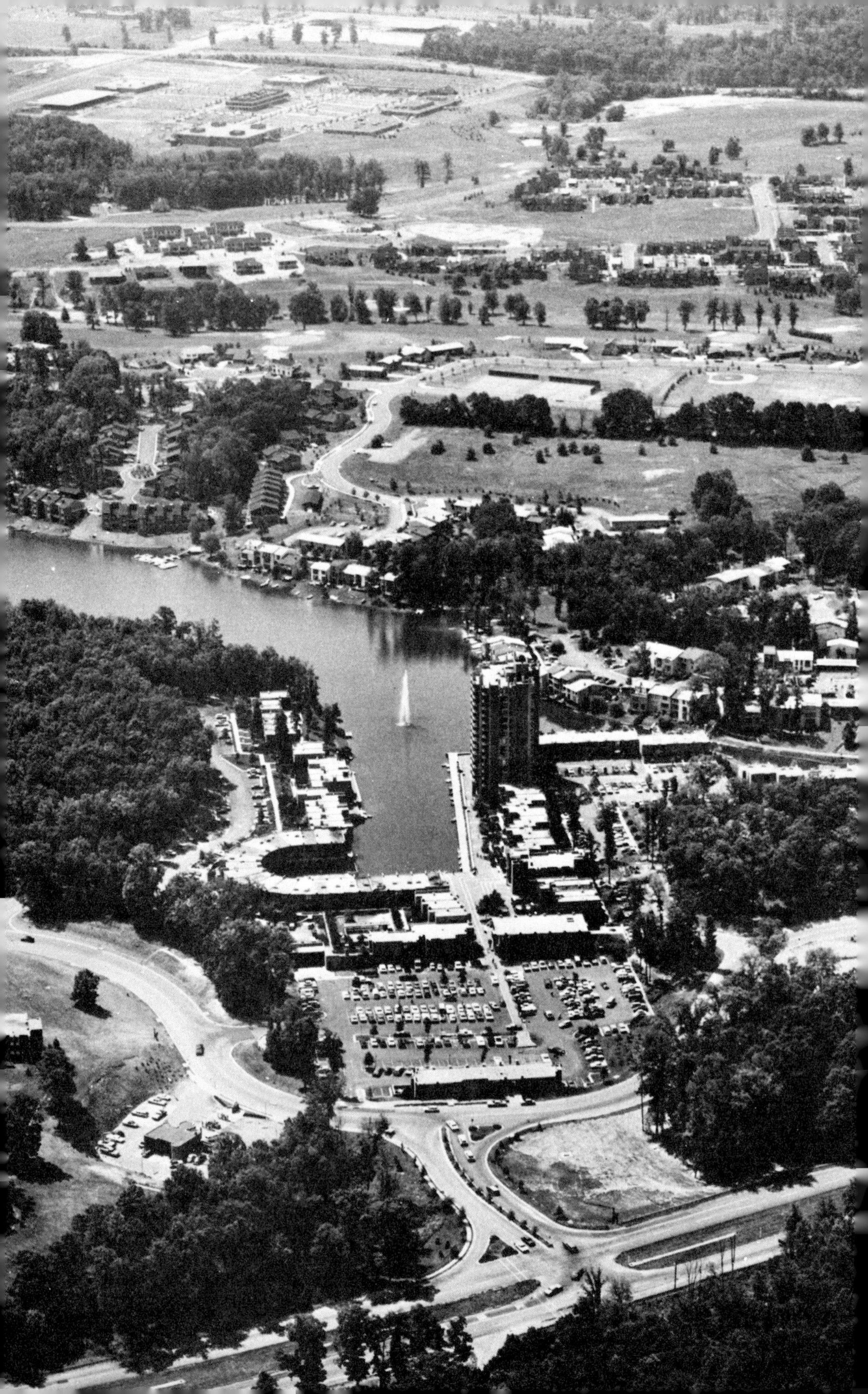

New Towns   15

Of great interest for urban planning are conceptually planned new towns. Of course, all cities were new at some point in historic time. But most of them grew up gradually, by chance, and with little or no planning.

In the history of urban society, new towns have been specifically planned for a variety of different reasons. In the sixteenth and seventeenth centuries, European colonial efforts in the New World, particularly those of the Spanish and English, involved planning and establishing new towns (Reps 1965). More recently, the Soviet Union has planned and built several hundred new towns, often as a specific part of the nation's larger planned efforts to develop natural resources and new geographical areas. In a somewhat similar manner, Canada has developed planned new towns as a part of resource development in sparsely settled territories. Starting at mid-century, Israel began to plan and build numerous new towns. Many of these new towns were a part of a broader national plan to defend the nation's frontiers, to develop agricultural production, and/or to systematically distribute population in locations other than Tel Aviv, Haifa, and Jerusalem (Strong 1971). Also in the mid-twentieth century, some notable new towns have been planned for political centers. Outstanding among these are the national capitals of Brasilia in Brazil, Islamabad in Pakistan, Canberra in Australia, and the provincial capital of Chandigarh in India.

From the middle of the twentieth century to the present, there has been a considerable upsurge in the planning and building of new

New town environments, such as the Reston development, emphasize housing, recreation, jobs, schools, health-care facilities, and shops. (Photo: Courtesy of Gulf Reston, Inc.)

towns for the express purpose of reducing slum conditions in older cities and improving the quality of the urban environment for people in new locations. This new town building effort was most specifically moved forward by the passage of the first British New Town Planning Act in 1946. It was an outgrowth of pressure from social reformers. The Ebenezer Howard garden city model is extensively used in this type of new-town planning. Most of these garden city new towns are being located in or near major metropolitan regions, in effect in ecumenopolizing channels. Also related to this quality of the environment-humanistic motive for garden city new towns is the new-town-in-town development. Most new-towns-in-town are related to urban renewal, but they are more than urban renewal.

New towns are built with private capital and by government financing. In some situations, government planning and financial support are combined with private capital. New towns are usually planned for populations between 50,000 and 300,000. Many new towns have a satellite relationship to larger and older existing cities.

Planned new towns house a very small proportion of the world's urban population. Indeed, the new town movement is small. By current scale it will provide for far less than one-quarter of the world's new urban population by 2000. New towns as examined in this chapter are only a part of the late twentieth-century urbanization process. They are intended to contribute to higher quality urban environment. They are not conceptualized as the major mechanism for overcoming urban slum problems and urban environmental imbalances.

By definition new towns involve (1) a designated land area; (2) a predetermined maximum population; (3) systematic land use; (4) provision for social institutions including family-housing, education, economics-jobs, recreation, religion, government, and health; and (5) a specified sociophysical relationship to their larger geographical environment.

NATURE AND SOCIAL ORGANIZATION

From Ebenezer Howard's 1898 garden city concept through the British New Town Planning Act in 1946 to the present, new towns have been conceived as total environments (Howard 1966). Even rural areas around a new town are planned in support of the town. The urban-rural balance is to contribute to low density and the minimizing of pollution. In some cases green space is preserved in the form of greenbelts or greenwedges. Residential sites and industrial sites are specifically planned in the new towns. Jobs are planned for a designated proportion of the working population. Special effort is usually made to minimize commuting and where possible to have jobs in a walking proximity to residences. Much new town planning effort is placed on separating pedestrian traffic from auto traffic. Indeed, public transportation may be more extensively planned for than private transportation.

New towns focus carefully on planning for schools, recreation, shopping centers, and health services. Planning for religion receives less attention. Provision for government, in the sense of local citizen control, is often the least effective of the institutional planning efforts. Sociologically, new towns are planned to accommodate the major activity systems for societal existence. Physical plans need to support the social activities of people who live in cities and urbanized areas.

It is typical for new towns to be planned for completion in a twenty-year period. New towns may become economically viable and self-supporting within a decade and a half, and paid for in a fifty- to sixty-year period. The British have had particularly good experiences regarding the economics of their development.

Size of new towns

The appropriate size of new towns continues to be a matter of conjecture. Howard's original garden city new town model proposed populations of 30,000. The first generation of British new towns (1947 – 1956) were planned for populations ranging from 60,000 to 80,000. The second generation of British new towns (1961 to the 1970s) are planned for 150,000 to 200,000 persons. Indeed, by the 1960s in many parts of the world, new towns were being planned for populations of 200,000 or more. Social organizationally, if new towns are to have relatively complete social systems and be more than satellites, larger populations are required in order to provide for an adequate range of plural urban culture and services. Even communities of 200,000 population are too small to support advanced hospitals, large universities, major league spectator sports, great museums, and quality symphonies.

It is argued that urban areas of approximately 200,000 population can effect economic efficiency, allow significant citizen participation, and provide high-quality social control. Accordingly, in ecumenopolizing areas new towns can be planned large enough to function as freestanding areas, rather than as satellites, for most daily needs of their populations. Yet they are sufficiently proximic to larger urban places so their populations may utilize major regional airports, hospitals, museums, recreation programs, and so forth.

Social stratification and social interaction

Stratification and social interaction are two major areas of specific attention in new towns. From Howard's garden cities, Letchworth in

1903 and Welwyn in 1919, through the development of Tapiola, Finland in 1951, to the American federally supported new towns of the 1970s, special emphasis has been placed on provision for all social classes. This ideal has been only partially achieved (Osborn 1969). In fact new towns have become havens for the middle classes. Often there is a full range of middle classes from lower-middle through middle-middle to upper-middle. The nature of the planned residential environment makes little provision for the economically poor. Regulations on space and land use largely negate the possibility of estates of sufficient size and status to attract the upper classes.

Social interaction is encouraged and planned for by using low-density designs combined with many common areas. In the British new towns, an average of fifteen persons per acre is the goal. Often in new towns, more than half of the places of residence are rented rather than owned. Accordingly, it is easy to maximize common areas both in buildings and outdoors.

Additionally, pedestrian traffic and auto traffic are largely separated by the use of the superblock (Stein 1969). The superblock of the 1930s has been modified into the Planned Unit Development in the 1970s. In addition to separating foot traffic and auto traffic, superblocks and Planned Unit Developments can offer a range of housing types, often extending from detached housing through row housing to high-rise units juxtaposed with convenience shopping facilities, schools, churches, recreational facilities, and sometimes health facilities as well. Social interaction is sometimes specifically facilitated by age-specific groups, for example in residential spaces for the elderly or for singles only. In other cases planning facilitates the integration of social interaction among all ages and both sexes.

A primary mechanism for facilitating social interaction is the planned neighborhood (Keeble 1972; Bailey 1973). In 1929 C.A. Perry related the neighborhood to physical planning. It was centered around a school to be within a ten-minute walk of all students (a distance of one-quarter mile). By the time of new town planning in the 1940s, the neighborhood was seen as a population of approximately 10,000 around a service center that included schools, shopping centers, health services and open recreation spaces. Superblocks and cul-de-sacs became the standard design elements for facilitating this social interaction. As many people have become more mobile and less family centered, less time has been spent in residential neighborhoods. The social space for neighborhoods with schools at their center has eroded in countries like the United States, where school integration is implemented by busing students across neighborhood lines. The neighborhood may now have to share more sociophysical space with something like Herbert Gans' "social intensive unit." The social intensive unit is an area of fifty to one hundred families where residents may choose persons for face-to-face interaction. Services would be planned at the community or larger level rather than at the neighborhood or social-intensive-unit levels.

Comparing the new town of Reston, Virginia and the West Springfield area — also suburban to Washington, D.C., but not a new town — illustrates relevant differences for planned and nonplanned developments (Cuthbertson 1976). As of 1970, Reston and West Springfield had populations of 8,315 and 9,755 respectively, in census tracts 4092 and 4042. Reston's population was 5.7 percent black, while West Springfield's was only 0.2 percent black. The median school years completed in Reston were sixteen and in West Springfield fifteen. The median number of rooms in housing units in Reston was 6.4 compared to 7.8 in West Springfield. Housing in Reston was only 42 percent owner occupied compared to 85 percent in West Springfield. The median value of owner-occupied units was higher in Reston than in West Springfield, $44,500 compared to $42,800. In West Springfield 96 percent of the housing units were single-family, compared to only 59 percent single-family units in Reston. In the new town, 9 percent of the population rode buses to work while only 3 percent in West Springfield rode buses. Occupationally, 81 percent of the residents of Reston were professional, clerical, or managerial, while only 75 percent in West Springfield were in these categories. The 1969 mean family income in Reston was $17,540, compared to $19,331 in West Springfield. In sum, there is more diversity of population in Reston and more opportunity for social interaction.

Density

Densities in new towns generally range from 12 to 15 persons per acre. This is even lower than the 19 in Letchworth and 22 in Welwyn as planned by Howard. Density in America's federally funded new towns is closer to 10 persons per acre ("Failure of the New Densities" 1953). The British urban sociologist Ruth Glass asserts that "the assessment of density is evidently an art and not a science" (p. 358). She notes the folk wisdom that urbanism equals high density, urbanism equals bad living conditions, and therefore high density equals bad living conditions. But the situation, she suggests, is more complex than the folk wisdom implies. Generally there is confusion because density may be computed as the number of rooms per acre, the number of persons per acre, the floor space or building densities per acre, with variations for gross and net densities. All of these may be correct, but they have considerably different meanings.

Physical densities and social densities must be differentiated. While the meaning of density for urban culture may vary, it is clear that the gross land use for the garden city new towns is greater than in traditional urban areas. Within the garden city, the actual number of people per room and the number of rooms per acre in the built-up areas may vary considerably, as they do in traditional urban areas. But due to the greater homogeneity of population in the garden city new towns, the social densities of population are greater than in traditional urban areas. This is to say that in many new towns one must encounter a larger number of people or travel over a greater physical distance to experience a diversity in people and social circumstances similar to that in nonplanned cities.

Youth and the elderly in new towns

Garden city new towns of the late 1940s and the 1950s were disproportionately inhabited by young adults with small families. Accordingly, provisions were made for totlots and other early childcare needs. Only very limited provision was made for teenagers and "young singles." Similarly, few provisions were made for gerontological needs. There were few single-bedroom and efficiency residential units. As new towns have matured into their second and third decades, there are increased demands both for youth facilities and for facilities for married couples and single individuals outside of the childrearing experience. The planning matrix for new towns which develops over a fifteen-to-thirty-year period can systematically anticipate age-specific growth. Costly physical facilities can be constructed and phased into use at a time period appropriate for their age-specific need.

In a similar manner, hotel-type accommodations are not typically planned in the early sociophysical phases of the new towns. These facilities remain for construction in later phases.

In the second generation British new towns, more planning emphasis is placed on the anticipated needs of youth and of older citizens. Nevertheless, in most respects the built environment to provide for implementation of teenage and elder-citizen needs remains for later stages of development. Family-center activities, more than facilities for single adults, continue to dominate new town development.

Arts and recreation in new towns

Opportunities for new town inhabitants to participate in the arts and recreation are extensively planned. Little theater groups, chamber and popular music groups, choral groups, hobby painting activities, and so forth are extensively developed (Pritchard 1964). Open spaces for outdoor recreation are a cardinal feature of the garden city new towns. Sports fields for organized games, tennis courts, swimming pools, and golf courses are typical facilities. There are also hiking, bicycle, and horseback riding trails. Picnic areas and nature-study areas are frequently designated.

NEW TOWN MODELS

There are three major new town models, namely, the garden city, the linear city, and the megastructure city. The father of the garden city is Ebenezer Howard (Howard 1966). In 1899, the Garden City Association was organized. In 1946 the garden city was embodied in the first British New Town Planning Act. From 1946 to the present, this model has received more use than any other.

The linear-city model originated with Arturo Soira y Mata in 1882 (Doxiadis 1967). This model has had limited use in Madrid, Spain; Volgograd, Russia (Miliutin 1975); and Santiago, Chile. An extensive linear-city development was proposed for London, but it never materialized. While Doxiadis asserts that the "linear city is unfeasible," there is considerable world urban pressure to perfect its development. Its elements are similar to those of the garden city except that the town center is in a long strip. On either side of the strip center are transportation, residential areas, and industry, with agriculture on the outer edges, also serving for open green space. All institutional activities for urban societal life are planned for, as in the garden cities.

The megastructure model is sharply different from garden cities and linear cities. It is the most urban of the three models. A megastructure is a very large building within which an urban societal-sized population can have their total life experience. Inhabitants need not be restricted to the megastructure, but they will have no life-support needs outside of them. In the megastructure, spaces will be designated for residence, manufacturing, commerce, food production, education, health, recreation, worship, and government. Soleri's megastructures are designed to support populations larger than those of Denmark, Finland, or Norway. The average density in an arcology would be 440 persons per acre. They are designed to be built floating at sea, to be built over earth crevices like the Grand Canyon in the United States, to orbit the earth like a space capsule, or to be built in traditional city locations (O'Neill 1976).

Two other megastructure proposals illustrate this model. They are the Minnesota Experimental City (Experimental City Project 1969) and the Compact City (Dantzig 1973). These megastructures would have populations in the 250,000 range.

In sum, the nature of new towns, regardless of the model, involves the careful conceptual integration of all the social-institutional needs for human survival. Ideally, new town plans are societal in scope. In some cases they are free-standing, and in other cases they are satellites or even new-towns-in-town. Even when the satellite new towns draw upon older urban populations in metropolitan regions, the relationships to the older and larger metropolitan regions should be planned.

BRITISH NEW TOWN EXPERIENCES

The British new town experience is of considerable importance. It is of the longest duration and the most extensive national commitment found anywhere to date (Howard 1966; Osborn 1969; Corrigan 1971; Bar 1973; Tyrwhitt 1973). The British new town experience effectively starts with Howard's garden city model in 1898. In 1903 Letchworth was founded some thirty-five miles north of London. In 1919 Welwyn Garden City was founded some twenty miles northwest of London. These new towns were designed for populations of about 30,000 and 50,000 respectively. They were each planned to have an agricultural greenbelt.

Raymond Unwin was one of the designers of Letchworth. He continued an interest in new towns. By 1933 Unwin was involved in the Greater London Planning Commission, which recommended eight to ten new towns in a ring around London. There continued to be other commissions and reports, in varying ways pointing to the need for new towns. Parliament finally passed the New Towns Act of 1946. This historic Act provided for the central government to establish development corporations. It also provided the authority to acquire land for development, and provided for the financing and building of housing and other community facilities. The central treasury lends money to the development corporation at the going rate of interest. It is to be repaid in a sixty-year period. In fact, the first generation British new towns began to make money within a little more than one decade.

The London ministry drafts the designation orders for new towns. Public inquiries are then held concerning the site selection. Subsequently the minister appoints a nine-person, part-time, salaried development corporation. Some of these appointees must reside in the development area. The development corporation in turn selects a general manager and brings together a full-time paid new town planning staff, which is approved at the ministry level. After most of the planning and construction is completed, the development corporation is phased out and a development commission is established to further the operation.

British new towns are designed to maximize employment within their urban limits and to reduce daily commuting to London and other adjacent larger urban areas. Indeed, in the London ring new towns, people are given priority advantages for improved residence facilities if they will move from designated areas in London to a designated new town and agree to accept employment there. A majority of the migrants to the new towns have been under age thirty-five. Typically, they are married couples with small children and still in the childbearing ages. Few new town migrants are singles and fewer still are oldsters (Kellaway 1969; Roderick 1971). From 1946 to 1976, the London ring new towns grew from their collective 100,000 population at the time of designation to over 500,000, most of which was the result of migration.

In addition to the London ring new towns, there is a northward expansion toward Liverpool. This is an ecumenopolizing corridor. A second corridor in which new towns have been established is between Glasgow and Edinburgh. In effect British new town planning is being used to systematically improve the urban environment at crucial pressure points.

By 1961 a second generation of new towns was launched. These are about twice the size of their first-generation counterparts, ranging between 150,000 and 200,000 population. They are specifically designed to provide more social benefits and social amenities. Most of the new town and agree to accept employment there. A majority of the migrants to the new towns have been under age thirty-five. Typically, they Greenbelt critics assert that they are a type of neo-urban wall. It is also argued that they are a waste of time as people and goods are moved across them between the central cities and the satellites. There are also numerous ecology arguments rendered in support of greenbelts.

The physical building of new towns includes constructing housing, arranging for industries and jobs, providing schools, health care facilities, and other elements of the societal system of the master-plan matrix. In Britain there is a systematic effort to provide diversified employment opportunities in the new towns. Special efforts are made to provide for a range of job skills and specifically to provide employment opportunities for women. Special efforts are made to insure that individuals who take jobs in new towns are able to get housing there also. New industries are attracted, and expansion of existing industries is supported.

The British new town planners attempt to address the needs of social development as well as economic stability. In spite of this, the new towns are characterized by considerable socioeconomic homogeneity. There is an age-specific imbalance, with a disproportionate number of persons between the ages of thirty and forty. Few residents are from racial minorities. In the first generation new towns, insufficient planning emphasis was placed on social development. Since the 1960s, social development officers have been employed. Their functions vary considerably from little more than "welcome wagon" persons to directors of playgrounds and cultural activities.

The British new towns have both proponents and opponents. Their record of experience is sufficient to be worthy of careful examination. By the 1970s, the first-generation new towns are making money for the London government. They have not depopulated London, but they were not realistically intended to do that. They have demonstrated that a systematic movement of population can be achieved. While there have been short-range problems with housing, jobs, and social dissatisfactions, the overview evaluation of residents is that of satisfaction to high satisfaction.

NEW TOWN EXPERIENCE IN THE UNITED STATES

New towns in the United States have a troubled history. As the nation moved rapidly from dispersed agriculture to industrialism, housing for workers and the provision of other life needs near jobs increased. Industrial new towns followed. The negative experience in Pullman, Illinois illustrates the fate of this kind of community planning (Budder 1969). In 1880 George Pullman, the millionaire developer of the Pullman railroad car, decided to increase production and develop a new plant with a planned town and model housing in the South Chicago area. He steadfastly refused to call his development a new town. More modestly he asserted that it was good business and a part of a moneymaking scheme to provide a higher quality environment for workers and their families. He subsequently hired an architect and a landscape architect to plan the plant and the town. By 1881 some 1,700 people were living in Pullman. In spite of the many amenities in industrial new towns like Pullman, the towns were generally criticized as excessively paternalistic, and they subsequently failed. But the nation had become more urban than rural in 1920, and the need for higher quality urban environment continued to grow.

By the late 1920s the superblock concept appeared, first being used in Radburn, New Jersey (Stein 1969). In the mid-1920s builders around New York were experimenting with apartment complexes constructed around courtyards with green space for residents' relaxation and leisure. Success in this regard precipitated the idea of building a garden city in three superblock neighborhoods which would accommodate a total population of 25,000. The site was Radburn, New Jersey, just across the Hudson River from New York City. Radburn was in a still unspoiled rural area. Construction began in 1928, and the first homeowners occupied their new residences in 1929. Travel to New York City was to have been facilitated by the George Washington Bridge and connecting highways, but the ensuing depression of the 1930s interrupted these plans, and Radburn was never completed.

For innovation and new town planning, Radburn's impact was a success. Its superblock idea involved facing houses on lanes and parkways and providing an auto approach from small cul-de-sac streets. Children and others could play and relax in the safe interior parks, free from auto traffic and noise. Residents could walk to schools, shopping facilities, and recreation areas without crossing streets. This was a sharp and decisive sociophysical modification from the historic grid pattern of street development. It also separated social activity systems while placing them in a planned proximity.

Ironically, the depression years of the 1930s stimulated from the U.S. Department of Agriculture the next major new-town experiment in the United States. R.G. Tugwell, an agricultural economist on the faculty of Columbia University in New York, was called by President Franklin Roosevelt in 1935 to develop new towns under the Resettlement Administration, an agency in the U.S. Department of Agriculture (Myhra 1974). It was Tugwell's belief that America's rural poverty had to be corrected with innovation in the cities. Further, he believed that social planning in a democracy was an effective way to improve the human environment. Tugwell planned and started the construction of three garden city new towns. Initial construction was provided for under the Emergency Relief Appropriations Act of 1935.

In 1935, Tugwell and his staff studied one hundred cities as potential sites for planned new communities and submitted a list of twenty-five to the President. Later that same year, Roosevelt approved eight cities for greenbelt new towns. Only half of the money allocated by the President ever reached the construction agency, so the new-town sites were reduced from eight to five. They were located in St. Louis, Missouri; Cincinnati, Ohio; Milwaukee, Wisconsin; Washington, D.C.; and New Brunswick, New Jersey. Later that same year, construction was begun at the sites in Cincinnati, Milwaukee, and Washington, D.C..

Greenbelt, Maryland, ten miles north of Washington, D.C., was first. It was built on a 5,400-acre tract of land. Initially it contained 1,000 residences. It was expanded during World War II. Greenhills, Ohio, twenty miles north of Cincinnati's central business district, was the second. Its land area was 5,930 acres, and it was initially designed to accommodate 1,000 homes and related facilities. Greendale, Wisconsin, eight miles northwest of Milwaukee, was the third and last of the new towns. It was built on 3,410 acres containing 750 home sites and related facilities.

The greenbelt towns were deluged with opposition from the outset. Court appeals and Congressional harassment were roadblocks. Tugwell resigned in 1936. The planning and construction organization was dismantled, and the towns were finished by other agencies. In 1955 the Federal Government finally sold its interests to private developers, and another phase of America's new town building experience was laid to rest.

Also in the 1930s there was some new town development under the Tennessee Valley Authority. Norris, Tennessee, now in metropolitan Knoxville exemplifies this development (Scott 1969). Norris was planned for a 1,000-home site. Due to its rugged terrain, superblocks were rejected in favor of curvilinear streets and cul-de-sacs. Given Southern residential preferences, row houses were rejected in favor of detached housing. A 2,000-acre greenbelt was established, and 14 acres of common ground were set aside. A school, community auditorium, and shopping center were constructed. Norris was sold to private developers in 1946.

Following World War II, massive amounts of suburban and strip-housing development took place in an unplanned way in the United States. Middle-class whites accelerated their exodus from older central cities. Persons lower on the socioeconomic scale, often blacks and browns, moved into the decaying central cities, and slum problems were exacerbated. Many urban renewal schemes were tried; they were often evaluated as too physical and too insufficient. The call for new towns grew again in the 1960s. Government bureaucrats and private citizens made trips to Europe to see and study new town experiences there. Subsequently the American Congress found itself once again confronting proposals for new town support.

It was apparent by the middle and late 1950s that the British new towns were making significant profits. Indeed, from the mid-1940s through the 1960s, private capital corporations were building new towns in America (Turner 1974). In 1969 the U.S. Department of Housing and Urban Development listed sixty-three new communities in twenty states developed by private capital. Most of these were in California, Arizona, and Florida (*Survey and Analysis of Large Development and New Communities* 1969). Many of the privately developed projects are more advanced residential developments than actual new towns. Nevertheless, the point is that from the 1880s to the 1970s, new-town experiences in America never have been totally extinguished.

The Housing Act of 1968 under Title IV gave authority for the U.S. Department of Housing and Urban Development to issue loan guarantees to assist developers building new towns. The Act placed a ceiling of $250 million on the guarantee program and a $50 million guarantee limit for any one new town. This program enabled private corporations to borrow money at favorable interest rates and also gave the lending institutions security. While the government itself continued to invest no money directly in new towns, supplementary HUD grants paid for sewerage, water facilities, and related kinds of support. Only Jonathan, Minnesota, was initiated under this 1968 legislation.

The Urban Growth and New Community Development Act of 1970, through its Title VII, superseded the 1968 Act. The 1970 Act increased the amount of guarantee to $500 million, and it also extended the guarantee privileges to public agencies. Fifteen new towns were supported under this Act (Mields 1973). Title VII specified the following goals: (1) the new towns should be well planned, large-scale developments that include all of the basic institutions normally associated with towns; (2) the new towns should be self-sufficient in the sense of providing jobs, education, health facilities, cultural opportunities, and commercial facilities; (3) employment and other social opportunities are to be opened to all races and income groups; (4) the new towns should be technologically innovative; (5) older urban areas should be revitalized through new-town-in-town developments; and (6) the new towns should encourage population growth and relocation in predominantly rural areas. Also the 1970 legislation required at the outset social input in the form of citizen advisory groups, housing distribution plans designed to avoid segregation, and specific designation of educational and social facilities. Table 15–1 summarizes the extent of Federal commitment to new towns under this legislation.

By the mid 1970s, federal support for new towns in the United States was again under heavy attack and was near its demise. The rhetoric against new towns was clear: "HUD should back no additional new towns" (*Housing and Development Reporter* 1974). Such a definitive view is based on the judgment that federally assisted new communities cost more than they are worth and that they provide only limited innovation. Critics of the program point out that new communities like Jonathan and Cedar-Riverside in Minnesota have been for sale early in their development. Also, it is noted that communities like Jonathan (Minnesota), St. Charles (suburban Maryland), and Riverton (near Rochester, New York) have had to be bailed out of financial troubles by HUD.

Much of the criticism of America's federally supported new towns is specifically aimed at their housing. Yet the 1970 legislation clearly indicated that they should be total urban social systems, not just housing developments. Most new-town experiences in both Europe and the United States are based on a fifteen-to-thirty-year building schedule. Accordingly, there an insufficient amount of time has elapsed to make

TABLE 15—1 Summary of New Communities Guaranteed by HUD (Dollars in Thousands)

Community	Type	Guarantee Commitment Amount & Date	Guarantee Amount & Date	Issue Interest Rate	Population (projected)	Dwelling Units (projected)	Location
Jonathan, Minnesota	Satellite/ Growth center	$21,000 2/70	$ 8,000 10/70[a]	8.50%	50,000 in 20 years	16,500 in 20 years	20 mi. S.W. of Minneapolis
St. Charles Communities, Maryland	Satellite	$24,000 6/70	$13,000 6/72 $18,000 12/70	7.20% 7.75%	75,000 in 20 years	25,000 in 20 years	25 mi. S.W. of Washington D.C.
Park Forest South, Illinois	Satellite	$30,000 6/70	$30,000 3/71	7.00%	110,000 in 15 years	35,000 in 15 years	30 mi. S. of Chicago
Flower Mound, Texas	Satellite	$18,000 12/70	$14,000 10/71	7.60%	64,000 in 20 years	18,000 in 20 years	20 mi. S.W. of Dallas
Maumelle, Arkansas	Satellite	$ 7,500 12/70	$ 4,500 6/72	7.62%	45,000 in 20 years	14,000 in 20 years	12 mi. N.W. of Little Rock
Cedar-Riverside, Minnesota	New-town-in-town	$24,000 6/71	$24,000 12/71	7.20%	30,000 in 20 years	12,500 in 20 years	downtown Minneapolis
Riverton, New York	Satellite	$12,000	$12,000 5/72	7.125%	25,600 in 16 years	8,000 in 16 years	10 mi. S. of Rochester

TABLE 15—1 (continued)

San Antonio Ranch, Texas[b]	Satellite	$18,000 2/72	—	88,000 in 30 years	28,000 in 30 years	20 mi. N.W. of San Antonio
The Woodlands, Texas	Satellite	$50,000 4/72	$50,000 9/72	7.10%	150,000 in 20 years	49,160 in 20 years	30 mi. N.W. of Houston
Gananda, New York	Satellite	$22,000 4/72	$22,000 12/72	7.15%	50,000 in 20 years	17,200 in 20 years	12 mi. E. of Rochester
Soul City, North Carolina	Free-standing	$14,000 6/72	—	—	44,000 in 30 years	12,906 in 30 years	45 mi. N. of Raleigh-Durham
Harbison, South Carolina	Satellite	$13,000 10/72	—	—	23,000 in 20 years	6,750 in 20 years	8 mi. N.W. of Columbia
Lysander, New York	Satellite	[c]	[d]	—	18,300 in 8 years	5,000 in 8 years	12 mi. N.W. of Syracuse
Welfare Island, New York	New-town-in-town	[d] 12/72	—	—	18,000 in 7 years	5,000 in 7 years	in New York City
Shenandoah, Georgia	Satellite/Growth center	$40,000 2/73	—	—	70,000 in 20 years	23,000 in 20 years	35 mi. S.W. of Atlanta

[a] Guaranteed under Title IV; all other guarantees under Title VII.
[b] Contingent on water protection studies.
[c] Eligible for 20% grant from HUD supplementing basic federal grant programs.
[d] First to receive a determination of eligibility for grant assistance rather than federal guarantee of its debt; receives federal assistance under Title VII, Housing and Urban Development Act of 1970.

Source: Hugh Mields, Jr., *Federally Assisted New Communities* (Washington, D.C.: Urban Land Institute, 1973), p. 27.

definitive evaluations. Nevertheless, by 1978 the U.S. Department of Housing and Urban Development terminated the new-town program and moved to sell its participation to private investors.

CONTINENTAL EUROPEAN NEW TOWN EXPERIENCES

The Netherlands

When examining European new town development, an appropriate starting place is the Netherlands. Town planning there dates from the seventeenth century. Furthermore, the Netherlands have one of the world's greatest national population densities (Davis 1969; Strong 1971). The Netherlands expect their population to grow from 13 million to 20 million by the year 2000, and to have a density of 1,500 persons per square mile, compared to 75 persons per square mile in the U.S.A. Therefore, getting on with planning in the last of the twentieth century is a high-priority item.

In 1963 the Dutch began to expand the 10,000-population town of Zoetermeer, nine miles from the Hague, to provide for a population of 70,000 by 1980 and 100,000 ultimately. West of Amsterdam six garden city suburbs are being built to provide for more than 140,000 people. South of Amsterdam new towns are also being planned, one using a megastructure model, which will provide for 140,000 persons. Additionally, new towns are being built in the Polders (Vink 1955).

Sweden

In Sweden a satellite garden city new town planning model is being used around Stockholm. Sweden has a land area and a shape similar to California's. But its 8 million population is considerably smaller than California's 20 million. Like much of the rest of the world, Sweden is rapidly shifting from a rural to an urban society. In 1870, 75 percent of the Swedish population was agricultural. By the second half of the twentieth century, 75 percent of all Swedes live in cities (Strong 1971). The city of Stockholm has a population of 800,000 and its metropolitan area is a little over 1 million. Planning in Sweden dates from the sixteenth century. More recently, Stockholm has netted significant advantages from an 1874 Land Planning Act. From that time on, the city of Stockholm has purchased land on its periphery for systematic expansion (Beggs 1955). Accordingly, Stockholm has had a minimal land acquisition problem for its new towns. Five new towns — Vällingsby, Farsta, Skärholmen, Täby, and Spånga — are being developed in a satellite relationship to the capital city, and more are being planned

(Strong 1971; Sidenbladh 1975). In the Stockholm region only 20 percent of the housing is for single-family residences. By 1990 that proportion is expected to increase to 30 percent.

Vällingsby was opened in 1954. It is planned for a core population of 44,000 and is nine miles from central Stockholm. Most housing is in apartments, up to twelve stories; there is some row housing three to six stories, a limited amount of single-family row housing, and even fewer detached units on the outer fringes. The Vällingsby town center provides for commercial activities, theaters, church, a library, a post office, social services, and parking for 1,250 automobiles. The shopping center and facilities are large enough to provide for a total peripheral population of some 60,000 (Smith 1957). It is designed to employ 25 percent of its resident population. Also, it is connected with central Stockholm by rapid transit and by a major highway. Unlike in the London ring new towns, diurnal commuting is an acceptable part of the planning for the Stockholm satellite cities (Pass 1973).

Finland

Finland's 5 million population is half rural. The country was ravaged by World War II, lost population and territory, was faced with 400,000 refugees to house and employ, and was required to pay reparations to the Soviet Union. The Helsinki region has a population of 700,000 people. It is growing, particularly in its suburban fringe areas. The problem of housing construction has been critical. The size of the average dwelling is small, some 650 square feet (Strong 1971). In view of these problems, the new town of Tapiola has been built in suburban Helsinki. It has become internationally famous.

Residential spaces in Tapiola are small, generally under 1,000 square feet per family unit. Ninety percent of residences are owner-occupied. Half of Tapiola's residents will be employed there. The city's target population, in the 20,000 range, is divided into three neighborhoods. The town center, however, is designed to serve not only Tapiola but also peripheral areas with a total population of 80,000.

Tapiola was developed by private capital. It was started by a foundation established in 1951 which acquired 670 acres of land just six miles from Helsinki (von Hertzen 1973). Tapiola is a garden city new town. Large areas of land are retained for green space and as wooded areas. There will be multiple-use open spaces for recreation and for gardening. Tapiola provides a range of housing sizes and a range of prices. Social and recreational facilities are provided for children, teenagers, and the middle-aged.

In sum, although Tapiola is a somewhat isolated example and small for new towns in the last of the twentieth century, it is a nearly perfect illustration of balancing people and services in a planned environment that is a satellite to a larger urban population.

France

Urban population pressures have come only recently to France (Hughes 1971). Half of the French population continues to live in rural areas or small towns. But in the last of the twentieth century, urbanization is progressing rapidly. The Paris region is expected to grow from 8 million in the early 1970s to 14 million by 2000 (Pressman 1973). Accordingly, in the late 1950s the French government established the Priority Urbanization Zone Policy (ZUP — Zonne à Urbaniser de Priorité) (Kinsey 1969).

There are five new towns in the Paris region. They are designed to accommodate large populations. Pontoise is thirty kilometers northwest of Paris and is planned for 450,000 people by 2000. Evry is located thirty kilometers south of Paris and is also designed for 450,000 people. Melus-Senart is thirty-five kilometers southeast of Paris. It is planned for 330,000 people. Fifteen kilometers east of Paris is Marne-la-Vallée. It is designed to accommodate 550,000 by the year 2000. St. Quentin-en-Yvelline is twenty-five kilometers southwest of Paris and is designed to accommodate 275,000 inhabitants. These new towns will be linked to Paris by rapid rail service as well as by highways. They are designed to be full-service towns rather than dormitories. Resident populations will be provided with employment opportunities, shopping facilities, educational institutions, and so forth. Nevertheless, the towns will not have complete autonomy but will be a systematic part of the total Paris region.

Norway

Norway's new town experience is limited, but nonetheless exemplary. Fyllingsdalen is a new community planned for a population of 25,000 as a satellite to the old city of Bergen, which has a population of 120,000. Bergen had little land on which to expand. Alternatives included building land in the sea, razing old buildings and replacing them with high-rise buildings, building higher buildings on the mountainside, or tunneling through a mountain to give access to an adjacent valley. The last option has been followed. By building Fyllingsdalen, the ancient beauty of Bergen and the ecology of the area have been saved. The new town involves extensive separation of pedestrian and vehicular traffic. Public bus service connects it to Bergen. Housing prices vary, and the styles include high-rise, middle-rise, and low-rise apartments, plus row housing and single-family-detached units. All of the housing structures are sited to maximize views of the mountains, valley, and fjord.

Fyllingsdalen is designed to provide for a town center, neighborhood convenience stores, schools, churches, light industry, offices, and recreation. The construction of Fyllingsdalen is supported by both private capital and public enterprise (Davis 1969).

Soviet Union

Building new towns in the Soviet Union has been a serious enterprise from 1926 to the present. It is reported that more than 800 new towns have been constructed (Shvarikov 1964). About a third of the Soviet new towns have been constructed on new or vacant sites. Others are expansions of existing cities or are satellite cities to large central places like Moscow. Most of the new towns have between 50,000 and 100,000 population. Currently the view is held that 100,000 to 200,000 population is an optimum size (Mellor 1963; Osborn 1969). A number of notable Soviet new towns are considerably larger, however: for example, Saporozhje has over 500,000 people, Karaganda has 500,000, Novokuznetsk has over 400,000, and Magnitogorsk has over 300,000.

Sites for new towns in the Soviet Union are chosen to facilitate the development of new sources of fuel and electric power, to transform the Asian regions into industrial areas, to facilitate creating new metallurgical industries, to stimulate chemical and oil industries in the Ural and the Volga regions, and, generally, to expand the population east of the Ural Mountains.

Once the new towns are sited, their planned internal social organization is generally similar to that of the garden city model. Typically, towns are surrounded by extensive green zones, and there is an extensive provision of parks and playground facilities. They are organized into microdistricts. These are intended to be self-contained residential neighborhoods ranging in population size between 5,000 and 20,000. Residential structures are typically apartments ranging from a few floors to twelve to fifteen stories high. This scale is used to facilitate mass construction techniques, specifically prefabrication. Planning is facilitated by state ownership of land and by centralized authority.

The new town of Togliatti illustrates the development pattern (Ruzhnikov 1969). It is located five hundred miles southwest of Moscow and planned for a population of 400,000. The town is laid out in areas providing for residence, recreation, education, commerce, and so forth. Public buses provide the main source of transportation. Togliatti is divided into microdistricts with populations between 2,000 and 4,000. Three to five housing blocks are organized around courtyards.

Prefabricated housing units range from five to sixteen stories high. Floor space in the residential units is minimal.

The Moscow satellite new towns are smaller, generally in the 60,000 population range (Hojayev 1957). Moscow's satellite new towns are intended to help curb the growth of the capital city. While satellite towns in many respects, they are constructed to have employment opportunities and not to be just dormitory towns. In sum, Russian new town experience is more significant for its extensive development than for its innovation.

Poland

Poland was devastated during World War II so that town building in Warsaw, and elsewhere, was a necessity. Nowa Haut is a prime example of Polish new town building (King 1955; Schneiderman 1956; Malisz 1962; Gorynski 1973). Planning in Poland is from the top down. In 1949, it was decided to build a new steel mill in the area of Krakow. In order to do this, new housing had to be provided for workers. Accordingly, the decision was made to build a total new town. Originally, Nowa Haut had a master plan that would accommodate 100,000 inhabitants plus an alternate reserve for an additional 30,000. By the mid-1970s the town actually housed 170,000. It is designed on a neighborhood basis. In each neighborhood there are blocks of flats or residential units. Additionally, the neighborhoods provide for kindergartens, schools, shops, movies, and youth facilities. All of these were built simultaneously so that when the population moved to the new town it had a full range of facilities. Much of the construction in the Polish new towns is prefabricated, similar to the techniques used in Russia. Most of the structures are built by a central authority.

NEW TOWNS IN AFRICA, LATIN AMERICA, THE NEAR EAST, AND THE ORIENT

New town experiences outside of Europe and North America are limited. Nevertheless, some of them are innovative and instructive.

Ghana

Planning for Tema started in the 1950s (Kirchherr 1969). This new town is built in conjunction with the development of a port. It is seventeen miles from Accra and in effect forms a metropolitan population with it. The initial plan was for a city of 75,000 people. By the late 1960s Tema was scaled upward to support a population of 250,000. Tema generally follows a grid pattern. In the town center, vehicular and pedestrian traffic are separated. The city is divided into seven communities, each made up of four neighborhoods (Vincent 1962).

Brazil

One of the most controversial new town examples is Brasilia. It is instructive because its scale is so massive. Its large scale and baroque form express the power of the nation. Brasilia was started in 1957. It is located inland, 925 kilometers from Rio de Janeiro (Stephenson 1970; Epstein 1973).

Brasilia is planned for 500,000 people. It has a major axis for government buildings and a second perpendicular axis for residential areas. The government-building axis is grand in style. The residential axis follows primarily a superblock design. There are neighborhoods with convenience facilities, schools, churches, and so forth. Most of the residences are in middle-rise apartment buildings. There are some row and some detached units. Housing was primarily designed to accommodate the needs of government bureaucrats and officials. Insufficient housing was provided for construction and service workers. Accordingly, so-called free towns, which are poverty areas, have grown up on the fringes of Brasilia to house the poor people.

Israel

The Israeli experience with new towns is different by degree. They have been rapidly built to distribute population away from Tel Aviv, Haifa, and Jerusalem; to accommodate the large number of immigrants; to stimulate agricultural production; and to assist in securing national boundaries (Morris 1970; Ash 1974).

Israel gained independence in 1948. At that time its population was only 870,000, and by the 1970s it had increased to more than 3 million. Planning is coordinated nationally. Cities are planned in hierarchies ranging in inhabitants from 500 to 100,000 or more. Thirty new towns are being built. Many are sited where there was no previous urban development. Since the national government assumes ownership of the land outside of the big cities, the usual problems of land acquisition for developing new towns do not obtain. In other respects, the Israeli new towns generally follow the garden city model with low densities and large open spaces. Dwelling units are built at approximately sixty per hectare and are essentially in four-story blocks.

By the mid-1960s, the new towns have a combined population of over 600,000. The small size of Israel's new towns has caused considerable economic inefficiency. Moreover, their lack of socioeconomic and cultural opportunities causes migration trends to the older and larger cities to be larger than the planners desire. Indeed, some two-thirds of the inhabitants are immigrants. Immigrants are referred to specific new towns and given few alternatives (Doudai 1965; Silkin 1967; Marans 1969).

India

A notable example of new town building is Chandigarh, the capital of Punjab Province in India (Chowdhury 1965; Evenson 1966). Chandigarh was started in 1950. It is approximately 150 miles northwest from Delhi. Initially, it was planned by architects from California. In its second year, control of the planning and development shifted to Le Corbusier.

Chandigarh is planned for a population of 150,000. In its main public sector, grandiose buildings constitute a city magnificent. The capital complex buildings include state government offices, the High Court, the Secretariat, the Legislature, and the Museum of Knowledge. Beyond the government buildings, the city is laid out linearly with a major long shopping street plus linear parks. Within the linear format, superblocks are developed. The superblocks become neighborhood units in which housing is allocated by occupational or status rank. Each superblock contains housing for approximately 1,150 families. This small population is consistent with the small village background experience of many of the inhabitants. Similarly, the architecure of the residential units is designed to be reminiscent of the villages from which many of the inhabitants have come. Roofs are flat because of tradition and also because they are then desirable supplemental sleeping areas. In spite of the superblock development, it is found that there is little neighboring among residents. This is generally attributed to sharp occupational and status differentials, which inhibit open and free social interaction.

Pakistan

In the northwest of West Pakistan, a few miles from the town of Rawalpindi, Doxiadis planned Islamabad as the new capital. The plan was started in 1959 and work was initiated in 1961 (Doxiadis 1965; Jamoud 1968). Islamabad is planned for 400,000 people in twenty years. The layout of the city utilizes the grid pattern. It is related to a large national park and to the existing city of Rawalpindi. It is also designed to grow linearly. Within the grids, the community structure is paramount. Ultimately the city will include residences, classrooms, laboratories, nurseries, swimming pools, playgrounds, tea houses, mosques, and service centers. Housing is traditional for the area with flat roofs, high walls, and patios for outdoor living.

Japan

Since World War II, Japan's population has grown rapidly. Accordingly, there has been a need to build satellite cities as well as more independent new towns (Inouye 1952; Omori 1964; Iton 1964). The first of Tokyo's satellite new towns was designated in 1958. More than a dozen additional new towns have now been started. The satellite new towns have populations ranging from 50,000 to 200,000. For example, Senri new town is located fifteen kilometers north of Osaka. Its area is 1,150 hectares and it is planned for 30,000 households or a population of 150,000.

The plans of these new towns are in and of themselves not strikingly innovative. They do, however, illustrate societal attempts to provide for an orderly and high-quality environment.

Australia

Canberra was founded in 1913 in the southeastern part of Australia. Initially it was planned to accommodate 75,000 people. It is now expected to expand to 250,000 population by the mid-1980s (Barney 1963; Holford 1963). Canberra, like Brasilia, is planned around a manmade lake, and like Rome it is a city built between multiple hills. Government buildings are located on one side of the lake. They include the Parliament House, the High Courts, the National Library, and supporting offices. On the opposite side of the lake is the town center. On the central business district periphery on one side is the Australian National University and on the opposite side is a technical college. Hospitals, hotels, and other services for urban life support are in the central area. Employment, shopping facilities, infant care centers, and primary schools are dispersed through the residential districts. The residential areas are constructed in a garden city model with maximum open space. Interdistrict transportation is facilitated by a four-tier road system.

In sum, the non-European and non-North American new towns illustrate more planning that is regional and national in scope. Indeed, they are often related to resource development.

IMPLICATIONS

We now have a brief worldwide sketch of new-town-building experiences essentially spanning the years from 1946 to the present. Broad as this experience is, it is limited. Most new towns are planned for physical completion within a fifteen-to-thirty-year period. Therefore, in only a few cases do we have experience with second generation sociophysical relationships in new towns. Evaluation of new town experience is accordingly limited.

There is evidence that new towns can be economically viable. Similarly, there is some evidence showing that residents have high satisfaction with new towns. But some have had serious economic problems and provided poor social environments. New towns have not depopulated major older cities, but most urbanologists did not expect them to do that. In most cases they are in satellite relationships to larger, older municipal areas and/or in an ecumenopolizing channel of population growth. Nevertheless, in the Soviet Union, Brazil, Venezuela, Australia, and other places, there are examples of new towns that have been successfully established outside of satellite and ecumenopolizing areas.

In terms of urban growth policy, to date new towns have played only minor roles. Even in places like the Soviet Union and England, where the governments have supported some 800 and some 30 new towns respectively, they have been insufficient to massively redirect urbanizing populations. Nevertheless, in most places where new towns exist, they do demonstrate that population centers can be established on a planned basis and that this can create high-quality urban environments. Only limited citizen participation has been a part of new town planning to date. Also, new-town models are greatly limited. Most of the world's new towns utilize Howard's antiurban garden city model. There is a need for linear cities and megastructure cities to be constructed for research purposes.

By the 1970s, new towns are an important experiment on the world's urban landscape, but they are nowhere typical or normative.

REFERENCES

ASH, J. The progress of new towns in Israel. *Town Planning Review*, 1974, 45, 387–400.

BAILEY, J. (Ed.) *New Towns in America*. New York: Wiley, 1973, 60–61.

BAR, W. Designing new and expanding communities in Britain. 1946 – 1971. *Ekistics*, 1973, 37, 8–13.

BARNEY, S. Canberra — a fast growing capital. *Town and Planning Review*, 1963, 38, 3–24.

BEGGS, V. W. P. Operation Vallingby — Sweden experiments with planned decentralization. *The American City*, 1955, 70, 117–19.

BUDDER, S. *Pullman: An Experiment in Industrial Order and Community Planning 1880 – 1930.* New York: Oxford University Press, 1967.

CHOWDHURY, E. Le Corbusier in Chandigarh: creator and generator. *Architectural Design,* 1965, 35, 504 – 14.

CORRIGAN, A. W. *Learning from British New Towns.* Washington, D.C.: U.S. Department of Labor, 1971.

CUTHBERTSON, I. D. Fiscal impact of new town and suburban development: an empirical study of Reston, West Springfield, and Fairfax County, Virginia. *Urban Land,* 1976, 35, 5 – 12.

DANTZIG, G. B., & SAATY, T. L. *Compact City: A Plan for a Livable Urban Environment.* San Francisco: W. H. Freeman, 1973.

DAVIS, J. M. European new communities. *Building Research,* 1969, 6, 8 – 15.

DOUDAI, A., & OELSNER U. Maccabit: a conceptual framework for a new town — Israel. *Ekistics,* 1965, 29, 286 – 89.

DOXIADIS, C. A. Islamabad: the creation of a new capital. *Town Planning Review,* 1965, 36, 1 – 28.

DOXIADIS, C. A. On linear cities. *Town Planning Review,* 1967, 38, 35 – 42.

EPSTEIN, D. G. *Brasilia: Plan and Reality.* Berkeley: University of California Press, 1973.

EVENSON, N. *Chandigarh.* Berkeley: University of California Press, 1966.

Minnesota Experimental City. Minneapolis: University of Minnesota, 1969.

Failure of the new densities. *Architectural Review,* 1953, 114, 355 – 61.

GORYNSKI, J. The problem of participation in new town development: Nowa Haut, Poland. *Ekistics,* 1973, 37, 40 – 41.

HOJAYEV, D. Soviet Union to build new towns. *Town and Country Planning,* 1957, 25, 373 – 87.

HOLFORD, W. The growth of Canberra. *Town Planning Review,* 1963, 38, 3 – 24.

Housing and Development Reporter, 2 (December 2, 1974), 687 – 97.

HOWARD, E. *Garden Cities of Tomorrow.* Cambridge: M.I.T. Press, 1966.

HUGHES, D. W. New town progress in France. *Town and Country Planning,* 1971, 39, 79 – 85.

INOUYE, T. Tokyo needs new towns. *Town and Country Planning,* 1952, 24, 69 – 71.

ITON, S. The outline of Kozoji new town. *Ekistics,* 1964, 28, 115 – 20.

JAMOUD, L. Islamabad — the visionary capital. *Ekistics,* 1968, 32, 329 – 33.

KEEBLE, L. *Principles and Practice of Town and Country Planning.* London: The Estates Gazette, Ltd., 1972, 218 – 237.

KELLAWAY, A. J. Migration to eight new towns in 1966. *Journal of the Planning Institute,* 1969, 55, 196 – 202.

KING, R. H. Contemporary work in Poland. *Town Planning Institute,* 1955, 41, 265 – 68.

KINSEY, D. N. The French ZUP technique of urban development. *American Institute of Planners Journal,* 1969, 35, 369 – 75.

KIRCHHERR, E. C. Tema 1950 – 1962: the evolution of a planned city in West Africa. *Ekistics,* 1969, 33, 226 – 31.

LEE, M. Islamabad — the scale of the city and its central area. *Ekistics,* 1962, 13, 148 – 61.

MALISZ, B. *Poland Builds New Towns.* Warsaw: Polonia Publishing House, 1962.

MARANS, R. W. Planning the experimental neighborhood at Kiryath Gat, Israel. *Ekistics*, 1969, *33*, 70 – 75.
MELLOR, R. E. H. The Soviet new town. *Town and Country Planning*, 1963, *31*, 90 – 94.
MIELDS, H., JR. *Federally Assisted New Communities: New Dimensions in Urban Development*. Washington, D.C.: Urban Land Institute, 1973.
MILIUTIN, N. A. *Sotsgorod: The Problem of Building Socialist Cities*. Cambridge: M.I.T. Press, 1975.
MORRIS, M. D. New towns in the desert: Israel demonstrates how to create them. *The American City*, November 1970, pp. 94 – 96.
MYHRA, D. Rexford Guy Tugwell: initiator of America's greenbelt new towns, 1935 – 1936. *American Institute of Planners Journal*, 1974, *40*, 176 – 88.
OMORI, K. Tokyo's satellite towns. *Town and Country Planning*, 1946, *32*, 190 – 194.
O'NEILL, G. K. Space colonies: the high frontier. *The Futurist*, 1976, *10*, 25 – 34.
OSBORN, F. J., & WHITTICK, A. *The New Towns*. Cambridge: M.I.T. Press, 1969.
OSBORN, R. J. How the Russians plan their cities. *Ekistics*, 1967, *33*, 175 – 78.
PASS, D. *Vallingby and Farsta – From Idea to Reality*. Cambridge: M.I.T. Press, 1973.
PRESSMAN, N. French urbanization policy and the new towns program. *Ekistics*, 1973, *37*, 17 – 22.
PRITCHARD, N. The arts in a new town. *Town and Country Planning*, 1964, *32*, 15 – 18.
REPS, J. *The Making of Urban America*. Princeton: Princeton University Press, 1965.
RODERICK, W. P. The London new towns. *Town Planning Review*, 1971, *42*, 323 – 42.
RUZHNIKOV, Y. A new town on the Volga. *Architect and Building News*, 1969, *3*, 61 – 62.
SCHNEIDERMAN, S. L. Behind the scenes in Poland's model cities. *Reporter*, 1956, *15*, 15 – 17.
SCOTT, M. *American City Planning Since 1890*. Berkeley: University of California Press, 1969.
Serri new town neighborhood center, Senriyama, Osaka. *Japan Architect*, 1964, *39*, 32 – 35.
SHKVARIKOV, V., HAUCKE, M., & SMIRNOVA, O. The building of new towns in the U.S.S.R. *Ekistics*, 1964, *28*, 307 – 19.
SIDENBLADH, G. Stockholm: three hundred years of planning. In H. W. Eldredge (Ed.), *World Capitals*. New York: Doubleday Anchor Books, 1975.
SILKIN, L. Israel's new town program. *Town and Country Planning*, 1967, *35*, 146 – 47.
SMITH, G. E. K. Vallingby: the new section of Stockholm. *Architectural Record*, 1957, *212*, 173 – 84.
SOLERI, P. *Arcology*. Cambridge: M.I.T. Press, 1969.
STEIN, C. S. *Toward New Towns for America*. Cambridge: M.I.T. Press, 1969.
STEPHENSON, G. V. Two newly created capitals: Islamabad and Brasilia. *Town Planning Review*, 1970, *41*, 317 – 32.
STRONG, A. L. *Planned Urban Environments*. Baltimore: Johns Hopkins Press, 1971.
Survey and Analysis of Large Developments and New Communities. Washington, D.C.: U.S. Department of Housing and Urban Development, 1969.
TURNER, A. New communities in the United States: 1968 – 1973. *Town Planning Review*, 1974, *45*, 259 – 73.

TYRWHITT, J. Changes in new town policies in Britain 1946–1971. *Ekistics*, 1973, *37*, 14–16.
VINCENT, L. G. Tema: Ghana's new town and harbor. *Town and Country Planning*, 1962, *30*, 113–16.
VINK, J. New towns and expanding towns in the Netherlands. *Town and Country Planning*, 1955, *23*, 42–46.
VON HERTZEN, H., & SPREIREGEN, P. D. *Building a New Town – Finland's New Garden City, Tapiola*. Cambridge: M.I.T. Press, 1973.
Youth in the new towns. *Town and Country Planning*, 1960, *28*, 231–34.

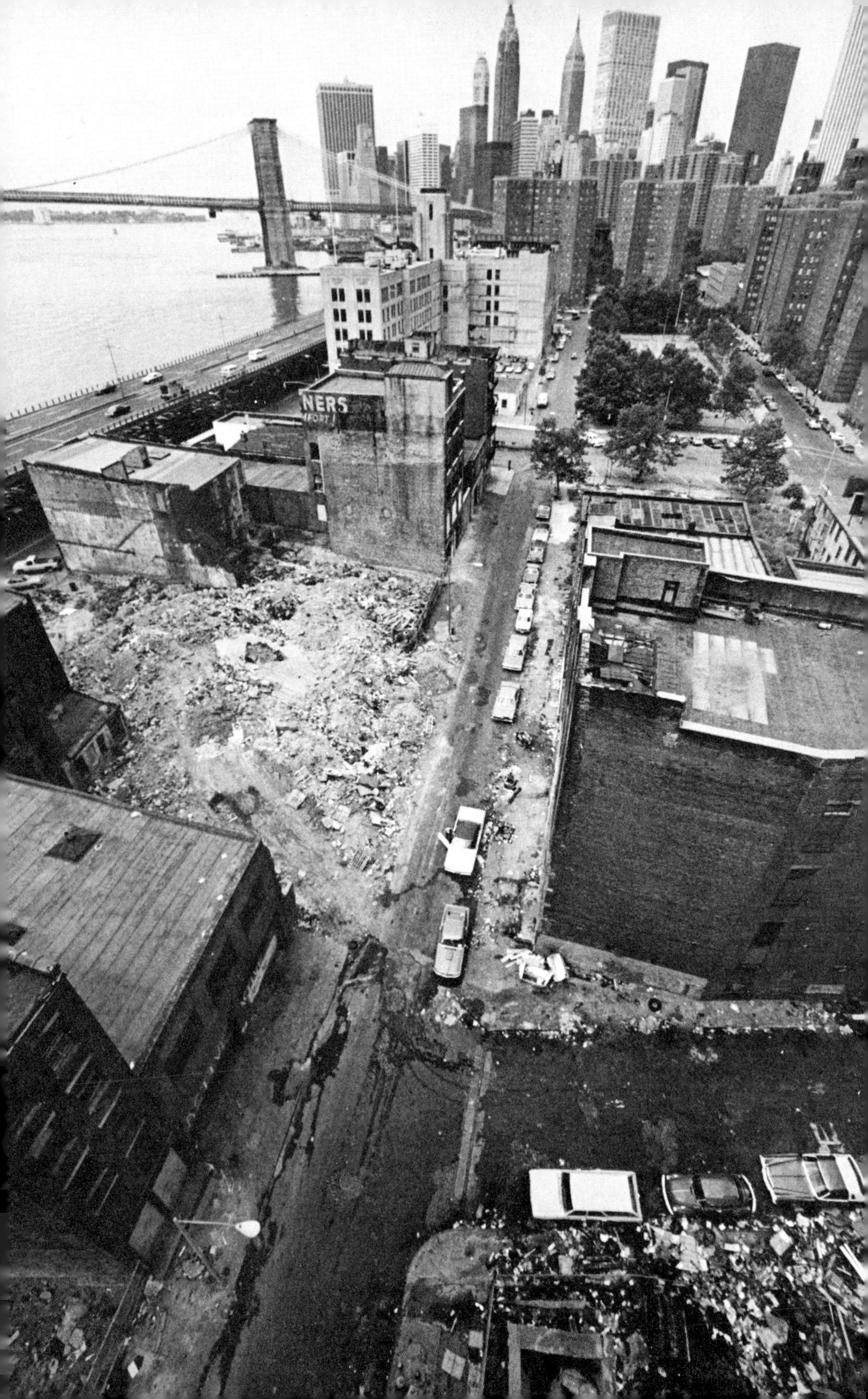
NERS

Urban Policies   16

Most nations of the world lack anything close to unified urban policies. The United Nations lacks clear urban policy directions. At regional and local levels, since the middle of the twentieth century many so-called comprehensive plans have been developed, but few have been significantly implemented. Urban policy matters ultimately need worldwide attention. But there remains much mistrust and little cooperation between the "have" and the "have not" nations of the world. While human populations spread into megalopolis regions and toward ecumenopolis, social relationships and political structures remain underdeveloped. A large-scale suburbanization "policy" has implicitly evolved in many nations. This has been "implemented" most by the rush to build superhighways enabling many people to move from central cities to the urban fringe. In many places there are reports of people being alienated from nations and being frustrated from urban overload. The very thought of worldwide cities, a constitution for the world, a world language, and so forth offers more of a threat than security to many.

Realistic urban policies must offer local citizen participation and identification that can be integrated with regional policies, national policies, and international policies. Data presented in previous chapters reveal that the Earth is becoming an urbanized planet. Realistic urban policies therefore, must be built of component units that interface on a worldwide scale. Urban policies necessarily must deal with people and space issues ranging from individual privacy to the balanc-

Progressive urban policies help to avoid the kind of slums and blight shown in this New York City neighborhood. (Photo: Ellis Herwig for Stock, Boston.)

ing of world population with resources and with the distribution of goods and services. Urban policies from local to world levels must clearly address each of the societal activity systems utilized by urban people.

Demographers and urbanologists suggest that within the next one hundred years, world population may increase from the current 4 billion to between 35 and 50 billion (Doxiadis 1966). Some scholars estimate that the earth has the potential to feed between 30 billion and 80 billion people (Meier 1956). It is also suggested that the proportion of world population which is urban, currently some 40 percent, will increase to 98 percent in the next one hundred years. There are also countervailing arguments that massive starvation and disorder will cause this degree of urbanization and this magnitude of population never to obtain. More positively, some suggest that the world's population rate of growth is slowing down. In any event, this is the bold profile of world trends which challenges and humbles policy builders.

URBAN POLICY ELEMENTS

At the outset, urban policy elements are divided into two major categories, namely, social and physical. The social elements of urban policies include all of the societal activity systems that support urban living. Physical elements concern man-land relationships related to urban design. Physically the proportion of low-, medium- and high-density built environment must be related to resource use, delivery of goods and services, recycling of environments, and maximization of the range of living styles.

Urban policies must address each of the following activity systems: socialization, from day-care and preschool arrangements through professional training; production and distribution of goods and services, including both agricultural and nonagricultural; family and social living relationships; recreation and leisure; science, the generation of new advanced bodies of knowledge; health activities, including preventive medical services and disease and ailment recovery; welfare activities for individuals who need rehabilitation, reorientation, and custodial care; the arts, as apex expressions of urban civilization; government, at multiple levels; religion and expressions of civil meaning in society. As urbanization intensifies in the years ahead, additional activity systems may be generated, for example in areas like gerontology, pollution control, or environmental recycling. Realistic urban policy must anticipate an expansion rather than a contraction of activity systems. Urban policies must also address the following range of physical elements: land-use ecology and population density; transportation and people-movement systems; urban renewal and new urban development; megastructure environments versus dispersed low-density environments; and physical spaces for each of the activity systems. Citizen involvement and participation in developing urban planning elements needs to be insured at all levels. The elements of urban policy need to interface locally, regionally, nationally, and worldwide in such a way that both professional and citizen identification is achieved at these several levels.

WORLD URBAN POLICIES

World leaders and urbanologists see the planet being made small by science, communication, and transportation. Multinational business and industry increasingly make the world a common urban market. Urbanized societies increasingly exploit resources on a planetary scale (Freedman and Berelson 1974).

The world's current rate of population growth is about 2 percent per year — the highest in history. Some scientists believe that this population increase is a grave catastrophe now. Others suggest the real challenge is a matter of urban social organization. Concerning the latter view there is no question. The urban invention is relatively new and still organizationally incomplete.

By the middle of the twentieth century, a few cities reached societal size. Also a half-dozen megalopolis regions have reached substantial societal size. Some of the multifunctional regions physically overlay multiple national areas. By the end of the twentieth century, societal-sized cities and urban regions are expected to be widespread. Accordingly, urban policies need to be established so that they address cities and regions societally while interfacing on an urban scale. This is not necessarily to suggest that city-states should be anticipated. The possible return to city-states can be treated as a separate matter. But viable urban planning and urban policy must now confront all social institutions for societal life simultaneously.

Some observers assert that urban man's challenge is to shift from population growth to equilibrium (Forrester 1971). Others suggest that the real goal ought to be reduction in worldwide population in order to bring natural resources, capital investment, and pollution into a balance which will support a higher quality of life. An alternate view is presented by Doxiadis and his associates. They suggest that the world population may grow to between 35 and 50 billion as ecumenopolis or worldwide city is achieved. Some futurologists suggest that even with these larger population projections, a higher quality urban environment is easily within the grasp of contemporary humanity. More equality may be possible between the less developed ruralized societies and the more developed urbanized societies. For example, Powell suggests that ten to fifteen billion dollars annually for a period of twenty years would be required to achieve radical transformation and advancement in the less developed areas of the world. This resource could be made available by some disarmament among the advanced urbanized nations where collectively some two hundred billion dollars are annually spent for defense (Ackoff 1974).

The phenomenon of urbanization will be most critical for the welfare of mankind during the next four to five decades. If urban culture is to be an apex of civilization, the balancing of population, natural resources, mobility, science, meaning, government, education, and leisure require the critical and urgent attention of the world's growing family of some one hundred seventy nations. Specific proposals for a world constitution surfaced in the twentieth century (Borgese 1965). But world constitution ideas for cooperation and federation still receive little serious attention outside of intellectual circles.

Dynamic world urban policies are tested by those who call for limits of growth now and by those who see danger in zero population growth and who anticipate more people living in space than on earth by 2150 (Forrester 1971; Meadows 1974; Mesarovic 1974; Kahn 1975; Sauvy 1976; O'Neill 1976). World urban policy is strengthened by the intellectual wrestling between these extreme positions. Within these extremes, policies for each of the societal activity systems need to be articulated down to local planning levels.

NATIONAL URBAN POLICIES

We reiterate that most nations do not in fact have a national urban policy. The Netherlands, Great Britain, and Israel, some may argue, are close to the use of a full national urban policy. Many other nations have addressed some of the fundamental elements of urban policy.

The Netherlands offers one of the strong examples of national urban planning. Indeed a national master plan was adopted in 1966. It offers a general outline for development through the year 2000. Planning policy in the Netherlands is shared at three levels, the nation, the twelve provinces, and the thousand municipalities. The 1966 national urban policy also dealt with implementation. First it specified that the policy implementation would require close cooperation between various departments of government, including housing, transportation, public works and water supply, finance and economic affairs, industry, agriculture, and social and cultural activities. This cooperation is achieved through the Government Planning Council. Additionally, im-

plementation of the national policy specifies participation by citizens, particularly with local authorities. The creation of consulting planning councils is a technique used for this part of the policy implementation. Thus far in the Netherlands, administration of the national urban policy has moved forward without special laws creating a fourth tier of government.

National policy in the Netherlands focuses on directing the regions in which the greatest amount of population growth can take place through the year 2000. While most recent growth has been in the western part of the nation, the national urban policy will bring about a shift so that by 2000 more than half of the urban growth will be in the east and the north of the nation. The national policy anticipates a population of one-half million in the polder areas. Motor vehicles are expected to triple in number by 2000, increasing mobility and requiring physical space. New urban housing will be required in many parts of the nation. The national policy anticipates that a majority of the housing will be detached, but without excessive space use (Merlin 1971).

In Great Britain, national planning is largely embodied in new-town developments. In 1940 a Royal Commission Report on the Distribution of the Industrial Population was presented. It referenced the growth of the great industrial cities in Britain and their subsequent large slums. In the late nineteenth century, Charles Booth and Ebenezer Howard, in their respective publications *London Life and Labor* and *Garden Cities of Tomorrow,* called for national action. In 1947 the Town and Country Planning Act in effect gave birth to a national British urban policy. It is supplemented with many other pieces of legislation, like the Special Roads Act of 1949, the Clean Air Act of 1956, the New Towns Act of 1965, Leisure in the Countryside — England and Wales, 1966, the Civic Amenities Act of 1967, and the Town and Country Planning Act of 1968.

Britain's urban policies focus on decentralization as well as renewal of housing, commerce, and industry within the great cities. Each new town that is given London approval is carefully sited in terms of its location in a planning region and in relation to the entire nation. British urban policies focus overtly on activity systems related to jobs and economics, housing and family lifestyles, leisure and recreation, health, education and welfare, and churches.

The advantages of national urban policy are clearly illustrated in the case of Israel. By nationwide urban planning, Israel has been able to reduce the proportion of its population in its three largest urban areas while systematically expending the distribution of urban growth throughout the rest of the nation. Tel Aviv, Haifa, and Jerusalem have a smaller proportion of the nation's population in the 1970s than they did when the nation was established. In Israel urban policy also systematically addresses activity systems including housing and family space, schools, industry, health and welfare, and so forth.

In the United States there continues to be no viable urban policy (Moynihan 1970). However, in the 1960s a Department of Housing and Urban Development was established. The Housing and Urban Development Act of 1970 required the president to submit to the congress a biannual Report on National Growth. In 1972 the first of these reports was submitted. It included a discussion on the formation of a single comprehensive national growth policy.

In 1968 the National Committee on Urban Growth Policy was formed under the joint sponsorship of the National Association of Counties, the National League of Cities, the United States Conference of Mayors, and Urban America Incorporated (Canty 1969). In terms of a national urban policy, this committee recommended that the federal government give financial assistance to the creation of one hundred new communities averaging 100,000 population each plus an additional ten new communities of at least 1 million population each. In terms of the population growth expected by the year 2000, these new urban areas would accommodate only 20 percent of the new inhabitants. More specifically, the committee recommended the following: (1) new towns should be developed which are specifically designed to increase housing, education, and employment; (2) the new towns should be designed specifically to include places for low- and moderate-income persons as well as for the more affluent; (3) the new communities should be sited in terms of local, state, regional, and national objectives for orderly urban growth; (4) the new town development should provide full opportunity for the private sector; (5) the new town development, to the fullest extent possible, should take place within existing jurisdiction of governments and not require additional special district governments; (6) new town developments should stimulate advances in technological development; and (7) new towns should follow the highest standards of urban planning and design. In effect this committee report stimulated the passing of the New Communities Act of 1968 and the New Communities Act of 1970. Only fifteen new communities were supported by these Acts before they were phased out. Moreover, little attention was focused on urban renewal and even less focus was placed on population distribution and industrial locations. No planning policy mechanisms exist in the United States to bring the urban activity systems related to housing, education, health, welfare, leisure, the arts, and so forth together. There continues to be uncoordinated urban sprawl, governmental fragmentation, decline of central city centers, increased pollution, and rampant unemployment.

The New Community Acts that were passed in the United States were insufficient in scope. Additionally there was a lack of organization to provide for interface between national planning legislation, state urban policy, and local planning. Also, there has been insufficient direction for siting and expansion of industry, the relation of transportation systems to urban development, and the relation of educational activity systems to urban growth policy. In reiteration, a social system of urban policy does not yet exist in the United States.

Urban policy in Poland exemplifies centralized planning in Eastern Europe. In the post-World War II years, the national economy, land development, and urban growth all have been part of Poland's centralized planning. The nation has 32,000,000 people. Only 1,300,000 are in Warsaw. Most of the remainder of the population is rural or in small towns. The national urban policy is designed to systematically direct new industrial development in rural regions in order to encourage the development of middle-sized municipalities, namely those with populations of about 100,000. National planning in Poland is carried out at four administrative levels: the central government, seventeen regions, two hundred fifty local districts, and local municipalities. Poland's national planning policy is aimed at decongestion of specified areas and development of other areas. Considerable satisfaction has been achieved in planning for the urban systems of housing, education, jobs, health, welfare, and recreation (Malisz 1962; Merlin 1971).

REGIONAL URBAN POLICIES

Urban regional policies have experienced considerable utilization in the last half of the twentieth century. The major British new-town planning dating from 1946 utilizes regional considerations extensively in designating sites for new towns. Early in the 1950s, Poland was divided into seventeen planning regions for urban expansion and for shifting population from rural to urban areas. In the United States, the Area Redevelopment Administration was established in 1961 as a step toward regional planning. Even more specifically the Appalachian Regional Development Act was passed in 1965. Yet in face of both of these Acts, America remains a long way from strong regional policies. Many of the redevelopment areas are too small to guide viable regional policy planning. Larger regions like Appalachia and the Ozarks overlap multiple states where there is little or no enabling legislation to support broad planning.

In Europe, where urban population growth and pressure have a much longer history than in many other parts of the world, six nations signed the Treaty of Rome in 1957 with three others joining in 1973 (Hall 1975). Although this agreement is primarily economic (creating the European Economic Community), the implications are broadly societal. Within this European Economic Community the experience of France illustrates the interrelationships between local planning, regional planning, national planning, and multinational planning. The French planning policy extends from local authority through the national government to the multinational level via the Treaty of Rome. In the implementation of this kind of planning strategy, France is now divided into twenty-one planning regions. Using this kind of planning policy, the French are attempting to address the following kinds of situations: in the 1960s the Paris region constituted only 2 percent of the national land area, but nearly 20 percent of the national population and nearly 30 percent of industrial jobs. In effect, France was rapidly becoming a nation with one overwhelmingly dominant city. With the new regional policy, further expansion in the Paris area will be carefully planned rather than haphazard. Furthermore, urban and industrial development will be systematically located throughout other parts of the nation.

The scale of regional policies may vary sharply from one geographical area to another. That which may be regional, for example, in the smaller Scandinavian nations may be at a smaller scale than local planning in some of the larger nations of the world. Copenhagen's well known 1948 Finger Plan is regional in scope, but it deals with a population of just over one million. By contrast a city plan for New York, Chicago, or Los Angeles must address the needs of multiple millions of people in one political jurisdiction. And when the larger cities of the world engage in regional planning with populations in their hinterlands, their effort is at a societal scale. Regional planning in the Great Lakes megalopolis area involves policies generated both by Canada and the United States. The northwestern European megalopolis area involves policy generated from the Netherlands, Belgium, Germany, and France (Gottman 1976). National policy and regional policy in a small nation like Israel is developed for a total population less than one-half that of any of the world's six major megalopolis regions.

The scale of regional policy must vary with the sociophysical environmental location. Some urban regions may be so small that they become ineffective. Other urban regions may become so large that their populations become alienated. Accordingly, urban regional policy must focus on areas sufficiently large to encompass all of the elements of sociophysical planning, while also utilizing policy mechanisms for citizen identification and participation that are meaningful. The value orientations of some urbanites enable them to deal with large and plural societies as stimulating, challenging, and rewarding rather than as situations of urban overload leading to alienation. Where the majority of citizens endorse such values, urban regions may be large.

In all cases, urban regional policy must deal effectively with local citizen participation and with the smaller units of society. In juxtaposition, urban regions must be large enough to contribute to societal equilibrium (Chapin 1965; McLaughlin 1969; Hall 1975).

An aspect of regional policy again gaining some attention is the city-state or the neo-city-state. In America this policy thinking is referred to as the development of metropolitan states (National Growth Policy 1972). Figure 16 – 1 shows where in the United States consolidated urban regions or metropolitan states might be significantly developed. It is submitted that in America metropolitan state policy could preserve polycentric local government by bringing the already elected officials into a new city-state legislative body under a new governor to be elected for the area. The metropolitan or city-state arrangements would be fiscally and constitutionally viable. City-suburban imbalances would be eradicated by this form of regional policy. Comprehensive planning could be meaningfully carried out in the area of a metropolitan regional state. Minorities and special interest groups would have full representation in the new metropolitan states. Finally, the metropolitan states would not be fragmented into small competing governmental jurisdictions.

In the Rio de Janeiro area of Brazil, there now exists a city-state region relating the city of Rio de Janeiro to its immediate rural land area. This quasi-city-state policy was developed there when the nation's capital was moved to Brasilia.

LOCAL URBAN POLICIES

Local municipal policies must be understood as partial even when city plans are titled comprehensive. Certainly in the urbanized society of the last of the twentieth century, individual municipalities do not exist in vacuums. Their local plans need to be comprehensive for the internal aspects of the municipality as a formal organization. Nevertheless, city urban activity systems only exist within larger social units at the regional, national, and multinational levels.

New town development offers one of the clearest ways to understand local comprehensive planning policies which interface at larger levels. British new town planning policies require that the siting of new towns be done in terms of planning regions and selected national services like highways, railways, and airports. Then within the new town, social activity systems concerning residences, jobs, health services, education, churches, recreation, and welfare are all planned in relation to each other in the municipality and to the larger society in which the municipality is located.

In the United States, policy recommendations have been made to plan 272 new communities between 1970 and 2000 (Pickard 1969). The average size of these new towns would be 110,000 persons. In urban regions they would be larger in population and in outlying regions smaller. They would range in size from 500,000 population to 75,000

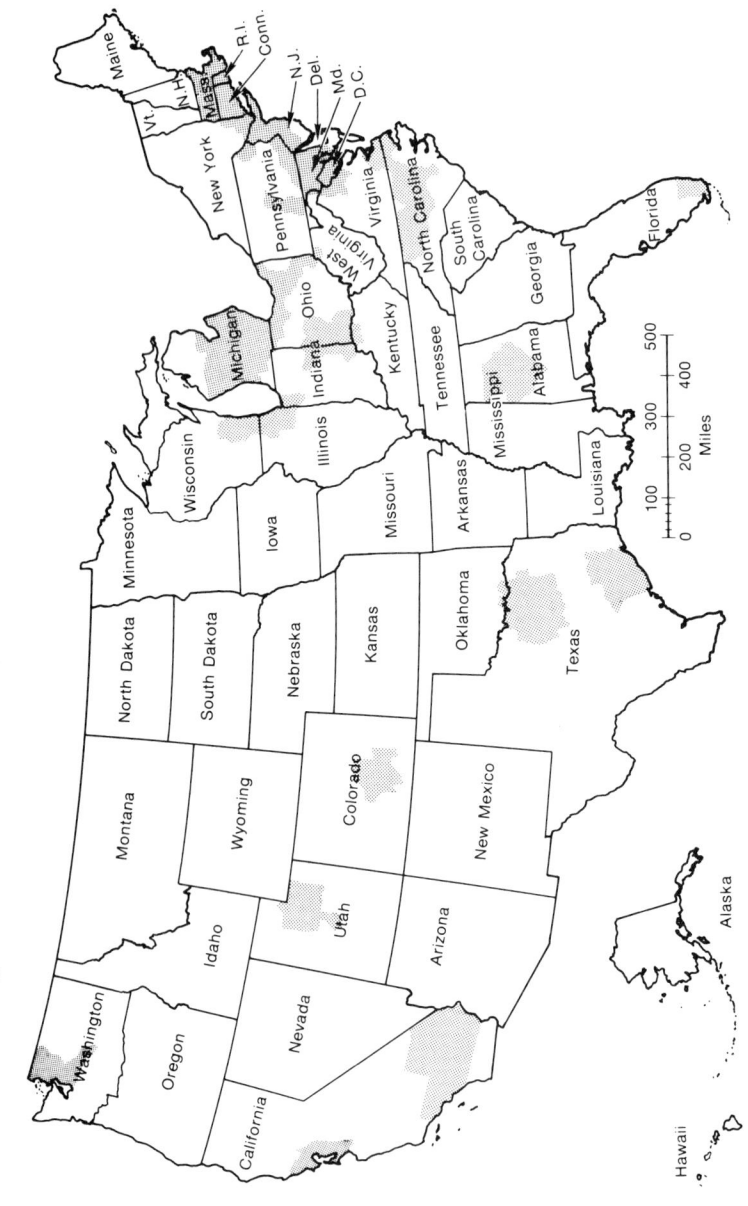

Figure 16-1 Possible Metropolitan State Locations in the United States

Source: National Growth Policy (Washington, D.C.: Committee on Banking and Currency, *House of Representatives, 92nd Congress, Second Session,* 1972).

population. Fifty-eight of the new towns would be planned for the northeastern urban regions, 25 in outlying northern regions, 43 in southern urban regions, 67 in outlying southern regions, 59 in western urban regions, and 20 in outlying western regions. Clearly, local planning policy for these new towns would articulate with regional planning policies and with national planning policies. During the thirty-year period, the nation is expected to add 100 million people. Seventy million would be accommodated in local areas but outside of the systematically planned new towns.

Much local planning policy concerns the socioeconomic effectiveness of urban renewal. At a minimum, this requires an environmental impact analysis. Locally, urban renewal projects need to be examined in terms of each of the urban activity systems required for subsistence in the area. It is inadequate to provide a new housing project or a new industrial park or a new highway system via urban renewal as if the project locally does not interrelate with all of the elements of social life.

IMPLICATIONS

The physical urban world is made small by technology. With the mass communication and the mass transportation of the twentieth century, urban people and urban ideas influence, indeed increasingly control, rural life the world over. Urban policies on one part of the planet now intricately relate to urban policies on other parts of the planet. Indeed there may be more differentiation between urban lifestyles within a given metropolitan area than between metropolitan areas on opposite sides of the planet. Telstar communication and jet travel are two illustrations of the technology which, in effect, forces the urban world into a planetwide international network. This world urban network needs integrated and coordinated urban policy guidelines.

The social urban world remains large and diverse. Urban society by definition is plural and complex. High-quality urban lifestyles and cultural apexes contribute extensively to the proliferation of diverse urban values. Some areas of the urban world may achieve great excellence in ballet, while others are noted for athletic distinction; some urban areas may be famous for their support of education leading to scientific breakthroughs, while in other urban places expressions of religious passion may be the hallmarks of achievement; still other urban locations are known for high achievements for social class and individual equality, while other urban areas may be renowned for symphonies and art museums and so forth. As urban centers grow through the metropolis experience in an ecumenopolizing direction, diverse sociocultural values are increasingly experienced in the same urban regions. For some people this urban diversity is a matter of frustration, leading to urban overload and alienation. For other urbanites, the wide-ranging diversity becomes a matter of exhilaration, challenge, and opportunity. In either event, the world made small by technology is made large by sociocultural differences. The socialization institutional space, therefore, needs to be expanded so that people can be trained to understand and be enriched by plural culture. Broad-gauged urban policies are needed to guide this enriching development.

The urban world is in a time of precipitous biological expansion — some say a population explosion. In fact it is the worldwide reduction of the death rate and the preservation of life which produces most of the population increase. The urban people of the world in the last of the twentieth century know more about family planning and human biology, and have more effective contraceptive devices at their disposal, than ever before. Furthermore, in the early period of urbanization, birth rates in inner city areas were distinctly lower than in rural areas. In spite of more contraceptive knowledge and larger urbanized populations, population growth is greater now than in the past. Sociocultural values concerning the right to procreation are highly diverse and conflicting — particularly those relating to abortion and sterilization. Today, adult bisexual social relationships that fall outside of the historic procreative family present another problematic urban policy area. Moreover, with expanding population there are increasing social conflicts between and among youth, persons in the middle years of life, and older individuals. These role conflicts are further frustrated by cybernating trends, which contribute to reduced work hours. The procreative social institutional space of urban society needs policy direction to help urbanized people "know who they are."

The urbanized world is highly systematic in its organizational development. Ruralized society was highly individualistic. Early city experience was transitional from rugged rural individualism to what is now being understood as planned urbanism. The plural urban society involves the utilization of a large number of specialists. Urban specialists become highly dependent upon one another in making the support activity systems operate effectively. In order to produce and distribute the wide range of ideas and social services needed for quality urban life, urban organizations developed in the past must be in cooperative equilibrium.

Urban planning policy must be societal planning at multiple levels. Local policies must relate to regional policies and regional policies to national and international policies. And with mature world urbanization, there must be policy planning reciprocity from the top levels of world organization to the local urban units. The structure of policies coming up from local levels and policies being articulated

down from worldwide levels must be motivating to support the development of new apexes in urban life quality. In sum, urban policies must be integrative of social-institutional activity systems at multiple levels.

REFERENCES

ACKOFF, R. L. *Redesigning the Future.* New York: Wiley, 1974, 216.
BELL, G., & TYRWHITT, J. *Human Identity in the Urban Environment.* New York: Pelican, 1972.
BORGESE, E. M. *A Constitution for the World.* Santa Barbara, Calif.: Center for the Study of Democratic Institutions, 1965.
CANTY, D. (Ed.) *The New City: National Committee on Urban Growth Policy.* New York: Praeger, 1969.
CHAPIN, F. S. *Urban Land Use Planning.* Urbana: University of Illinois, 1965.
DAVIDOFF, P. Working toward redistributive justice. *Journal of the American Institute of Planners,* 1975, *41,* 317 – 18.
DOXIADIS, C. A. *Urban Renewal and the Future of the American City.* Chicago: Public Administration Service, 1966.
FORRESTER, J. W. *World Dynamics.* Cambridge, Mass.: Wright-Allen Press, 1971.
FREEDMAN, R., & BERELSON, B. The human population. In *The Human Population.* San Francisco: W. H. Freeman, 1974.
GOTTMAN, J. Megalopolis systems around the world. *Ekistics,* 1976, *41,* 109 – 13.
HALL, P. *Urban and Regional Planning.* New York: Wiley, 1975.
KAHN, H., & BROWN, W. A world turning point — and a better prospect for the future. *The Futurist,* 1975, *9,* 284 – 89.
MCLOUGHLIN, J. B. *Urban and Regional Planning: A Systems Approach.* New York: Faber, 1969.
MALISZ, B. *Poland Builds New Towns.* Warsaw: Polonia Publishing House, 1962.
MEADOWS, D. et al. *Dynamics of Growth in a Finite World.* New York: Wright-Allen, 1974.
MEIER, R. L. *Science and Economic Development.* Cambridge: M.I.T. Press, 1956.
MERLIN, P. *New Towns.* London: Methuen, 1971, Chapter 3.
MESAROVIC, M., & PESTEL, E. *Mankind at the Turning Point.* New York: Dutton, 1974.
MOYNIHAN, D. (Ed.) *Toward a National Urban Policy.* New York: Basic Books, 1970.
National Growth Policy. Washington, D.C.: Committee on Banking and Currency, House of Representatives, 92nd Congress, Second Session, 1972, 664 – 666.
National Municipal Policy. Washington, D.C.: National League of Cities, 1969, p. 666.
O'NEILL, G. K. Space colonies: the high frontier. *The Futurist,* 1976, *10,* 25 – 33.
PICKARD, J. P. Trends and projections of future population growth in the United States. Paper presented to Urban Growth Committee on Banking and Currency, U.S. House of Representatives, Washington, D.C., July 22, 1969.
SAUVY, A. *Zero Growth?* New York: Praeger, 1976.

Index

A

Abrams, Charles, 173, 178
Advocacy planning, 264
Air rights, 151, 156
Albrecht, Milton, 216
Alienation, 243
Anonymity, 187
Antisocial behavior, 29, 138, 143, 156, 247
   defensible space, see also conflict
   mug, 31, 145
   protective electronic devices, 31
   rape, 31, 145
   social control, 145
   space, 145
   urban centers, 92
Antiurban, 164
Apartments, 146, 163, 181
   double-load corridor, 146
   electronic surveillance, 146
Architectural determinism, 10
Arcology, 139, 151, 242, 257
   see also Soleri
   see also megastructure
Art, 216
   apex of urban civilization, 216, 223
   artist-in-residence, 21
   auditoriums, 216
   Brasilia, 222
   churches, 222
   civic center, 221
   community theater, 223
   conservatories, 216
   facilities, 224
   libraries, 216
   Lincoln Center, 24, 216
   literature, 230
   malls, 222
   Mexico City, 222
   museums, 216, 217, 218, 219
   opera companies, 223
   opera house, Sidney, 24
   parking, 217
   performing art centers, 217
   schools, 216
   subway access, 217, 224
   supergraphic, 216
   symphony orchestras, 223
   Toronto Airport, 223

B

Bacon, Edmund, 223
Bailey, James, 87, 164, 208, 284
Baroque urban forms, 29

Bathrooms, 134
Bay Area Rapid Transit
  System, 266
Bell, Daniel, 115
Bollens, John, 103
Boston
  West End, 174, 244
Bracey, Howard, 68, 129
Brazil, 185
  Brasilia, 9, 29, 138, 226
Broadacre City, 44, 158
Broady, Maurice, 50, 153, 254
Brockman, John, 6
Built environment, 10, 143, 182
  crowding, 142
  high rise, 143
Buttimer, A., 256

C

Calhoun, J., 139
Campbell, Carlos, 87
Canada, 9, 281
Canty, Donald, 131, 315
Caro, Robert, 258
Cavalli-Sforza, L. L., 16
Central business district, 22, 23,
  60, 153, 155, 247, 263
Chandigarh, 10, 138
  Baroque design, 10, 29
Chapin, Stewart, 153, 256
Chicago
  John Hancock Center, 189
China, 35, 238
  health systems, 237
  patriotic health campaign, 238
  worker doctors, 238
Churches, 157, 197, 263
  art, 222
Cities
  Acropolis, 16
  ancient, 3, 16
  Baroque design, 17
  centers, 23

classic, 26
commerce, 24
complex social organization, 3
concept, 35
congestion, 28
Dark Ages, 4
disease, 27
home rule charter, 51
human invention, 4
industrial, 29
life style, 4
literacy, 23
Mesopotamia, 28
Medieval, 4
pageantry, 17, 28
plural culture, 51
Pre-Columbian, 16, 23
pre-urban society, 4
purpose, 16
Renaissance, 5, 28
urban-rural differences, 3
Citizen participation, 10, 264
  see advocacy planning, 264
City states, 169
Clawson, Marion, 9
Cloward, R. A., 78
Clustering, 159
Codes, 156
  building, 156, 182
  enforcement, 264
  housing, 156, 182
Cognitive maps, 65, 156
Community, 31
  face-to-face, 20
  suburban, 20
  territoriality, 144
  theater, 223
  therapeutic, 237
Commuting, 78, 172, 173, 263
  automobiles, 5
  cost, 188
  daily, 5
  streetcars, 5
  worker, 174, 190

Compact City, 151, 257
  see also Dantzig
Comprehensive planning, 154, 155, 260
  air rights, 156
  base maps, 156, 262
  central business district, 154
  churches, 72, 157, 262
  de Chiara, 72, 154
  densities, 263
  easements, 263
  fire departments, 157
  flood plains, 162
  Gallion, 154
  health, 155
  Housing Acts, 255, 261, 273
  land use maps, 73
  neighborhood centers, 155, 262
  plat, 162
  police departments, 157
  public buildings, 262
  public utilities, 263
  trailer parks, 155
  view rights, 156
  welfare, 156
  workable programs, 263
Condominium, 180, 185, 270
  Brazil, 185
  Egypt, 185
  Europe, 185
  lower class, 187
  Paris, 185
  South America, 185
  United States, 185
  vacation, 187
Conflict, 16, 31, 131, 174, 255, 258
  see also antisocial behavior
  Marxian, 20
  turf, 131
Conurbation, 37
Cooley, Charles Horton, 138
Copenhagen, 193
  Louisiana Museum, 220

Crime, 233
  antisocial, 31, 145, 247
  closed circuit television, 31, 143
  defensible environment, 247
  electronic surveillance, 31, 146
  mug, 31, 145
  rape, 31, 145
  social control, 145
  urban ecology, 246
Crowding, 141, 142
  antisocial behavior, 143
  built environment, 143
  high rise, 139
  Hong Kong, 142
  lobby areas, 143
  roof gardens, 143
Cul-de-sac, 77, 174, 184, 284
Cumbernauld, 193
  transportation, 193

D

Davids, L., 103
Davis, Kingsley, 9
Dantzig, George, 20, 151, 257, 287
  see also Compact City
Deasy, C. M., 255
de Chiara, J., 155, 158, 160, 227, 261
Delvin, G. A., 192
Density, 5, 30, 50, 57, 106, 139, 140, 158, 262
  Calcutta, 5
  crowding, 141
  Delhi, 5
  ecology, 70
  high, 5, 158
  housing, 171
  Howard, E., 73
  industrial, 153
  Le Corbusier, 73
  low, 157, 158

residential, 68
urban centers, 92
Wright, F. L., 73
DiMaio, A. J., 171
Double load halls, 247
Downs, A., 200, 206
Doxiadis, C. A., 9, 31, 43, 278, 310
Duggar, G. S., 274
Dumazedier, J., 224
Dykman, John, 191, 247

E

Ecology, 5, 24, 57
  Boston, 57
  central business district, 60
  concentric circle, 60
  daily movement, 5
  density, 70, 73
  greenbelt, 58
  Latin American, 61
  Mexico City, 61
  models, 60
    classic, 60
    factorial, 63
    social area, 63
  multi-nuclear, 60
  neighborhoods, 70, 74, 75
  nurseries, 5
  overload, 59, 64
  Paris, 63
  parks
    Central, New York, 57
    Golden Gate, San Francisco, 57
    Regency, London, 57
  population, 5
  poverty, 77
  Pruitt-Igoe, 57
  residential, 68
  rest homes, 5
  site planning, 57
  size of place, 57
  social class, 61
  sociophysical, 5
  suburbs, 57
  symbolic meaning
    Boston Commons, 57
    Boston West End, 57
    privacy, 65
    restrooms, 57
    sex, 57
    Teotihuacan, 57
    turf, 57
Ecumenopolis, 7, 29, 35, 42, 43, 193, 283
  Asian Highway, 40
  Canada, 43
  Europe, 43
  Trans-Siberian Railroad, 40
  United States, 42
Education, 197
  busing, 131
  day-care centers, 199
  docents, 199
  education parks, 205
  ethnicity, 204
  guild, 198
  libraries, 203
  literacy, 23
  neighborhood schools, 199, 203, 205
  new towns, 205
  on-the-job, 200
  recreational, 199
  school
    board, 205
    rooms, 199, 203
    urban, 204
    yards, 199
  science museums, 203
  space, 203
  walking distance, 202
  Watts, 204
Effrat, Marcia, 131
Elevators, 25

urban centers, 92
vertical movement, 25
Energy, 45, 265
England, 174, 261
Environment, 157
Erber, Ernest, 255

F

Field, M., 235
Foley, John W., 176
Formal organization, 38, 153, 160, 165
  urban centers, 92
Forrester, J. W., 35, 173, 179, 260, 271, 278, 311
France, 274
Freedman, R., 20
Fuller, Buckminster, 240

G

Gallion, Arthur, 26, 261
Gans, Herbert, 138, 174, 244, 256
Garden city, 6, 158, 178, 286
  antiurban, 164
Geddes, Patrick, 20
Glass, Ruth, 285
Goodman, William, 161, 233, 244
Gottmann, Jean, 20, 115, 154, 273
Government, 103
  annexation, 117
  Bollens, 112
  Census of Governments, 104
  citizen participation, 119
  city councils, 119
  city states, 121
  city-county consolidation, 117
  councils, of, 119, 263

  federated, Toronto, 118
  Greater London Council, 116
  special districts, 118
  two-tier, 117, 118
  urban county, 117
Greenbelts, 59, 111, 158, 225, 262, 288, 289
  1938 Greenbelt Act, 112
  London greenbelt, 112
Guttman, R., 10

H

Hall, Richard, 141
Halprin, Lawrence, 192
Hamblin, D., 4
Hammond, N., 21
Hauser, Arnold, 216
Haussmann, Georges-Eugene, 258, 269
Health, 157, 162, 233, 241
  care, 235
  China, 235
  clinics, 157, 235
  communicable disease, 144
  departments, 233
  disease control, 241
  family physicians, 234
  healthing, 242
  hospitals, 153, 157, 235
  medical districts
    gynecology, 237
    pediatric, 237
  medical facilities, 157
  obsolete doctors, 240
  officers, 160
  out-patient care, 237
  pay-as-you-go, 241
  planning, 237
  pollution
    air, 235, 238
    noise, 238
    radiation, 238

water, 235, 238
service free, 241
socialized medicine, 235
Soviet Union, 235
supermarket hospital, 235
therapeutic communities, 237
United States, 235
World Health
  Organization, 234
world health planning, 239
Herbert, D., 91, 240
High quality environment,
  38, 157
High rise, 22, 23, 30, 31, 160,
  182, 187, 247
  cost, 188
  crowding, 142
  double-load halls, 146
  electronic surveillance, 146
  elevators, 143, 146
  high income, 87
  low income, 188
  Olympic Tower, 188
  religion, 211
Historic urban forms, 15
History, 15
  classic cities, 25
  Dark Ages, 16
  Hanseatic League, 16, 23
  industrial cities, 29
  Medieval cities, 16, 28
    churches, 28
    pageantry, 28
    plazas, 28
  Pre-Columbian, 23
  preservation, 263, 273
  Roman Empire, 21, 23
  Ur, 8
Hoke, B., 241
Hopkins, Henry, 224
Housing, 24, 171, 178
  Abrams, 173
  African, 180
  apartments, 181

Asian, 180
bedrooms, 178
building codes, 183
children, 181
clustering, 181
condominiums, 180, 184,
  185, 186
densities, 172, 181
design, 182
detached, 178, 181
double load halls, 174, 184
exterior halls, 174
government, 172
high rise, 183, 186, 188
Latin American, 180
livability, 134
low income, 172, 178, 184, 186
meaning, 172
middle income, 172
nationalized, 178
neighboring, 184
open, 133, 173
open plan, 133
ownership, 185
planned unit developments,
  181
prestige, 172, 184
privacy, 132, 174
Pruitt-Igoe, 174
residence patterns, 45
rooms, 181
satisfaction, 135, 184
single family, 135, 178
slum, 173, 180
squatments, 180
street sleepers, 180
subsidized, 172, 178
substandard, 172, 178
suburban, 172
tax base, 181
tenement, 181
upper class, 181
upper income, 183, 184
U. S. department, 172

Howard, Ebenezer, 6, 44, 73, 158, 178, 233, 258, 282, 283, 304
Hoyt, Homer, 60
Huntoon, M. C., 76

I

Israel, 9
  Jerusalem, 281
  new towns, 9
  Tel Aviv, 281

J

Jacobs, Jane, 8, 146
Japan, 174
Jensen, R., 20, 30
Jobs, 156, 160, 171, 174, 187
  creation, 188
  employment, 263
  job training, 175
  labor force, 173
    female, 173, 176
    male, 173
  manpower planning, 174
  manual, 174
  municipal employees, 171, 187
  new manpower model, 178
  new towns, 188
  occupational class, 173
  on-the-job training, 175
  professional, 174
  short work week, 175, 176
  social class, 175
  transportation, 188
  unemployment
    central city, 175, 188
    suburbs, 175, 188
  urban ecology, 174
  walk to, 193
Jones, Ernest, 5
Jus, A., 234

K

Kaplan, Marshall, 223, 255, 261, 264
Keeble, Lewis, 105, 284
Kennedy, R. W., 133, 134
Kira, A., 133

L

Land use, 151
  air rights, 151, 160
  codes, 151
    cultural, 152
    manufacturing, 152
    residential, 152
    transportation, 152
    utilities, 152
  England, 153
  highways, 155
  industrial densities, 153
  leisure, 151
  new town, 162, 165
  recreation, 151
  recycling, 151, 158
  sanitary land fills, 158
  solid waste, 158
  Soviet Union, 153
  subsurface rights, 151
  surface, 156
  Sweden, 153
  traffic, 152
  view rights, 151
Lang, J., 238
Larson, C. T., 178
Le Corbusier, 133, 139, 158, 187
  La Ville Contemporaine, 139
  open plan residence, 133
Life styles, 131
  busing, 131
  friends, 135
  guest rooms, 133
  husbands and wives, 132
  privacy, 132

teenagers, 131
unmarrieds, 131
Linear city, 178, 247, 287
Los Angeles
    Watts, 204
Lot size, 160, 161, 162
    set backs, 163, 164
    zero lot lines, 164
Low income, 271
Lynch, Kevin 65, 76

M

Malls, 193
    art, 222
McGrath, N., 143
Meadows, D., 41
Megalopolis, 9, 29, 84
    Bo-Wash, 9, 30, 43
    Eastern Seaboard, 43
    regions, 37
    Tokyo, 9, 26
    Tokaido, 26, 30, 259
Megastructure, 30, 32, 140, 151, 189, 242
    see also arcology, 151, 140, 9
    high rise, 9
    John Hancock Center, 188
    new towns, 140
    religion, 209, 210
Merlin, Pierre, 87, 107, 205
Mexico
    Chichen Itza, 4
    Mexico City
        art, 222
        ecology, 61
        high rise, 187
        pollution, 26
        recreation, 226
        social class, 66
    Uxmal, 3
Meyerson, 179, 183
Michelson, W., 130

Mields, Hugh, 87, 164, 205, 208
Milgram, S., 64, 234
Minneapolis, 273
    Arts Complex, 217
    Walker Art Center, 217
Minnesota Experimental City, 5, 86, 257
    formal organization, 10
Moscow, 21, 42
    see also Soviet Union
Multinational industries, 43, 179
    Barnet, R., 43
    Muller, J., 43
    Tavel, C., 43
Mumford, Lewis, 29, 73, 134
Museums, 216, 219, 222
    Amon Carter Museum, 219
    children participation, 221
    circulation patterns, 219
    crowds, 141, 219, 223
    docents, 221
    films, 221
    Ft. Worth Art Center, 219
    Hirshhorn, 218
    lectures, 221
    Louisiana Museum in Copenhagen, 221
    personal space, 141
    restaurants, 223
    Walker Art Center, 218

N

Neighborhood, 31, 136, 138, 262, 270
    centers, 87, 154
    friendships, 255
    neighboring, 68, 184
    parks, 228
    primaryness, 138
    residential, 174, 184
    schools, 173
    social class, 67
    territoriality, 174

Netherlands, 9, 261
  Rotterdam, 270
Newman, Oscar, 8, 31, 174, 247
New towns, 152, 164, 269, 282
  arts, 285
  Brazil
    Brasilia, 9, 193, 205, 300
    Epstein, 300
  British, 288
    1946 New Town Planning Act, 282
  Canada, 282
  Canberra, 282
  Chandigarh, 9, 282
  Ciudad Guayana, 9
  Columbia, 205
  Cumbernauld, 193
  density, 68
  ecology, 68
  education, 205
  elderly, 286
  England, 10, 68
  Finland, 297
  France, 298
  garden city, 228, 282, 286
  Ghana, 300
  Howard, E., 282, 287
  India, 302
  Islamabad, 282
  Israel, 9, 301
  Japan, 303
  job planning, 190
  Kingsport, USA, 9
  Kohler, USA, 9
  land use, 165
  Los Alamos, USA, 9
  megastructure, 140, 287
  Miliutin, 287
  Minnesota Experimental City, 287
  neighborhoods, 165
  Netherlands, 296
  new-town-in-town, 88, 273, 282
  Norway, 298
  Pakistan, 302
  planners, 174
  Poland, 300
  Pullman, USA, 290
  Radburn, 290
  recreation, 228
  religion, 107
  Reston, 228, 284
  social class, 66, 67, 304
  Soviet Union, 281, 299
  superblock, 302
  Sweden, 296
  Tapiola, 283, 296
  town centers, 87
  Tugwell, Rex, 291
  United States
    Greenbelt, 291
    1968 Housing Act, 292
  Welwyn, 283, 285, 288
  youth, 285
New York City
  Empire State Building, 140
  Lincoln Center, 24, 216, 274
  Olympic Tower, 188
  Paley Park, 225

O

Open space, 163
  Babylon, 159
  California, 159
  Hawaii, 159
  planning, 159
  Rome, 159
Osborn, Frederic J., 87, 164, 288
Overload, 243

P

Palen, J., 246
  Papaioannou, J. G., 20, 42

Paris, 185
  Champs Elysées, 17
  ecology, 63
  Haussmann, 17, 269
  population, 47
Parking, 192, 263
  churches, 208
Parks, 157, 164
  Central, New York, 158
  City Park, New Orleans, 158
  Disneyland, California, 226
  Golden Gate, San
    Francisco, 158
  green space, 158
  greenbelts, 225
  Lake Front, Chicago, 158
  linear, 158, 228
  metropolitan region, 225
  Paley Park, New York
    City, 225
  parkitecture, 226
  Tivoli, Copenhagen, 226
Pawley, M., 178, 181
Pedestrian, 161, 179, 191, 193
  malls, 193
  movements, 161
  urban centers, 95
Perry, Clarence, 139, 284
Personal space, 141
  clothing, 142
  examinations
    anal, 142
    vaginal, 142
  genital organs, 142
  homosexuality, 141
  masturbation, 141
  museums, 141
  nude swimming, 144
  Playboy Clubs, 142
  privacy, 141
  proximities, 141
  restrooms, 141
  striptease, 141
  voyeurism, 142

Pirenne, H., 36
Planned unit development, 30,
    76, 137, 159, 160, 163, 181, 247,
    255, 264, 284
  clusters, 163
  detached units, 163
  townhouses, 163
Planning, 254
  701 Comprehensive
    Planning, 255
  social activity systems, 256
Plat, 161
Pollution, 25, 26
  air, 26, 158, 193, 235
  Los Angeles, 26
  Mexico City, 26
  noise, 26, 193
  parks, 228
  water, 235
Popenoe, D., 184
Population, 42, 43, 44, 45
  China, 50
  control, 50
  daily variation, 156
  health, 157
  India, 50
  longevity, 157
  Moscow, 47, 48
  Paris, 47
  projections, 156
  Tokyo, 48
  twenty-four hour
    variation, 156
  United States, 48
  women, 157
Post-industrial, 40, 83, 171
Poverty, 78, 244
  see slum
  see social class
Privacy, 132, 133, 173
  anonymity, 181
  bathrooms, 133
  closet space, 133
  confessionals, 133

ecology, 65
hospital rooms, 132
invasion of, 133
lower class, 133
middle class, 133
reading, 132
religion contemplation, 208
sex books, 132
study carrels, 132
theater boxes, 133
Pruitt-Igoe, 138, 174, 185, 244, 264, 278
Purloff, H. S., 27

R

Radburn, 37, 137, 290
  superblock, 290
Rainwater, Lee, 130, 173, 185, 244
Recreation, 224
  balconies, 224
  bird watching, 228
  boating, 229
  campsites, 228
  family rooms, 224
  golf, 228
  hiking, 228
  linear parks, 228
  mass leisure, 224
  music, 224
  neighborhood parks, 228
  novels, 225
  Olympic Games, 24
  parlor games, 224
  patios, 224
  playing fields, 228
  pocket parks, 224
  television, 224
  vacation trips, 224
  water games, 225
  winter sports, 228
Recycling, 50, 140, 151, 158
  urban centers, 95

Redstone, L. G., 221
Reiner, S., 10
Religion, 16, 197, 206
  Acropolis, 197
  apexes in cities, 197
  cathedrals, 197, 210
  China, 206
  civil religion, 197
  high rise, 211
  house type, 210
  mosque, 211
  neighborhood, 210
  optimum size
    congregation, 209
  pageantry, 210
  parking space, 209
  schools, 197, 209
  Soviet Union, 208
  space, 209
  store front, 208
  symbols, 209
  synagogue, 209
  theocracy, 197
  U.S.A., 208
  ziggurats, 197
Reps, John, 281
Residence patterns, 45
  see housing
Reston new town, 137
  recreation, 228
Runcorn, 138, 164
  neighborhoods, 138
Rutledge, A. J., 226

S

Saalman, H., 19, 258
San Francisco, 184
  cannery, 270
  central business district, 89
  ecology, 70
  Ghirardelli Square, 196
  Golden Gateway Center, 95
  St. Francis Square project, 184

St. Mary's Cathedral, 211
Scale, 41, 140
  Brasilia, 29, 196
  industrial cities, 29
  Mumford, L., 73
  pedestrian, 196
  Pruitt-Igoe, 73
  Spanish Steps, 5
  suprahuman, 29, 196
  urban centers, 99
Schools, 153, 160
  art, 212
  job training, 176
  neighborhood, 173
  officials, 160
Science, 43, 44
Scott, Mel, 222, 292
Sessions, Elena, 15
Sex, 144
  bathrooms, 132
  books, 132
  erotic, 134
  goddess, 16
  heterosexual, 144
  homosexual, 144
  nudity, 134
  sexuality, 16
  slum, 134
Shevky, E., 63
Shomon, J. J., 224
Sirjamaki, John, 16
Sjoberg, G., 16
Skyscrapers, 21
  see high rise
  food production, 45
Slum, 29, 57, 139
  housing, 172
  segregated, 173
Social class, 20, 26, 31, 65, 66, 283
  bourgeois and proletarian, 20
  English new towns, 68
  exclusive suburbs, 20
  lower class, 283

Marx, K., 20
Mexico City, 66
middle class, 256, 260, 283, 292
Middletown, 65
neighborhoods, 66, 68
privacy, 133
segregation, 29
social mobility, 66
stratification, 65
uniforms, 26
Yankee City, 65
Social institutions, 20
Social mobility, 66
  see social class
Social planning, 160
  social impact, 160
Social problem, 178
Social space, 140
Societal size, 139, 169
  urban areas, 169
  urban centers, 99
Sociophysical, 5, 44, 131, 139, 152, 173, 186, 241, 247, 255, 259, 304
  art facilities, 217
  education planning, 202
Soleri, Paolo, 6, 32, 50, 151, 241, 257
  see also megastructure
  see also arcology
Sommer, Robert, 141, 143, 144, 203
Soria y Mata, Arturo, 178, 287
Soviet Union, 7, 153, 174, 178, 235, 281
  health systems, 237
  Moscow, 21, 42, 237
  welfare, 244
Space
  airport terminals, 144
  air space, 127
  antisocial, 145
  art museums, 144

bathrooms, 76, 144
Boston Commons, 128
church sanctuaries, 144
defensible, 144
elevators, 143
Ghirardelli Square, San Francisco, 128
Islamic purdah, 128
isolation, 143
kitchen eating space, 137
Kremlin, 127
livability, 133
living room, 129
meaning, 127
   Boston's West End, 128
   house, 128
   London Regency Park, 128
   Mexico City's Chapultepec Park, 128
   San Francisco Golden Gate Park, 128
night clubs, 144
nurseries, 137
open plan residence, 133
parks, 143
privacy, 132, 137
single family, 129
Soviet Union, 136
space amenities, England, 128
stratification, 129
symbols, 125, 128
Spillhaus, Athelton, 7, 50
St. Louis
   Pruitt-Igoe, 138, 174, 185
Standard Metropolitan Statistical Area, 35
Stein, Clarence, 66, 284, 290
Stratification
   see social class
Strauss, A., 6
Strong, A. L., 281, 297
Subdivision, 160
   air rights, 160
   cluster, 160
   cul-de-sac, 160
   fire protection, 160
   formal organization, 160
   health, 162
   hillside, 163
   jobs, 162
   lot size, 162
   major street plan, 161
   mobile home, 162
   ordinances, 160
   plat, 162
   regulations, 160
   restrictive covenants, 162
   schools, 162
   set backs, 162
   sidewalks, 160
   social welfare, 162
   utility right of ways, 160
Suburbs, 29, 273, 274
   affluent, 20, 173
   Ur, 20
Superblock, 30, 68, 137, 138, 164, 174, 247, 284, 292, 302

T

Taylor, Lee, 35, 68, 70, 118, 154, 155, 163, 176, 216, 224
Territoriality, 143
   box seats, 144
   communicable disease, 144
   home, 143
   homosexuals, 144
   private, 144
   public, 143
   turf, 144
Thomlinson, Ralph, 20, 39
Toffler, Alvin, 222
Toronto, 21
Townhouses, 163
Trailer parks, 154
Transportation, 152, 158, 178, 191, 263

Bay Area Rapid Transit
  System, 266
car pools, 111
Champs Elysées, 19
commuters, 263
congestion, 158
cost, 188
dial-a-bus, 112, 158
ecumenopolis, 193
elevators, 26
express system, 158
freeway, 260
highways, 178, 192
minibus, 112
municipal system, 172
parking facilities, 263
peak travel hours, 25
pedestrian, 98, 161, 178, 192, 193, 284
people movement systems, 25
private cars, 158
public, 162, 191, 192, 193
publicos, 110
rapid, 193, 274
road system
  African, 192
  Asian, 192
  European, 192
  Inca, 192
  megastructures, 193
  Middle East, 192
  parking, 192
  Roman, 192
  Roman traffic, 19
social impact, 162
social problems, 178
street plans, 5, 161
street types, 158, 178
traffic congestion, 19, 158
transit corridors, 158
trip lengths, 158
urban centers, 98
vertical and horizontal, 26
Travel, 144

jet, 178
recreation vehicles, 224
steps, 5
streetcars, 5
tourist accommodations, 224
vacation, 224
Tugwell, Rex, 292

U

United States, 174, 261, 271
  health, 235
  Tugwell, Rex, 292
Unwin, Raymond, 288
Urban activity systems, 171, 253, 256
Urban centers, 83
  air pollution, 98
  auto free zones, 98
  central business district, 88, 89, 95
  central place theory, 88
  civic center, 88
  Compact City, 87
  community centers, 85
  cybernated, 96
  density, 94
  downtown, 83
  elevators, 94
  employment, 88
  formal organization, 88, 94
  functional space, 87
  Ginza, Tokyo, 98
  Glatt Center, Zurich, 95
  Golden Gateway Center, 95
  megastructures, 85
  Minnesota Experimental City, 87
  multifunctional, 85, 88, 91, 92
  neighborhood centers, 85
  new towns, 4
  noise pollution, 94, 98
  pedestrian ways, 95, 96, 97

Place Bonaventure,
  Montreal, 95
planned unit
  developments, 85
San Francisco, 89
shopping mall, 89
size of place, 88
traffic, 98
transit, 88
unifunctional, 85
urban cores, 99
urban sprawl, 96
Urban ecology, 246
Urban landscape, 31
Urban overload, 135
Urban police powers, 162
  codes, 155
  subdivision regulations,
  155, 162
  zoning ordinances, 155
Urban policies, 309
  Doxiadis, 309
  Forrester, Jay, 311
  Kahn, H., 312
  local, 317
  Meadows, Paul, 312
  national, 312
    Britain, 312
    Israel, 312
    Netherlands, 312
    Poland, 315
    United States, 314
  regional, 315
Urban problems, 35
  housing, 171
  jobs, 171
  transportation, 171
Urban regions, 103
  Greater London
    Conurbation, 110
  greenbelts, 111
  green wedges, 113
  high density, 110
  London Ring new towns, 110

megalopolis, 115, 116
Netherlands, 106
pedestrian, 108
planned unit
  developments, 116
plural culture, 116
Poland, 106, 108
sociophysical, 110
Soviet Union, 108, 121
Standard Metropolitan
  Statistical Areas, 113
suburbanization, 111
transportation systems, 110
Urban renewal, 136, 138, 152,
  172, 269, 271, 273, 281
Urban-rural differences, 6
  Bracey, H., 6
  Sorokin, P., 6
  Strauss, A., 6
  Taylor, L., 6
Urban sprawl, 152
Urban utopianists, 44
Urbanization, 1, 30, 35, 36, 37
  England, 39
  European continent, 47
  mass urbanization, 20
  one hundred years, 3
Urbanized Area, 36
Urbanized society, 51
U. S. Department of Housing
  and Urban Development,
  171, 183
  Operation Breakthrough, 182

V

View rights, 156, 159, 162
  Lynch, K., 75
  visual environment, 73
  visual impact, 73
Views, 141
von Hertzen, H., 164

W

Ward, Barbara, 40, 44
Warsaw, 263, 270
Webber, M., 71
Wedgwood, R., 177
Welfare, 222
  alienation, 243
  cycles of poverty, 244
  day-care, 244
  departments, 234
  dependent children, 243
  gerontological facilities, 244, 255
  old age assistance, 243
  overload, 243
  Soviet Union, 244
Wolstenholme, G. E. W., 240
Wooley, L., 16
Wright, Frank Lloyd, 139, 158
  Broadacre City, 139

Z

Zoning, 5, 29, 26, 77, 155
  ordinance, 155, 182
  spot, 163
  variances, 163